1

A-Cand

MY JEWISH WORLD

The Encyclopaedia Judaica for Youth

editor in chief
Rabbi Dr. Raphael Posner

ENCYCLOPAEDIA JUDAICA

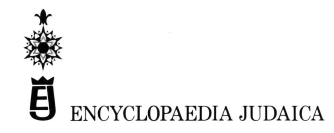

ISBN 0 7065 1411 4
Catalogue Number 51041

Set by Isratypset, Jerusalem
Printed and bound by Keterpress Enterprises, Jerusalem
Printed in Israel

MY JEWISH WORLD

a word to the reader

My Jewish World is a book for continuous reading as much as it is a reference book. In it you will find entries on all the important concepts and ideas of Judaism, on all the festivals of the Jewish calendar, on all the great events of Jewish history, on hundreds of great Jews who have made significant contributions to their people and to the world at large, and on the countries, cities and towns that have special meaning for the Jewish people. In addition you will find out how other religions and cultures have acted towards the Jews and what Judaism thinks about them. *My Jewish World* is just what its name says it is – a description of the Jewish world in the past and the present. You can read *My Jewish World* from beginning to end, or you can just open it and browse at random. You can also use it as an aid in your studies; to find out more about the things you study at school.

The information in *My Jewish World* is taken from and based upon the incomparable treasure of Jewish knowledge that was assembled to create the monumental *Encyclopaedia Judaica* that was published in Jerusalem in 1972. That work, written by the greatest scholars in their fields, has been distilled and reshaped for you by an expert staff under the supervision of the Editorial Board of the *Encyclopaedia Judaica.* We hope that *My Jewish World* will whet your appetite and that you will turn more and more frequently to the *Encyclopaedia Judaica. My Jewish World,* however, is not intended to be a comprehensive encyclopaedia but rather a selective, representative work from which you will be able to gain a general view and understanding of the wonderful heritage of the Jewish people.

In *My Jewish World* each article is a separate unit designed to give an overall view of the subject it deals with. When a subject mentioned has its own entry which will add something to the one you are reading, it is marked with an asterisk. Very often we suggest at the end of the entry (or in the middle, if it is relevant) that you look at other entries which will help you understand the subject better.

A very great deal of care has been taken with the illustrations. These consist of photographs, diagrams, maps and charts and are all intended to add to what you read in the entry. Read the captions carefully; you will find more interesting information in them.

At the end of Volume 6 there is a comprehensive index to *My Jewish World.* This tells you where the entries are and shows where you will find more information. It also includes descriptions of many items that are not in the six volumes. Whenever you come across a Hebrew or foreign language term you do not understand, look in the index, for it also contains a glossary that will help you. It is generally a good idea to consult the index first on any subject you are interested in. Read the main entry first and then look at all the other places referred to.

Now, all that is left to be said is : "Read and enjoy !"

Raphael Posner

Raphael Posner

Editor-in-Chief

There are many Hebrew words in *My Jewish World;* some are printed in Hebrew letters but all are given in transliteration, that is, spelled out in English. The following table shows the system we have used in all cases except in a very few where there is an accepted English spelling.

Consonants :

א	not transliterated
בּ	b
ב	v
ג	g
ד	d
ה	h
ו	v; when it is not a vowel
ז	z
ח	ḥ; pronounced like the "ch" in Loch Lomond
ט	t
י	y; when it is not a vowel
כּ	k
כ	kh; pronounced like the hard German "ch" as in *Ach!*
ך	kh; this is the final form of כ, i.e., the way it is written at the end of a word.
ל	l
מ	m
ם	m; final form of מ
נ	n
ן	n; final form of נ
ס	s
ע	not transliterated
פּ	p
פ	f
ף	f; final form of פ
צ	ẓ; pronounced "ts" as in tsetse fly
ץ	ẓ; final form of צ
ק	k
ר	r
שׁ	sh
שׂ	s
תּ	t
ת	t

Vowels:

*ָ *ַ *ֲ	a; as in glad
*ֶ *ְ *ֱ	e; as in bed
*ִ *ִי	i; as in tin
*ֵי	ei; like the "a" in take
*ֹ *וֹ	o; a little softer than owe
*ֻ *וּ	u; as in zoo

א and ע as pronounced by most Hebrew speakers have no sound but take the sound of the vowel. Occasionally, when they appear inside a word we use an apostrophe (') to indicate that the two vowels should be pronounced separately

AUSTRIA. Drawing of Polish Jews in the ghetto of Vienna. They are standing in front of a used clothes shop, c. 19th century.

AARON. It is difficult to grow up in the shadow of a famous and successful brother. To have been the brother of Moses, the man who received the Torah from God Himself, must have been many times more difficult. Yet Aaron was greatly respected by the Jews of his time, both for his priestly functions as given by God and for the love and compassion which he gave his people.

There is no biblical account of Aaron's birth and nothing is known of his early life. He married Elisheba of the tribe of Judah, and his brother-in-law, Nahshon, a chieftain of that tribe, was a direct ancestor of King David. Thus the two main hereditary institutions of Israel were linked: the House of Aaron (the priesthood) and the House of David (the kingship).

Aaron was clearly given a lesser role than Moses. Aaron experienced revelations from God and, being an eloquent speaker, acted as prophet and miracle-worker before Pharaoh in the matter of the *Plagues of Egypt. However, it is significant that even where he plays an active role in performing the miracles, it is not a result of his own ability or initiative, but solely by divine command given through Moses. Aaron is not mentioned during the escape from Egypt or the crossing of the Red Sea, but he appears later with the incident of the *manna. At the revelation on Mount Sinai, when the Torah was given to Israel, Aaron was a minor participant, permitted to ascend the mount, but with the same status as his sons and the seventy elders of Israel.

Aaron was involved in the sin of the creation of the *Golden Calf. He made no attempt to stop the would-be idol worshipers, and it was he who fashioned the Calf, built the altar and proclaimed a religious festival. However, he did not regard the Calf as a god and did not participate in its worship. It seems that he realized he could not control the people and wanted to forestall any catastrophe until Moses returned. He was neither punished nor disqualified from the priesthood for his role in the affair.

It was as founder of the hereditary priesthood that Aaron served his most significant function. In fact, all of today's *kohanim* are direct descendants of Aaron on their father's side. Because of the importance of the priestly succession, the biblical account of the death of Aaron is detailed. Three years older than Moses, Aaron died at the age of 123, never having been permitted to enter Ereẓ Israel. The Israelites had arrived at Mount Hor from Kadesh and by divine decree Aaron ascended the mount with Moses and Eleazar, Aaron's son. Aaron then had the satisfaction of seeing his son succeed him in his priestly office as he handed him the garments of priesthood. Aaron died a peaceful death on the summit of the mount, and the entire community mourned him for 30 days.

Aaron played an important part in the exodus from Egypt, as depicted in these two scenes from the *Sarajevo Haggadah* (Spain, 14th century). Above, Moses and his flock approach the burning bush to receive God's instructions. Because Moses was reluctant to accept the divine commission, this encounter ultimately led to Aaron's role as Moses' spokesman before Pharaoh and the people of Israel.

In the lower illustration, performing in the presence of Moses, Pharaoh, and the royal court, Aaron turns his rod into a serpent that swallows the serpent rods of the Egyptian magicians.

In the rabbinic tradition Aaron is seen as a man of love and compassion who always tried to make peace. Thus Hillel, the great rabbi, declared: "Be of the disciples of Aaron, loving peace and pursuing peace, loving one's fellow man and bringing him near to the Torah."

AARON OF LINCOLN, who lived in England (1123-1186), was a financier who lent money on a large scale. The king of Scotland was one of his clients. He kept careful records of his financial transactions which were carried on over much of England, and which included loans to bishops, earls and barons.

He advanced money to the king on the security of future revenues. He also lent money to church foundations such as the Monastery of St. Albans, for their ambitious building programs. At one time nine

Medieval Jewish moneylender — an image often distorted and caricatured by Christians to represent craftiness and cruelty. A 15th century woodcut.

abbeys owed him 6,400 marks for mortgages which he held.

After Aaron's death his vast estate was seized by the king. It included many properties and bills of debt owed him by churchmen, noblemen and others. A special branch of the exchequer, or treasury — the *Scaccarium Aaronis* — was formed to administer the estate until 1191. Since it was not dignified for the king to press his noblemen to repay him, some of these bills of debt were sold to Aaron's son Elias, who was able in this way to recover a part of his inheritance.

A typical receipt, now in the British Museum, and written in Latin, reads: "Aaron the Jew of Lincoln, and Benedict Grossus, son of Pucella, send their greetings to all who may see this note. Know that the men of Barton (upon Humber) returned ten pounds sterling to us last Michaelmas (an old feast on September 29), after the death of Roger, Archbishop of York (who died on November 26, 1181). And therefore we have drawn up this, our brief, as proof of it; and beside this, they returned ten shillings to us on the same date."

ABBASIDS was the name of a dynasty of Arabian-Muslim caliphs who ruled the Arab world during the years 750 to 1258. In addition to having a great impact on the life of the Islamic peoples, the Abbasids' rule also influenced the life of Jewry since, on the whole, they permitted the Jews to have their own internal organization. During this period, the *exilarchs headed the Jewish community undisturbed and the two great Babylonian yeshivot of Sura and Pumbedita flourished under the leadership of the *geonim* (see *Gaon). In fact, with the exception of one series of anti-Jewish and anti-Christian decrees during the years 847-861, the rights of all religious minorities were assured and there are no known cases of forced conversion to Islam in this era.

ABBAYE. In Babylon, in the year 278 c.e., a lately widowed woman died giving birth to a son. The orphan, whose real name is not known, was nicknamed Abbaye. He was brought up by an uncle who was an outstanding scholar.

Abbaye grew up to become one of the greatest sages of the Talmud and ultimately became the head of the Pumbedita Academy in Babylonia. There are very many statements by him in the Talmud and he had dozens of discussions with his contemporary *Rava. In six of those disputes the legal decision follows Abbaye's opinion. Abbaye's main teacher was Rabbi Joseph whom he succeeded as head of the Academy. Rabbi Joseph suffered a serious illness and became blind. As a result, he forgot much of his own learning, and Abbaye used to help him to recall it.

Abbaye was a poor man. At night he worked in his fields so that he could study during the day. It was his belief that a man must live a productive life by working as well as studying.

When asked a question in *halakhah,* Abbaye often answered: "Go out and see what the people say," meaning that one should follow the popular tradition of the time. He taught that the commandment to love God means that "God should come to be loved by other people through your behavior." That is, a person should live a good life, studying Torah and treating other people well, so that anyone seeing him will think: "The life of a person who has studied Torah is a pleasant one."

Kindness was an important part of Abbaye's teaching. "A soft answer turns away anger," he would say, and tried to impress upon his students that to be loved in Heaven and on earth, a man must act kindly and gently towards his fellow men.

Abbaye died in 338 c.e.

A page from the *Mocatta Haggadah,* Spain, 13th century, listing the order of procedure at the Passover *seder* ceremony in abbreviation. Each intricately drawn letter is made up of animal forms. The order is slightly different to the generally accepted one.

ABBREVIATIONS. The abbreviation of words originated in antiquity, probably soon after the alphabet developed. While originally rare, their use increased with time because of their many advantages. They relieved the shortage of space and precious writing materials, served the convenience of the scribe, and preserved a certain degree of secrecy. An abbreviation also prevented the constant repetition of the full name of God. Various methods of abbreviating evolved in the course of time although occasionally they caused confusion and misunderstandings.

The expression *notarikon* (derived from the Greek term for stenography) occurs in the Mishnah and refers to the use of initial letters (known as *rashei tevot*) and dots and dashes to indicate abbreviation. The Mishnah regularly uses abbreviations, such as ר׳ for רַבִּי and the Talmud also employs them as memory devices, or *mnemonics.

Abbreviations appear on Jewish *coins of the Jewish War (66-70) and the Bar Kokhba War (132-135) and on documents recovered from the Dead Sea Caves and Masada.

In the Middle Ages, the names of frequently quoted scholars and their works were abbreviated and made pronounceable, for example, Rashi (Rabbi Shelomo Yiẓḥaki), Rambam (Rabbi Moses ben Maimon), Rosh (Rabbenu Asher). Even in later periods, famous personalities continued to be called by an abbreviation such as the Ba'al Shem Tov (Besht, בֶּעשׁ״ט) and Elijah of Vilna (הַגְּרָ״א– הַגָּאוֹן ר׳ אֵלִיָּהוּ).

Since the 19th century some authors' initials have almost superseded their actual names (even the poet

Judah Leib *Gordon, for example is known as יַלַ״ג). The initials with which the historian and journalist Shneur Zalman Rubashov (later president of the State of Israel) signed his articles eventually became his Hebrew name שַׁזַ״ר *Shazar).

Many 19th- and 20th century Jewish organizations and institutions have become known by their abbreviated titles. The ḥasidic movement emanating from Lubavich is known by the initials of their motto Ḥabad (חָכְמָה, בִּינָה, דַעַת–חַבַ״ד "wisdom, understanding knowledge"). The habit of calling international bodies by their initials (e.g. UN, UNESCO, UNSCOP) has found an echo in the Hebrew או״ם for אֻמּוֹת מְאוּחָדוֹת (United Nations). In Israel constant use is made of abbreviations: (e.g. Mapai, מַפַּא״י–מִפְלֶגֶת פּוֹעֲלֵי אֶרֶץ יִשְׂרָאֵל which means "the Israel Labor Party"; Zahal, צְבָא הֲגַנָּה לְיִשְׂרָאֵל–צַהַ״ל which means "Israel Defense Forces"). These groups have adopted abbreviations which have virtually become independent words. Military ranks, units, and equipment are expressed almost exclusively by abbreviations, such as the word for sergeant סֶגֶן מִחוּץ לַמִּנְיָן–סַמָּ״ל (=non-commissioned lieutenant). A member of the Israel Parliament is abbreviated חֲבֵר כְּנֶסֶת–ח״כ , a publisher מוֹצִיא לְאוֹר–מו״ל, Land of Israel אֶרֶץ יִשְׂרָאֵל–א״י, the rest of the world is חוּצָה לָאָרֶץ–חו״ל. Cities with a compound name are often abbreviated (e.g. תֵּל אָבִיב–ת״א Tel Aviv). An orange is called תַּפּוּז , the abbreviation for תַּפּוּחַ זָהָב a golden apple.

Abbreviation of the Name of God. The name of God is probably the most often abbreviated word, due to its frequent appearance in Jewish writing and the reverence which is accorded it. It was abbreviated in antiquity, mishnaic, and talmudic times as ה׳ or י״ in Targum Onkelos as ה׳ and ד׳ and in the Middle Ages it was represented by ה׳ and varying numbers of *yod's, vav's,* strokes, and dots, from which developed the use of *yod's*. It has been estimated that there are over 80 substitutes for the Divine Name.

Abbreviation of Names. In the same way that in medieval times the names of famous rabbis were abbreviated, in the emancipation period, when the Jews had to adopt surnames, Hebrew abbreviations often formed the basis of "secular" names. The name Katz כֹּהֵן צֶדֶק–כַּ״ץ stood for families of priestly descent, and Segal סְגַן לְוִיָּה–סֶגַ״ל for those of levite origin. When referring to deceased persons, such abbreviations became common: עָלָיו הַשָּׁלוֹם–ע״ה may he rest in peace, זִכְרוֹנוֹ לִבְרָכָה–זַ״ל may his memory be a blessing, חֲכָמֵינוּ זִכְרוֹנָם לִבְרָכָה–חֲזַ״ל our sages of blessed memory, ה׳ יִנְקוֹם דָּמוֹ–הי״ד (for martyrs) May God avenge his blood, פֹּה נִקְבָּר–פ״נ (on tombstones) here lies buried.

In correspondence it became usual to prefix letters and occasionally also printed matter and books with בְּעֶזְרַת ה׳–בעז״ה, בע״ה, ב״ה "With the help of God," and in modern times the concluding greetings are דְּרִישַׁת שָׁלוֹם–ד״ש "regards" and כָּל טוּב–כ״ט "all the best."

Book Titles. The best known abbreviations are those for the Hebrew Bible, תַּנַ״ךְ composed of the initial letters of תּוֹרָה, נְבִיאִים, כְּתוּבִים and שִׁשָּׁה סְדָרִים–שַׁ״ס for the Babylonian Talmud.

Many other Jewish classics have become known by the abbreviations of their titles to the extent that some students would not recognize the full name. This is also true for the abbreviations of the names of medieval rabbis mentioned above.

Misunderstandings and Misinterpretations. The increasing and inconsistent use of abbreviations has inevitably led to occasional confusion and made the study of Hebrew texts more difficult. Difficulties arise when an abbreviation can be read in more than one way and, because of the risk of misrepresentation, no abbreviations may be used in a bill of divorce, or other religious documents. Many abbreviations were misinterpreted (often quite intentionally) and caused misunderstandings which became part of Jewish folklore. For example, the *Yaknehaz* abbreviation in the Passover *Haggadah,* denoting the order of the benedictions *(yayin, Kiddush, ner, Havdalah, zeman),* was understood as the German *jag'n Has* ("hunt the hare"), and pictures of a hare hunt sometimes accompany the relevant passage in the printed *Haggadah.* (See also *Acrostics and *Mnemonics).

ABDULLAH IBN HUSSEIN (1882-1951), first king of the Hashemite kingdom of Jordan, was born in Mecca. He was the second son of Hussein ibn Ali of the Hashemite family that had been rulers of Mecca from the 11th century C.E. and traced its descent from the prophet Muhammad.

Abdullah grew up in Constantinople, where he received the traditional education of a Muslim gentleman, and later became his father's political secretary. After his father, Hussein, was installed as emir of Mecca in 1908, Abdullah secretly negotiated with the British in a struggle for power against other Arab rulers. This resulted in the "Arab Revolt" of 1916 and the Allies' recognition of Hussein as king of the Hejaz (a region in Saudi Arabia).

1

Towards the end of 1920, Abdullah moved north with a Bedouin army in an attempt to restore his brother Faisal to the throne of Syria, from which the French had deposed him. In Jerusalem in March, 1921, he met Winston *Churchill, the British colonial secretary, who offered him the administration of Transjordan. It was about this occasion that Churchill remarked, "On a Sunday afternoon I created Transjordan with a stroke of my pen!" Abdullah then became the hereditary ruler of what came to be known as Jordan. This included parts of Judea and Samaria, which the Zionists had justifiably claimed as traditionally parts of Ereẓ Israel.

The police of Jordan were soon called the "Arab Legion." They were developed into an elite fighting force during World War II under John B. Glubb, a British Army officer. Glubb had such a strong attachment to the Arabs that they called him Glubb Pasha and considered him one of their own.

In 1946 a treaty with Britain ended *Mandate rule and gave Jordan independence. Abdullah became king. He was one of the more moderate of the Arab leaders and conducted secret negotiations with Jewish leaders, including Golda *Meir, before and after the *War of Independence – but nothing came of them. Nevertheless, he acted in defiance of the *United Nations' decision of November 29, 1947, and in 1949 annexed the West Bank and part of Jerusalem, and refused free entry to Jews.

In 1951 he was murdered in Jerusalem and succeeded by his son Talal, who was soon deposed on grounds of mental illness by his own son, Hussein, the present King of Jordan.

2

1. Abdullah, shortly after becoming the emir of Transjordan, standing between Sir Herbert Samuel, the high commissioner for Palestine and Transjordan (left) and Sir Wyndham Deedes, chief secretary. Photo taken about 1921 in Jerusalem.
2. The Inquisition, from which Abenatar Melo suffered greatly, claimed many victims. In this detail from a painting entitled "Auto da Fé" (Act of Faith), a Judaizer, though not necessarily born a Jew, is interrogated simply for having practiced certain Jewish customs.

ABENATAR MELO, DAVID. A poet who suffered years of imprisonment and torture during the Spanish *Inquisition, David Abenatar Melo finally lived to compose songs of praise to God.

Abenatar Melo managed to escape the torture of the Inquisition by becoming a *Marrano – one who pretended to accept Christianity but continued to practice Judaism secretly. In 1616 he was one of the founding members of the Eẓ Ḥayyim Talmud Torah Society of Amsterdam. In 1617 he was instrumental in arranging for the publication of a prayer book in Spanish, and later, for printing a Passover *Haggadah.*

In 1626 he published a remarkable translation of the Book of Psalms into Spanish verse, which he dedicated to "the Blessed God and the Holy

Company of Israel and Judah, scattered throughout the world." The introduction contains an account of his sufferings. This Book of Psalms is not a direct translation, as it contains several references to the current events of those days, and especially to the tyranny of the Inquisition. At the end of Psalm 30, for example, he mentions the trial (or auto da fé) at which he appeared, and where 11 Jews were burned.

His descendants grew up to be Jews who were able to practice their Judaism openly. Abenatar Melo, who died in about 1646, is believed to have been the father of Immanuel Abenatar Melo, the *ḥazzan* of the Sephardi community of Rotterdam until 1682 and then of Amsterdam, and grandfather of David Abenatar Melo, the preacher and *ḥazzan* in Amsterdam.

ABNER OF BURGOS abandoned his Jewish religion and caused the Jews of Spain great suffering. He was born in 1270, in an age of confusion for the Jews. When Abner grew up and became a doctor, many Jews who had seen the false messiah of Alvia came to Abner for advice. They were not sure whether they had seen real miracles or not. Abner, however, was unable to help them, as he himself was confused. He always wondered why Jews, especially the righteous ones, suffered so much, and why the Jews were exiled from their homeland.

For 25 years he puzzled over these questions and finally, unable to find answers in the Bible or the Kabbalah, or in the works of Arab philosophers, turned to the New Testament and the Christian philosophers. Finally, at the age of 50, he converted to Christianity.

Abner spread many lies about the Talmud. One such untruth was that the Talmud had ten evil commandments. He treated the Jews badly because he wanted to convince them that it was better to convert to Christianity. He even argued with great Jewish scholars such as Moses ben Joshua of Narbonne. On one occasion, in 1334, he tried to convince the Jews of Toledo that they had made a mistake in the date of Passover.

His pupil, Isaac ben Joseph ibn Pulgar, helped to spread his ideas amongst the Spanish Jews. Most of Abner's writings were lost. The only Hebrew work left is his *Sefer Teshuvot li-Meḥaref* ("Refutation of the Blasphemer"). His other main remaining work is in Castilian, *Mostrador de Justicia* ("Teacher of Righteousness").

Abner was the first Jew to publish such anti-Jewish writings. After his death in 1340, many Spanish Christians used his writings as a basis from which to attack Jews and Judaism.

Medieval Jewish scholars, distinguishable by their knobbed hats, dispute a point of faith with their Christian counterparts, who may well have bolstered their arguments with some of Abner's controversial works. From a woodcut by Johann von Armssheim, 1483.

ABRABANEL, ISAAC BEN JUDAH (1437-1508) was a statesman, philosopher, and a scholar of great versatility in both Jewish and secular studies. (His name often appears as Abarbanel). By the age of 20 he had written articles on vital religious questions as well as on the original form of the natural elements.

The son of a wealthy and influential family, Abrabanel succeeded his father as treasurer to King Alfonso V of Portugal. When Alfonso conquered parts of North Africa, he brought back 250 Jewish captives. Abrabanel contributed largely to the fund to free the captives and personally arranged for collections throughout Portugal and Italy to help support them.

With the death of Alfonso, a period of tranquility ended for the Jews. Abrabanel was accused of conspiracy and sentenced to death. He fled to Spain

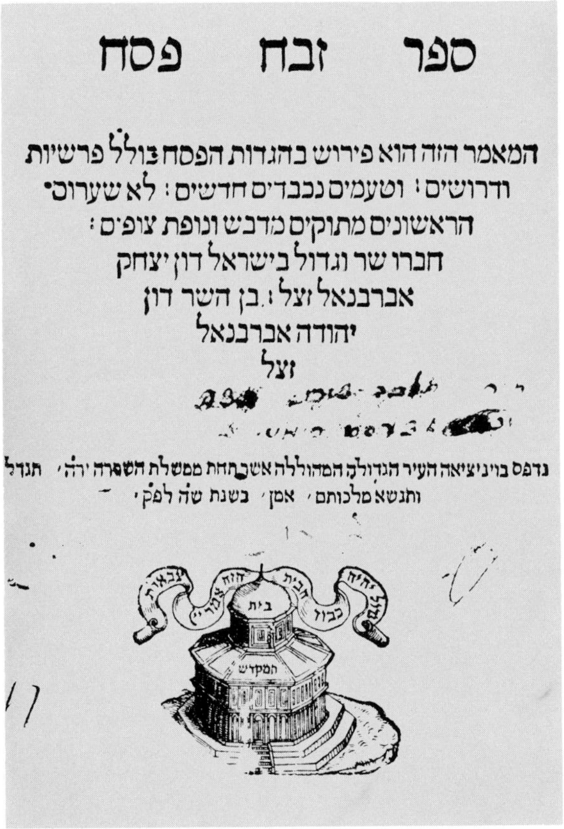

ספר זבח פסח

המאמר הזה הוא פירוש בהגדות הפסח כולל פרשיות
ודרושים: וטעמים נכבדים חדשים: לא שערום
הראשונים מתוקים מדבש ונופת צופים:
חברו שר וגדול בישראל דון יצחק
אברבנאל זצל: בן השר דון
יהודה אברבנאל
זצל

נדפס בויניציאה העיר הגדולה המהוללה אשר תחת ממשלת השררה יר״ה׳ תגדל
ותנשא מלכותם׳ אמן׳ בשנת שה לפק׳

Title page of *Zevaḥ Pesaḥ,* in which Abrabanel poses 100 questions about the Passover *Haggadah* and answers them at length. Venice, 1545.

where he had managed to transfer much of his fortune.

He thought that his troubles might have come because he had wasted his time in the service of an earthly ruler, so he decided to spend the rest of his life in religious study. He began to write about the earlier prophets in the books of Joshua, Judges and Samuel, thinking that his political experience in Portugal would help him to interpret them.

Abrabanel had not finished his writing when he was called to the service of Ferdinand and Isabella of Spain in 1484. He was faithful to their interests and lent them a great deal of money. But when Ferdinand and Isabella issued their decrees in 1492 that all Jews must convert to Christianity or be expelled from Spain, his pleas to them failed. They allowed Abrabanel to take 1,000 gold ducats with him, and in return for that favor cancelled a very large sum of money which they owed him. Shall we guess that this money of Abrabanel's helped finance Christopher Columbus' voyage to the New World that same year?

Abrabanel fled to Naples and tried to devote himself to study but was again called on to be adviser to the king of Naples. As a result of looting and other anti-Semitic episodes, Abrabanel moved from place to place, writing commentaries on the prophets, on the Haggadah, and on religious philosophy. He wrote articles expressing a hope for redemption to end the exile and the wandering of the Jews.

Even in death he had no peace. He was buried in Padua, but because of vandalism in the cemetery in 1509 his grave is unknown.

ABRAHAM, the father of the Jewish people, was born in Ur of the Chaldees, in Babylonia. It is impossible to fix his exact dates but it is estimated that he lived between the 19th and 17th centuries b.c.e. He was the son of Terah who, like everyone else in those times, was a worshiper of idols. It puzzled Abraham to see people praying and making their entreaties to images of wood and stone. An *aggadah* related that when he smashed his father's idols to demonstrate that they were powerless, King Nimrod had him thrown into a fiery furnace, from which he was saved by the angel Gabriel.

Abraham was keenly perceptive of the world around him. The forces of nature and the cycles of the heavenly bodies led him to grasp that a great unseen power ruled the world. He spread the idea of monotheism and won over many converts. His own spiritual growth gave him a prophetic insight and made him receptive to the word of God.

At God's command Abraham left his home and all his relatives in Ur of the Chaldees, and set out for Canaan with his wife, Sarah. On the way God appeared to him and promised him that he would become the founder of a great nation. With his nephew Lot, he continued to Canaan, where he built several altars to God – at Shechem, Beth-El, and Ai.

Driven by famine to Egypt, the patriarch represented the beautiful Sarah as his sister to avoid any threat to his life. Sarah was taken to Pharaoh's palace, but was released when God informed Pharoah that she was another man's wife. Abraham returned to Canaan and Lot went on his own way. On one occasion Abraham had to resort to battle to rescue Lot who had been captured by a coalition of eastern kings. He won the war despite the strong odds against him.

God repeatedly promised Abraham abundant offspring, but for long years Sarah remained childless. Discouraged, she presented her maidservant Hagar to Abraham as a second wife. Ishmael was born of the union and became the father of desert tribes, and the ancestor of today's Arabs.

1

1. According to some interpretations, Abraham's recognition of God stemmed from his knowledge of astronomy. That may have been the inspiration for this pen and ink drawing entitled "Abraham Looking at the Stars," by the Austrian artist Ephraim Moshe Lilien, c. 1908.
2. On his return from the battle to rescue Lot, Abraham received bread and wine from Melchizedek, priest-king of Salem. Illustration in an Italian manuscript, 17th-18th century.
3. This map of Israel, drawn by Abraham ben Jacob, was the first to be printed in Hebrew and was included in the *Amsterdam Haggadah,* 1695. It shows the division of Ereẓ Israel among the 12 tribes, and the route followed in the exodus from Egypt.

Years passed and Abraham was commanded to circumcise himself and all male members of his family as a permanent token of God's covenant with Abraham and his descendants. Abraham accepted this new commandment without faltering. Until the *mitzvah* of circumcision, the patriarch had been known as Abram and his wife as Sarai. Another sign of the covenant was the inclusion in their names of the Hebrew letter *heh,* which is one of the abbreviations for the name of God.

One day three messengers from God appeared, assuring Abraham that a son would be born to him within a year. They also brought word of God's decision to destroy Sodom and Gomorrah because of their wickedness. Abraham prayed for those cities but could not save them, although he was able to save Lot. The following year, at the age of 90, Sarah bore Abraham a son, whom they named *Isaac. She then asked that Hagar and Ishmael be banished because of their harmful influence on Isaac. God told Abraham to follow Sarah's wish.

The climax of Abraham's life was the command to sacrifice Isaac on Mount Moriah – a supreme test of his faith. (This test is discussed in the article on the **Akedah.*) Without hesitating Abraham obeyed, but his hand was stopped at the last moment by an angel. Here again the patriarch received the divine blessing that his descendants would be as numerous as the stars of heaven and would conquer their enemies.

Sarah died in Kiriath Arba (or *Hebron), where Abraham bought the cave of Machpelah as a family burial place. To this day Jews go to the site to pray.

Abraham then sent his servant Eliezer to Haran to find a wife for Isaac. After Isaac's marriage to Rebekah, Abraham took Keturah as his wife and they had nine more children. The Midrash identifies Hagar with Keturah.

In Jewish tradition, Abraham's life is an example to this day of supreme faith and devotion to God, and of love for one's fellow man. Abraham is also the personification of hospitality; his tent was open on all four sides. He himself waited on guests, and taught them Grace after Meals to bring them to faith in One God. Because he converted so many people to his belief, Abraham is considered the father of all proselytes, who are often given his name.

2

ABRAHAM BEN JACOB, who lived in the late 17th century, was a brilliant copper engraver who worked in Amsterdam, Holland. Once a Christian pastor in the Rhineland, he converted to Judaism.

He was famous for his art work in Jewish books. The celebrated *Haggadah* which was printed in Amsterdam in 1695 includes a number of his copper engravings, which set a new fashion, and served as a model for the printing of *Haggadot* for more than 200 years.

Abraham ben Jacob also engraved the title pages of two books. One was the *Arba'ah Turim,* the basic work on Jewish law written by *Jacob ben Asher; the

3
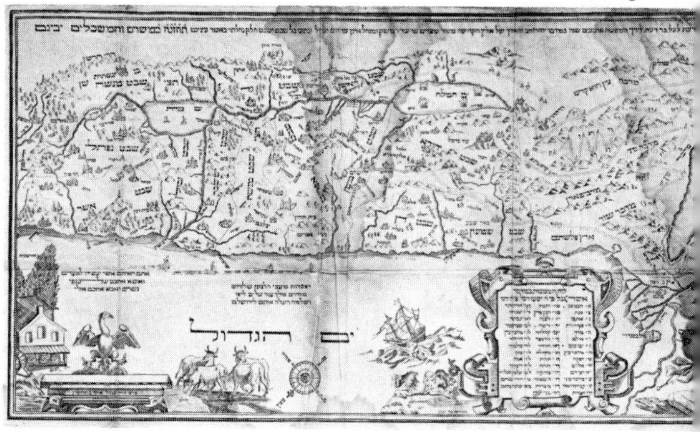

other was *Shenei Luḥot ha-Berit* ("Two Tablets of the Covenant"), which was the main work of the kabbalist, Rabbi Isaiah ben Abraham Ha-Levi *Horowitz.

Other engravings by Abraham ben Jacob include a *ketubbah* (the document which a husband presents to his wife upon marriage), and a map of Israel with Hebrew lettering, which was included in a *Haggadah*.

ABRAHAMS. The three Abrahams brothers were English athletes. The eldest, Sir Adolphe Abrahams (1883-1967), was a doctor of medicine and author who had studied at Cambridge, where he was sculling champion in 1905. He was medical officer in charge of British Olympic teams from 1912 until 1948, and president of the British Association of Sports and medicine. Together with his younger brother, he wrote *Training for Athletes* in 1928, and *Training for Health and Athletics* in 1936.

The second brother, Sir Sidney Abrahams (1885-1957), was a colonial official. After studying at Cambridge, he became a magistrate in Zanzibar, advocate general in Baghdad, and chief justice of Uganda. He represented Cambridge in the long jump and the 100-yard dash, and ran for Great Britain in the 1908 and 1912 Olympics. He also served as honorary legal adviser to the Amateur Athletic Association.

Harold Maurice Abrahams (1899-) was an athlete and lawyer who became the first European to win an Olympic sprint title when he won the 100-meter dash in 1924. While at Cambridge, he won the British long jump championship in 1923, and in 1924 set a British long jump record that lasted for 30 years. He captained the British Olympic team in 1928 and was chairman of the British Amateur Athletic Board in 1969. He reported on athletics for the English press and radio, and wrote books such as *Sprinting* (1925), *Athletics* (1926), and *The Rome Olympiad* (1960).

ABU GHOSH is an Arab village in the Judean Hills eight miles west of Jerusalem. The village has a population of some 2,000 people, mainly Muslims, who earn their living by growing grain, vegetables, vines, olives and fruit.

It was here, on the site of the biblical town of Kiriath-Jearim, that the Ark of the Law rested in the house of Abinadab (II Sam. 6:21; 7:1,2) when it was rescued from the Philistines and before it was brought to Jerusalem. Abu Ghosh was also significant during the Crusades, and the village still contains a well-

Window in the western wall of the Romanesque church built by the Crusaders at Abu Ghosh.

preserved Crusader church dating from the year 1142. Amazingly, one of the stones inserted in its walls bears the imprint of the Roman Tenth Legion, apparently stationed in the Abu Ghosh area in the first century c.e.

After the building of the nearby kibbutzim Kiryat Anavim (1920) and Ma'aleh ha-Ḥamishah (1938) relations between the villagers and Jews were friendly and remained so in the Israel *War of Independence. Some of the villagers even cooperated with the Israel forces.

ABULAFIA. Famous families have appeared throughout Jewish history, among them *Sassoon, *Rothschild, *Soloveitchik and many more. The Abulafia family of Spain included rabbis, poets, statesmen, and communal leaders. After the expulsion from Spain in 1492, the family scattered to various Mediterranean countries. One distinguished rabbinical branch of the family settled in Israel.

Meir Abulafia (1170?-1244), talmudist, thinker and poet, was the foremost Spanish rabbi of the thirteenth century. A member of the Toledo *bet din* at thirty, he organized various Jewish communities. His writings cover *halakhah*, **Masorah* and Hebrew poetry, as well as the works of *Maimonides, with whose concept of resurrection Abulafia disagreed very strongly. His greatest work, an extensive commentary on the Talmud, was considered the summation of the talmudic school of the Spanish rabbis.

Meir's nephew, the rabbi and kabbalist Todros ben Joseph ha-Levi Abulafia (1220-1298), was the spiritual leader of the Castilian Jews of Spain, and an intimate adviser to Alfonso X.

1. Florid Hebrew inscription on the stucco wall of the Toledo synagogue (later the Church of El Transito) honoring Samuel Abulafia for his help in financing the building in the 14th century. Above it is the coat of arms of the Kingdom of Castile and Leon.
2. Lavishly decorated interior of the same Toledo synagogue, c. 1375.

1

Todros ben Judah ha-Levi Abulafia (1247-1295), Hebrew poet and financier, was close to Alfonso X and Sancho IV. His works offer revealing insights into life and literature in the thirteenth century.

An important personality in Kabbalah was Abraham ben Samuel Abulafia (1240-1291). Based in Navarre, Spain, he traveled extensively in Mediterranean countries, proclaiming prophecies and heralding the coming of the Messiah.

Samuel ben Meir ha-Levi Abulafia (1320-1361) was a wealthy Spanish financier, communal leader and philanthropist. He was financial and political adviser to Pedro the Cruel, and served as a diplomat as well. He did much to improve the financial state of Pedro's monarchy, thus reinforcing its power against the rebellious nobility. Yet in 1360, Pedro suddenly turned against him. Abulafia was imprisoned and tortured to death and his fortune confiscated. His beautiful home in Toledo is today the El Greco museum.

Jacob ben Solomon Abulafia (1550-1622) was a noted rabbi in the city of Damascus, with many ties with Safed, the holy city of scholars and mystics in Palestine. His son Ḥayyim (1580-1668) was a talmudist who moved to Jerusalem and, at seventy, to Hebron where he directed the yeshivah.

Ḥayyim ben Moses Abulafia (1660-1744), moved from Hebron to Jerusalem where he studied. He then served as rabbi in Safed, and in Smyrna, Turkey, for many years.

2

In 1740 he returned to Palestine with the conviction that the era of the Messiah was coming, and that the holy city of Tiberias, in ruins for 70 years, must be rebuilt before the Messiah could come. Although he was eighty, he began to organize this work, sending his sons and sons-in law abroad to raise funds for the restoration. His son Isaac (died 1764), a leading talmudist, succeeded him as rabbi, leader, and rebuilder of Tiberias.

Ḥayyim Nissim Abulafia (HANA) (1775-1861), rabbi and communal worker, was born in Tiberias and succeeded his father as leader of the Jews there. In 1854, he was elected *Rishon le-Zion* (Sephardi chief rabbi) in Jerusalem.

ACQUISITION, or *kinyan* (as it is known in Hebrew legal parlance), is the act whereby a person obtains legal rights. Acquisition of rights by way of a *kinyan* can be divided into three groups: (1) acquiring ownership over ownerless property *(hefker)*, for example, fish in the ocean or lost property which the owner has abandoned hope of finding; (2) rights over property which has an owner, e.g. when the acquisition is by way of a sale or gift; (3) contractual or personal rights such as debts or hiring of workmen.

The purpose of the formalities of acquiring title is to demonstrate beyond doubt that the property is in the unrestricted possession of the person acquiring it. An oral agreement is not an absolute transfer of rights; therefore, even though it is immoral to break an oral agreement, it is not legally binding. In some cases the *kinyan* does not demonstrate possession but rather indicates a finalization of the agreement, and only then is the agreement binding. In general, the acquisition of rights requires the intention of the acquirer. Usually a *kinyan* cannot be performed by one who is under 13 years of age.

The act of *kinyan* can be performed in a variety of ways. The most common are *hagbahah,* lifting the object to be acquired three handbreadths into the air, and *shetar,* the signing of a deed by the giver and handing it over to the acquirer. These, as well as the other methods, are based on various interpretations of biblical texts as well as on business practices in talmudic times. The important consideration is to have acts of acquisition which are absolute and not open to cancellation. In line with talmudic practice, rabbinic courts of law still enforce certain methods of sealing a deal, if they are widely recognized, such as

1

2

1. Acre fishermen, outside the old city walls, mending their nets. Their occupation is one followed by residents of Acre for thousands of years.
2. Northwest tower, known as the "English Bastion," which is part of the seawall of Acre. It was built by Ahmad al-Jazzar, governor of Acre in the late 18th century.

the practice among Jewish dealers in certain diamond exchanges of shaking hands, while wishing each other *mazal u-verakhah* ("good luck and blessing").

The laws of acquisition are very complicated; they are developed and elaborated in the Talmud and their study has always constituted an important part of the yeshivah syllabus.

ACRE. The remains of a Crusader breakwater and the massive Ottoman seawalls still protect the ancient city of Acre from the ocean rollers of the Mediterranean. Acre is situated 14 miles north of Haifa and is built on the Bay of Haifa. Its geographic position has caused it to be occupied by every army waging campaigns in Syria and Ereẓ Israel.

During the conquest of Canaan under Joshua, Acre was in the territory of the tribe of Asher who could not conquer it, and it therefore remained an independent Phoenician city. When conquered by the Persians, Acre served as an important military and naval base in their campaigns against Egypt. It had its own coinage: gold and silver coins were minted there in 332 b.c.e. When an association of citizens loyal to the Greek tyrant Antiochus was living there, the city became hostile to the neighboring Jews in Galilee. In 164 b.c.e. Simeon the Hasmonean had to beat off its attacks, and his brother Jonathan was treacherously taken prisoner there in 143 b.c.e.

In the Middle Ages Jewish scholars arrived in Israel through the port at Acre and some settled in the town. In 1211, 300 rabbis from France and England arrived, and in 1260 Rabbi Jeḥiel ben Joseph of Paris remained in the town together with his son and 300 pupils, and promptly founded a yeshivah. Scholars of Israel and Babylon addressed their questions to the "scholars of Acre." The town became a center of study and attracted many scholars, such as Rabbi Abraham *Abulafia and *Naḥmanides. In time the community dwindled but was revived again in the 18th century. It became a political and military center strong enough to resist Napoleon's advance in 1799, and cause the collapse of his Middle Eastern expeditions.

During the British Mandate, a fortress in the town served as a prison where members of the *Haganah including Moshe *Dayan, as well as Vladimir *Jabotinsky, were imprisoned.

Today Acre has been rebuilt as a modern industrial center, but still contains an Old City with remains from the Ottoman period (1516-1918) which include the double wall of the city, the citadel, and a beautiful mosque still used by Acre's Arab population.

ACROSTICS is the name given to a style of writing in which successive or alternating verses, or clusters of verses, begin with the letters of the alphabet in sequence. Sometimes the sequence follows the order of the alphabet and thus makes it easier to remember the composition by heart; sometimes the letters make up the name of the author. Shelomoh ha-Levi *Alkabez, for example, used the letters of his name as the initials of the respective verses of *Lekhah Dodi,* the hymn sung on Friday evening to welcome the Sabbath.

In the Bible there are many examples of acrostic compositions although some of them lack a letter or two of the alphabet. The most elaborate ones are Psalm 119, in which each letter of the alphabet has eight verses, and Lamentations 3, where each letter has three verses.

In post-biblical literature the acrostic device is very common, particularly in Hebrew poetry. Often the key letters which make up the author's name are the

זְמִירוֹת לְשַׁבָּת :

יָהּ רִבּוֹן עָלַם וְעָלְמַיָּא · אַנְתְּ הוּא מַלְכָּא מֶלֶךְ
מַלְכַיָּא : עוֹבַד גְּבוּרְתֵּךְ וְתִמְהַיָּא · שְׁפַר קֳדָמָךְ
לְהַחֲוָיָה : יה רבון

שְׁבָחִין אֲסַדֵּר צַפְרָא וְרַמְשָׁא · לָךְ אֱלָהָא קַדִּישָׁא
דִּי בְרָא כָל־נַפְשָׁא · עִירִין קַדִּישִׁין וּבְנֵי אֱנָשָׁא ·
חֵיוַת בָּרָא וְעוֹפֵי שְׁמַיָּא : יה רבון

רַבְרְבִין עוֹבְדָיךְ וְתַקִּיפִין · מָכֵךְ רְמַיָּא זָקֵף כְּפִיפִין ·
לוּ יְחֵא גְבַר שְׁנִין אַלְפִין · לָא יֵעֹל גְּבוּרְתֵּךְ
בְּחֻשְׁבְּנַיָּא : יה רבון

אֱלָהָא דִּי לֵהּ יְקָר וּרְבוּתָא · פְּרֹק יָת־עָנָךְ מִפֻּם
אַרְיָוָתָא · וְאַפֵּק יָת־עַמָּךְ מִגּוֹא גָלוּתָא · עַמָּךְ דִּי
בְחַרְתְּ מִכָּל־אֻמַּיָּא : יה רבון

לְמִקְדְּשָׁךְ תּוּב וּלְקֹדֶשׁ קֻדְשִׁין · אֲתַר דִּי בֵהּ יֶחֱדוּן
רוּחִין וְנַפְשִׁין · וִיזַמְּרוּן שִׁירִין וְרַחֲשִׁין · בִּירוּשְׁלֵם
קַרְתָּא דְי־שֻׁפְרַיָּא : יה רבון

Yah Ribbon Olam, a Sabbath table-hymn written in Aramaic in acrostic form. The first letters of each of the five verses spell the word "Israel." Composed by the 16th-century poet, Israel ben Moses Najara.

middle or last letters of the sentence. Some poets built their poems on the basis of the alphabet backwards, or in a double alphabetical form. Many prayers are in an acrostic form; besides making them easier to remember, the acrostic also ensures that mistakes and deletions will not occur.

In the Middle Ages, and even later, entire works were composed in which every word began with the same letter. The most famous of these is *"Elef Alfin"* ("A thousand *alefs*"), attributed to Abraham Bedersi. A common form of acrostic is the use of the initial letters of the first few words of a work to spell the name of God.

ACTION FRANÇAISE. The trial of Alfred *Dreyfus was a reflection of the anti-Semitism in French society at the very end of the 19th century. At this time, a movement called Action Française was formed and lasted some forty years. Action Française was in favor of French monarchy, and of wiping out Jews.

It claimed that the Jews were causing the evils in French society, and that because of the Jews, the French people were not united. Jews, Freemasons, Protestants and other foreigners, the anti-Semites said, were using slogans of liberty and revolution to disguise their own interests, and to fragmentize France into political units. Thus, to fight these groups was for the good of France. The Action Française was particularly harsh against Jews; the Jew for them was a barbarian, and they tried to cause the failure of any economic enterprise in which Jews were concerned.

Although the movement did not consider itself specifically anti-Semitic, its ideas nevertheless inspired the anti-Semitic laws passed by the Vichy government after France's surrender to Germany in World War II. These laws, aimed at keeping Jews out of French politics and society, were later repealed.

The movement newspaper, *L'Action Française,* appeared from 1908 until 1944. Today neither the movement nor the paper exist, but their spirit is kept alive in racist and Fascist publications.

ADAM AND EVE. When the first man was to be created, says the *aggadah,* God consulted the angels. Some favored his creation, because of the love and mercy he would show; others were opposed — because of the falsehood and strife he would stir up. In the end, for reasons best known to Himself, the Holy One decided to create man.

The early chapters of the Book of Genesis (see *Bible) describe the creation of man as the climax of the Six Days of *Creation. After the completion of heaven and earth, God fashioned the man from dust of the ground, breathed life into his nostrils, and placed him in the Garden of Eden to be its caretaker. He was given permission to eat freely from any tree of the Garden except, under penalty of death, from the Tree of Knowledge of Good and Evil. The man was commanded to give names to all the animals, but among them found no suitable companion. God then put the man to sleep, removed one of his ribs, and fashioned it into a woman, whom Adam found to be a companionable helpmate. He called her Eve, which means "the mother of all living."

The naked couple had no feeling of shame. However, once the artful serpent had induced the woman to eat the fruit of the forbidden tree, and she had shared it with her husband, they became aware of their nakedness and hid from God. As punishment for this transgression, the serpent was condemned to crawl on its belly and eat dust; the woman was sentenced to the pangs of childbirth and to being subject to her husband; and the man was destined to toil and sweat in order to wrest his bread from an accursed and hostile soil, until his return to the dust whence he came.

Having eaten of the Tree of Knowledge of Good and Evil, the man had now become like a divine being, "knowing good and evil." In order to prevent him from eating of the Tree of Life which was also in the Garden, and thereby acquiring the other quality that distinguished the divine beings – immortality – God expelled him from the Garden of Eden and barred access forever to the Tree of Life.

In the Aggadah. In their search for lessons on man's place in God's universe, the rabbis discussed at great length the biblical account of the creation of Adam, which is outlined above. Thus, for example, the Midrash observes that each newly created form of life ruled over what preceded it in the order of creation. Adam and Eve were thus created last in order that they should rule over all creation, and in order that they should be able to enter a banqueting hall that was waiting ready for them. In the words of the Midrash, "The matter may be likened to an emperor's building a palace, consecrating it, preparing the feast, and only then inviting the guests." On the other hand, the rabbis taught that Adam was created last, so that if he should become conceited, he could be told: "The gnat was created before you."

In Medieval Jewish Philosophy. For most of the medieval Jewish thinkers, the biblical story of Adam has both a literal and allegorical meaning. *Judah Halevi wrote that in addition to the loftiest intellect ever possessed by a human being, Adam was endowed with the divine power that enables man to achieve communion with God. *Maimonides held this to be possible through the development of the intellect alone, no other special gift being required. Adam's sin is understood allegorically by Maimonides as a failure to resist the demands of physical passion.

In much the same way Joseph *Albo interprets the whole of the story of the Garden of Eden allegorically, regarding it as a "symbolic allusion to man's fortune in the world." Thus Adam represents all of mankind; the Garden of Eden, the world; the Tree of Life, the Torah; and the serpent, the evil inclination. Just as Adam is placed in the Garden, in the midst of which stands the Tree of Life, so man is placed in the world in order to observe the commandments of the Torah. Having eaten from the forbidden fruit, Adam is banished from the Garden – in the same way, writes Albo, as man is punished if he disobeys the divine commandments. (See also *Creation.)

ADAR, THE SEVENTH OF. According to talmudic tradition, the seventh day of the month of Adar is the anniversary of both the birth and death of Moses. In Oriental communities it became a day of fasting and commemoration for the pious, based on the belief that a spark of the soul of Moses is found in every righteous person.

In medieval Egypt the day signaled a central event in the life of the community. Celebrations were held at the ancient synagogue in the village of Damwah near Cairo, believed by the villagers to be the spot where Moses prayed before going to Pharaoh. The Seventh of Adar was devoted to prayers and supplication, while the following day was a lively carnival. The custom in 17th-century Turkey and Italy was to observe this date as a fast day and to recite specially selected passages from Scripture, the Mishnah and the Zohar.

Today, Sephardi Jews still light candles for the "ascent of the souls of the righteous" on the Seventh of Adar. Some traditional communities recite special *piyyutim,* or hymns, while for the **ḥevra kaddisha* (those who prepare the dead for burial) it is a fast day which is concluded by a special banquet at which new members are admitted.

In Israel this has become the official day for commemorating the death of Israeli soldiers whose last resting place is unknown.

ADLER, ELKAN NATHAN (1861-1946), was a lawyer by profession, and his practice permitted him opportunities for travel to places which could further his real interest: book collecting. As a result he built

1. Adam and Eve beside the forbidden Tree of Knowledge, surrounded by the animals of the Garden of Eden. The words above their heads read, "Adam and Eve, Out Lilith," referring to the legendary demon Lilith who wanted to kill all newborn infants. This 17th-century engraving by Abraham ben Jacob of Amsterdam is accompanied by a prayer for women in childbirth.
2. The *ḥevra kaddisha* (burial society), for whom the Seventh of Adar plays an especially somber role, are depicted in this funeral scene, painted on a glass wine beaker. Prague, 1713.
3. Bookplate used by Elḥanan Ha-Kohen Adler (Nathan Elkan), with the Tomb of Rachel in Bethlehem in the background.

up a remarkable library. He was among the first persons to realize the importance of the Cairo **Genizah*. Adler visited Egypt in 1888 and again in 1895-96, and returned to his native England with about 25,000 fragments of manuscript. Ultimately his library contained 4,500 manuscripts, which he cataloged. He also had a collection of some 30,000 books on Judaica and general fields of interest.

Adler's vast collection was sold in 1923 to the Jewish Theological Seminary and to the Hebrew Union College in order to make good the embezzlements of a business partner. These acquisitions raised both of these libraries to positions of significance. Books acquired by Adler after 1923 passed, after his death, to the Jewish Theological Seminary.

He was an active member of Ḥovevei Zion (see *Ḥibbat Zion), the early forerunner in the 19th century of the Zionist movement.

This versatile son of Great Britain's Chief Rabbi Nathan Marcus Adler was also an author. His published writings were based mainly on his many travels and on materials in his own collection. Many of his books were on Jewish subjects. Among his works are: *History of the Jews of London, Jewish Travellers,* and *About Hebrew Manuscripts,* as well as articles on the Samaritans, and on Egyptian and Persian Jews.

Title page of *Torat ha-Bayit,* by Solomon ben Abraham Adret in which he discusses the laws of most Jewish ritual observances. This 1608 Venice edition also includes Aaron ha-Levi's criticism of the book, called *Bedek ha-Bayit,* and Rashba's answer to the criticism, called *Mishmeret ha-Bayit.*

ADRET, SOLOMON BEN ABRAHAM (c. 1235-c. 1310), was one of the outstanding rabbinic scholars and communal leaders in Spain in the Middle Ages. Many students of rabbinic literature would not recognize the name Adret, for he is usually known, as are many great scholars, by the acronym formed from the Hebrew initials of his name: **Ra**bbi **Sh**elomo **B**en **A**braham = Rashba.

Adret was born to a well-to-do family in Barcelona, where he lived all his life. He studied under the famous *Naḥmanides, being considered one of his outstanding students.

While still young, Adret engaged extensively in financial transactions: the King of Aragon was among his debtors. After a few years he withdrew from business and accepted the position of rabbi in Barcelona, which he held for more than 40 years. Adret was recognized as the leading figure in Spanish Jewry before he was 40. He was a man of great accomplishments, strong character, and incorruptible judgment. Yet he was a humble man, with a warm, sensitive heart.

Questions were addressed to Adret from all parts of the Jewish world including Germany, France, and Palestine. The communities gathered his responsa into special collections and kept them as a source of guidance. He explained the most complicated matters in clear and simple terms. Many of his responsa deal with the clarification of problematic biblical passages, and some of them touch on questions of philosophy and the fundamentals of religion. Adret's responsa are also a primary source of information for the history of the Jews of the period.

Adret had a considerable knowledge of Roman law and local Spanish legal practice and played a vital role in providing the legal basis for the structure of the Jewish community and its institutions.

Although Adret was well-versed in philosophy and the scientific literature of his day, he forbade the study of philosophy by the young (less than 25 years old) because he felt that such study could mislead the unlearned.

Adret headed a yeshivah to which students flocked even from Germany and other countries. His famous commentary on the Talmud is the result of his lectures. Adret's responsa which are extant today have at all times been highly influential and are a major source of Jewish *Law.

ADVERTISING. In modern times Jews have had great influence on the art of advertising, especially in America. Originally, businesses wrote out their own advertising copy, and the advertising agencies only arranged for the sale of space in which to advertise. This was changed by Albert D. Lasker, who had joined the Chicago advertising agency of Lord and Thomas in 1898. He provided his own first-rate copywriters, who used a great deal of imagination in their work. In 1904, when he was only 24 years old, Albert Lasker became a partner in the firm, and by 1912 he was the sole owner.

In 1918 Milton H. Biow (1892-) started a modern one-man advertising agency, which conducted advertising business for 40 years, becoming one of the largest and best known agencies in the United States and abroad. He was the first to use radio and television "spots" for short advertisements.

Grey Advertising was founded in 1917 by Lawrence Valenstein (1899-) when he was only 18 years old. He later took in two partners, and all three advertised a product before it went onto the market, in an attempt to produce a demand for that product even before it appeared. In 1936 this agency circulated a newsletter called *Grey Matter,* which was read by many people in the advertising industry and in the business world. The agency became most successful, with branches in Canada, Japan and Europe.

A former director of Grey Advertising, William Bernbach (1911-), who was born in the Bronx, New York, started his own agency in 1949 together with two partners. In less than 20 years the agency became the sixth largest in the United States. William Bernbach introduced new methods and won many awards, and his style was often copied by others. In

1

2

1. The poster is one form of advertising widely used in Israel. This one, incorporating a photo by contemporary French photographer Israel Bidermanas (Izis), is intended to encourage student tourism in the Holy Land.
2. A page of classified ads from the "Forward," an American Yiddish daily. June 13, 1920.

1955, when Norman B. Norman (1914-) bought control of the business, the name of the agency was changed to Norman, Craig and Kummel.

Several other Jews have made important contributions to advertising. One of them, Monroe Green (1905-), is an advertising vice-president of the *New York Times*. In Britain, Jews only held important positions in advertising after World War II. In Europe, Jewish participation in this field was brought to an abrupt end by the Nazi Holocaust. However, since World War II, Jews working in American and British advertising agencies have extended their work to Europe, where they compete with European agents.

In Ereẓ Israel there was very little advertising during the time of the British Mandate. The first advertising agency was set up in Jerusalem by Benjamin Levinson in 1922. He was soon followed by a few others. Immigrants coming from Germany between 1933 and 1939 opened a few more modern agencies. Large-scale advertising only began in the 1950s, as industry developed in Israel.

Most agencies in Israel place their advertisements in the daily press. In fact, Israel's 25 newspapers receive two-thirds of all advertising. Other media are the radio, exhibitions, shop windows and cinemas. There is no commercial TV in Israel.

AERONAUTICS, AVIATION, AND ASTRONAUTICS. Every aviation-minded country in the world has benefited from the aircraft designs of outstanding Jewish citizens.

One of the earliest inventions by a Jew was the "Zeppelin"; designed in 1892 by David **Schwarz**, a Zagreb (Yugoslav) timber merchant, who taught

himself the principles of engineering and mechanics. His airship was cigar-shaped and had an aluminum framework. He died of shock when he learned that the German government had agreed to take up his project. The designs were carried through to production by Count Zeppelin.

Emile Berliner (1851-1929), who emigrated to the U.S. in 1870, was the first man to make lightweight revolving-cylinder internal-combustion engines and to equip airplanes with them. Between 1919 and 1926 he built and tested three helicopters. His son, Henry Adler Berliner (1895-), an aeronautical engineer, was chief of war plans for the Eighth Air Force during World War II.

Marcel Bloch (1892-), who later changed his name to Marcel Dassault, became a major aircraft manufacturer in France during the two World Wars. He designed one of the first four-engined transport planes, and also the Mystère and Mirage fighter jets, among the best in the world, which were used by the Israel air force during the *Six-Day War and the *Yom Kippur War.

World War II found a number of Jews in key aircraft positions. In England, Sir Ben Lockspeiser (1891-) conducted research at the Royal Aircraft Establishment in Farnborough from 1920 to 1927, when he became head of the government air defense department. During World War II he headed research at the Air Ministry, and became Director-General of the Ministry of Aircraft Production

In France, René Bloch (1923-) was Director of Aviation in the French navy and later in the Ministry of Defense.

The Israel aircraft industry manufactures training jets and is reportedly producing a first line jet fighter powered by an American engine. The industry does a great deal of renewing and rebuilding passenger planes and produces a small transport and an executive jet.

Astronautics. In the U.S.A., the National Aeronautics and Space Administration (NASA), operates the

1

1. Only known photo in existence of David Schwarz's aluminum "Zeppelin," the first such ship made of rigid materials.
2. *Rumplertaube* – observation plane designed by German pioneer aircraft manufacturer Eduard Rumpler in 1908, capable of flying at what was then the great height of 25,000 feet.

United States astronautical program. Abe Silverstein is a director of its Lewis Research Center; Abraham Hyatt directs program planning and evaluation; Leonard Jaffe is director of Communications Systems of Satellites.

In Russia, too, it is assumed that Jews are involved in the space program. Lieutenant-Colonel Boris Volynov is said to be Jewish. In 1969 he commanded the spaceship "Soyuz-5," which performed the first link-up in space, when cosmonauts transferred from one spaceship to another.

AFGHANISTAN is a Muslim state in Central Asia which some early Bible commentators regarded as the home of the Ten Lost Tribes of Israel. In the Babylonian era persons unwanted by the Jewish leadership, rival candidates for example, were exiled to Afghanistan because of its distance.

Medieval sources mention several Jewish centers. Balkh was the most important, and there is evidence from Moses Ibn Ezra and *Benjamin of Tudela that there were 40,000 Jews living in Ghazni in the year 1000 C.E.

About 20 recently-discovered stone tablets, with Persian and Hebrew inscriptions dating from 1115 to 1215, prove the existence of a Jewish community in the town of Firoz Koh. However, the Mongol invasion in 1222 annihilated the town and its community.

Little is known about the Jews of Afghanistan until the 19th century when, because of forced conversions, many Jews fled from Persia and settled in Herat and Kabul where they could live as Jews. They were traders in skins, carpets and antiquities and they spoke a Judeo-Persian dialect, in which they produced fine religious poetry. At the end of the 19th century they moved to Ereẓ Israel.

About 5,000 Jews were living in Afghanistan in 1948. Of these, about 300 remained in 1969, some 4,000 having emigrated to Israel, and the rest to Iran or to India. Most of them were poverty-stricken tailors and shoemakers. At the beginning of the 20th century Afghanistan families living in Jerusalem published Judeo-Persian commentaries on the Bible and other works.

AGE AND THE AGED.

In the Bible. The Bible regards long life as a blessing and it is promised as a reward for observing certain commandments. To this day, in Hebrew and in Yiddish, people sometimes wish their friends life "to 120 years." This figure is based on a verse in Genesis (6:3) which says: "Let the days allowed man be one hundred and twenty years." The prophet Zechariah gives a happy description of old age when he speaks of the days to come. "There shall yet be old men and women in the public squares of Jerusalem," alongside "boys and girls playing in its public squares" (8:4).

On the other hand, the Bible mentions that Isaac's eyes were dim with age (Genesis 27:1) and some of the descriptions of old age are grim indeed, as in the Book of Ecclesiastes (12:1-6). The psalmist expressed the prayer of countless ageing folk when we wrote: "Do not cast me away in the time of old age; when my strength is failing, do not forsake me."

In his youth King Solomon wrote the lyrical Song of Songs, in his maturity the wisdom of Proverbs, and in his old age he wrote Ecclesiastes, in which he looks back and realizes what emptiness there is in many people's lives. The sages saw this as a symbol of the changes which take place in a man's way of thinking as he ages: "When a man is young, he quotes poetry; when he matures, he quotes proverbs; when he grows old he speaks of the things he has found to be worthless."

Because of the experience of the aged, old age and wisdom are sometimes regarded as going together. Thus, throughout the Bible and Talmud, the word "elder" means judge, leader, or sage. On the other hand, the Book of Job also stresses that there are young men who are wiser than old men. Nevertheless, respect for the aged is always a *mitzvah*: "You shall rise before gray hairs, and show respect to the old man" (Leviticus 19:32). Indeed, the prophet Isaiah speaks of disrespect for the aged as a sign of a corrupt generation (3:5).

In the Talmud. There are passages in the Talmud which describe the later years of life as unattractive, because of the disabilities that often accompany old age: "The rocks have grown tall, the near have become too distant to visit, two legs have become three [by the addition of a cane], and the peacemaker of the house makes peace no longer." Most of the rabbis held that with age there also comes a dimming of mental ability. Thus Elisha ben Avuyah said: "What does learning when old resemble? It is like writing on blotted-out paper."

Some rare instances may be found of praise for age itself. According to Rabbi Johanan, for example, only elders sat in the Sanhedrin supreme court – though not beyond a certain age. Another sage points out that age itself is not a virtue: its value depends on wisdom and knowledge of the Torah. Thus in a

1

2

1. Aged Soviet Jewish farmer in the Ukraine, 1936.
2. A contrast of youth and old age – grandmother and grandchild in Karczew, Poland.

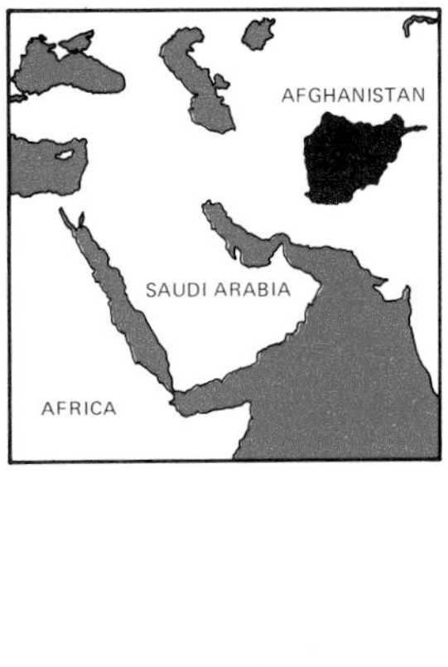

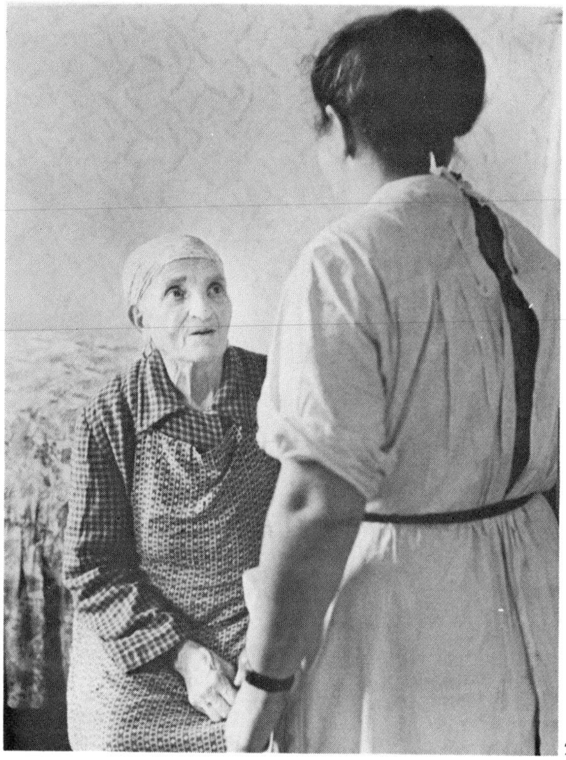

1. A talmudic *aggadah* dealing with Asmodeus, "king of the demons," who is seen here abducting Sarah. *Regensburg Pentateuch,* c. 1300.

2. Resident of an old-age home in Lodz, Poland, 1960.

certain discussion Rabbi Abbahu claimed that because he was older, the law should be decided according to his way of thinking. To which Rabbi Jeremiah answered: "Is the matter decided by age? It is decided by reason." On another occasion one of the sages taught that "the learned, as they grow older, grow wiser; the ignorant, as they grow older, become more foolish."

There were therefore two opinions among the sages as to the meaning of the verse: "You shall rise before the aged." Some held that this really meant the learned, arguing that "none may be called venerable except for the wise." Hence honor would be due to a young scholar, but not to an old ignoramus. Others disagreed. Rabbi Joḥanan, for example, used to stand in order to show respect for aged gentiles. One talmudic sage suggested the following compromise: "At the Academy respect wisdom; in company – respect age." In the case of the exceedingly old, Maimonides rules that one must always honor them by rising, even if they are not wise.

Thinking back on their younger years, some of the sages once said: "Happy is the old age that atones for the follies of youth; but happier still is the youth for which old age need not blush."

Care of the Aged. The problem of earning a livelihood in old age is discussed in the Talmud: "Every profession in the world is of help to a man only in his youth, but in his old age he is exposed to hunger." The rest of the community is obligated by the Torah to support the aged, like all other needy persons.

In the Middle Ages, authors of Jewish ethical works and communal regulations (*takkanot*) stressed the special need of the aged for charity and tender treatment. The suffering of the aged grew in this period, as families were broken by persecution and forced migrations, such as after the Chmielnicki massacres of 1648.

A home for the aged was founded in Amsterdam by the Sephardi community in 1749. The practice of establishing such a *moshav zekenim* soon spread throughout Europe. In Germany, for example, there were 67 homes for the aged by 1938, with 3,568 beds. American Jewish communities often provide welfare services that enable the aged to remain in their familiar surroundings. In 1966 there were 70 American Jewish homes for the aged, with about 12,500 beds, attending to the needs of nearly 16,000 elderly people.

The Nazi Holocaust, and the forced mass migration of Jews from Arab countries to Israel, have brought special problems. In Israel, the Malben organization strives to solve the special problems to be expected among the many refugees in the country. These include premature ageing, and the difficulties of aged people who have been uprooted from one society and have to adjust to another way of life which they often did not choose freely. Nearly two-thirds of the aged from Oriental families live with their children, compared with about one-third of the aged of European families. The 7,500 elderly persons who do not live alone or with their families, live in various institutions.

AGGADAH. Although there is a great deal of legal discussion in the *Talmud, more than half of that monumental work is devoted to what is known as *aggadah.* This is the name given to the material that tells historical stories and personal anecdotes, as well as homiletic interpretations of verses from the Bible. Much of the talmudic *aggadah* is also found in the *Midrash.

The sages used the *aggadah* to influence their listeners, and the stories usually set a moral and ethical standard. A particular story might not be reality, but it is nonetheless truth insofar as it teaches moral truths. The aim of much of the *aggadah* is to teach a person Judaism's most important commandments – *love and fear of God, and faith. This is what the rabbis meant when they said: "If you wish to know God, study the *aggadah.*"

Aggadah takes many different forms. It can be a narrative, a short or even lengthy story. It may be a legend, enhanced and embellished through the ages. Often, too, the *aggadah* expresses doctrines or maxims. On the surface many of the *aggadot* are simple, even childish, but they usually contain symbolism, and it is this which makes the *aggadah* so difficult to understand. Today we are so far removed from the source of the *aggadah* that this deeper message has often been lost to us. Only a concentrated study of the rabbinic sources can regain the hidden or lost meaning.

"Abraham's Bosom," relief on the north facade of the Cathedral of Rheims, 13th century. In Christian mythology, as in Jewish aggadic literature, Abraham is the warden of paradise and the protector of souls. He is therefore depicted here as the one who receives the souls from the angels.

Much of the *aggadah* dates from Second Temple times or even earlier. The sages repeatedly added to the *aggadah,* each generation making its special contribution. Throughout the mishnaic and talmudic period, the sages would devote their sermons not only to legal matters but also to *aggadah.* The rabbis often chose this method to repudiate criticism of Judaism made by its enemies. Many *aggadot* were sermons which seem to be harmless stories, but which in fact present political views that could not be expressed openly, either because of an oppressive foreign government or (at a later period) because of the ruling Church. For example, when Roman suppression of Judaism threatened to shake the loyalty of certain Jews, Rabbi *Akiva told them the following *aggadah* in order to warn them of the dangers of deserting their faith:

A cunning fox, strolling along the banks of a river, saw that the fish in it were greatly agitated.

"What do you fear?" he asked.

"We can see the fishermen with their fearsome nets. They're coming to catch us!" they cried.

"Then, my dear friends," said the fox, "do me the courtesy of joining me up here, and enjoy with me the safety of the dry land."

The fish were quick to decline his seemingly kind invitation: "Fool!" they retorted. "If we are in danger in the water, which is our native element, how much more will we be in danger if we exchange it for a foreign environment!"

Another type of *aggadah,* also often disguised in simple form, was in reality a mystical message. Since mysticism does not lend itself well to exact expression, the rabbis would use a parable or an allegory to make themselves understood.

In the times of the Mishnah and Talmud – in the early centuries of the Common Era – *aggadah* was an essential part of Jewish learning, being listed side by side with the Bible, Mishnah, and *halakhah.* However, unlike the *halakhah, aggadah* has no binding force. It is not heretical to hold opinions different from the *aggadah* and there are numerous contradictions in the *aggadah* itself. Obviously, one story cannot be used to question a different *aggadah,* as the total body of the *aggadah* represents views of different sages over more than a thousand years, and many *aggadot* were meant for a specific time or event. The total sum of the *aggadah,* however, represents Jewish thought and tradition over one of the most important periods of Jewish history and is itself one of the pillars of Judaism.

AGNON, SHMUEL YOSEF (1888-1970). Agnon was the first Hebrew writer to be awarded the Nobel Prize for Literature. One of the central figures in modern Hebrew fiction, his works deal with the conflict between traditional Jewish life and the modern world, and attempt to recapture the fading traditions of the European shtetl, or township.

Shmuel Yosef Czaczkes (Agnon's original name) was born in the Jewish shtetl of Buczacz, Galicia, where his father was a fur merchant and follower of the ḥasidic *rebbe* of Chortkov. Agnon did not go to school but received his education from his father who taught him *aggadah,* and from his mother who taught him German literature. When he was eight years old he began to write in Hebrew and Yiddish, and at 15 published his first Yiddish poem. In the following years he began to publish regularly and wrote 70 pieces in Hebrew and Yiddish within three years.

2

As a young man, Agnon left his shtetl of Buczacz and immigrated to Israel, where he temporarily left his religious way of life. Shortly afterwards, however, he returned to Jewish tradition and remained an observant Jew for the rest of his life.

His first short story *Agunot* ("Forsaken Wives") was published in Palestine in 1924 under the pen-name Agnon, which bears a resemblance to the title of the story, and which became his official family name thereafter.

In 1913, Agnon left Israel for Germany where he remained for 11 years. Zionist young people liked his combination of traditional and modern ways of writing. In Germany Agnon met the wealthy businessman Salman Schocken, who became his admirer, supporter, and publisher. Free from financial worries Agnon lived comfortably, wrote much, and collected rare and valuable Hebrew books. This happy period ended in 1924 when a fire swept his home and destroyed most of his books and manuscripts. In the same year, Agnon settled again in Jerusalem, but again his valuable library was destroyed, this time when his home was plundered during the Arab riots of 1929.

In 1931, he became recognized as one of the central figures of modern Hebrew literature when he published the first edition of his collected works, including the folk-epic *The Bridal Canopy,* considered to be a cornerstone of modern Hebrew literature. Running through his stories is the ever-recurring conflict between old and new, and many of his stories have a nightmarish quality, as they leave the reader wondering what is real and what is fantasy. Characters talk to themselves in an attempt to understand themselves and their puzzling surroundings. In *A Guest for the Night,* an anonymous narrator visits his town in Galicia after an absence of many years, and witnesses its desolation. The factual core of this story was Agnon's own visit to his native town of Buczacz in 1930. Although the novel mirrors the hopelessness of the Jewish world during this time, Agnon even in his youth had called Buczacz a "city of the dead."

What is considered to be Agnon's greatest novel *Temol Shilshom* ("Yesterday and the Day Before"), is a powerful description of Palestine in the days of the Second Aliyah, but its spirit reflects the period in which it was written, the years of the Holocaust.

In addition to his other works Agnon published about half a dozen new short pieces every year, mostly in the Hebrew newspaper *Haaretz.* Many of his books are about Buczacz, while others are popular collections of rabbinic lore and ḥasidic tales. One of these collections is *Days of Awe,* "a treasury of traditions, legends, and learned commentaries concerning Rosh Ha-Shanah, Yom Kippur, and the days between, culled from 300 volumes ancient and new." Another collection of stories, and the major novel *Shirah,* were published after his death.

Agnon received many awards including the Israel Prize in 1954 and 1958. The crowning honor was the Nobel Prize for Literature in 1966, the first granted to a Hebrew writer.

1

1. Cover of a children's book by S.Y. Agnon, *Ma'aseh ha-Ez* ("The Story of the Goat"). Published in 1925.
2. Shmuel Agnon (right) being applauded by King Gustaf VI of Sweden, upon receiving the Nobel Prize for Literature in Stockholm, 1966.

AGRICULTURE. "Judah and Israel dwelt safely, every man under his vine and fig tree from Dan to Beersheba" (I Kings 4:7). The history of Jewish farming has fluctuated since biblical times, but Jews have retained an attachment to the land in spite of drought, dispersion, wars, the Holocaust, and a modern civilization of industry and commerce.

The Jewish agricultural tradition is clearly found in the Bible. Farming was not easy work. Much of the land was stony or thickly wooded with forests, and when cleared land was not used for farming or grazing, forests began to grow and wild animals would invade those areas. Nevertheless, the early Hebrews were successful; the Patriarchs were wealthy farmers and herdsmen. The tribe of Reuben, the son of Jacob, is described as "living among the sheepfolds, to hear the bleating of the flock" (Judges 5:16).

Rain was the most important element in successful farming. Ample rainfall was a blessing and a reward. The Bible frequently repeats the warning that rain would be withheld because of sin. For many centuries the synagogue service of Shemini Aẓeret has included a prayer for rain. There are more details on this under the heading *Rain and Dew.

Although the country is described as "a land of brooks of water, of fountains and depths springing forth in valleys and hills" (Deuteronomy 8:7) there is no evidence that in ancient times there were more than the hundreds of small springs and the few significant water sources which now exist. The ancient Israelites were careful in their use of rain, which was often stored in cisterns. They mastered the cultivation of the soil, often farming the hills as well. In order to protect the topsoil from erosion, they built contoured stone terraces, some of which may still be seen today. However, many were unfortunate, as the Torah had predicted: "The poor shall never cease out of the land" (Deuteronomy 25:11). For the poor, farmers were required by the Torah to leave the gleanings, the forgotten sheaves, the corners of the field, and a percentage of their crop. The article on *Charity discusses this further.

Every seventh year, and every fiftieth year, the land had to lie fallow. Other special laws (some of which also benefit the poor) apply to the land and its produce, and these are set out in the article on *Sabbatical Year and Jubilee.

When Israel returned from exile in Babylonia in the time of Ezra and Nehemiah in the fifth century b.c.e., farming difficulties increased. The rich had taken lands from the poor. In the talmudic period, a few centuries later, Josephus wrote about the Galilee: "The land is so rich in soil and pasturage, and produces such a variety of trees, that even the laziest are tempted to devote themselves to agriculture." But Roman conquerors seized land from the Jews and many areas were laid waste. From the fourth century c.e. farming became progressively more difficult and only those farmers who enjoyed the favor of the rulers could maintain themselves.

After the destruction of the Second Temple in 70 c.e. Jews in exile in Babylonia became farmers. The climate there was better than in Ereẓ Israel and rain was more bountiful. In Palestine prayers for rain were usual; in Babylonia public prayers were offered against floods. In the rest of the Diaspora, severe restrictions and heavy taxes were levied against Jewish farmers. From the end of the eighth century agriculture became a marginal Jewish occupation in both Christian and Muslim lands. Nevertheless, Jews continued to farm the land, often owning large farms with hired labor. Some dealt in livestock and farm produce, or engaged in crafts based on agricultural materials, such as hides and fibers.

1

2

1. Picking plums on an Israel agricultural settlement. The varied climates in Israel permit the cultivation of a wide variety of fruits, 80% of which are grown on irrigated land.
2. This youngster is proudly bearing a crate of live chicks, grown by the Israeli Poultry Breeders Union, to be shipped to Nicosia.

Arab farmer plowing a rocky hillside, using a primitive agricultural implement similar to those used by his ancestors thousands of years ago. Though oxen are generally used to pull such plows, this farmer chose to use his camel.

In 18th and 19th century Europe some Jews were involved in agriculture through the marketing of farm products, and in the West Indies there were Jewish plantation owners. In Eastern Europe Jewish farm owners and tenant farmers became numerous; their presence prompted the movement to settle numbers of Jews on the land. The projects of Baron de *Hirsch assisted greatly, and by 1930 about 6% of the Jews in Eastern Europe were farmers.

In the United States Jewish farming was known as early as 1820 when Mordecai Manuel *Noah was granted permission to found Ararat, his model community near Niagara. To help absorb the massive immigration from Russia in the 1880s, farming was encouraged and assisted by Baron de Hirsch and by welfare organizations such as HIAS (Hebrew Immigrant Aid Society). Poultry farming was especially popular and was used to absorb large numbers of immigrants. Vineland and Woodbine, N.J., early in the 20th century, and later Toms River and Farmingdale, N.J. were known as "Chickenville." At the end of World War II there were about 20,000 Jewish farming families. The number has since diminished as the general farm population in the U.S. has decreased.

Agriculture in modern Israel is discussed in the article on *Israel.

Ancient Agricultural Methods. A farmer in the 1970s would not get very far with the use of farm tools available to our ancestors. Yet on the lands of ancient Israel farmers were able to produce an abundance in crop yields that has been approached again only in our day. Many of their primitive implements are still used by Arab peasants.

The soil was plowed twice, first to allow the rainwater to penetrate, and then to level the ground before planting or sowing. The ancient wooden plow used in Israel had a plowshare made of bronze, or later of iron. The heads of the oxen were framed in a wooden yoke, which was tied to the plow, and a hoe was used to remove weeds in mountain areas where the plow could not reach. Water for irrigation was drawn from a well in earthenware or metal pitchers attached to a rope or chain.

For harvesting, a curved blade with short teeth bent backward was inserted into a short handle, to make a sickle. The reaper grasped the stalks in his left hand while cutting, and would lay the grain on the ground in bundles tied together with straw, and later tied into larger sheaves ready to be sent to the threshing floor.

When threshing, in order to separate the kernels from the husks, a large wooden board whose underside was set with basalt stones was dragged over the grain by a pair of oxen. The grains could then be shaken horizontally in a round sieve with a fiber net attached. This winnowing caused the lighter elements to be carried away by the wind while the heavier kernels fell down in a heap. The kernels were then milled or crushed.

Among other implements in use were churns to make milk into butter, and presses for wine and olive oil. An ancient olive press which was recently excavated is on display at the Israel Museum in Jerusalem, while other ancient implements may be seen in Jerusalem's Agricultural Museum.

AGRIPPA I (10 b.c.e. - 44 c.e.) became a beloved and respected king of Judea although his early life was one of quarreling, drunkenness and flight from debt. The son of Aristobulus and Berenice, grandson of King Herod of Judea, and Mariamne, the Hasmonean princess, he was educated in Rome with the princes of other courts. These connections were important to him later in his life. During periods of political turmoil among the vassal states of Rome, Aggripa was rewarded with appointment as ruler of parts of the Kingdom of Israel (37 c.e.) and later of Judea and Samaria (41 c.e.).

His three-year reign was a period of relief and benefit for the Jews. He was sympathetic to the Pharisees and careful to observe Jewish laws. Thoughtful and sincere, Agrippa once stopped his own procession to let a bride's pass first. He was not proud, and celebrated the festival of First Fruits with other residents of Jerusalem. When called to read the Torah he stood, although a king was allowed to sit. When he read the passage: "One from among thy brethren shalt thou set a king over thee: thou mayest not put a foreigner over thee" (Deuteronomy 17:15), his eyes filled with tears, since he was not of pure Jewish descent. But the rabbis called out, "Agrippa, you are our brother."

His death (44 c.e.) was sudden and mysterious. It was thought that he had been poisoned by Romans who feared his popularity with his subjects.

AGUILAR, GRACE (1816-1847) was an English author of Portuguese Marrano extraction, who wrote a number of novels on Jewish themes and some religious works addressed primarily to Jewish women. Her first book was a volume of poems, *The Magic*

Two ivory lions from King Ahab's "House of Ivory," built in Samaria in the ninth century. Ahab rebuilt the city of Samaria, after fighting off an invasion by King Ben Hadad of Damascus, and erected an acropolis, a royal palace, and a high protective wall. The use of expensive materials such as ivory is evidence of the economic prosperity during Ahab's reign.

Wreath, which she published anonymously when she was only 19 years old. Her truly creative period, however, began in 1842, and in the five years until her death at the age of 31 her literary output was remarkable, particularly because at the same time, although very ill, she was helping her mother run a private school in London.

Most of Grace Aguilar's books were not published until after her death. The best known of her Jewish novels was *The Vale of Cedars,* a romantic, highly idealized picture of the Marranos in Spain. Twice translated into German and twice into Hebrew, it long retained popularity. She also wrote stories and sketches based on Jewish life and family traditions. In a more serious vein, she translated from French the apologetic work of an ex-Marrano, Orobio de Castro, *Israel Defended* (1838). She herself wrote *The Spirit of Judaism: In Defense of Her Faith and Its Professors,* and *The Jewish Faith.* The latter took the form of letters addressed to a friend wavering in her religious conviction. Her *Women of Israel* was a series of biographical sketches of biblical characters, intended to arouse the pride of young Jews in their heritage. Grace Aguilar was one of the first English Jews to attempt to write a history of the Jews in England; it appeared in *Chambers' Miscellany.* She died while on a visit to Germany. Her collected works, in eight volumes, appeared in 1861.

AHAB (c. 874-852 b.c.e.). "Ahab denies the God of Israel" were the words that Ahab, king of Northern Israel for 22 years, inscribed over the gates of the city of Samaria. It is no wonder that the Bible (I Kings) says that Ahab did more to anger God than all the kings of Israel before him.

Although Ahab, son of *Omri, became an idol-worshiper, he was not entirely corrupt. He believed in the prophets of Israel and consulted them before military campaigns. He built Samaria and fortified Jericho and other cities. But when he extended the army's power and put its commanders in charge of provinces, he upset the traditional rule of the elders of Israel.

Ahab became rich. He stimulated commerce, and during his reign Israel became prosperous. But the wealth was limited to the nobility and to traders. They ignored the plight of the small farmers who were impoverished by many years of war. Some of them had to sell their children into slavery in order to pay their debts. Discontent grew into active opposition, led by *Elijah the Prophet.

The most bitter criticism of Ahab, however, was that he did not restrict the wicked activities of his wife Jezebel, a Phoenician idol-worshiper. It was Jezebel, permitted by her husband to do as she pleased, who introduced worship of the idol Baal, and had many temples built to his honor. Many Israelites who remained faithful to God were persecuted. One of Jezebel's tricks convinced her husband to put an innocent man to death because of her selfishness.

The Bible (I Kings 21) tells how Ahab coveted the vineyard of Naboth the Jezreelite and offered to buy it or exchange it for another. But Naboth was not willing to give up his family inheritance. Ahab accepted this, but Jezebel would not. She arranged to have two unprincipled witnesses testify falsely at a public trial that Naboth had cursed God and the king. As a punishment, Naboth was stoned to death. Jezebel then told Ahab that Naboth was dead. The vineyard was his.

Elijah rose in anger against Ahab: "Hast thou killed, and also taken possession?" The prophet foretold that Jezebel's body would be eaten by dogs, which would also lick Ahab's blood in the place where they licked the blood of Naboth. And indeed when the King was killed in a battle against Aram, dogs licked the blood from the royal chariot.

The *aggadah* tells that because of Ahab's sins, he was one of the three or four kings who would have no share in the world to come.

In his novel *Moby Dick,* Herbert Melville names his chief character Captain Ahab, a complex personality like this king of Israel.

1. Photo of Aḥad Ha-Am taken in 1925, three years after he settled in Ereẓ Israel, where he remained until his death. During this period he completed the work on *Al Parashat Derakhim,* dictated his memoirs, and edited his letters for later publication.

2. Title page of the first volume of *Ha-Shiloa'aḥ*, the Hebrew literary journal founded by Aḥad Ha-Am in 1896. It served a broad Jewish readership in Eastern Europe.

Aḥad Ha-Am

AḤAD HA-AM (1856-1927). It has been said that the pen is mightier than the sword. In modern Jewish history one man who really accomplished great things with his pen was Aḥad Ha-am. As a writer, he definitely changed the history of the Jewish people through the many essays and articles he wrote. Aḥad Ha-am lived in Odessa in Russia where he worked for a tea company, and also in London. He travelled several times to Ereẓ Israel, and finally settled in Tel Aviv in 1921. His numerous works are now collected in four volumes called *Al Parashat ha-Derakhim,* which means "at the crossroads." He felt that the Jewish people stood at a crossroad in its history and undertook to point out the way which he felt was the right one. "Aḥad Ha-Am" means "one of the people," and was not his real name. He was given the name Asher Hirsch Ginsberg at birth and took the pseudonym when he began to write. He wanted to show that he was really one with the Jewish people when he talked about matters that concerned the whole future of the nation.

When Aḥad Ha-Am was a young man, Jews were beginning to settle farms and villages in Palestine. An organization called Ḥovevei Zion ("Lovers of Zion") was urging Jews to leave Russia and establish a homeland in Ereẓ Israel. Aḥad Ha-Am joined this organization because he too believed in the goal of Zionism – establishing a Jewish homeland. He soon visited the young settlements and then wrote his first famous essay, *Lo Zeh ha-Derekh,* in which he claimed that the settlements were doing very poorly and would not draw many Jews to them. Aḥad Ha-Am held that the first task of Ḥovevei Zion must be to educate Jews so that they would want to live in Ereẓ Israel. He felt that people would not become pioneers in a strange land where life was extremely hard if they were not especially inspired. They needed some special purpose if they were going to make that great sacrifice.

Aḥad Ha-Am believed that the reason for settling in Ereẓ Israel and for being a loyal member of the Jewish people must come from Judaism itself. In many of his essays he tried to explain what he thought the meaning of Judaism really was. He taught that Judaism had contributed some great and unique ideas to the world, of which the most important was

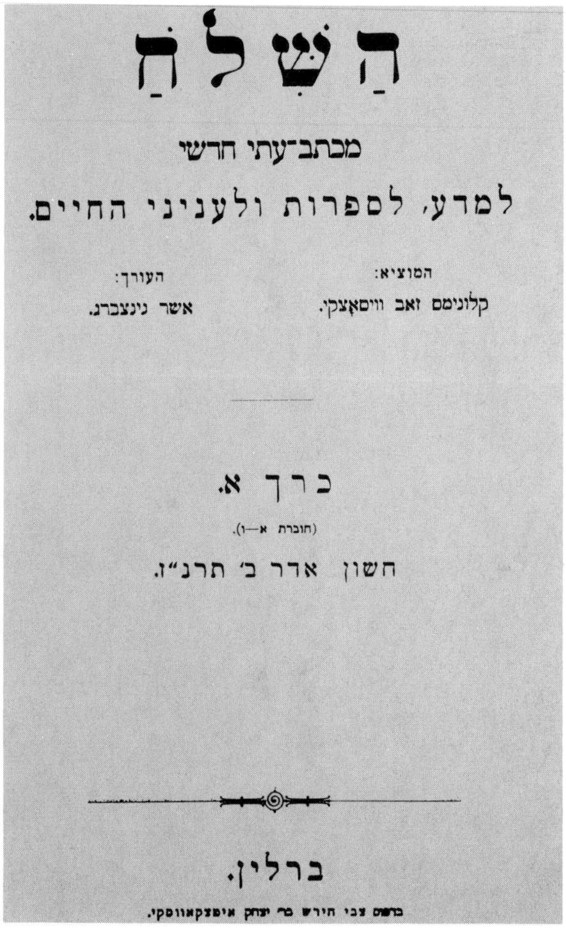

הַשִׁלֹחַ

מכתב־עתי חדשי

למדע, לספרות ולעניני החיים.

המוציא: קלונימס זאב ויסאצקי.

העורך: אשר גינצברג.

כרך א.

(חוברת א—ו).

חשון אדר ב׳ תרנ״ז.

ברלין.

בדפוס צבי הירש בר׳ יצחק איטצקאווסקי.

that complete justice should be everywhere, among all men, and that Jews must try to set an example to all men by living a just life and building a good society themselves. In Ereẓ Israel Jews who were proud of this ideal would establish a society based on honesty and justice. In such a society new life would be given to Judaism. Jewish history and culture would be studied, and teachers would go out from Israel to all areas where Jews lived. In this sense, Ereẓ Israel would be a spiritual center of a renewed Jewish life, and would breathe this life into all the communities of the Exile. This ideal of Aḥad Ha-Am was very powerful and many Zionists followed his teachings, although others opposed and fought his views.

AḤIMAAẒ BEN PALTIEL (1017-c. 1060) was a chronicler and poet of Capua, south Italy. In 1054 when he removed to Oria, the place of origin of his family, he compiled *Megillat Yuḥasin* ("The Scroll of Genealogies"), also known as *Megillat Aḥi-ma'aẓ* ("The Chronicle of Aḥi-maaẓ"). In rhymed prose it describes the genealogy of his family from the ninth century to his own time. The Aḥimaaẓ family counted among its members prominent personalities, who had been leaders of their generation in the different communities of Italy, as well as in North Africa. They actively participated in some of the most important events in those countries. *Megillat Aḥi-ma'aẓ* is consequently a significant Jewish historical source covering several periods and countries. It also includes legends and fantastic tales but, despite some inaccuracies, it is a reliable historical document. The one known manuscript is in the library of Toledo Cathedral, where it was discovered by A. Neubauer in 1895. It has since been edited three more times.

AKAVYAH BEN MAHALALEL (first century c.e.).

Reflect upon three things and you will not sin: know where you came from; where you are going; and before Whom you are destined to give account. (*Avot 3:1*).

Akavyah's maxim illustrates his awareness of the presence of God and his understanding of the human condition. He was offered the position of chief of the *Sanhedrin on condition that he renounce four of his decisions in which he disagreed with the majority, but he refused, declaring: "It is better for me to be called a fool all my days than I should become even for one hour a wicked man in the sight of God; and that men should say, 'He withdrew his opinions for the sake of power.' " One of his opinions resulted in his excommunication. Although he remained firm in his convictions until death, Akavyah admonished his son to accept the opinion of the majority. His son's entreaty "Commend me to your colleagues," elicited the reply: "Your own deeds will bring you commendation or your rejection." According to the Mishnah Akavyah died while still under the ban, but two great sages denied that Akavyah was ever put under a ban. One declared: "God forbid that we should think that Akavyah was excommunicated, for the Temple court was never closed (a consequence of excommunication) in the face of a man so great in wisdom and in fear of sin as Akavyah ben Mahalalel."

AKEDAH. The story of the *Akedah*, Abraham's readiness to sacrifice his beloved son Isaac, has become the supreme example of self-sacrifice in obedience to God's will, and the ageless symbol of Jewish martyrdom. The Bible opens the story in these words: "Some time afterward God put Abraham to the test. He said to him, "Abraham," and he answered, "Here I am." And He said, "Take your son, your favored son, Isaac, whom you love, and go to the land of Moriah, and offer him there as a burnt offering on one of the heights which I will point out to you" (Genesis 22:1-2).

Abraham was obedient to the divine command even though Isaac represented his only hope for the fulfillment of God's promise to make of him a great nation. He took Isaac to Mount Moriah as he was told, and bound him on an altar. An angel of the

Mosaic from the floor of the sixth-century Bet Alfa synagogue in the Jezreel Valley, Israel. Abraham stands pointing a knife at Isaac, who is bound near the altar. Behind Abraham, a ram is tied to a tree, the hand of God is seen between the sun's rays above, and Abraham's two servants and donkey wait on the left.

Lord bade Abraham stay his hand, and a ram was sacrificed in place of Isaac.

Abraham's willingness was unprecedented: he was not guided by any previous example, nor was he governed by any motive but the love of God. Tradition teaches that it is on the very site of the *Akedah* on Mount Moriah in Jerusalem, that the Holy Temple was built many centuries later.

In Religious Thought. Rabbi Isaiah Horowitz (1565?-1630), author of *Shenei Luḥot ha-Berit*,

1. A modern rendition of the *Akedah,* as depicted in a 20th century poster. This artist follows the traditional view that Isaac was already a bearded young man rather than a small child when the incident occurred. Framing the picture are Hebrew quotes from the biblical account.

2. In this 19th-century painting, British artist Simeon Solomon was more concerned with the tragic tenderness of the relationship between Abraham and his son, than with the details of the *Akedah* itself.

observed that the *Akedah* teaches that everything must be sacrificed to God, if need be. Moreover, whenever man has an opportunity to do good or to refrain from evil he should reflect that perhaps God is testing him as He tested Abraham.

According to Maimonides, however, the *Akedah* is not a test in the usual meaning of the word. Maimonides explains that even though man has free will to act as he chooses, God knew in advance that Abraham would choose to obey. Thus, God was not so much putting Abraham through a test, as making his unswerving obedience a shining example of man's devotion to the word of God.

In the Liturgy. In the early rabbinic period, in the first centuries of the common era, special prayers for mercy included references to Abraham's sacrifice. And since the Middle Ages, a recital of the *Akedah* has been part of the daily morning services.

The *Akedah* is also recalled in several ways on Rosh ha-Shanah, which according to tradition is the day on which it took place. This explains why the Torah portion read in the synagogue on the second day of Rosh ha-Shanah is the account of Abraham's sacrifice. In the Musaf additional service of Rosh Ha-Shanah, the *Zikhronot* ("remembrance") prayer includes an appeal to God to remember the Akedah: "Remember unto us, O Lord our God, the covenant and the lovingkindness and the oath which You swore unto Abraham our father on Mount Moriah; and consider the binding with which Abraham our father bound his son Isaac on the altar, how he suppressed his compassion in order to perform Your will with a perfect heart. So, too, may Your compassion prevail over Your anger against us." And it is on Rosh Ha-Shanah that we sound the *shofar,* or ram's horn. One of the explanations given for this is that as we pray the *shofar* reminds us of God's lovingkindness in substituting a ram for Isaac.

In the Arts. The dramatic power of the *Akedah* has inspired a rich variety of expression in art and music. Good examples are Rembrandt's etching *Abraham's Sacrifice* (1635) which shows Isaac kneeling as the angel stays Abraham's hand. This work is housed in the Israel Museum in Jerusalem. The Russian composer Igor Stravinsky, composed a "sacred ballad" entitled *Akedat Yiẓḥak.* It was first performed in Jerusalem in 1964.

AKIVA (c. 50-135 c.e.). Few life stories are as spectacular or indeed as romantic as that of Rabbi Akiva. Akiva ben Joseph rose from the status of a poor, outcast shepherd to become one of the most outstanding authorities of Judaism who ever lived.

His disciples, who were extremely devoted, numbered in the thousands. Many of them, like Rabbi *Simeon bar Yoḥai and Rabbi *Meir, were among the great teachers of the generation which followed. Akiva was the expert in *hermeneutics, the science of interpreting the text of the Bible, and was able to find solutions to many of the halakhic problems of his day. In this way his teachings influenced later talmudic thought and were a major factor in the development of Judaism.

As a young man, Akiva worked as a shepherd for Kalba Savua, one of the wealthiest men of Jerusalem, who had a beautiful daughter, Rachel. Akiva and Rachel fell in love, but her father opposed the marriage because Akiva was unlearned and illiterate. He promised to learn, but Kalba Savua was stubborn in his opposition. He refused to see the young couple or to give Rachel any dowry when she left home to marry Akiva. Instead of beds, they had straw to sleep on. Akiva told Rachel: "I wish I could afford to give you a Jerusalem of Gold." (This was a gold design of the city which was popular as an ornament.) According to a legend, Elijah then appeared to them as a poor man begging for a bit of straw on which he could lay his newborn infant. Akiva told Rachel, "See, we are not really so poor – that man doesn't even have straw!"

When their own son was old enough to be taught *aleph bet* Akiva attended first grade with him and also began to learn. He made very rapid progress and was soon ready for advanced study. With Rachel's encouragement and blessings, he left home to study Torah at one of the great academies in Lydda. He was forty years old at the time.

In 12 years Akiva had become a great scholar. He opened his own yeshivah in Bene-Berak. On his return to his village, he was followed by 12,000 students. Before he could reach his home, however, Akiva overheard his wife tell a neighbor that she would gladly wait 12 more years if he could double his knowledge. He left without revealing himself to her. Twelve years later, accompanied by many students, and met by crowds of admirers, the renowned Rabbi Akiva returned to his home. Rachel, overjoyed, ran to join the throng which greeted her husband. Some of his followers were impatient with the poor, shabby woman who dared to approach the great man. But Akiva drew her near. "All that I have and all that you have," he told them, "comes from her."

In 132 C.E. when *Bar Kokhba led a full-scale revolt against Rome, Akiva thought Bar Kokhba might be the Messiah who would liberate Israel from her oppressors. In spite of strict Roman edicts against studying the Torah, Akiva continued to teach, saying: "Torah is thy life and the length of thy days."

The Romans imprisoned him, and later condemned him to death by slow torture. Akiva recalled the passage of the **Shema*: "And thou shalt love the Lord thy God with all thy heart, with all thy soul and with all thy might." On this he himself had taught: " 'With all thy soul' means loving God even in that moment when he takes your soul from you." And indeed, when he was led to the execution, it was the time for the *Shema* to be recited. The Romans tore his flesh with iron combs, but Akiva, who was 85 years old, bore his torment with serene dignity. He was reciting *Shema* as his soul departed.

ALBO, JOSEPH (15th century, Spain). Albo's book, *Sefer ha-Ikarim,* is one of the representative Jewish books of its period. It reflects its author's troubled reaction to the wavering faith among his fellow Jews, both in his native Spain and abroad, which stemmed from philosophical discussions. Albo keenly felt the need to restore the morale of his people by offering them a reasoned presentation of Judaism and by formulating the basic beliefs of the Jewish religion. He brought to this task a wide knowledge of both rabbinic literature and Jewish philosophy. He was also at home in Islamic philosophy and in Latin Christian scholasticism. In addition, he was versed in mathematics and medicine.

The *Sefer ha-Ikarim* is divided into four parts. The first is a critique of earlier attempts (such as that by Maimonides) at formulating the principles of the Jewish religion. Albo gives three fundamental principles of Judaism, namely, the existence of God, divine revelation, and reward and punishment. Albo reduced the belief in the coming of the Messiah to the level of an ordinary belief, a rank below the principles, perhaps to refute Christian teaching which made that belief a central one. Albo had already hinted at this view at the Tortosa Disputation where

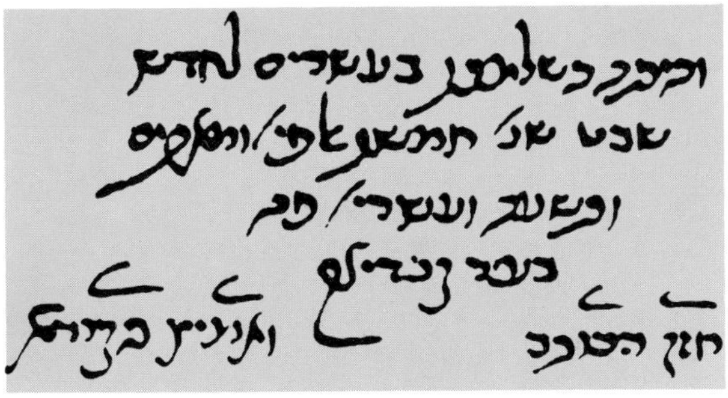

Excerpt from a handwritten copy of Joseph Albo's *Sefer ha-Ikarim* ("Book of Principles"), made in 1469. The original was written in 1425.

1. W.F. Albright, son of an American Methodist minister, who became one of the foremost biblical archaeologists and Semitic scholars.
2. The Bible relates how Ham, son of Noah, found his father drunk and naked. But, whereas Ham was insensitive to his father's honor and openly drew attention to the disgrace, his brothers at once covered Noah with the utmost delicacy, keeping their faces discreetly turned away. Illustration by an Italian artist for an 18th-century Hebrew prayer book.
3. Medieval Hebrew authors called alchemy a craft, and in this last page of a Hebrew manuscript of biblical commentaries, these "craftsmen" are said to be manufacturing pearls. c. 16th century.

1

2

he was the representative of the Jewish community. (See *Disputations).

Albo's work achieved great popularity in Jewish circles and was translated and commented on in several languages.

ALBRIGHT, WILLIAM FOXWELL (1891-1971), was one of the greatest biblical archaeologists of our times, a Christian who combined faith in the Old and New Testaments with a belief in modern science. His archaeological research led him to conclude that many of the dates indicated in the Bible are correct. (Abraham, for example, lived between 2,000 and 1,500 b.c.e.) The evidence from his work showed him that the biblical stories are good descriptions of actual events. In his book *The Excavation of Tell Beit Mirsim* he described step by step how he uncovered the ancient Canaanite royal city of Debir. This city was originally inhabited by descendants of the Anakim (giants) and was conquered by Joshua.

For 13 years Albright directed the American School for Oriental Research in Jerusalem. In tribute to his scholarship, it was renamed after his death the W.F. Albright Institute of Archaeological Research.

ALCHEMY. Just as scientific laboratories of today are bustling with the activity of daily new discoveries, those of ancient times were filled with the spirit of the science called alchemy. Alchemists were scientists who worked hard trying to transform simple metals

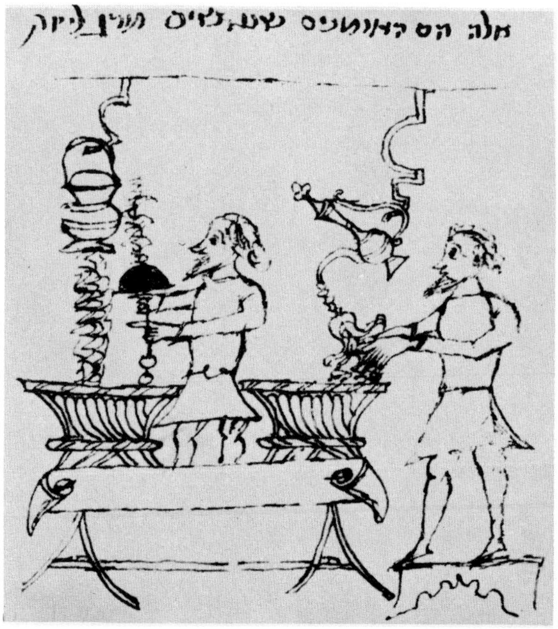
3

into precious gold, and produce the mystical "philosopher's stone." By the end of the Middle Ages many alchemists lost hope of ever producing the "philosopher's stone," and began to believe that only deeply religious people knew its secret. They considered Abraham to have been an expert in making gold, for it says in the Bible that "Abram was very rich in cattle, in silver and in gold." Moses, King David, Solomon, and the prophet Elijah were among other experts, they believed. Many Christian alchemists found roots to their theories in the Kabbalah. They would hopefully inscribe Hebrew words and letters on the pots in which they melted metals. The "philosopher's stone" is sometimes symbolized as a circle around a six-pointed star, which we know as the "Star of David."

Actually those who believed that alchemy was a Jewish art, or that the Kabbalah is at all based on alchemical theories, were greatly mistaken. The idea of creating gold would certainly be tempting to people of all kinds, so it was natural that Jews shared the enthusiasm of the ancient alchemists, just as we might enter fields of knowledge that interest and challenge us.

Certain Jewish scholars believed in this mystical science, while others such as Maimonides and Judah Halevi considered it to be nonsense. Although its goal was never achieved – no-one could really turn silver or mercury into gold – many of the methods used by alchemists became important and useful to chemists in the laboratories of later generations.

ALCOHOL. Moderate use of alcohol has always been regarded by Jewish authorities as an important and, at times, necessary feature of life and religious observance. *Wine is an integral part of many rituals and no feast is considered complete without it.

The ceremonies of *Kiddush, Havdalah,* and circumcision are accompanied by a brimming cup of wine; two cups are drunk at the wedding ceremony; and for the Passover *seder* each person is required to drink four cups of wine. The festivals of Simḥat Torah (see *Sukkot) and *Purim are occasions for companionable public drinking.

The Talmud discusses drinking on Purim until the merrymaker cannot distinguish between "Blessed be Mordecai" and "Cursed be Haman," although later authorities urged that this not be taken literally. The Aramaic words for "cannot distinguish" are *ad delo yada.* This is the origin of the term Adloyada which is often applied to Purim festivities and masquerades.

In Ereẓ Israel, Jews have always drunk wine in preference to other alcoholic beverages, but in other countries their taste extended to other drinks. In ancient Babylonia the brewing of beer was common. Some of the *amoraim* were brewers, notably Rav Papa, who become wealthy because of his expertise.

Jews drink wine, beer, or spirits freely, according to their tastes, but few Jews are heavy drinkers or alcoholics. The tendency toward moderate use of alcohol is also reflected in the Jew's degree of assimilation. This may be because traditional Judaism involves the use of alcohol on certain occasions (with a blessing pronounced before drinking), and this encourages moderation.

While the rabbis of the Talmud opposed over-indulgence, they were quick to point out the many beneficial uses of alcohol. In the days before aspirin and miracle drugs, various alcoholic beverages were used as pain-killers, tranquilizers, and anti-depressants. The Book of Proverbs recommends: "Give strong drink to him that is ready to perish, and wine to the bitter of soul" (31:6) but condemns overindulgence, especially by those in responsible positions (31:4). Whether a person was capable of addressing a king properly was considered a test of drunkenness.

Judges must not render decisions after drinking wine. In capital cases, where a man's life was at stake, the Sanhedrin court had to abstain from wine during the entire hearing. A person who is drunk is forbidden to lead prayer or conduct a service. When Hannah comes to the Sanctuary and weeps as she prays for a child (I Samuel 1:10-15) Eli, the high priest, reprimands her because he thinks she is drunk.

Kohanim (*priests) are prohibited from drinking any alcohol before or during the performance of their priestly duties. *Nazirites, in order to approach a level of priestly purity, used to vow to abstain from wine or any product of the grapevine. Such extreme abstinence, however, was a rare exception, and not encouraged.

ALEXANDER THE GREAT (356-323 b.c.e.), King of Macedonia, Greece, began a career of conquest when he was 21. In a little over 10 years, he had subjugated all the lands from Egypt to India. By introducing Greek culture into the Middle East he greatly influenced the development of Judaism. The philosophies of Plato and Aristotle, Greek drama and history entered Jewish culture with Alexander's conquest of Israel.

A legend, told by Josephus, describes Alexander's visit to Jerusalem. Jaddua, the high priest, had a warning from God in a dream, that he should wear a purple robe and his priestly hat when he would go to meet Alexander. When they met, Alexander knelt before Jaddua. Alexander's general asked him why the great conquering Greek king should adore the high priest of the Jews. Alexander replied: "It was not he I adored, but the God who honored him with high priesthood. For I saw this person in a dream dressed exactly in this way ..... telling me to make no delay but to boldly cross over the sea. He promised that he would conduct my army, and would give me dominion over the Persians." Alexander then gave the high priest his right hand and went into the Temple and offered sacrifice to God. He rejoiced when he was shown the Book of Daniel in which Daniel declared that one of the Greeks would destroy the empire of the Persians. He was sure he was that Greek. The next day Alexander gave the Jews the right to live according to their own laws.

The Talmud tells a similar story, with different names. The high priest, *Simeon the Just, meets Alexander. After Alexander kneels before him and

2

1

1. Hellenistic bust of Alexander the Great near the end of his reign.
2. Another illustration of Noah, lying drunk and naked, being covered by his sons, Shem and Japheth. From the Spanish *Golden Haggadah*, c. 1320.

says: "The image of this man wins my battle for me," Simeon expresses his fear that Alexander will let the Samaritans demolish "the House in which prayers are said for you and your kingdom that it may never be destroyed." Alexander replies to Simeon: "The Samaritans are delivered into your hands."

Both stories indicate that the Jews tried to cooperate with Alexander, and thereby preserve Israel; and that the greatest of conquerors, according to Jewish tradition, recognized that he got his power from the God of Israel.

Jews often acknowledged Alexander's favors to them by naming their children after him.

ALEXANDRIA was once the most important city in Egypt; it was a center of Hellenism, the brand of Greek culture that spread through the world in the wake of the conquests of Alexander the Great. Jews settled in Alexandria at the beginning of the third century b.c.e. and during Roman times many became citizens of the city. Some Jews were extremely rich, but most were artisans.

There was a strong local *bet din,* an office for drawing up documents, and synagogues were built in every part of the city. The splendid central synagogue was so large that the voice of the cantor could not be heard by some worshipers, and flags had to be waved to tell them when they should make responses.

There was a great deal of anti-Semitism in the city and in 38 b.c.e. serious riots broke out against the Jews. In 66 c.e., influenced by the outbreak of war in Ereẓ Israel, the Alexandrian Jews rebelled against Rome. The revolt was crushed, and 50,000 Jews were killed. During the widespread rebellion of Jews in the Roman Empire in 115-117 c.e., the great synagogue was burnt down. As a consequence, the economic situation of the Jewish community deteriorated and the population diminished.

The Eliyahu ha-Navi Synagogue in Alexandria.

During the period of the Second Temple, there was a sizable community of Alexandrian Jews in Jerusalem, where they were influential. Simeon, who was Herod's high priest, was of this community. Nicanor built the gates in the Temple walls from gates he brought back from Alexandria.

The Jews of Alexandria spoke Greek and were influenced by Greek culture. For example, *Philo of Alexandria, the great philosopher, attempted to present a synthesis of Judaism and Hellenism. The Greek translation of the Bible, the Septuagint, was the basis of Jewish-Hellenistic literature. After Philo, Alexandrian Jewish culture declined. In the Byzantine era, the Jews were persecuted by the church, and in 414 expelled from the city.

The Jews returned to Alexandria after the Muslim conquest, and in the seventh century there was still a large Jewish community. In 1170, 3,000 Jews lived there, among them rabbis, scholars and *dayyanim.* During the medieval period the community appealed to the Jews in other Egyptian cities for help in ransoming co-religionists captured by pirates. Many Spanish exiles settled there in the 15th century. But the community continued to dwindle, suffering from the plague, an earthquake, and the French conquest in the late 18th century; Napoleon even ordered the ancient synagogue to be destroyed.

During the 19th century, under the rule of Muhammad Ali, there was a new period of prosperity, and in 1915 the Zion Mule Corps was organized in Alexandria. After the *Sinai Campaign in 1956, thousands of Jews were banished from the city. Since then the number of Jews has dwindled rapidly, and by 1970 very few remained.

ALFASI, ISAAC BEN JACOB (known as Rif; 1013-1103), was the author of the most important code prior to the *Mishneh Torah* of *Maimonides. In a sense, Alfasi brought the geonic period to a close: the last of the Babyonian *geonim,* Hai Gaon, died when Alfasi was 25 years old. Alfasi himself was called *"*gaon"* by several early halakhic authorities.

Alfasi was a native of Algeria and after a period of study in Kairouan, he settled in Fez. (Hence his surname "Alfasi" or Rif, initials of Rabbi Isaac Fasi). He remained in Fez until 1088 when, in his 75th year, he was denounced to the government by enemies and was forced to flee to Spain. After a few months in Cordova he moved to Lucena where shortly after his arrival, he became head of the yeshivah (1089). He remained in Lucena until his death.

Moses ibn Ezra, one of the great Spanish Hebrew poets, described Alfasi as a man unsurpassed in keenness of intellect, whose wisdom was deep beyond compare, whose pen was swift, outdistancing that of any rival, and whose equal in intensity of religious feeling could scarcely be found. Alfasi dedicated his life to the study of the *Talmud and its dissemination among the masses. Long before he came to Spain his intellectual stand was decided and he was not influenced by the cultural life of Spain.

Hundreds of Alfasi's responsa have survived. Many of them were written while he was still in Fez, the majority in Arabic. His fame, however, rests on his great work *Sefer ha-Halakhot* (or *Halakhot Rabbati*). This is a sort of abbreviated Talmud which leaves out all the sections which are no longer relevant in practice, and gives decisions in the various differences of opinion. The work became known as the *Talmud Katan* ("Little Talmud") and many great scholars have written commentaries on it, explaining the Rif's opinions and their sources.

Later generations were unstinting in their admiration of Alfasi and his book. Maimonides wrote: "The *Halakhot* of the great rabbi, our teacher Isaac, of blessed memory, has superseded all these works (geonic codes) . . . for it contains all the decisions and laws which we need in our day . . . and, except for a few *halakhot,* not exceeding ten, his decisions are unassailable." Abraham ben David of Posquières, who tended to be severely critical of other authors, wrote of him: "I would rely on the words of Alfasi even if he should say that right is left."

ALGERIA. After the Arab conquest of North Africa in the seventh century, many Oriental Jews came to Algeria to settle. Their early economic and cultural life was vigorous and they were in contact with the mainstream of Jewish life of the Near East, including the *geonim* of Babylonia and Palestine. It was in part due to the Algerian Jews that the teaching of the great academies of Sura and Pumbedita spread to Morocco and from there to Spain. The city of Qal'at Hammad was the birthplace of Rabbi Isaac *Alfasi (1013), author of the most important compilations of laws before *Maimonides. For two centuries, little was known about the Jews of Algeria. In the mid-13th century, we find that Tlemcen was a busy seaport with a small but lively Jewish community. It thrived on the trade and on the visits of wealthy Jewish merchants.

1

2

3

1. 2. 3. 19th-century etchings of Algerian Jews in their native dress.

Christian kings of Spain often appointed Jews as ambassadors to Muslim countries. In the port cities of Algeria, these ambassadors joined the wealthy, well-educated local Jews to form a small but active group of intellectuals. It was this nucleus, as well as economic opportunity, which attracted many Spanish refugees in 1391. At first the new immigrants were resisted because of the fear of business competition, and because their customs and prayers were different. But in time the gap was narrowed. Their trading brought prosperity. Their learning and dedication, their talent for organization and leadership helped strengthen and revitalize the masses of Algerian Jewry whose educational and cultural level was very low. There were some periods of persecution, but the organization of community life, begun in the 14th century, was sustained for 500 years and enjoyed the cooperation of Muslim authorities.

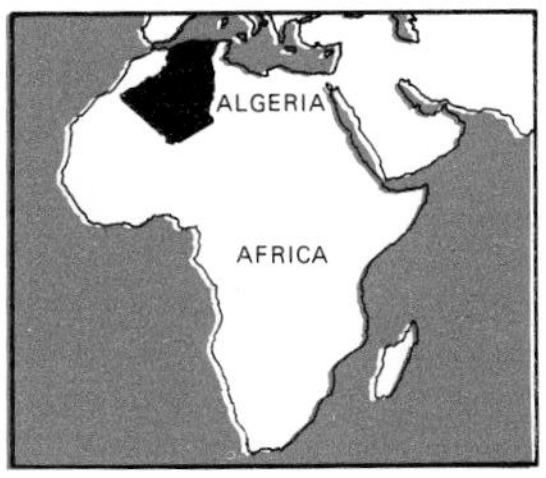

This community life was especially strong in the capital city of Algiers where the Spanish Jews prospered and became a majority.

By the 15th century, Algiers was a major religious center. Many *Marranos moved there. After years of observing their religion in secrecy under the Spanish *Inquisition, the Marranos wanted to practice Judaism openly.

In the 16th century, Algeria came under Turkish rule. Wealthy Jews were appointed to influential positions, such as the treasury and the minting of coins. But the masses of Jews fared badly under the Turks. Many were reduced to poverty by plagues, famine and heavy taxes.

In the early 19th century, community leaders were actively persecuted, beheaded or dragged to the stake. With the French conquest in 1830, a new era began for Algeria's 30,000 Jews. Their communal structure was disrupted and their authority turned over to the French. Assimilation was encouraged, and in 1870 Algerians were declared citizens of France. Anti-Semitism spread. Killing of Jews and looting of synagogues was common. Some Jews resisted, strengthening their faith and establishing new schools. During the *Hitler period they were severely persecuted under the racial laws of Vichy. Later, during the struggle for Algerian independence (1961-62) Jews were in the middle, caught between the Arab Muslims and the European French, the victims of both.

Most Algerian Jews emigrated – 70,000 to France, 5,000 to Israel. Their property was abandoned. About 1,000 old people remain. Algeria has adopted an extremely anti-Israel attitude and gives full support to Palestinian terrorists.

ALKABEZ, SOLOMON (c. 1505-1576). Look down from the edge of a sheer cliff in the old city of *Safed in the Upper Galilee, to the calm, quiet valley where Alkabez lies buried. This is the valley where, on Friday at dusk, accompanied by other kabbalists, Alkabez used to go walking, singing hymns to welcome the Sabbath. On one of these walks *Lekhah Dodi* was composed, and it is now sung in communities throughout the world, as part of the Sabbath evening service. The hymn is full of longing for the *Shekhinah* ("Divine Presence.")

In 1530, at the age of 25, Alkabez had left his native Turkey and set out for Ereẓ Israel. In 1536 he arrived in Safed and in time became a leading rabbi, and a prolific writer. He studied *Kabbalah all his

ואחר כך יעמדו כל העדה הקדושה לכבוד שבת מלכתא · לשורר
הפיוט נאה ומסובח אשר חברו ויסדו הרב הכולל האלקי מהר"ר שלמה
הלוי ז"ל אלקבץ ושמו חתום בראשי חרוזות שהי' בק"ק צפת תוב"ב
לכה
דודי לקראת כלה פני שבת נקבלה:
לכה דודי לקראת כלה פני שבת נקבלה:
שמור וזכור בדבור אחד : ה
השמיענו אל המיוחד : יי אחד
ושמו אחד : לשם ולתפארת ולתהלה:
לכה דודי לקראת כלה פני שבת נקבלה:
לקראת שבת לכו ונלכה : כי היא
מקור הברכה : מראש מקדם נסוכה:

Alkabez's *Lekhah Dodi* hymn ("Come, My Beloved"), as it appears in an 18th century manuscript. The hymn was officially introduced into the Sephardi prayer book in 1584.

life, and wherever he went he stopped to preach and to study with eager students and with learned men. In one of his writings he tells that, while learning Torah with Joseph *Caro on the night of *Shavuot, a mystic angel (called a *maggid* by kabbalists), appeared to Caro. From then the practice became established of staying awake to learn Torah all through the night of Shavuot. The custom, still observed today, is called *Tikun Leil Shavu'ot.*

In his writings on the Bible, Alkabez asked difficult questions in order to show the deep thoughts beneath the surface which had been handed down from generation to generation.

After Alkabez's death in 1576, few of his manuscripts survived. Some of them are commentaries on the Bible, others are kabbalistic. His commentaries on the laws concerning meals are also still widely studied today.

ALKALAI, JUDAH (1798-1878), rabbi and forerunner of modern Zionism. Alkalai was born in Sarajevo (now in Yugoslavia) and brought up in Jerusalem. He felt that the Jews should not wait for the Messiah to restore them to the Land of Israel but should make every effort to go there themselves to settle. The outstanding feature of his first book is his revolutionary attitude toward redemption as opposed to the traditional religious interpretations. *Teshuvah* ("repentance") which, according to the Talmud is the precondition for redemption, is interpreted by Alkalai in its literal sense, i.e. *shivah,* the return to Ereẓ Israel.

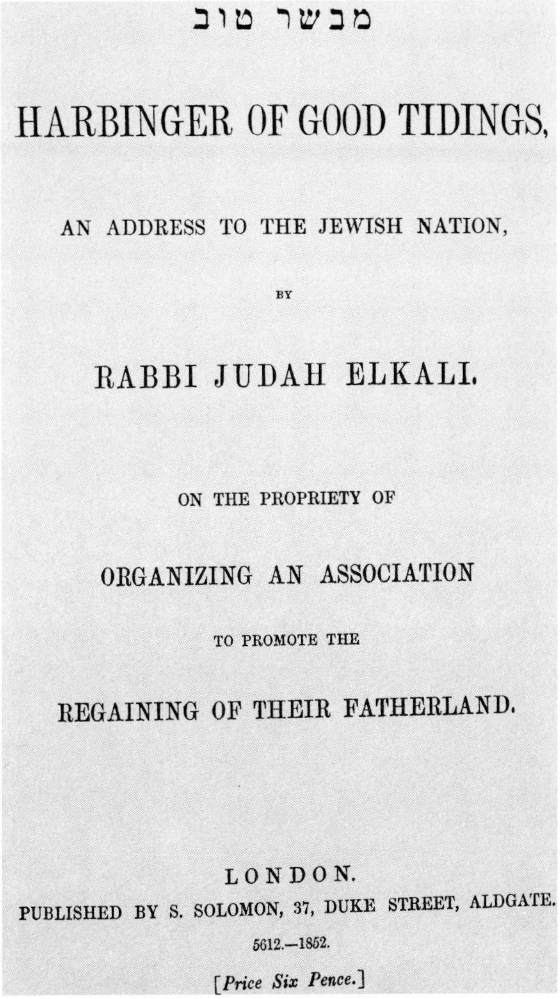
מבשר טוב

HARBINGER OF GOOD TIDINGS,

AN ADDRESS TO THE JEWISH NATION,

BY

RABBI JUDAH ELKALI.

ON THE PROPRIETY OF

ORGANIZING AN ASSOCIATION

TO PROMOTE THE

REGAINING OF THEIR FATHERLAND.

LONDON.

PUBLISHED BY S. SOLOMON, 37, DUKE STREET, ALDGATE.

5612.—1852.

[*Price Six Pence.*]

Alkalai aroused strong opposition in Orthodox circles, which rejected this modern concept of redemption. However, he continued to publish pamphlet after pamphlet, stressing that the settlement of Ereẓ Israel was the primary solution to the Jewish problem in Europe. Alkalai called for the introduction of the tithe for financing settlement, for the achievement of international recognition of Jewish Ereẓ Israel, for the restoration of the assembly of elders as a Jewish parliament, for the revival of Hebrew (particularly spoken Hebrew), for Jewish agriculture, and for a Jewish army. He expressed the hope that Great Britain would supervise the execution of the program.

In 1852 Alkalai visited England in order to propagate his idea for a return to Ereẓ Israel, and later traveled to several other West European countries seeking support for his plan. In all, he published 18 pamphlets as well as many articles in Hebrew newspapers.

ALLENBY, EDMUND HENRY HYNMAN, VISCOUNT. Viscount Allenby (1861-1936) was a British soldier who commanded the Egyptian Expeditionary Forces which in 1917-18 defeated the Turks in Palestine by employing superior strategy. He was a man of massive build and forceful personality, known to his troops as "The Bull."

In June, 1917, he was sent to Cairo as commander of the British forces in Egypt and Palestine. British troops were then held up on Gaza after two unsuccessful battles. Deceiving the enemy into thinking he would launch a third frontal attack, he took Beersheba instead, thus forcing the Turks to withdraw from Gaza, and leading to the capture of Jaffa and of Jerusalem.

By the fall of 1918, troops transferred from the Far East to Palestine were ready for forays across the Jordan, in which the Jewish Legion took part. Allenby again deceived the Turks into thinking that he would attack once more with his right wing but, having secretly transferred the bulk of his forces

1. English version of one of Judah Alkalai's pamphlets. His original writings are in Ladino and Hebrew.
2. Crowds line the streets of Jerusalem to get a glimpse of Allenby and his troops on their arrival in 1917.
3. Judah Alkalai, who traveled all over Europe to urge Jews to return to Ereẓ Israel.

3

2

(some 35,000 men) to the orange groves north of Jaffa, he broke through at night to reach Nazareth via the Megiddo Pass before the Turks realized what was happening. Thousands of Turkish troops were taken prisoner in this decisive victory.

For his achievements in forcing Turkey out of the war, he was made Viscount Allenby of Megiddo and Felixtowe, and was given a state grant of 50,000 pounds sterling. One of the main streets in Tel Aviv is named after him, and so is the main bridge over the Jordan river between Jordan and Israel.

ALLIANCE ISRAELITE UNIVERSELLE was founded in 1860 and centered in Paris. Its Hebrew name is כָּל יִשְׂרָאֵל חֲבֵרִים which means "All Israel are friends." Its aim was to develop among Jews an international organization to fight discrimination, and to raise the political, social and educational level of Jews everywhere. Adolphe Crémieux, the French statesman and minister of justice, was its president from 1863-1880.

The Alliance began to work effectively in communities where Jews were oppressed, mostly in Eastern Europe and the Near East. It was able to improve their legal status through contacts with international diplomatic conventions. In 1869 it began to assist the emigration of Jews, chiefly from Russia and Rumania, where they were being persecuted. Other relief organizations helped, but they were overwhelmed by the mass exodus following the Russian pogroms.

In the 1890s, emphasis shifted to education which developed rapidly, thanks to the generosity of Baron Maurice de *Rothschild. The Alliance was most active in the Near East and North Africa. In 1912 there were 71 schools for boys and 44 for girls in Turkey, and 5,500 pupils in 14 schools in Morocco. Education programs included social welfare, as the Alliance sought to improve the living conditions of students and their families.

After World War II and Israel's War of Independence (1948), the Alliance faced difficulties. The great upheaval and the mass exodus of Jews from North Africa upset the foundations of its institutions. In Israel its schools were incorporated into Israel's educational system. But Alliance activities were intensified in France where many North Africans had moved. In 1968 there were over 20,000 students in 64 schools, and a new seminary was established to train teachers and directors for them.

1. Yigal Allon, appointed Israel's Foreign Minister in 1974.
2. Children learning to dance the *hora* at a school of the Alliance Israelite Universelle in Tunis, 1953.

1

2

ALLON, YIGAL. An Israel statesman and military commander, Yigal Allon (1918-   ), was born at Kefar Tavor in the Lower Galilee. In 1937 he graduated from the Kadoorie Agricultural School, and in the same year, became a member of Kibbutz Ginnosar.

His activities in underground defense began during the Arab riots of 1936-1939, when he served under Yiẓḥak *Sadeh in the special units of the *Haganah.

In 1941 he was among the founders of the *Palmaḥ, the crack commando unit of the Haganah; he became its commander in 1945.

During the *War of Independence he commanded decisive operations in all parts of the country, and in the final stages of the War he commanded the southern front, driving the invading Arab armies from the whole of the Negev, including Eilat and part of the Sinai peninsula. He came to be regarded as the most experienced field commander in the Israel Defense Forces and left his stamp on the standards that characterize Israel's army officers.

After the War of Independence, he studied at the Hebrew University and at Oxford. Turning his attention to political activity, he became one of the leaders of the Aḥdut ha-Avodah political party, and in 1954 was elected to the Knesset.

From 1961 to 1968 he served as minister of labor, where he improved the state employment service, extended the road network and introduced legislation on labor relations. In June, 1967, he was a member of the inner war cabinet that mapped out the Six-Day War strategy. In 1968 Allon became deputy prime minister, and in the following year became minister of education and culture as well.

According to Allon's ideas on a peace settlement with Israel's neighbors, Judea and Samaria should be reunited with Jordan, but no Jordanian troops should be permitted to cross the Jordan River westward, and there should be a protective belt of Israel settlements along the Jordan Valley. In 1974 Allon became Foreign Minister of Israel and retained the deputy premiership.

ALLUF is an honorary title that was conferred in the early Middle Ages on scholars of the Babylonian academies who had the privilege of sitting in the first row. The word is of biblical origin where sometimes it means "friend and companion," and at other times it means either "chieftain" or, more probably, "clan."

Nowadays the word is used for a rank in the Defense Force of the State of Israel, equivalent to major general.

ALSACE-LORRAINE. The provinces of Alsace and Lorraine lie on the French-German border. Today they are part of France but in the past they have been traded back and forth with Germany as a result of various wars which have punctuated the continuing rivalry between these two European powers. In these struggles the local Jews were always the first victims of the invading armies. The local population looked upon the Jews as itinerant strangers and did not defend them. Since they were also distrustful of Jews, they would not even permit them to organize for self-defense.

The presence of Jews in the area is first mentioned by the famous Jewish traveler and commentator, *Benjamin of Tudela, in 1170 c.e. The Jewish population grew steadily until 1306 when there was a heavy influx of refugees expelled from France. One generation later during the *Armleder* massacres, 20 Jewish communities in Alsace were victims of these marauding bands of *Judenschlaeger* ("Jew-killers") who murdered and looted their way through Germany from Franconia to Alsace between 1336 and 1339. They were stopped by the authorities only when they turned from Jews and began to attack the general population.

In 1349 the *Black Death swept through Europe. Jews were accused of spreading the epidemic and were slaughtered even before the plague reached Alsace. Only in Strasbourg were Jews defended by the local council until it was overthrown, and then this important Jewish community too was destroyed. These events set the tone for future relations between the Jews and the local population.

The Jews were not allowed to return to the large cities as residents. They had to leave each night after their work and return to their rural homes. They engaged mainly in small-scale moneylending to the peasants and they were heavily taxed. They could own no property except their homes, and they sometimes had to wear a Jewish *Badge, and in the courts they were compelled to swear the degrading *oath *more judaico.* The authorities tried to limit the Jewish population by forbidding Jewish immigration, and by requiring each marriage to be authorized by the government. Children of unauthorized marriage were declared illegitimate, taken from their parents, and forcibly baptized.

In the early 18th century, under the French monarchy the conditions of Jewish life changed little. Immigration policies continued, Jewish traders were forbidden to keep accounts in Hebrew and anti-Semitic cruelties continued.

When Napoleon emancipated the Jews of Europe there was intense local oppostion and there were even attacks upon Jewish settlements. In his zeal to transform Europe into a homogenous culture, Napoleon tried to force the Jews to integrate by regulations requiring the use of family names, and by government influence in religious institutions. Gradually the religious *heder* was forced to give way to secular state schools, and the local religious traditions and Jewish dialect disappeared. The Jews themselves had not been eager to integrate. They were happy just to be able to live where they pleased.

When Germany annexed all of Alsace and most of

Anti-Jewish riots in Durmenach, a village of Alsace, on February 28, 1848. The caption to the lithograph is written in both German and French, evidence of the constant struggle between these two nations to gain control of the area. Unfortunately, the Jews suffered under both administrations.

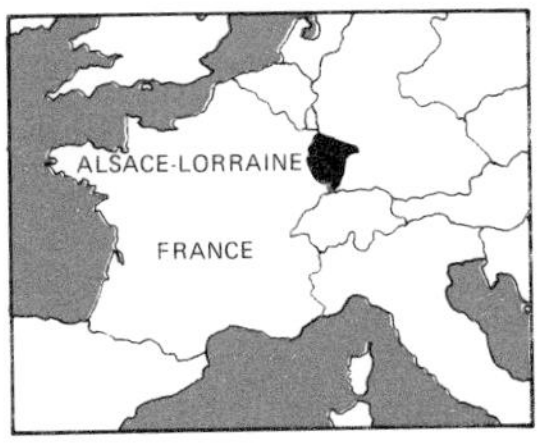

1

2

1. Watching the *Altalena* burning off the shore of Tel Aviv, June 1948.
2. The high priest dressed in his ceremonial garb, burning incense on the altar to offer as a "soothing odor" to God. Copper engraving from Amsterdam, 1713.

Lorraine in the Franco-Prussian war (1871) many Jews fled and resettled in other parts of France. France regained this lost territory after World War I, but during World War II the Germans took back this region which was a symbol of their earlier defeat, and proceeded to make it *Judenrein* (free of Jews). After the War, the greatly reduced Jewish community returned only to the large cities. The Jewish population was increased in 1962 by refugees from *Algeria.

ALTALENA, a ship carrying immigrants and ammunition, arrived at Israel's shores in June, 1948, and caused a bitter conflict between the newly formed Israel government and the underground *Irgun Ẓeva'i Le'ummi (I.Ẓ.L.)

During Israel's *War of Independence, a temporary truce was called with the Arabs between June 11 and July 9, 1948. However, during this time the Israel government under *Ben-Gurion faced a critical internal challenge to its authority. The *Altalena* was carrying arms and ammunition which had been independently bought by the I.Ẓ.L. without the approval of the government. When it arrived, the government demanded that the ship and its cargo be handed over to its jurisdiction. The I.Ẓ.L. refused, and a battle developed between the Palmaḥ (representing the government) and the I.Ẓ.L. The Palmah shelled the ship, and 83 people were killed and wounded when cannon fire sank it.

This incident aroused many bitter feelings, but made it clear that the Israel government would not tolerate any independent armed force in competition with the Israel Defense Forces.

ALTAR. In both the *Tabernacle and the *Temple the focal point was the altar. On it those parts of the sacrifices which had to be offered up were burned, and against it was sprinkled the blood of the sacrifices. (For more information see *Sacrifice).

According to the Bible the altar was made of stones joined together with earth, the wider stones being placed below and the narrower above. The stones of the altar of the Temple were smooth and were plastered over twice a year, and according to Judah ha-Nasi were smoothed down with a cloth every Sabbath eve. Four stones were placed at the four corners of the altar; these were known as the "horns" of the altar. On the altar a fire burned continuously. There was a ramp leading up to the altar enabling the priests, who alone were permitted to go on to the altar, to reach the top so as not to violate the prohibition: "Thou shall not go up by steps to my altar . . . " (Exodus 20:23). Though the dimensions of the altar did not have to be exact, the absence of the horns, base, ramp or the lack of a square appearance would disqualify the sacrifice. In the Temples it seems that the altar was plated with bronze; in the Tabernacle it was portable.

In addition to the sacrificial altar there was an altar for the burning of incense. The exact dimensions of this are given in the Torah: 1 x 1 x 2 cubits (a cubit is about 18 inches). This incense altar was made of acacia wood and plated with gold. Like the other altar it also had "horns." The one in the Sanctuary in the Wilderness had rings and staves for its transportation.

With the destruction of the Second Temple sacrifices were no longer made. It was then said: "Now that there is no altar, a man's table atones for him"; and prayer takes the place of the sacrifices.

AMALEK was an ancient people who lived in the Negev and adjoining desert areas. The Amalekites, as members of this nation are known, attacked the Jews when they left Egypt. The attack was for no apparent reason, as Amalek was not threatened by the Children of Israel. In the battle which took place at Rephidim, the Jews were led by Joshua while Moses stood on a nearby mountain with his arms held towards heaven. When he became tired and lowered his arms, the Amalekites succeeded and when he held them high the Jews won. Aaron and Hur helped Moses to keep his hands up. The Amalekites were not completely destroyed on that occasion and they became hereditary enemies of the Jews.

In the Bible there is an explicit command to "blot out" their memory and many of Israel's worst enemies, such as Haman of the *Purim story, were said to be descended from them. The section in the Torah requiring us to "remember what Amalek did to you" is read on the Sabbath before Purim. From a statement in the Talmud that Sennacherib, the Assyrian king, "mixed up" the ancient peoples in the course of his conquests, it would follow that it is impossible to identify this people since that time.

AMERICAN COUNCIL FOR JUDAISM. This anti-Zionist organization was founded by a group of Reform rabbis in 1942 in protest against a resolution by the Central Conference of American Rabbis, which supported the establishment of a Jewish army in Palestine. Its ideology, reflecting classical 19th-century Reform Judaism, treats Judaism only as a religion and not as a nationality.

Among the Council's activities have been: a quarterly journal, *Issues* (discontinued in November 1969), a religious education program free of Zionist influence, and a philanthropic fund separate from other Jewish charities, which it feels are under Zionist control. Its spokesmen have frequently denounced Israel in language reminiscent of Arab propaganda. Always an isolated minority in Jewish affairs, the Council's membership shrank further following the Six-Day War of 1967, when the reunification of Jerusalem caused a number of prominent Jewish anti-Zionists to have a change of heart and to lend their support to Israel.

AMERICAN JEWISH CONGRESS. The American Jewish Congress was formally organized in 1928 as an outgrowth of a series of meetings of Jewish religious, Zionist, and fraternal organizations begun in 1918. During the 1930s it was a leading force in the anti-Nazi movement, in efforts to aid the European victims of Hitlerism, and in combating American anti-Semitism. Together with the Jewish Labor Committee it set up the Joint Boycott Council directed against German goods and services.

Following World War II the major emphasis was on the encouragement of a liberal political and social

1. Aaron and Hur help Moses to hold his hands high (upper right) as the Children of Israel battle the Amalekites below.
2. Seven altars built by Balak, king of Moab, at the direction of his soothsayer, Balaam. 12th-century Byzantine art.

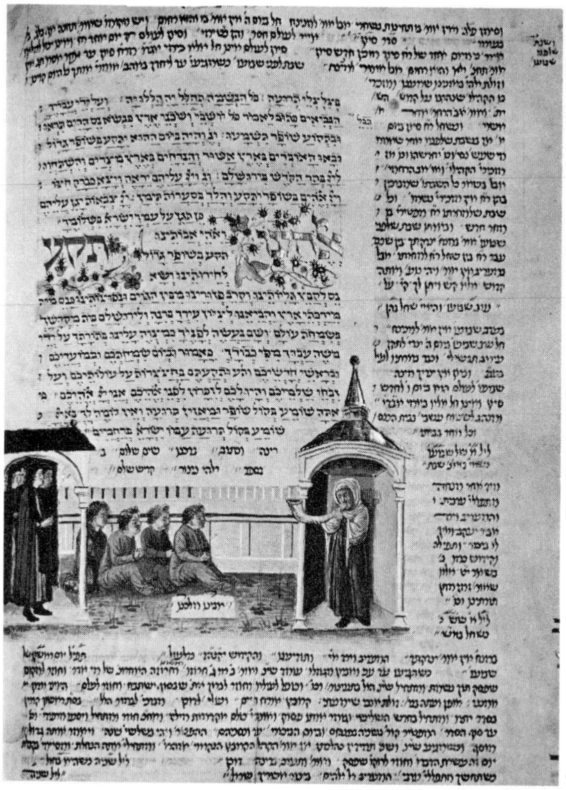

1. Thousands turn out for anti-Nazi demonstration organized by the American Jewish Congress in New York City, May 10, 1933.
2. Part of the *Amidah* prayer in the *Musaf* service for *Rosh Ha-Shanah* when, as the illustration shows, the *shofar* is blown. c. 1470.

climate. The A.J.C. backed social legislation and activities designed to eliminate racial and religious bigotry and to advance civil liberties. Two of its major concerns were Negro rights and the separation of Church and State. Today the A.J.C. sponsors regular tours to Israel as well as yearly "dialogues" between American and Israel intellectuals.

AM HA-AREẒ (Hebrew עַם־הָאָרֶץ) means literally "people of the land" but in both the Bible and later Hebrew literature it has quite different and specific connotations.

In the Bible, besides the general meaning of "population," *am ha-areẓ* has also been interpreted in different contexts as "the ancient Hebrew parliament," "the landed nobility," and "the free male property-owning citizenry."

In the Talmud the meaning of the term changed and mainly signifies someone who was not particular about tithing his produce to the priests and about the laws of ritual impurity. The term in this sense is used in opposition to the term Pharisee, and indeed there was a great deal of antagonism between the two parts of the population.

In modern usage, particularly in Yiddish, *am ha-areẓ* has come to mean "ignoramus." Indeed, its plural form – *amaraẓim* – was evidently coined by an ignoramus, for it is ungrammatical.

AMIDAH in Hebrew means "standing," and is the name given to the prayer which is recited while standing. The *Amidah* is a central element of the prayer services, second in importance only to the *Shema.

The *Amidah* is recited at every fixed service, three times daily at *Shaḥarit, Minḥah,* and *Ma'ariv* – details of which may be found in the article on *Prayer. It is recited on the Sabbaths and festivals as well. The *Amidah* is popularly known as the *Shemoneh-Esreh* ("Eighteen") because of the 18 benedictions it originally comprised. At *Shaḥarit* and *Minḥah* the reader or **ḥazzan* repeats the *Amidah* aloud after the silent recitation by the members of the congregation. This was initiated for the benefit of those congregants who did not know how to read Hebrew or, in the days before printing when books were rare, who did not know the *Amidah* by heart. They would, therefore, listen to the cantor's repetition and answer *"Amen"* to each of the benedictions. Nowadays, although many people do know how to read Hebrew, and recite the *Amidah* for themselves, it is still repeated. For the reader's repetition, the third benediction is enlarged to include a responsive reading between the cantor and the congregation. This is known as the *Kedushah.*

There are various forms of the *Amidah* for different occasions. On weekdays the *Amidah* contains 19 benedictions; on fast days one more is added in the reader's repetition. On Sabbaths and festivals there are only seven benedictions, except in the additional *Musaf* service of Rosh Ha-Shannah when there are nine. In cases of emergency or illness, the intermediate blessings of the weekday *Amidah* may be combined into one, which is explained below.

All of the various forms of the *Amidah* have the first three benedictions and the last three benedictions in common. The first three benedictions are devoted to praise of God, the last three to thanksgiving and to prayers for peace. On weekdays, the intermediate benedictions are petitions, and the *Amidah* is basically a prayer of supplication. On the Sabbaths and festivals, no petitions are recited, and the intermediate benedictions are devoted to the special sanctity of the day.

The *Amidah* is recited silently, being modeled after the prayer of *Hannah, who whispered her pleas inaudibly, only moving her lips. When reciting the *Amidah,* the worshiper faces Jerusalem; if he is in Jerusalem, he faces the Temple Mount. The requests in the *Amidah* are formulated in the plural. The pronoun "we" is thus used throughout the prayer, even when it is recited silently by one individual. This is done so that every individual worshiper prays not only on his own behalf but as a member of the congregation. The sequence of the benedictions of the weekday *Amidah* is described below.

THE OPENING BENEDICTIONS – PRAISES

1. The Mishnah calls the first blessing *Avot* which means "fathers," as God is addressed as the "God of Abraham, God of Isaac, and God of Jacob." This reference to ancestry is an expression of *zekhut avot,* "the merit of the fathers," and thus stresses the continuity of the Jewish people. It concludes with *Barukh . . . Magen Avraham* ("Blessed be . . . the Shield of Abraham").

2. The second benediction is in praise of God's love which is available to everyone, to the fallen, to the sick, to the imprisoned. These are examples of *gemilut ḥasadim,* "deeds of lovingkindness." This benediction also praises God for His power, or *gevurah.* Among the manifestations of God's power are His providing sustenance for all living creatures, His healing the sick, and His causing rain to fall. Stress is laid on the revival of the dead, and the benediction which concludes with *Barukh . . . meḥayyeh ha-metim* ("Blessed be . . . He Who revives the dead") is therefore also known as *Teḥiyyat ha-Metim* ("Resurrection of the Dead").

3. The third benediction speaks of God's holiness, and is amplified into the paragraph known as *Kedushah,* when the *Amidah* is repeated at public services. It concludes with *Barukh . . . ha-El ha-Kadosh* ("Blessed be . . . the Holy God").

THE INTERMEDIATE BENEDICTIONS – PETITIONS

(A) Individual Petitions.

4. The fourth benediction is a request for the gift of wisdom and understanding. It concludes with *Barukh . . . ḥonen ha-da'at* (Blessed be . . . the gracious giver of knowledge").

In this modernistic painting entitled "The Priestly Blessing," by Polish artist Jankel Adler, the *kohen* covers his head with the *tallit* and raises his hands in the traditional gesture used during this part of the *Amidah* service.

the synagogue. His life story inspired many Jews to martyrdom, rather than to accept Christianity. (See *Conversion, Forced).

Over the years a legend arose as to what followed. In the synagogue, as the *Kedushah* prayer was about to be recited, Rabbi Amnon asked the *ḥazzan* to wait while he sanctified the great name of God. He thereupon recited the hymn *U-Netaneh Tokef,* after which he died. Three days afterward he appeared in a dream to Rabbi Kalonymus ben Meshullam and taught him the entire prayer. Rabbi Amnon asked him to circulate it throughout the Diaspora for recital in synagogues on Rosh Ha-Shanah. The prayer, which describes in exalted language the procedure followed in heaven on the Day of Judgment, is actually older than the tenth century, for it is found in ancient liturgical manuscripts and in *Genizah* fragments. It apparently originates from an early Palestinian prayer which was later attributed to Rabbi Amnon.

AMOS, the shepherd, was called from following his flock to become a prophet of Israel. His prophecies began two years before the great earthquake in the days of Uzziah, king of Judah, and *Jeroboam, king of Israel, in the eighth century b.c.e.

The third of the twelve Minor Prophets, Ámos preached a powerful message that sounds as relevant in the Western world of the twentieth century as it did in Ereẓ Israel in Amos' own day.

The Book of Amos has three distinct parts. The first prophecy is a warning to Israel's neighbors – Syria and others – condemning their violence and aggression, especially against Israel. The exile and destruction foretold for the nations of the Near East were prophesied for Israel too, for similar sins against its own people.

The second section condemns the selfishness of the wealthy who regarded their affluence as a sign of God's favor. The idle rich oppressed and ignored the misery of the masses of poor people. Amos cried out against the careful observance of the Temple ritual when it ignored morality as an integral part of religion. Ritual alone does not please God, who demands that it go hand in hand with mercy and compassion.

The third section foretells disaster – earthquake, pestilence, famine, and the ultimate calamity of exile, with Israel scattered among the nations unless they would return to God. The book closes with the promise of reconciliation – that God will rebuild the fallen Tabernacle of David, and that his people will inherit all the land (9:12-15): "And I will turn the captivity of my people Israel and they shall build the waste cities and they shall inhabit them . . . and they shall no more be plucked up out of their land which I have given them, saith the Lord thy God."

Beginning of the prologue to the Book of Amos in a Latin Bible, France, 13th century. The illustration shows Amaziah, priest in the temple of Beth-El, and opponent of Amos. Amaziah drove Amos out of the northern kingdom, back to Judah.

AMRAM GAON, or Amram ben Sheshna, was a **gaon* of Sura, Babylonia, noted for his responsa and the oldest surviving order of prayer. He died c. 875 c.e. More than 200 of Amram's responsa are extant, some in collections of geonic responsa, others of the earlier rabbinic authorities; still others were discovered in the Cairo **Genizah.* His responsa include both practical halakhic decisions and comments on the Talmud.

Amram's fame, however, rests primarily on his *Seder* (commonly called his *Siddur*), "the order of prayers and blessings for the entire year . . . according to the tradition which we possess." The *Seder,* known also as *Yesod ha-Amrami* and as *Maḥzor de-Rav Amram,* originated in a responsum which was evidently sent to the community of Barcelona. From there it spread throughout Spain and to other countries. The *Seder Rabbi Amram* is the oldest order of Jewish prayers extant. As well as the text of the prayers for the entire year, it contains the laws and customs pertaining to the different prayers. The *Seder* served as the basis for later orders

2

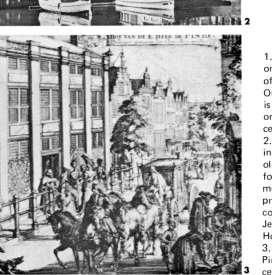

3

1. Opening page of one of only three surviving copies of *Seder Rav Amram.* Our present-day *Siddur* is a variation of Amram's original. Spain, 14th-15th century.
2. Jewish Historical Museum in Amsterdam, housed in the old Waaggebouw and forming part of the municipal museum. Its primary display is the art collection of the Portuguese Jewish community in Holland.
3. Amsterdam home of the Pinto banking family. 17th-century engraving.

of service and especially the liturgy of countries which came under Babylonian influence. (For further information see also *Prayer Books).

AMSTERDAM. In the late 16th century, when the northern provinces of Holland became independent of Catholic Spain, *Marranos of Spanish and Portuguese origin went to live in Amsterdam, where they soon lived openly as Jews. Here they were granted protection of life and property. Although the Jews of Amsterdam were barred from practicing all trades that were organized in guilds, they were allowed other professions.

In 1675 the community built a magnificent synagogue which became a model for Sephardi synagogues in other places. Amsterdam became a center for Jewish learning for all Marranos. The Talmud Torah school taught not only talmudic subjects, but also Hebrew grammar and poetry, and in the upper classes only Hebrew was spoken. Its pupils officiated as rabbis in numerous Sephardi communities in Western Europe and Mediterranean countries. Most of the religious literature in Spanish and Portuguese intended for the guidance of the Sephardi communities was written and printed in Amsterdam. The first Jewish printer there was *Manasseh ben Israel.

Most of the community became followers of the false messiah *Shabbetai Ẓevi in the mid-17th century. Even after the end of that movement, it remained a source of controversy in the community for many years.

The Jews took an active role in the economic life of Amsterdam, especially in the tobacco, printing and diamond industries. But the Jewish community was never very wealthy and after the French conquest of Holland in 1794, two-thirds of the 3,000 members of the Sephardi community depended on charity.

Ashkenazi Jews first arrived in 1620, mainly from Poland, and they depended, economically and socially, on the Sephardi community until they established their own community in 1636.

The Jewish community continued to grow in Amsterdam – by 1920 there were approximately 69,000 Jews there – and they maintained excellent relations with the non-Jewish population. When the Nazi terror started in the mid-1930s, many European Jews fled to Amsterdam, with the result that by 1941 there were 79,410 Jews in the city. The Germans occupied Holland in 1940 and most of the Jews were sent to concentration camps and murdered. All Jewish property was stolen.

In 1973 there were approximately 12,000 Jews in Amsterdam, but the rate of intermarriage with the non-Jewish population was very high. The old Portuguese synagogue was still in use and was on the itinerary of almost every visitor to the city.

AMULET. From earliest times, man has tried to protect himself from misfortune by the use of objects he considered holy or magically potent. One of the ways of doing this was to keep the object close to his person, frequently wearing it as a piece of clothing, or as an ornament. It was believed that no evil spirit would dare to attack someone who was protected by the object. There are some who hold that the desire for this protection is the source of the habit of wearing jewelry; women, being weaker and in greater danger, would feel a greater need for protection and as a result might wear several such objects.

It became the custom for people to wear amulets, which were pieces of paper or metal disks with inscriptions on them, which would protect the bearer from sickness, the "*evil eye" and other troubles. The inscriptions commonly consisted of verses from the Bible or names of various angels. The use of writings as a way to keep off evil spirits came from the belief in the holiness and power of certain words.

It is not known if amulets were used during the biblical period. The rabbis of the Talmud discussed whether written amulets were sacred objects, and they distinguished between amulets which worked and those which were not proved effective. An effective amulet was one which allegedly cured a sick person three times or cured three sick people.

2

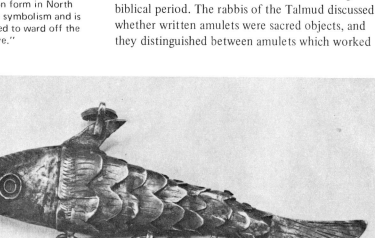

1

1. Amulet in the form of a fish, a traditional symbol of fertility, from 19th-century Morocco.
2. Silver amulet worn as jewelry in 19th-century Palestine. The hand is a common form in North African symbolism and is supposed to ward off the "evil eye."

Of course *tefillin* and *mezuzot* (see **Mezuzah*) are not amulets. Their use is a commandment by God "as a sign on your hand and . . . . on the doorpost of your house" (Deuteronomy 6:8-9). They are reminders to the Jew of his duty to bear witness to one God. Phylacteries, the common translation for *tefillin*, comes from a Greek word meaning protection against danger or disease, and is therefore incorrect.

During the Middle Ages the rabbinic attitudes toward amulets varied. Maimonides argued against the "folly of amulet writers." Naḥmanides however approved of the use of amulets. With the increased study and practice of *Kabbalah in the Middle Ages, their use spread from Spain to Eastern Europe and Ereẓ Israel. Over the centuries the belief in amulets gradually diminished in Europe, although in Eastern Europe it remained widespread until World War II. Among Oriental Jewish communities, however, this belief is still prevalent.

ANAN BEN DAVID was an eighth century sage in Babylonia. He founded the sect of Ananites and was regarded by the *Karaites as their founder. According to various accounts he was the older son of an *exilarch, the lay leader of the Babylonian Jewish community. He should have succeeded his father but the exilarchate was given to Anan's younger brother. Anan thereupon rallied a group of sectarians who set him up as their own exilarch. This led to his arrest. He was sentenced to death by hanging, for defying the caliph's confirmation of his brother in the office. A fellow prisoner advised him to bribe the officials and to obtain a hearing before the caliph in order to claim that he represented a different faith distinct from Rabbanite Judaism, and therefore was not guilty of the crime ascribed to him. Anan stressed before the caliph that in matters pertaining to calculation of the calendar his methods were akin to the Muslim system. He was thus released.

The only proven historical fact about Anan's life is that he was a learned Jew of aristocratic descent, who for some reason founded a sect of his own.

Anan's immediate followers, the Ananites, were never numerous. Only a few remained by the tenth century. They steadily decreased in number and were absorbed in the later Karaites. However, Anan's prestige among the Karaites increased until he was acknowledged by them as the father of the Karaite sect itself.

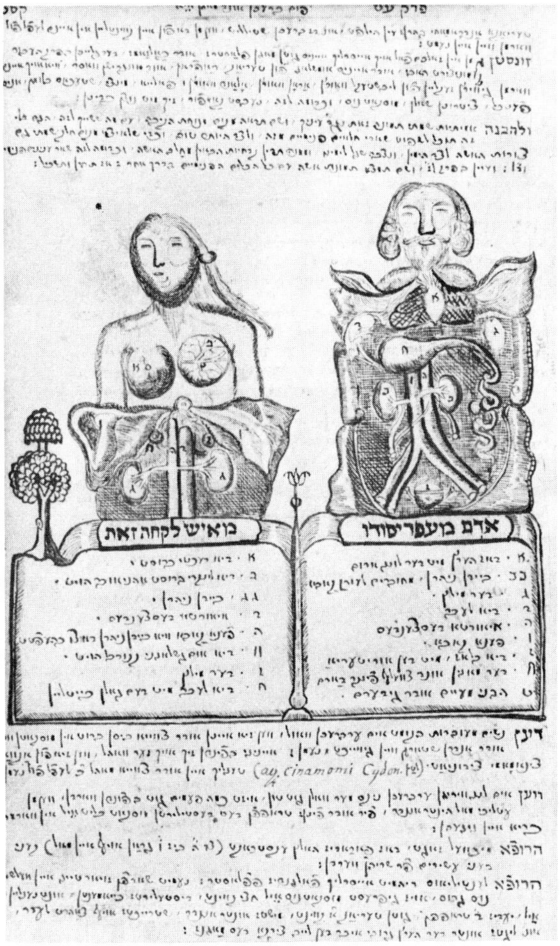

Anatomical drawing of male and female organs from a Yiddish medical manuscript, *Sefer Etz ha-Sadeh*. "Man comes from dust, woman is taken from man," reads the caption under the two diagrams.

ANATOMY. There is no systematic account of the anatomy of the human body in the Bible, although much use is made there of anatomical facts, metaphors, and expressions. Biblical anatomy is factual and based on observation. Talmudic treatment of anatomy, however, is very rich; the details are sometimes astonishing in their accuracy, as in the description of the small cartilage rings in the structure of the trachea (wind-pipe) which was discovered by Western anatomists only in the 18th century. At the same time, the anatomical information in the Talmud is incomplete, apparently because the subject was not studied systematically but only incidentally, as far as it was necessary for the solving of legal and ritual problems. Thus, for example, talmudic scholars were much occupied with the regulations concerning *kosher* meat, with physical disfigurement that disqualified a man from the priesthood, and with rules concerning the menstruous woman. This accounts for the fact that anatomical knowledge was so widespread among them. The dissection of animal carcasses to ascertain their ritual fitness revealed important facts and prevented the development of many of the fantastic notions prevalent among primitive peoples.

The Skeleton. The enumeration of 248 bones in the human body is well-known in rabbinic tradition. The names given to the bones in the Talmud are precise in their anatomical differentiation. The number of sinews (Hebrew: *gidim*, which may also mean muscles) is given as 365, the same as the number of days in the year. The two numbers together make 613, which is the number of commandments in the Torah.

The Digestive Organs. In an unusual passage the salivary glands are compared to springs of water and referred to as "the conduit that passes beneath the tongue." The ducts of the salivary glands were not described with such precision in scientific literature until the 16th and 17th centuries. The digestive tract of the human being is likewise described in the Talmud; the liver was regarded as one of the ruling parts of the human body, the other two being the brain and the heart. There is also a reference in the Talmud to the removal of the spleen by surgery.

The Respiratory Organs. Most parts of the respiratory system were identified in the Talmud. The identification of two small cartilages at the end of the thyroid cartilage is interesting since these were not discovered in the West before the 18th century.

The Heart. The Talmud contains few details on the anatomy of the *heart. The position of the heart is given as on the left side of the body.

The Genital Organs. These organs in the male are described in brief, and diseases connected with them accurately listed. However, because of the regulations concerning the menstruous woman, the talmudic scholars studied the anatomy of the female genitalia much more extensively. For reasons of propriety they used indirect terms to designate them, a fact that frequently causes great difficulty in understanding the anatomical details referred to.

Other Organs. The talmud does not deal much with the normal anatomy of the kidneys, but gives numerous accounts of kidney diseases. It describes the outer and inner membranes of the brain, recognizes the existence of motor centers in the spinal column, and records examinations of the spinal cord. There is also a mention of the fontanel: "the place where an infant's brain is soft."

From about the 10th to the 17th centuries, Jewish physicians shared the anatomical opinions of their neighbors. The reluctance of Jews to submit their bodies for dissection led to complications and ill-feeling in some universities, such as at Padua in the 17th and 18th centuries, and in Eastern Europe in the 20th. (On the question of postmortems, see *Autopsies and Dissection.)

The most outstanding Jewish physician of the Renaissance was Amatus Lusitanus, who in the 16th century, participated in the teaching of anatomy at the university of Ferrara. He was the first to describe the valves of the veins. Outstanding in the modern study of anatomy was Friedrich Gustav Jacob Henle (1809-1885), who did important research on the skin, the intestinal tract, and the kidneys. Another important figure was Benedikt Stilling (1810-1879), who did pioneer research on the spinal cord. (See also *Medicine.)

ANAV (or ANAU). According to its own tradition, the Anav family was one of four aristocratic Jewish families from Jerusalem whom Titus brought to Rome after he destroyed the Temple in the year 70 C.E. Between the ninth and 14th centuries members of the family distinguished themselves in Jewish learning. Jeḥiel ben Abraham, who died in 1070, was head of the yeshivah in Rome and a poet. His sons Nathan, Daniel and Abraham all taught at the yeshivah. Nathan built a beautiful synagogue and ritual bathhouse for his community, and wrote the *Arukh,* which is a very important lexicon of talmudic terms. Daniel was a poet and wrote a commentary on the Mishnah.

The brothers Benjamin and Abraham, descendants of the family, were 13th-century physicians and talmudists. Benjamin's son Judah, who died after 1280, was a talmudist and poet. He wrote on the laws of ritual slaughter and wrote some commentaries on the Talmud. Abraham's son, Benjamin, studied with his cousin Judah, and was an outstanding scholar. His main interest was *halakhah,* but he also had a thorough knowledge of mathematics and astronomy. He wrote poetic dirges when the Talmud was burned in Italy in 1244, when the gentiles there tore up the Torah scrolls, and when they desecrated the Jewish cemetery.

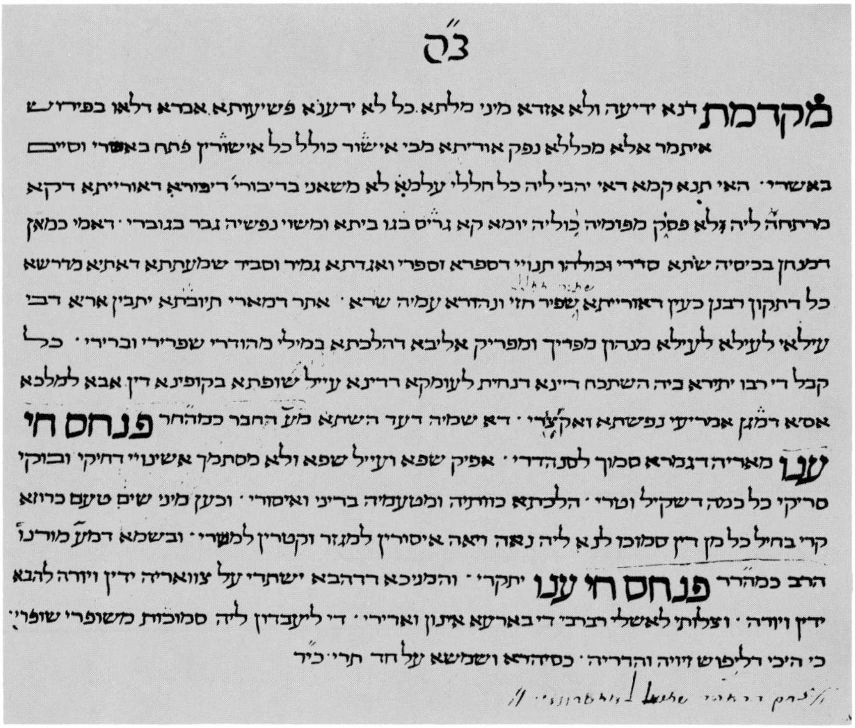
ב״ה
מקדמת דנא ידיעה ולא אזדא מיני מלתא. כל לא ידענא פשיעותא. אמרא דלאו בפירוש
איתמר אלא מכללא נפק אוריתא מבי אישור כולל כל אישורין פתח באשרי וסיים
באשרי׳ האי תנא קמא דאי יהבי ליה כל חללי עלמא לא משאני בדיבורי׳ דיבורא דאורייתא דקא
מריתחה ליה ולא פסק מפומיה כוליה יומא קא גריס בגו ביתא ומשוי נפשיה גבר בגוברי׳ דאמי כמאן
דמעתן בכיסיה שיתא סדרי וכולהו תנויי דספרא וספרי ואגדתא גמיר וסביר שמעתתא דאתיא מדרשא
כל דתקון רבנן כעין דאורייתא שפיר חזי ונהדרא עמיה שרא׳ אתר דמארי תיובתא יתבין ארא דבי
עילאי לעילא לעילא מנהון מפריך ומפריק אליבא דהלכתא במילי מהודרי שפירי ובירירי׳ כל
קבל די רבו יתירא ביה השתכח דיינא דנחית לעומקא דדינא עייל שופתא בקופינא דין אבא למלכא
אסא דמגן אבריעי נפשתא ואקצרי׳ דא שמיה דעד השתא מע״ החבר כמהר״ר פנחס חי
ענו מאריה דגמרא סמוך לסנהדרי׳ אפיק שפא ועייל שפא ולא מסתלק אשינויי דחיקי ובוקי
סריקי כל כמה דשקיל וטרי׳ הלכתא כוותיה ומטעמיה בדיני ואיסורי׳ וכען מיני שים טעם כרוזא
קרי בחיל כל מן דין סמוכו לתא ליה נאה ויאה איסורין למגזר וקטרין למשרי׳ ובשמא דמע״ מורנו
הרב כמהר״ר פנחס חי ענו יתקרי׳ והמניכא דדהבא ישתדי על צווריה ידין ויורה להבא
ידין ויורה׳ וצלותי לאשלי רברבי די בארעא איתון ואדירי׳ די ליעבדון ליה סמוכות משופרי שופרי׳
כי היכי דליפרש זויה והדריה׳ כסיהרא ושמשא על חד תרי׳ כ״ד

The ordination certificate of Phinehas Anav (1693-1768). This rabbi was involved in a controversy about the correct pronunciation of the Priestly Blessing.

Zedekiah ben Abraham Anav (1225-1297) was a noted scholar. He wrote an important halakhic compendium which is still considered to be a standard work. Jeḥiel ben Jekutiel (second half of the 13th century) was a poet and writer on Jewish ethics. He was also a copyist and copied out the Jerusalem Talmud; his is the earliest complete copy extant. A female descendant of the family, Paola, who lived at the end of the 13th century, was also a copyist.

ANGELS AND DEMONS. How many angels can stand on the head of a pin? Our familiarity with this question indicates that angels are a well-known concept. Similarly, phrases such as: "He runs like a demon," or "There is a demon in him," reflect our familiarity with the notion of demons. Though in modern times angels and demons are generally not taken seriously, in past centuries people did believe in them and they were actively discussed.

In the Bible. Many books in the Bible assume the existence of beings superior to man in knowledge and power but subordinate to the one God. These beings serve as His attendants and as His agents, carrying out His will. They are nowhere pictured as being independent. Many different terms are used in the Bible for angels, but the most common is *mal'akh,* which also means a messenger. Among other terms are cherub and seraph. These are depicted as winged creatures of an angelic nature. In the *Apocrypha there is mention of "fallen angels." In the Bible, the practice of *magic is completely prohibited and thus all the magical procedures which were common in the ancient world to protect people against demons hardly existed among Jews. There is reference to various demons, but they too are not described as independent beings.

In the Talmud. In the talmudic age both scholars and laymen believed in angels. Some sages believed that new angels are created every day; they praise God on that day and then disappear into a river of fire. Other sages believed that two angels, Michael and Gabriel, permanently serve God. In the Mishnah there is no mention of angels at all. According to the **aggadah* and **Midrash,* no angel may carry out more than one mission at a time; angels are assigned to countries, and thus there are angels who must not leave Ereẓ Israel; angels walk upright and speak Hebrew; and they have no needs or free will. Man, because he does have free will and must conquer his evil inclination, is considered more important than the angels.

The sages of the Talmud did apparently believe in demons but these, too, were regarded as carrying out God's will. In general it can be said that the belief in angels and demons is an attempt to understand how the incorporeal, unseen God of the Universe controls human history, the angels being a sort of metaphorical description of the process.

In the Prayers. The concepts concerning angels, as they developed in the *aggadah,* found their way into the liturgy and there are fairly frequent references to them as praising God. From the geonic times, certain prayers were introduced into the prayer book calling on the angels to "bring our prayers to God." This type of prayer has been, and still is, opposed by many important rabbis because Judaism believes that a man does not need any intermediaries between himself and God.

ANIELEWICZ, MORDECAI (1919-1943). Mordecai Anielewicz, who grew up to lead a Jewish revolt against the Nazis, was born in Poland to a hardworking Jewish family. As he grew older, he spent more and more time in his youth movement. So greatly did he believe in Zionism that when the German army was advancing toward Poland, he tried to escape to Palestine, but did not succeed as he was stopped by Rumanian guards at the border. Still a teenager, he returned to Poland and was determined to help the

1

1. Rembrandt's painting of Jacob wrestling with the angel of God.
2. Detail from a parchment amulet showing the female child-stealing demon, Lilith. 19th century.
3. The memorial to Mordecai Anielewicz by the Israel sculptor Natan Rapaport, overlooking museum dedicated to fighters of the Warsaw Ghetto, at Kibbutz Yad Mordecai.

2

3

Jews there. The first thing he did was to organize a type of kibbutz in the Warsaw Ghetto which made sure that everyone had equal rations of food and clothing. Children were given lessons and they even helped Mordecai publish a newspaper there. He then traveled to other parts of Poland helping Jews in similar ways.

While he was away on one of these trips in August, 1942, he was horrified to hear how cruelly the Germans were treating the Jews in the Warsaw Ghetto. He returned immediately and formed the Z.O.B. (*Zydowska Organizacja Bojowa;* "Jewish Fighting Organization"). As commander, he trained his forces to fight back against the Germans. In January, 1943, when his whole group of *Hashomer ha-Ẓa'ir friends were killed by the attacking Germans, he decided that the whole ghetto must fight back. Everyone in the ghetto was given a task. Mordecai had three secret code names – Marian, Aniol ("angel" in Polish) and Malakhi. Time and time again, the Germans attacked the ghetto, but the Jews were so well organized that they held them off from April till May.

Finally, on May 8, 1943, Mordecai was killed with many of his fellow fighters in his command bunker. His courage gave so much strength to other Jews that he was never forgotten. A kibbutz in Israel, called Yad Mordecai, was named after him.

Illustration of an animal fable in a 15th-century edition of *Mashal ha-Kadmoni,* a collection of folk tales originally written in the 13th century.

ANIMALS. There is a forest region in the world where a hiker, reaching out idly to pluck an unusual variegated flower, may be astonished to see it rise before his very eyes and silently disintegrate into scores of tiny, colored crumbs which then fly off in dozens of directions. As he instinctively reaches for his camera, he may be just in time to see the same colored crumbs converging on a nearby twig, and thereby instantaneously recreating the same flower.

The insects which protect themselves in this way are born into a family of brothers and sisters of many colors. The flower formation they coordinate to produce is patterned on no flower found in nature. Photographing this collective camouflage which is produced by instinctive group solidarity, the astonished hiker may well join in with King David's exuberant hymn of praise to God for his miracles of pattern and instinct in the world of nature: "How manifold are Thy works, O Lord! In wisdom hast Thou made them all; the earth is full of Thy creatures" (Psalm 104:24).

IN JEWISH LAW

Since animals are part of creation, man must bear responsibility for them. Thus the Torah demands that compassion and kindness be shown toward animals, both in routine dealings and in ritual matters. Thus the *dietary laws which remain to this day a distinctive feature of religious observance specify clearly which animals may be eaten and how they are to be prepared for food.

Although animal slaughter is permitted to provide food for man it must be done humanely. The Jewish method of slaughter, which is painless and instantaneous, is discussed under **sheḥitah.*

Other biblical laws repeatedly show concern for the wellbeing of animals. Man must rest on the Sabbath and may not work his animals either. "Thou shalt not do any manner of work, neither thy son . . . nor thy servant . . . nor thy cattle" (Exodus 20:10).

One may not muzzle an ox which is threshing grain (Deuteronomy 25:4). Farmers sometimes did this to keep the ox from nibbling. In fact a man must see to it that his animals are fed before he himself sits

1

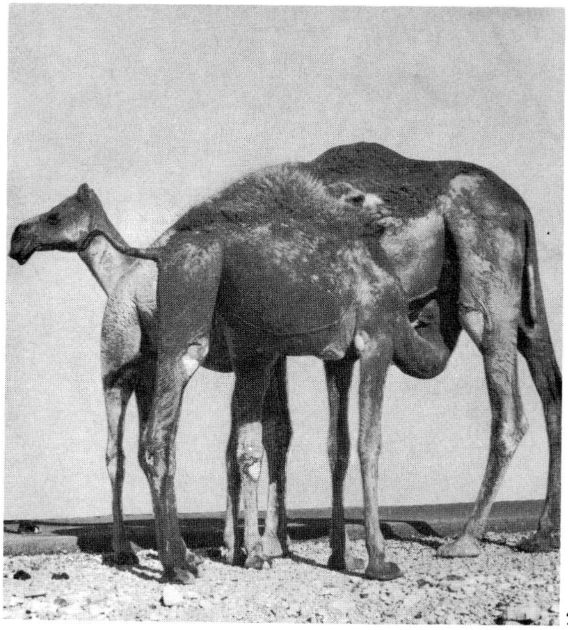
2

1. Drawing from a 13th-century children's book, illustrating the fable of the wolf and the crane. The crane is removing a bone caught in the wolf's throat.
2. Camels, among the first animals to be domesticated by man, thrive in the arid conditions of Israel's Negev region.

down to eat, and he may not buy animals unless he can care for them properly. If an animal is overburdened, even the animal of an enemy, it must be helped (Exodus 23:5). Hunting is frowned upon as not befitting the descendants of Abraham. The Torah further prohibits the slaughter of an animal and its young on the same day (Leviticus 22:28). One may not plow with an ox and an ass yoked together (Deuteronomy 22:10). To anyone who has seen this practice, the suffering of the smaller animal is quite plain.

Laws governing the sacrifices which were an integral part of Jewish worship in Temple times describe in detail the animals which were to be used in the Temple service.

ANIMAL MOTIFS IN THE BIBLE

Many of the banners of the ancient Tribes of Israel have animals as their symbols, and these are represented in a series of 12 stamps issued by the Israel Post Office. Some of these animals appear as well in the signs of the *Zodiac.

Animal metaphors are frequently used in the Bible. For example, the Almighty "is for them like the horns of the wild ox; they shall devour enemy nations . . . ; they crouch, they lie down like the lion" (Numbers 24:8-9). In the Book of Proverbs, the references to animals serve mostly to teach good behavior: "Go to the ant; thou sluggard; consider her ways, and be wise" (Proverbs 6:6-8).

The international peace of the Messianic era is described in a beautiful passage in Isaiah (11:6-7): animals which are natural enemies will live together in harmony. "And the wolf shall dwell with the lamb, and the leopard shall lie down with the kid; and the calf and the young lion and the fatling together; and a little child shall lead them. And the cow and the bear shall feed; their young ones shall lie down together; and the lion shall eat straw like the ox."

ANIMAL TALES

There are 36 Hebrew and Aramaic animal tales in talmudic and midrashic literature. These are known as the "fox fables," though the fox appears in only 11, mostly as a clever and sly trickster. Most of the animal stories found in the *aggadah* are also found in Indian and Greek fables; the Jewish version is usually closer to the Indian.

Tales in which animals were the main characters were often used as a device to teach a moral lesson or to protest against objectionable local conditions; (an example is the fable of the fox and the fish, which is to be found in the article on the **aggadah*). Animal fables were also used by European Jews to illuminate typical human behavior. Few such tales, however, have been preserved. Among the 8,000 stories in the Israel folktale archives, there are only 140 animal tales. In the Yiddish collection of 540 East European folktales of Naphtali Gross, only 24 are animal tales.

FAUNA OF EREẒ ISRAEL

A review of the animals which are mentioned in biblical and talmudic literature reveals that some of them have disappeared from the landscape of Israel in fairly recent times. This is particularly true of wild animals which were permitted for food, that is, those that chewed their cud and had cloven hoofs. Of the nine such animals referred to in the Bible, only two have survived in Israel and neighboring countries. These are the gazelle and the ibex, which were saved from threatened extinction by the State of Israel's fauna preservation laws.

Domestic animals permitted for food were sheep, goats and cattle. Among the prohibited ones which were common, the ass was the most valuable work animal, and the camel was useful in arid and desert regions.

Through the centuries, hunting led to the elimination of most of the large carnivorous animals. Their dens were the thickets of the Jordan (Jeremiah 49:19), the Lebanese mountains (Song of Songs 4:8), the Syrian desert and the Negev (Isaiah 30:6). From these regions they descended upon populated places. Bones have been uncovered, dating back to early geological periods, of animals no longer to be seen in Ereẓ Israel, such as the warthog, hippopotamus, rhinoceros, striped hyena, elephant and mastodon. The Biblical Zoo in Jerusalem has a collection of many of the above-mentioned animals, whose cages are labeled with the biblical verse in which their names appear.

Some bears still survive in Syria and in the Lebanese mountains, and leopards occasionally make their way into Upper Galilee. The last lions and wild

ANIMAL	HEBREW	SOURCE
Addax	יַחְמוּר	Deut. 14:5
Ant	נְמָלָה	Prov. 6 6 - 8
Ass	חֲמוֹר	Gen. 12:16
	עַיִר, אָתוֹן	Gen 32:16
Bat	עֲטַלֵּף	Lev. 11.19
Bear	דֹּב	I Sam. 17:34
Bee	דְּבוֹרָה	Deut. 1:44
Beetle	תּוֹלַעַת	Deut. 28:39
Bison	תְּאוֹ	Deut. 14:5
Boar, Wild	חֲזִיר מִיַּעַר	Ps 80:14
Buffalo	מְרִיא	II Sam. 6:13
Buzard	אַיָּה, רָאָה	Deut 14.13
Camel	גָּמָל	Gen. 12.16
	בֵּכֶר, בִּכְרָה	Isa. 60.6
Cattle	בָּקָר	Gen. 13:5
	שׁוֹר	Gen. 32:6
	אֲלָפִים	Deut. 7:13
	אַבִּירִים	Isa 34.7
	פָּר, פָּרָה	Gen 32:16
	עֵגֶל, עֶגְלָה	Gen. 15 9
Centipedes	מַרְבֵּה רַגְלַיִם	Lev. 11.42
Chameleon	תִּנְשֶׁמֶת (שֶׁרֶץ)	Lev. 11:30
Cobra	פֶּתֶן	Deut 32:33
	שָׂרָף	Num. 21:6
Cock	שֶׂכְוִי?	Job 38:36
	זַרְזִיר מָתְנַיִם(?)	Prov. 30:31
Corals	פְּנִינִים	Lam. 4:7
Crane	עָגוּר	Isa 38.14
Cricket	צְלָצַל	Deut. 28.42
Crimson	תּוֹלַעַת שָׁנִי	Ex 25:4
Worm	כַּרְמִיל	II Chron. 2:6
Crocodile	תַּנִּין	Ex. 7:9
	לִוְיָתָן	Job 40:25
Deer	יַחְמוּר אַיָּל, אַיָּלָה	Deut 14.5

ANIMAL	HEBREW	SOURCE
Dog	כֶּלֶב	Ex. 22:30
Dove	יוֹנָה	Gen. 8:8
Eagle	עַיִט	Gen. 15:11
Earthworm	תּוֹלַעַת	Isa. 14:11
Elephant	שֶׁנְהָב	I Kings 10:22
Fish	דָּג, דָּגִים	Gen. 9:2
	דָּגָה	Gen. 1:26
Flea	פַּרְעֹשׁ	I Sam. 24:14
Fly	זְבוּב	Isa. 7:18
Fox	שׁוּעָל	Lam. 5:18
Frog	צְפַרְדֵּעַ	Ex. 7:27
Gazelle	צְבִי	Deut. 12:15
Gecko	אֲנָקָה	Lev. 11:30
	שְׂמָמִית	Prov. 30:28
Gnat	עָרוֹב	Ex. 8:17
Goat	עֵז	Lev. 7:23
	שָׂעִיר	Gen. 37:31
	תַּיִשׁ	Gen. 30:35
	עַתּוּדִים	Gen. 31:10
	אַקּוֹ	Deut. 14:5
Goose	בַּרְבּוּר	I Kings 5:3
Grasshopper	חַרְגּוֹל, סָלְעָם	Lev. 11:22
	חָגָב	Num. 13:33
Gull	שַׁחַף	Lev. 11:16
Hare	אַרְנֶבֶת	Lev. 11:16
Hawk	נֵץ	Lev. 11:16
Heron	אֲנָפָה	Lev. 11:19
Hippo-potamus	בְּהֵמוֹת	Job 40:15
Horse	סוּס	Gen. 47:17
	פָּרָשׁ	Isa. 28:28
Hyena	צָבוּעַ	I Sam. 13:18
Hyrax	שָׁפָן	Lev. 11:5
Ibex	יָעֵל, יַעֲלָה	Ps. 104:18

asses were destroyed at the end of the 19th century. Crocodiles, however, survived in the western rivers of Ereẓ Israel up to the beginning of the 20th century.

The fauna of the country is very varied, because Ereẓ Israel is the meeting place of three climatic (and floral) regions: the Mediterranean, the Saharo-Sindic, and the Irano-Turanic. Unlike its flora, however, the fauna of Ereẓ Israel has not yet been thoroughly studied and surveyed. At present approximately 88 species of mammal are known, 359 of birds, 76 of reptiles, 434 of sweet and salt water fish, and seven of amphibia. In addition there are many thousands of species of invertebrates, chiefly insects. (See also *Birds.)

A few of the creatures mentioned in the Bible and Talmud are briefly discussed below.

Ant. The most common variety in Israel is the harvest ant, described in the Book of Proverbs as the symbol of diligence and wisdom, preparing for the future by storing food during the harvest. These ants actually caused such extensive damage to harvested grain that Rabbi Simeon ben Gamaliel permitted the destruction of anthills during the intermediate days of festivals, a time when such labor is normally not allowed.

Ape. Though it is not native to the land of Israel, the ape appears in biblical and rabbinic literature. Apes were among King Solomon's imported luxuries. The

ANIMAL	HEBREW	SOURCE
Jackal	שׁוּעָל	Judg. 15:4
Kestrel	תַּחְמָס	Lev. 11:16
Kite	דָּאָה	Lev. 11:14
	דַּיָּה	Deut. 14:13
Leech	עֲלוּקָה	Prov. 30:15
Leopard	נָמֵר	Isa. 11:6
Lion	אֲרִי	Isa. 38:13
	אַרְיֵה,כְּפִיר, שַׁחַל	Job 4:10
	לָבִיא	Gen. 49:9
	לַיִשׁ	Job 4:11
Lizard	לְטָאָה,כֹּחַ	Lev. 11:30
	צָב	Lev. 11:29
Locust	אַרְבֶּה	Ex. 10:12
	גָּזָם,חָסִיל, יֶלֶק	Joel 1:4
	גּוֹבַי	Amos 7:1
Louse	כֵּן כִּנִּים,כִּנָּם	Ex. 8:12-13
Maggot	רִמָּה	Ex. 16:24
Mole Rat	חֲפַרְפֵּרוֹת	Isa. 2:20
Monkey	קוֹף	I Kings 10:22
Moth	נֹסֵס	Isa. 10:18
	סָס ,עָשׁ	Isa. 51:8
Mouse	עַכְבָּר	Lev. 11:29
Mule	פֶּרֶד,פִּרְדָּה	Isa. 66:20
Nightingale	זָמִיר	Song 2:12
Onager	עָרוֹד	Job 39:5
	פֶּרֶא	Jer. 14:6
Oryx	זֶמֶר (?)	Deut. 14:5
Ostrich	יָעֵן	Lam. 4:3
	כְּנַף רְנָנִים	Job 39:13
Owl	תִּנְשֶׁמֶת (עוֹף) קָאָת	Lev. 11:18
	אֹחַ שָׂעִיר	Isa. 13:21
	בַּת־יַעֲנָה תַּנִּים (?)	Isa. 34:13
	שָׁלָךְ, כּוֹס ,יַנְשׁוּף	Lev. 11:17
	קִפּוֹד	Isa. 14:23
Owl (cont.)	קִפּוֹז (?)	Isa. 34:15
	לִילִית	Isa. 34:14
Ox	רְאֵם, רֵים	Num. 23:22
Partridge	חָגְלָה	Num. 26:33
	קֹרֵא	I Sam. 26:20
Peacock	תֻּכִּי	I Kings 10:22
Quail	שְׂלָו	Ex. 16:13
Rat	חֹלֶד	Lev. 11:29
Raven	עוֹרֵב	Gen. 8:7
Scorpion	עַקְרָב	Deut. 8:15
Sheep	צֹאן	Gen. 4:2
	אַיִל	Gen. 22:13
	רָחֵל	Gen. 32:15
	כֶּבֶשׂ, כִּבְשָׂה	Ex. 12:5
	כֶּשֶׂב, כִּשְׂבָּה	Lev. 3:7
	טָלֶה	I Sam. 7:9
Skink	חֹמֶט	Lev. 11:30
Snake	נָחָשׁ	Gen. 3:1
Sparrow	צִפּוֹר דְּרוֹר	Lev.14:4
Spider	עַכָּבִישׁ	Isa. 59:5
Stork	חֲסִידָה	Lev. 11:19
Swift	סִיס	Isa. 38:14
Swine	חֲזִיר	Lev. 11:7
Tahash	תַּחַשׁ	Ex. 36:19
Turtle Dove	תּוֹר	Gen. 15:9
Viper	אֶפְעֶה	Isa. 30:6
	שְׁפִיפוֹן	Gen. 49:17
	צֶפַע	Isa. 14:29
	צִפְעוֹנִי	Isa. 11:8
Vulture	פֶּרֶס,עָזְנִיָּה, נֶשֶׁר	Lev. 11:13
	רָחָם, רָחָמָה	Lev. 11:18
Wasp	צִרְעָה	Ex. 23:28
Whale	לִוְיָתָן	Ps. 104:26
Wolf	זְאֵב	Isa. 11:6

rabbis record that they were trained in simple chores such as keeping crawling things out of the house, and they are listed among the animals not permitted for food. The Mishnah, noting certain similarities between these "lords of the field" and man, discusses whether their carcasses are therefore sources of ritual uncleanliness as human corpses are.

Lion. If there is at all an animal symbol of the Jewish people, it is probably the lion. The king of beasts, often rampant, is one of the most common symbols of the Jews, and appears as a motif in religious art and on *ceremonial objects. The Holy Ark and its embroidered curtains, the ornate mantle of the Torah scroll, painted synagogue walls and mosaic floors, and designs for the *menorah,* frequently show a lion as part of their decoration.

When Jacob blessed his children (Genesis 49:9) he compared Judah to a lion in strength. The figure of a lion later appeared on the standard of that tribe and is today on the banner of the city of Jerusalem, which is partly situated in the territory of Judah.

The Emperor of Ethiopia, who claims descent from King Solomon and the Queen of Sheba, is called the Lion of Judah.

In biblical times lions roamed the countryside freely, often stealing sheep. Samson and David are depicted in the Bible as heroes who survived their respective encounters with desert lions.

Pig. Listed in the Bible among the unclean animals forbidden as food is the pig, or swine. It has only one of the two signs that characterize animals permitted for food: although cloven-hooved, it does not chew its cud (Leviticus 11:7; Deuteronomy 16:8). It was eaten by the Canaanites before the Israelite conquest. The practice of offering it as a sacrifice in idolatrous worship provoked a protest from the prophet Isaiah (66:3).

As early as Antiochus IV Epiphanes in the days of the Maccabees (second century b.c.e.), refusing to eat swines's flesh was a test of the Jew's loyalty to Judaism. Likewise, as a deliberate insult during the Romans' siege of Jerusalem in 70 c.e., a pig was hoisted over the walls of Jerusalem instead of an animal fit for sacrifice. It was then that the rabbis decreed: "Cursed be he who breeds pigs."

The pig has always symbolized something repulsive, and in the Talmud the words "pig breeders and usurers" are often used together, since both are regarded with a feeling of revulsion and disgust. Indeed in Yiddish, the very word for pig is even avoided by some people, who prefer to substitute a euphemism which literally means "something else."

Species of the chameleon lizard found in Israel. It changes the color of its skin to match that of its surroundings.

In the Midrash, the Roman kingdom is called "pig," possibly because the boar or wild pig was the symbol of the Roman legion in Israel. "The swine when it lies down puts out its hooves as if to say 'I am clean;' so Rome," say the rabbis, "plundered and robbed under the guise of establishing a judicial tribunal."

In modern Israel pig-breeding is regarded with abhorrence, and the Jewish National Fund's contracts forbid pig-raising on Jewish National Fund land. In 1962, a law was passed forbidding the breeding, keeping or slaughtering of pigs, except in Nazareth and other specified places with a sizable Christian population.

ANOINTING with oil is a very ancient custom. It was done for both practical and symbolic reasons. The practical use was cosmetic, to soften and protect the skin, as well as medicinal, to heal various afflictions. Anointing also figured in the coronation of the king, in the ordination of Aaron and his sons as priests, and in the purification of a person suffering from *leprosy. These anointings were not for practical purposes but of symbolic value; they symbolized the new rank and power given to the anointed person and they evoked God's blessing on him.

The anointing oil was holy and made according to

a special formula. It could be used for no purposes other than those outlined above. In the case of leprosy, the oil used was not holy. According to the Talmud, the anointing oil was compounded only once in history – by Moses, who made enough to last for the whole period from the anointing of Aaron until the residue was hidden away by King Josiah. After that time no anointing took place.

In the case of kings, the whole head was anointed, i.e. covered with the oil, whereas the priests had only a mark made on the head with the oil. For King David and his descendants the oil was poured out of a horn; for King Saul it was from a phial since "his kingdom was not a lasting one." The kings of the Northern Kingdom of Israel were not anointed with oil but with balsam.

The word messiah literally means "the anointed one."

Samuel anointing David in the presence of his brothers, as depicted in a wall panel from the Dura-Europos synagogue, dating back to the third century c.e.

ANTHROPOLOGY is the name given to the study of man; physical anthropology is the study of the physical characteristics of man. When applied to the Jews, it means the study of the physical characteristics of the Jew and is obviously concerned with those that can be considered "Jewish."

Although the Bible is quite precise about the origins of the Jewish people – it started with Abraham who came from Mesopotamia – there were, over the ages, many additions to the people, so that it is impossible to consider the Jews as one clearly defined biological or genetic group. The Bible itself records the marriage of the sons of Jacob with women who were not members of the clan; Joseph, for example, married an Egyptian. Furthermore, in the Exodus from Egypt, a "mixed multitude" accompanied the Jews and were presumably assimilated into them. Also, in the course of history, whole groups – as well as individuals – have been absorbed into the Jewish people; a good example is the Idumeans who converted in Hasmonean times. Thus no racial purity can be claimed by the Jews, and indeed, Jewish tradition would not see any source of pride in it if it could be claimed. Any person who accepts the fundamentals of the Jewish religion, and who undergoes the conversion ceremony is completely accepted into the Jewish people. (For more on this see *Conversion to Judaism.).

From all this it follows that it is incorrect to state that "so-and-so looks Jewish," because there is no specifically Jewish appearance. There are blond Jews as well as darkskinned ones; some Jews have long noses and others have bobbed, upturned noses; there are blue-eyed Jews as well as black- and brown-eyed Jews; and some Jews are tall while others are short. In brief one could say that the Jews tend to have the same characteristics as the people among whom they have been living. This is true even with regard to blood types; the frequencies of blood type among Jews is very much the same as among the surrounding population. Nowhere is this lack of uniformity so striking as in modern Israel, where Jews are gathered from all over the world. (See also *Racial Discrimination.)

ANTI-SEMITISM is a term which was coined in 1879 to designate the then current anti-Jewish campaigns in Europe. Since that time, the term has come to denote all forms of hostility shown towards Jews throughout history. Although the word Semite includes many more races than the Jewish – the Arabs, for example, are also Semites – the term anti-Semitism is always used only with regard to Jews. Hatred of the Jews may stem from many causes and thus anti-Semitism can be classified as "religious anti-Semitism," "economic anti-Semitism," "social anti-Semitism," and "racial anti-Semitism."

In history, hostility towards the Jews has manifested itself in many different ways: violence against Jewish persons or property; expulsions from countries; legislation discriminating against Jews: and even attempts – often successful – to annihilate Jewish communities.

Lithograph of the second trial of Alfred Dreyfus in 1899. Dreyfus was a French Jew falsely accused of treason, in an atmosphere of anti-Semitism that shocked the modern Jewish world.

Prejudice against Jews already appeared in the ancient world. Jews not only refused to worship pagan idols: they even refused to respect them. In a world where every people was expected to respect other nations' gods, the Jews' belief in one, unseen God Who is absolutely supreme, set them apart. The Jewish laws forbidding the consumption of non-kosher foods prevented any real social contact between Jews and non-Jews. This led non-Jews to consider the Jews as anti-social and heretical; the main claim of ancient anti-Semites was that the Jews were against mankind and against the gods. This further led to falsification of history. For instance, it was claimed that the Jewish nation descended from a group of lepers who had been driven out of Egypt.

After the rise of Christianity and its acceptance as the official religion of the Roman Empire, anti-Semitism received a new impetus. The Christians, who themselves had been persecuted by the pagan empire, could not accept independent Jewish religious existence. They were unable to reconcile themselves to the fact that the Jews did not accept their messiah and their religious teachings. They claimed that they, the Christians, superseded the Jews and that they were the true People of Israel. Wherever Christianity spread through Europe, laws were passed discriminating against the Jews, who were forced to wear distinctive clothing (see *Badge, Jewish) and were often forced to live in separate areas. The Church took over the biblical law against moneylending on interest, but since the growing capitalist economy needed a steady flow of credit, the various Christian states made the Jews into the moneylenders by outlawing other occupations, and later persecuted them for being moneylenders.

During the *Crusades, the Jews suffered in Europe and in Ereẓ Israel. The knightly Crusaders, on their way to liberate the holy places from the Muslims, took the opportunity of murdering Jews and wiping out whole Jewish communities throughout Europe. In this way they were also able to free themselves from debts owed to Jews by killing the creditors. Although some church leaders objected, the killings went on. In Ereẓ Israel itself the Crusaders did not distinguish between the Muslims whom they had come to fight, and the local Jews who were really not a party to the war.

Although the treatment accorded to the Jews in Islamic countries was generally a little better than in Christian countries, the Muslims could never forgive the Jews for not accepting Muhammad and their new faith. Jews were very definitely second-class citizens and suffered from a variety of disabilities. Special heavy taxes were levied on them and they were forbidden to engage in all kinds of occupations.

The *Black Death which raged through Europe between 1348 and 1350, and which killed off between one quarter and one half of the total population, had a terrible effect on anti-Semitism. No one really knew what was causing the catastrophe and a convenient scapegoat was found in the Jews. Countless numbers of Jews were massacred because it was claimed that the Jews caused the plague by poisoning the wells.

The Reformation in the 16th century also had serious effects on the position of the Jews, although they were certainly not involved in the actual movement. Martin *Luther was at first sympathetic to the Jews, but when they refused to accept his new version of Christianity, he turned against them and became viciously anti-Semetic. He even advocated burning synagogues and killing as many Jews as possible. The Catholic Church suspected the Jews of having something to do with the Reformation, and persecuted them even more.

Perhaps the most outstanding act of anti-Semitism of the Middle Ages, with the exception of the Crusades, was the expulsion from Spain in 1492. There the Jews were told to accept the Christian faith or leave the country. Many took the first choice but continued to practice Judaism in secret. These *Marranos were one of the main subjects of investigation of the *Inquisition.

With the Enlightenment in some European countries, many of the discriminatory laws against the Jews were lifted, but anti-Semitism continued to exist, particularly in Eastern Europe. In Russia, for example, the domicile of Jews was limited to specific areas and they needed special permits to be able to live outside the *Pale of Settlement. The ancient *blood libel – surely one of the most disgusting lies ever invented – continued into the 20th century.

Often throughout history, the Jews – because they were a weak, defenseless minority – were used by governments to distract the attention of the general population from their real problems. Both in Czarist Russia and, later, in Hitler's Germany, this tendency was very marked. The Jews were blamed for all the ills of society and the government incited the populace to violence against the Jews in order to save themselves.

The rise of modern *Zionism was due, in great measure, to anti-Semitism. The founders could see no relief for the Jews from anti-Semitism until the Jews would have their own state and cease to be "guests" everywhere. Not even the most pessimistic thinker, however, could foresee to what extent anti-Semitism would go in Nazi Germany. The Jews there were stripped of all protection of the law. They were considered to be an inferior race which was responsible for all the troubles of the world. Paradoxically, they were accused of being at the same time both Communists and capitalists. The infamous forgery, the *Protocols of the Learned Elders of Zion, was revived to show how the Jews wanted to take over the world. The climax was reached in what the Nazis called "the final solution," which was intended to destroy all the Jews in the world. In their inhuman concentration and extermination camps they succeeded in killing – in the most terrible ways imaginable – 6,000,000 of Europe's Jews.

In a sense, the unbelievable excesses of Nazism shocked the world for a while. People began to realize what anti-Semitism could lead to. But only for a

View of Babi Yar in the Soviet Union where in 1941, the Nazis killed over 100,000 persons and then destroyed all evidence of the massacre. Soviet anti-Semitism forbade building a memorial to the murdered Jews on the site.

1. Russian caricature of Moshe Dayan, symbolizing the Israelis and their supposedly bloodthirsty expansionist tendencies.
2. Anti-Semitic headline in an American newspaper, published by Henry Ford, which for almost seven years waged a propaganda campaign against the Jews. May 22, 1920.
3. Anti-Semitic cartoon from Egyptian daily "Al-Massa," April 19, 1964, entitled "The Great Festival is Drawing Near," referring to the Arab intention of slaughtering the Israelis.
4. "The God of the Jews is money," says the caption in this Nazi caricature of the Jewish stockbroker sitting atop a huge bag of cash. "And in order to earn that money," the caption continues, "they commit the gravest crimes."
5. A 16th-century woodcut of a Jewish moneylender, often the object of ridicule by anti-Semites.

АРАБСКИЕ СТРАНЫ
"The Israeli extremists' appetite".
— *Sovetskaya Moldavia*, June 4, 1968
1

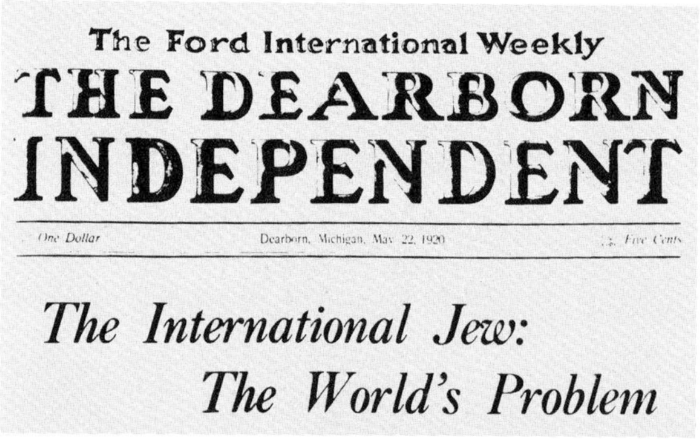
The Ford International Weekly
THE DEARBORN INDEPENDENT
One Dollar — Dearborn, Michigan, May 22, 1920 — Five Cents

The International Jew: The World's Problem

2

3

BÖRSE
GELD
4

ach dem vñ iüdisch listikeyt
yr fursetzt gar on all arbeyt
mit gãtzer faulkeit sich zu nern
5

1

2

3

1. **Bar Mitzvah.** Grandfather shows his grandson how to put on *tefillin,* a duty he will assume at his *bar mitzvah.* Painting by Avraham Bender.
2. **Ben-Yehuda.** Israel stamp issued on November 25, 1959 to commemorate the centenary of the birth of Eliezer Ben-Yehuda, the father of modern Hebrew.
3. **Bonds.** Israel stamp issued on April 30, 1951, the tenth anniversary of Israel Bonds. The worker holds the geographical outline of Israel (as it was then), symbolizing the upbuilding of Israel through physical labor and financial aid.

Das größte Getreide-Wucherthier der Welt.
Neueste zoologische Entdeckung des Kikeriki.

1

3

4

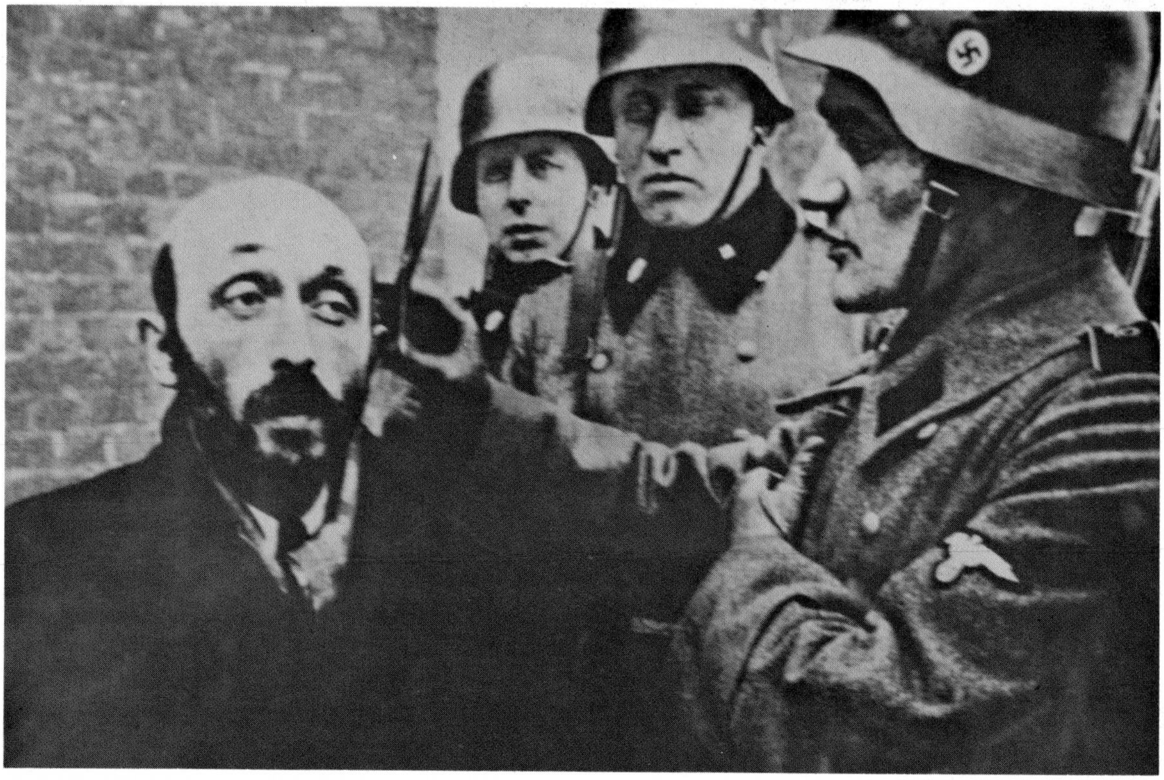

2

1. The Jew as a world-devouring vampire. Vienna, 1921.
2. Nazi S.S. men torment and ridicule a Polish Jew by cutting off his beard.
3. 4. Sculptured figures of "synagoga" and "ecclesia" – anthropomorphic representations of the synagogue, blinded to the truth, and the church, wearing a crown of glory. Bamberg Cathedral, 13th century.

while. Anti-Semitism began to rear its ugly head again, particularly in Soviet Russia under Stalin and, because of their conflict with the State of Israel, many Arab countries adopted anti-Semitic propaganda. Indeed, many of the Nazis who managed to escape from Europe found refuge in Arab countries, where they continued to spread vicious lies and hatred.

It seems that one of the main causes of anti-Semitism is the inability of some people to accept the existence in their midst of a non-conformist group that insists on maintaining its own beliefs and its own identity. The anti-Semite is an irrational person who generally cannot explain why he hates the Jews. Perhaps he does not know himself.

For more information on specific manifestations of anti-Semitism see the following entries: *Action Française; *Armleder; *Black Death; *Blood Libel; *Chmielnicki, Bogdan; *Concentration Camps; *Conversion, Forced; *Crusades; *Desecration of the Host; *Disputations; *Ecclesia et Synagoga; *Expulsions; *Ghetto; *Haidamacks; *Holocaust; *Minority Rights; *Nazism; *Numerus Clausus; *Oath More Judaico; *Protocols of the Learned Elders of Zion; *Rindfleisch; and *Self-Defense.

1. Cover of a Spanish edition of *The Protocols of the Learned Elders of Zion,* a violently anti-Semitic publication which claims that the Jewish plan is to "destroy Christianity and enslave humanity."
2. Bas-relief of Judah Maccabee, whose story is part of the Apocrypha. This sculpture is in the West Point Military Academy in New York.

APOCRYPHA is the name given to a body of ancient literature which was not included in the canon of the Hebrew Bible. For example, the story of *Judah Maccabee is not found in the Bible; rather, it is one of the pieces of literature which make up the Apocrypha. These historical and ethical works were written during the time of the Second Temple by authors who are now unknown.

There are 13 books in the Apocrypha. One of them, Susannah and the Elders, is the popular story of a righteous woman who is falsely accused by the wicked elders of her city but is saved by the young Daniel from the death verdict. Bel and the Dragon, another book of the Apocrypha, is an account of Daniel's success in demonstrating the futility of idol

worship to Nebuchadnezzar, king of Babylon, and Darius the Mede. From the literary point of view, by far the most important book in the Apocrypha is the Wisdom of *Ben Sira, a book of hymns and proverbs.

The books of the Pseudepigrapha, also written in the time of the Second Temple, are more numerous than those of the Apocrypha. The difference is, that whereas all of the apocryphal books are accepted as sacred by certain churches, only individual books of the Pseudepigrapha are included in the canons of various churches. Probably the most important work in pseudepigraphical literature deals with Enoch the son of Jared. It is an account of the visions revealed to him in the heavens. It deals as well with astronomical material and establishes the "correct" calendar at 364 days, making 52 weeks. Many works of the Pseudepigrapha also concern ethical matters. One such work is the Testaments of the Twelve Patriarchs, in which the sons of Jacob warn their children against sin, especially that particular sin which each had committed.

The Talmud considers both the Apocrypha and Pseudepigrapha as non-holy works. There is, however, a distinction drawn between them: the Apocrypha deals mainly with Jews, while the Pseudepigrapha is more universal.

In the Middle Ages apocryphal stories appeared in Hebrew literature. The story of *Hannah and her Seven Sons who refused to worship idols and died as martyrs was one narrative found in almost every medieval collection of Hebrew stories. In Renaissance times Jewish scholars continued to study apocryphal and pseudepigraphical material in their quest for historical sources.

APOSTASY means rejecting one's loyalties to the Jewish faith and nation in order to join the ranks of another religious faith. Throughout the ages there have been many different circumstances in which Jews left their religion.

In 175 b.c.e. in the ancient Middle East, the Seleucid Empire was engulfing the tiny Jewish state of Judea, and everywhere the influence of the idolatrous Greek culture was felt. The Royal Seleucid commissioner and his treacherous Jewish followers (known as Hellenizers) set up a pagan altar in the town of Modi'in, and demanded that the people desert their Jewish faith and make sacrifices there to the Greek gods. As one of the local Jewish nobility stepped forward to comply, the old Jewish priest Mattathias ran up to the traitor and slew him. He and his sons the Maccabees went on to defeat the Seleucid power in Ereẓ Israel and reestablish the Jewish religion with its Temple worship.

A century later *Elisha ben Avuyah, a great rabbi of early talmudic times, cynically renounced his Jewishness, and joined Roman society. His fellow Jews who bravely endured the persecutions they suffered for being Jewish were outraged by his action and felt utter contempt for him. Yet his brilliant student and follower, the kindly Rabbi *Meir,

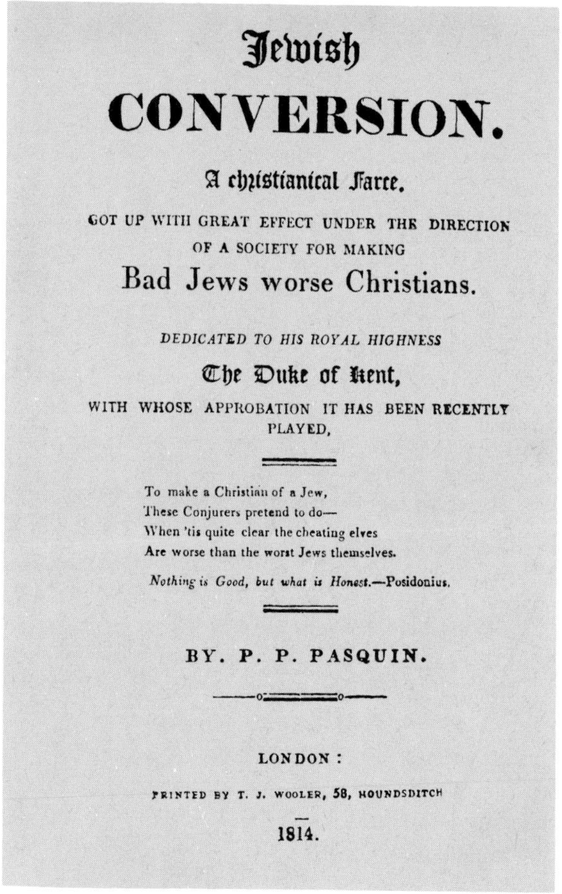
Jewish
CONVERSION.
A christianical Farce.
GOT UP WITH GREAT EFFECT UNDER THE DIRECTION
OF A SOCIETY FOR MAKING
Bad Jews worse Christians.
DEDICATED TO HIS ROYAL HIGHNESS
The Duke of Kent,
WITH WHOSE APPROBATION IT HAS BEEN RECENTLY PLAYED.

To make a Christian of a Jew,
These Conjurers pretend to do—
When 'tis quite clear the cheating elves
Are worse than the worst Jews themselves.

Nothing is Good, but what is Honest.—Posidonius.

BY. P. P. PASQUIN.

LONDON:
PRINTED BY T. J. WOOLER, 58, HOUNDSDITCH
—
1814.

Apostasy was the subject of ridicule by many non-Jews, as this title page from a "Christianical farce" on Jewish conversion shows. London, 1814.

continued to address him with tender respect, hoping that Elisha would repent and return to the Jewish people.

These are two early examples of Jewish apostasy, and they illustrate the two extremes of the Jewish people's response through history to its apostates. On the one hand, the apostate has been contemptuously regarded as a coward or traitor who chose to take the easy path of converting to the religion of the majority rather than continuing against all odds to keep strong

1. Woman from Habban, a town in the central South Arabian Peninsula, wearing traditional hair net and heavy silver jewelry.
2. Arabian Jew, photographed shortly after his arrival in Israel, 1951.

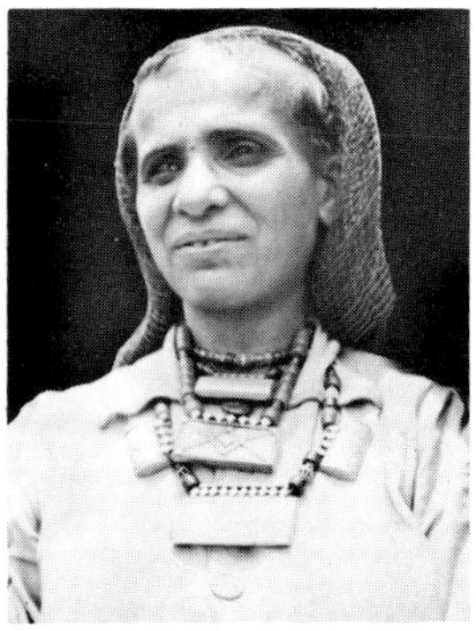
1

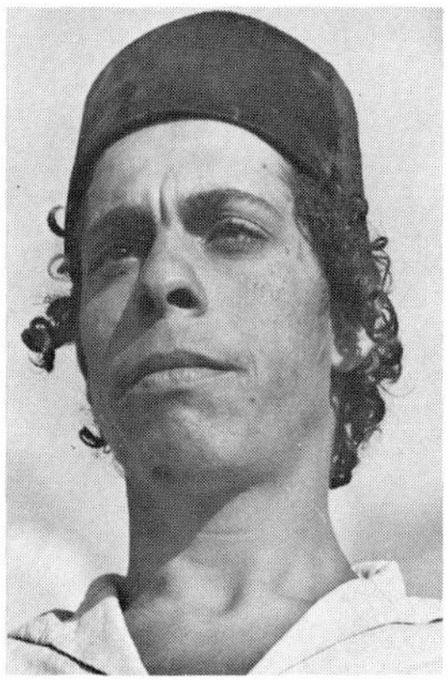
2

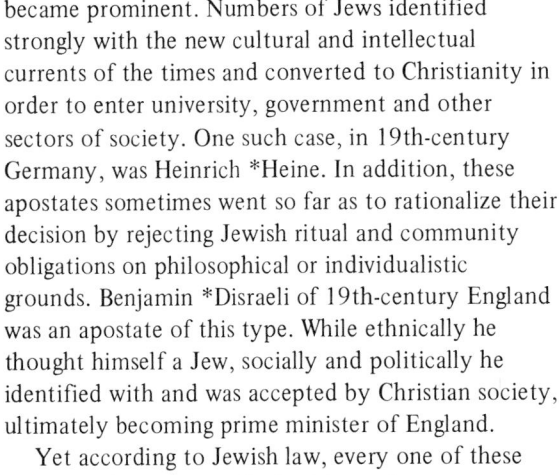

his faith in the God of Israel. In rebelling against Judaism he defiled the memory of those Jews in past history who fought and died to preserve their faith in their one God. On the other hand, other Jews like Rabbi Meir treated the apostate sympathetically in the hope that their misguided brother would repent and rejoin his Jewish religion and community.

The reasons for Jewish conversion to other faiths varied according to time and place. Sometimes the compelling factors were poverty, high pressured missionary activity, or oppression. In medieval Germany, many Jews were so poverty-stricken that in order to lure them away from their religion, missionaries used the motto: "Become baptized – we will get you plenty of money." Often, fear of expulsion or massacre was at the root of apostasy. Joining the majority religion also meant relief from special laws against Jews and achieving new social rights and privileges.

*Abner of Burgos was one of many who submitted to the pressures of poverty and went so far as to argue publicly with rabbis and to formulate new theological doctrines to prove that it was a Christian's duty to force Jews to convert.

In the late fifteenth century Spain a new kind of apostate appeared alongside the usual apostate – the *Marranos. Because of fear of death or expulsion, they and their families outwardly adopted Christian ways and worship while secretly practicing Jewish law and ritual. When the Marranos managed to escape to lands of religious freedom, they were usually reaccepted into the Jewish community without a reconversion ceremony.

With the onset of the Enlightenment in the eighteenth century, another form of apostasy became prominent. Numbers of Jews identified strongly with the new cultural and intellectual currents of the times and converted to Christianity in order to enter university, government and other sectors of society. One such case, in 19th-century Germany, was Heinrich *Heine. In addition, these apostates sometimes went so far as to rationalize their decision by rejecting Jewish ritual and community obligations on philosophical or individualistic grounds. Benjamin *Disraeli of 19th-century England was an apostate of this type. While ethnically he thought himself a Jew, socially and politically he identified with and was accepted by Christian society, ultimately becoming prime minister of England.

Yet according to Jewish law, every one of these apostates, being born of a Jewish mother, never lost his Jewish status through conversion. Indeed, as the Talmud teaches: "A Jew, even if he has sinned, remains a Jew." (See also the article *Conversion to Judaism.)

ARABIA. The Arabian peninsula was inhabited by a variety of ancient peoples who raided the countries of the Fertile Crescent – Ereẓ Israel, Syria, and Mesopotamia, and was a significant area for the development of both the Hebrew and Islamic civilizations. For Islam, it is Mecca, where Muhammad was born and spread his teachings, that has a special position in the Arab World – every Muslim is obliged to visit Mecca at least once in his lifetime. Medina, to which Muhammad fled in 622 and where he was buried in 632, also has the status of a holy place.

In the Bible, from the days of the patriarchs, there are many references to the dealings of the ancient Hebrews with Arabia. These include family ties, relations in war and peace, and trade between the Israelites and the various tribes of Arabia. The names of nomadic tribes and settlements and the genealogical lists of the sons of Abraham and Esau (or Edom) can be read on various inscriptions found in Israel and in Arabia. In addition, we can find descriptions of Jewish-Arab relations in the literature of the Second Temple period and in the Talmud.

Since there were great political and social differences between the north Arabian peninsula, called the Hejaz, and Yemen in the south, *Yemen is discussed in a separate article. As for the Hejaz, its history is vague and shrouded in legend. However, we have evidence to indicate that after the destruction of the First Temple, in the sixth century b.c.e., 80,000 *kohanim* (priests) who were saved went to live in Arabia and joined those Jews already settled there. Tomb inscriptions of Jews found at al-Ula and at al-Ḥijr contain such biblical names as Manasseh, Samuel, and Shalom.

The names and works of Jewish poets who lived in Arabia a generation before Muhammad, have been preserved in classical Arabic poetry, especially in connection with events in Medina, where about 20 Jewish tribes lived, including the "Two Tribes of Priests." Many Jews also lived in Khayber and other oases, and in the port of Maqua on the Gulf of Eilat.

Much of the other information we have about Jewish life in Arabia comes from inscriptions. The excavations of the ancient Jewish cemetery of Bet She'arim (near Haifa) reveal a series of graves of "the

people of Himyar," Himyar being another name for Southern Arabia. Inscriptions discovered in Himyar itself give archaeologists reason to believe that some of the kings of Himyar actually converted to Judaism in the 5th and 6th centuries c.e. However, after Himyar turned Muslim in the 7th century c.e. we have practically no information about Jewish life in Arabia – until the 20th century.

In 1948 about 54,000 Jews lived in hundreds of small communities in Southern Arabia, mostly in Yemen, but also in Aden, Bahrein, Saudi Arabia and Kuwait. By 1968, following emigration and a series of expulsion orders, there were only a few hundred Jews left in the entire peninsula.

Aden is a port and city in south western Arabia. In medieval times there were business, communal and religious ties between the Jews of Aden and all other Jewish communities of the Islamic Empire. Thus Jewish merchants and craftsmen in India and Ceylon were under the jurisdiction of the rabbinical court in Aden. This court in turn regarded itself as subordinate to the court in Cairo, which was appointed by the head of the Palestinian academy.

The Jews of Aden were ardent collectors of books written in Hebrew, so much so that travelers often went to Aden for Hebrew books they could not get elsewhere. Aden's businessmen were also well versed in Hebrew literature as evidenced by the long Hebrew poems pinned on to their ordinary business letters.

The community flourished as a trading center and Jews prospered, their community reaching the size of 3,000 families during the 18th century. However, in the 19th century Indian trade was at its lowest, and Aden fell into decay, its community dwindling to 500 persons in 1839.

Under British rule Aden began to develop again, especially after the opening of the Suez Canal in 1869. The Jewish population increased to 4,750 in 1947, but after the United Nations declared the partition of Palestine, Arab mobs attacked the Jewish Quarter, murdering and wounding many persons, and destroying buildings. From 1948 on, Aden Jews left the country, most of them immigrating to Israel, and following the Six-Day War in 1967, there were no Jews remaining in Aden.

ARABS. The Arabs are a Semitic people who originally lived in *Arabia and the surrounding countries. They are mentioned in the Bible and are descended from the same stock as the Jews; according to their own traditions, their ancestor was Ishmael, the son of the patriarch Abraham. Before the seventh century the Arabs were pagans, although a few tribes did accept Judaism. The religion of *Islam, which in part draws on Judaism, started in the seventh century and was accepted by the overwhelming majority of Arabs (see also *Muhammad). The Arabic language, which is related to Hebrew, has undergone many changes in its history, which accounts for the very diverse dialects spoken at the present time in different Arab countries.

With the adoption of Islam, the Arabs set out to conquer the world and indeed they did succeed in subjugating the whole of the Middle East as well as large areas of Europe such as *Spain. In their conquests, all pagans were forced to accept the Islamic religion, but Jews and Christians were allowed to continue in their faiths because they were monotheistic. Because of this conquest, many peoples who were not originally Arabs racially are now so considered. The populations of Egypt, Syria, Iraq, and North Africa are thus nowadays considered to be Arabs.

Not all Arabs are Muslims; because of Christian missionary activity there are also Christian Arabs. Thus "Arab" is today an ethnic term which includes far more than it originally did.

The Arab conquests included many lands in which there were old, well-established Jewish communities. The Jews generally welcomed the Arabs and even aided them. Although the Jews were considered inferior to the Muslims and had to pay a special poll tax for the privilege of continuing in their ancestral faith, by and large they were better treated than in Christian countries. Islam brought with it an amazing

Hajj Muhammed Amin al-Hussein (second from left) mufti (Moslem religious leader) of Jerusalem, at a meeting with Arab leaders, c. 1935. He became the chief spokesman of Palestinian Arabs during the Mandate period and, in his extreme antagonism towards the Jews, served as a close ally of Hitler. He even bragged of having had a private dinner with the Fuerher. He also incited large scale anti-Jewish riots in Jerusalem.

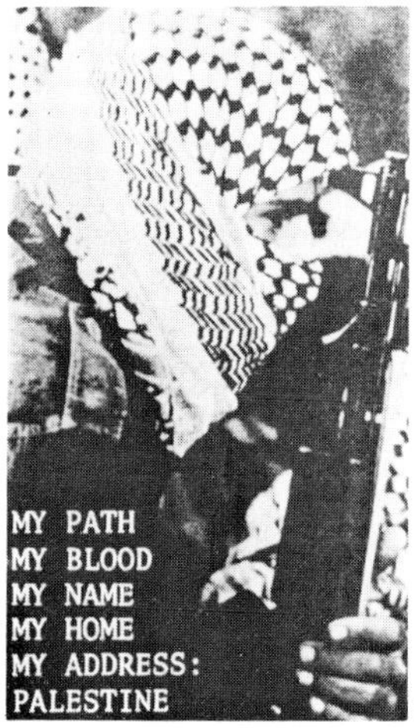

1

"Bondor" Ring Clear All-Silk Stockings AT Spinney's Limited

16 Pages

THE PALESTINE POST

The Negus Returns Home PAGE SEVEN

In Four Days TO CENTRAL EUROPE 48-HOUR SEA VOYAGE BY THE LARGE WEEKLY MAIL STEAMERS T.S.S. POLONIA (15,000 Tons) AND T.S.S. KOSCIUSZKO (13,000 Tons) to Piraeus, Istanbul and Constanza SAILING EVERY TUESDAY FROM HAIFA AT 3 p.m.

JERUSALEM FRIDAY, MAY 8, 1936

VOL. XII. 3035. PRICE: TEN MILS

Arabs Decide on Civil Disobedience

Palestine Greets Emperor Today

Scores of Journalists Congregate at Haifa

by J. L. MELTZER (Palestine Post Staff Writer)

HAIFA, Thursday. — Elaborate preparations are being taken by the British Admiralty, the Haifa Port authorities and the District Administration in anticipation of the arrival of the Emperor and Empress of Ethiopia and a large suite on board H.M.S. "Enterprise" tomorrow.

The section of the harbour which fronts the Port Manager's office will be clear of all traffic at ten o'clock in the morning, when the warship is expected to arrive. Only officials, notables and a record gathering of pressmen and photographers will be allowed on a warehouse platform opposite the quay-side at which the ship is to anchor, to watch the Negus and his entourage as they pass by to the special train which will be waiting to take them to Jerusalem.

It is reported here that the party will stay either at the King David Hotel or at the Ethiopian Convent in Abyssinian Street.

Journalists have arrived from all parts to witness the Royal arrival. One London correspondent

Business Behind Closed Doors

PEDLARS AND SHOPKEEPERS RESUME WORK

While most of the Arab shops in the country were closed yesterday, many of the shopkeepers in the Old City, Jerusalem, were doing business behind closed shutters.

Hawkers of agricultural products from the villages came to Jerusalem in large numbers yesterday and squatted, as usual, in David Street and the Mahne Yehuda Market with their wares. A new type of hawker selling cuts of meat also made an appearance yesterday in the Old City, and many of the Arab restaurants had meat yesterday for the first time in many days.

Inquiries at the Jerusalem Municipal abattoir revealed that the Arab butchers are not slaughtering there, and it is feared that the meat sold yesterday was not slaughtered under proper sanitary conditions.

Renewal of Municipal Works

Through the efforts of the District Commissioner and the Municipal Engineer, work on sewerage in the Old City was resumed yesterday. Police

VILLAGE ELDERS TRIED FOR ARSON

(From Our Own Correspondent)

HEDERA, Thursday. — A collective fine of LP. 10 was today imposed on the Village of Burelka, whose elders appeared before the Assistant District Commissioner, Mr. Pirie-Gordon, on a charge of arson.

The villagers were found guilty of setting fire to haystacks in Zichron Jacob, on the evidence of the police who had traced the tracks of the incendiaries to Burelka.

Jerusalem Mayor Supports Strike

A request to the District Commissioner of Jerusalem to instruct the Mayor, Dr. Khalidi, to "abstain from acts which bring damage to the city of Jerusalem," has been sent by the Agudath Israel, the Orthodox Jewish Association. This action has been taken in protest against the Mayor being a signatory to the appeal urging continuation of the Arab Strike.

The letter was sent on April 30, but submitted for publication only yesterday.

Dr. Khalidi's assistance in the strike is seen as an act which is utterly incompatible with his

REFUSAL TO PAY TAXES AFTER MAY 15

A resolution to refuse to pay taxes, if by May 15 the Government does not grant the Arab leaders' demands, was passed at a meeting of some 150 organizers of the Arab strike held in Jerusalem yesterday afternoon.

The Mufti, Haj Amin El Husseini, who is President of the Moslem Supreme Council, presided. The mover of the far-reaching proposal was the Chairman himself, a Government official, and it is understood that there was little discussion and virtually no opposition.

OFFICIAL COMMUNIQUE

THURSDAY, MAY 7, 7:30 P. M.

At about 7.20 last evening a shot was fired at a Jewish bus on the Ramle-Jaffa road near Beit Dajan, and a few minutes later an Arab car was fired on at almost the same spot. No one was injured.

This morning a fire broke out at an envelope factory at Athlit, and was still burning at 4 p. m. Two suspected persons have been arrested.

There are no other incidents to report.

7 Years for Stabbing Constable

The three persons arrested in connection with the trouble at Jenin yesterday were tried by the District Court there today. One,

CONTINUE STRIKE

The meeting decided also to call upon the Arabs to continue the strike in protest against Government policy.

The Central Strike Committee will visit a number of towns with a view to strengthening the strikers' determination. The first town to be visited is Haifa where breaches in the strikers' ranks have been specially prominent during this week.

During the week's notice which the Mufti and his followers have given the Government, the High Commissioner, in accordance with yesterday's decision, must on pain

THE CHALLENGE LEADER, PAGE EIGHT

2

3

1. Al Fatah poster, published after the Six-Day War by the terrorist organization, reaffirming the Arab claim to Palestine and "justifying" the use of violence.
2. Newspaper report on the general strike and political action taken by Arabs to protest Jewish immigration and settlement, May 8, 1936.
3. Arab delegates, who refused to sit with the Jews, at the London Round Table Conference of 1939 to discuss the partition of Palestine.

flowering of literature, philosophy and science, and this influenced the Jews a great deal. Very many great rabbinic scholars such as *Saadiah Gaon and *Maimonides wrote some of their major works in Arabic, and Arabic poetry had a major effect on the development of Hebrew poetry. Hebrew grammarians also labored mightily to show that Hebrew was as perfect a language as Arabic. In many countries, notwithstanding Islamic law, Jews reached high positions in government and it was under Arab rule that the Jews of Spain enjoyed what is known as their Golden Age.

The Arabs conquered Ereẓ Israel in 634 c.e. and maintained their rule there until 1099, when the Crusaders conquered the country. During this period the country was ruled by the caliphate in Baghdad. The rule of the Crusaders came to an end in 1291 when they were driven out by the Arabs. The period from then till 1516 is known as the Mamluk period. After that Ereẓ Israel still remained under the Muslim rule of the Turkish Ottomans until World War I, when it was conquered by the British.

In the course of the Middle Ages the Arab movement lost its thrust and with the industrial revolution and the enlightenment in Europe, Arab culture declined and Arab countries remained backward both economically and militarily. Most of the Arab countries were taken over by the Western European powers. Even the development of their oil resources did not help them a great deal since these were largely exploited by foreign powers.

At the end of the 19th century, a movement for Arab nationalism started. Young intellectuals, taking their cue from Central and Western European countries, began to organize in order to drive out the foreign powers and rule their own fate. Tragically, this clashed with the Zionist aspirations for a Jewish national home in Palestine. The British government – which had the League of Nations' *Mandate for Palestine – had promised the Jews, in the famous *Balfour Declaration, that they would be allowed to settle in Ereẓ Israel. The Arabs – both Palestinian and others – objected violently, and the British authorities adopted a policy of appeasement towards them, slowly but surely curtailing Jewish rights in Ereẓ Israel. When the U.N. decided in 1947 that the Jews should have their own state in Ereẓ Israel the surrounding Arab nations, Egypt, Jordan, Syria and Lebanon, invaded the infant state on the day of its birth in an all-out effort to destroy it. They were aided by the Arab countries further away, such as Saudi Arabia. When they failed and the State of Israel was firmly established, they still refused to accept its existence and have since done everything in their power to try to do away with it. Since 1948, nearly all the Jews who lived in Arab countries have emigrated, mostly to Israel, and the few who remain live in constant danger of persecution.

By and large the Arab countries have never been able to settle their own differences and unite. A major aim of Arab leaders, such as Nasser, has been to create a Pan-Arabism; that is, to persuade the Arabs that they are really one people. The way in which this has been done is to focus on the common hatred for the State of Israel. The Arab League, which was created in 1945, immediately began to enforce an economic embargo on Israel (see *Boycott). It ensures that no Arab country will do business with any corporation that does business in Israel, or even has Jews among its directors. Various terrorist groups

have been formed to continue guerilla warfare against Israel. Since this direct approach failed entirely, groups such as the Palestinian Liberation Organization (founded in 1964), Al Fataḥ (founded in 1967) and the Popular Front for the Liberation of Palestine have turned to terrorist activity against Israel installations, Israeli citizens and other Jews throughout the world. The terrorist groups are supported, morally and financially, by various Arab states, particularly Syria and Libya.

After the 1973 Yom Kippur War, some of the Arab states claimed that they would recognize the State of Israel if it would return all the territory it conquered in the 1967 Six-Day War and if it would also acknowledge the rights of the Palestinian refugees. These latter are the people who left Ereẓ Israel of their own volition during the 1948 War of Independence. They settled in Arab lands, mainly Jordan and Lebanon, where they were not allowed to integrate into the population but were kept in refugee camps where they were fed vicious anti-Israel propaganda.

In Israel there is a large Arab minority in addition to the population of the territories taken in the 1967 war. This minority, which numbers more than 450,000, enjoys equal rights with the Jewish population and has made tremendous strides forward in health, education and standard of living. The Israeli Arabs have their own schools in which the language of instruction is Arabic and the curriculum is planned by their own educators. There are several Arab members in Israel's parliament, the Knesset, and in the government of 1969-1973, two Arabs served as deputy ministers. Although some Israeli Arabs have been associated with various terrorist groups, these are a very small minority and are disowned by most of Israel's Arab population.

ARAD was a Canaanite city in the northern Negev, where important archaeological discoveries were made. The Bible records that on this site the invading Israelite tribes encountered strong opposition during their conquest of Canaan in the 13th century b.c.e.

In the 1960s archaeological excavations uncovered a large city from the Early Bronze Age II (c. 2900 - 2700 b.c.e.) which was built over a scattered, unfortified settlement. The city was surrounded by a stone wall, over eight feet thick, which was strengthened at intervals by semicircular towers. Well-planned, it was divided into various quarters by narrow lanes. The houses were uniform in design. Egyptian pottery was found on the site, indicating commercial ties with Egypt. According to all the evidence found, the town was destroyed not later than 2700 b.c.e., and the site remained deserted until the 11th century b.c.e. In the 10th century, probably during King Solomon's reign, a strong citadel was built on the site, which existed almost until the First Temple was destroyed in the 6th century b.c.e. The citadel was destroyed six times during this period. It was followed by a succession of Persian, Hellenistic and Roman fortresses. The latest stratum at Arad dates to the beginning of the Arabic period.

The most sensational discovery, however, was a complete Israelite temple, built on the lines of Solomon's Temple in Jerusalem, but resembling even more the biblical description of the *Tabernacle in the desert. Three steps led to the Holy of Holies, where two incense altars and other ritual structures were found. At the entrance to the hall there were two stone pillars, and an altar built of earth and unhewn stones stood in the yard.

Modern Arad, which lies six miles east of ancient Arad, was founded in 1961 in an area formerly inhabited by nomadic Bedouin tribes. Designed in six high-density neighborhoods, grouped around the civic center, with a separate industrial sector, resort area and suburbs, Arad was the first development town in Israel to be planned by a group of architects and engineers living on the site. The dry, pollen-free climate, the high altitude, and picturesque location have combined to attract tourists, and people suffering from respiratory diseases.

Local industries include the processing of potash, phosphates, gas and petrochemical products.

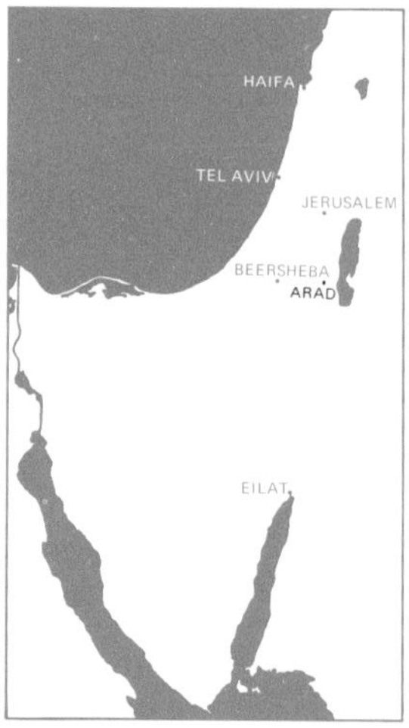

Aerial view of modern Arad, planned to eventually serve 50,000 inhabitants.

ARAMAIC is an ancient northwestern Semitic language which is, to a very limited extent, still spoken today. For the purposes of linguistic analysis the language is divided into five distinct periods starting from before 700 b.c.e. and ending with the modern Aramaic of today, often called Neo-Aramaic. From 700 b.c.e. till the early centuries c.e. documents and inscriptions have been found in places as far apart as Syria, Iraq, Egypt, Persia, India, Afghanistan, and the Caucasus, indicating that in the ancient world Aramaic was the *lingua franca,* the commonly accepted, language of nearly the whole civilized world.

1

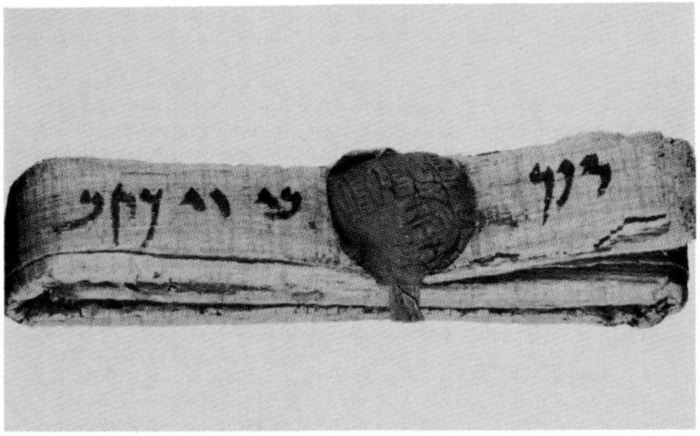

2

1. The unrolled scroll of an Aramaic papyrus of Jews in Egypt, fifth century b.c.e.
2. The above scroll closed.

For Jews, Aramaic has special significance. Parts of the biblical Books of Ezra and David are written in it, and there is a very important Aramaic translation of the Bible called Onkelos. (For more on this see *Bible). Both the Palestinian Talmud and the Babylonian Talmud are written in Aramaic except for the Hebrew quotations (see *Talmud). Certain of the prayers, such as the *Kaddish* and *Kol Nidrei* are also in Aramaic; for more information on this see *Prayer.

Aramaic is written in Hebrew characters and its grammar and vocabulary are quite like Hebrew. In Babylonia it was the vernacular of the Jews and continues in the present time as the language of Jews from *Kurdistan. In 1948 the total number of Aramaic-speaking Jews was estimated at 20,000; most of them are now in Israel.

ARCHAEOLOGY is a word which comes from Greek words meaning "ancient" and "knowledge." It has come to mean the study of the material remains of the past, and is usually restricted to the study of artifacts dating up to the end of the Middle Ages.

Although the discovery of written material is often the result of archaeological digging, its study does not belong to archaeology proper. In fact, the importance of archaeology decreases as written sources become more plentiful. For the period before our written records, archaeology is the sole source of information. This period is known as prehistory.

Not only the Land of Israel and Mesopotamia (Padan Aram of the Bible), but the whole Middle East is an archaeological center, because within it is the cradle of civilization, and many ancient towns lie buried in this region.

The written record of the Bible has been supplemented by the study of material remains. Mighty people like the Sumerians and the *Hittites, for example, would be almost unknown outside the Bible if it were not for the archaeological discoveries which document their way of life.

Archaeological research has been most instructive in all matters concerning economic life in ancient times, such as the transition from food-gathering to agriculture, the beginnings of irrigation, and the types of wheat and other products grown. It has also been possible to follow the development of *architecture from the earliest fortifications at *Jericho and other ancient *cities; the Israelite four-room house; and the architectural revolution that came about in the Hellenistic period by the introduction of Greek models.

Techniques. To decide upon a site, trained people search a promising area for likely places of interest. Unknown and deserted areas are explored, and if any ruins are found these are recorded. Then the site is thoroughly searched to see if any bits of pottery are lying around. These are sent to specialists for dating. Depending largely upon archaeological experience and instinct, those in charge of the search will then decide whether to dig at that spot or not.

Should they decide to dig, they will then start to excavate scientifically. This excavation is the main method of archaeology, and untrained hands are employed under supervision to systematically remove the layers of earth that accumulated over the centuries, and to remove the debris covering ancient remains.

This is done by digging trenches which reveal the various strata of soil deposited there at different periods of time. An entire cross-section of the strata is removed for study. Sections of the earth that accumulated against the foundations of any walls are next examined.

The dates of material such as pottery, lying on the surface of a "dig," or of deeply excavated material, can now be exactly established by means of Carbon 14 and other analytical methods of dating. This recently discovered method of dating is considered the most accurate of all methods and is carried out at the Hebrew University of Jerusalem and in the United States. Careful examination of bits of pottery, inscriptions found on pottery, walls, tombs, and coins also help to date the material and the site – as does a knowledge of events of the time.

Pottery breaks easily, but is not usually totally destroyed. Hence layers of soil are sure to be strewn with fragments corresponding to the surrounding soil at that date. Each piece is labeled, and an attempt is made to put the various bits together to form a whole object. As pottery styles change and develop through the ages, and a good deal about pottery styles through the ages is already known, these sherds (as the fragments are called) are the best means of dating an ancient settlement.

Biblical History. The destruction and total abandonment of *Shiloh mentioned by Jeremiah (7:12, 14), has been fully confirmed by archaeological evidence. Excavations at *Jerusalem show that the Jebusite town extended much further east than was previously believed, and that its conquest by way of its water tunnel was quite feasible.

Many traces of King Solomon's religious and administrative activity have survived, such as the temple at *Arad, and the fortress gates at Hazor, Gezer and *Megiddo. The *Siloam inscription and the Siloam tunnel itself show the waterworks of King *Hezekiah.

The finds at Samaria fully bear out the biblical account of the Phoenician influence at the court of *Ahab and Jezebel. The finds at Ramat Rachel, south of Jerusalem, show the spread of this influence to Judea.

There are remains, apart from coins, of the armed struggles against the Romans. Burnt debris dating from the war of the *Zealots has been found in the foundations of houses in Jerusalem's old city, and at *Masada evidence has been discovered of their pathetic last stand. Large numbers of everyday articles and written documents were likewise found in caves in the Judean desert where *Bar Kokhba and his men once hid.

Among the interesting sites that have been uncovered in Ereẓ Israel are *Abu Ghosh, *Acre, *Arad, *Bet Alfa, *Bet She'an, *Bet She'arim, *Jericho, *Lydda, *Masada, *Sepphoris, *Shechem and *Siloam.

A group of tourists reach the top of Masada overlooking the Dead Sea, where archaeological excavations have revealed the ruins of the last outpost held by the Zealots during the Jewish War against Rome in the first century b.c.e.

1

2

3

5

1. Pottery statue of a pregnant woman, from the sixth or fifth century b.c.e., found in the Phoenician cemetery at Achziv, north of Acre.
2. Remains of Robinson's arch, a monumental stairway ascending from the main paved street of Herodian Jerusalem to a gate in the west wall of the Temple area.
3. Glassware from Palestine of the fourth to first centuries b.c.e.
4. View of the Tel of Maresha, an important Judean town during biblical times.
5. Glass statue of goddess, found in Beersheba.

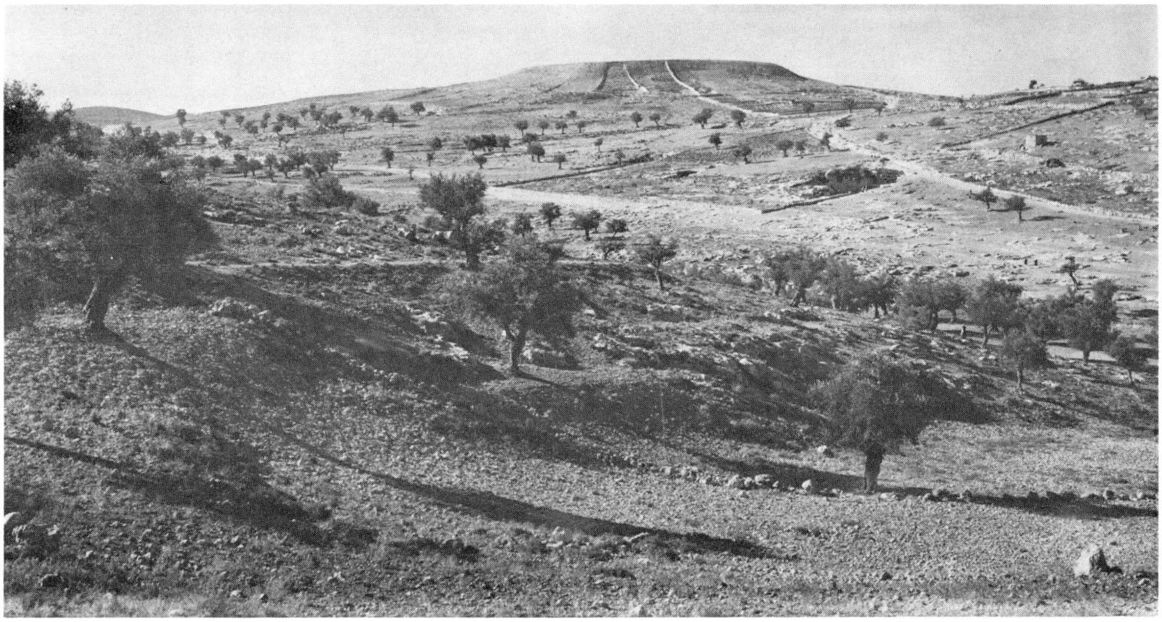
4

1

4

2

3

5

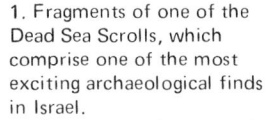

1. Fragments of one of the Dead Sea Scrolls, which comprise one of the most exciting archaeological finds in Israel.
2. Wall painting from a 17th century b.c.e. Egyptian tomb, showing agricultural activities.
3. Carving on a Jewish house in the Old City of Jerusalem.
4. Ruins of Qumran, ancient city near the caves in which the Dead Sea Scrolls were discovered.
5. Roman amphitheater (foreground) and forum at Gerasa, city in Transjordan.

1

3

1. Hellenistic facade of al-Khazna ("The Treasury") in Petra, Jordan. It was built directly into the red rock of the mountain in the second-first centuries b.c.e. when Petra served as capital of the entire region.
2. "Herodium," elaborate fortress built by Herod near Bethlehem in the first century b.c.e. and later used as his burial place.
3. Gate to a Neo-Babylonian palace decorated with 575 dragons and bulls and 120 lions on a background of blue glazed bricks. c. 625-539 b.c.e.

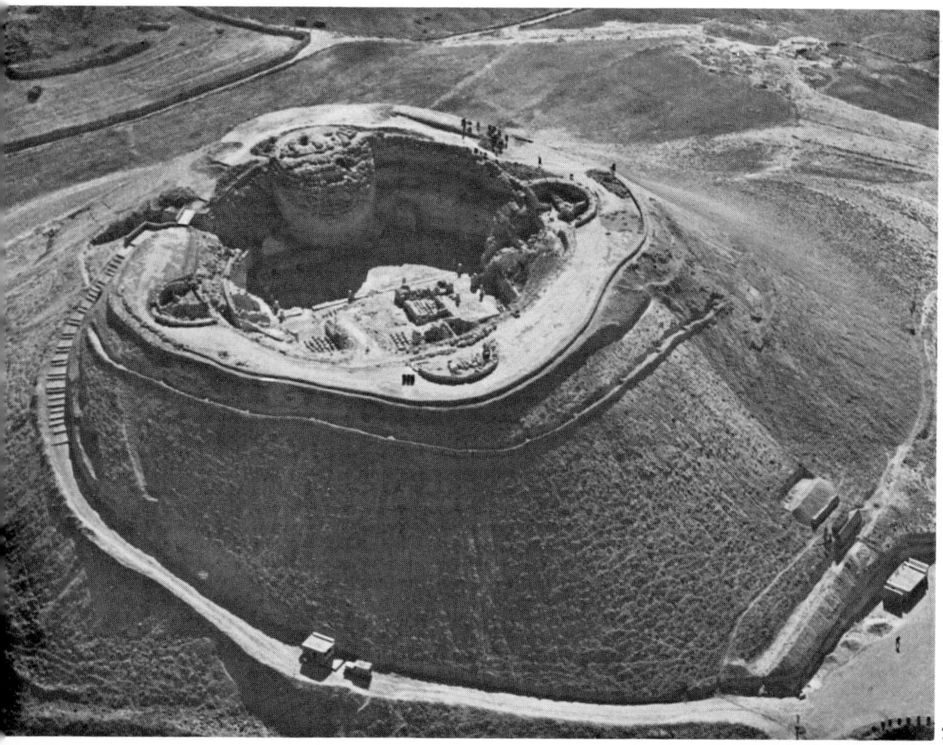

2

ARCHITECTURE. Modern archaeology has unearthed a wealth of information concerning Jewish architecture in Israel in the past. In ancient Palestine, the forerunner to Israelite architecture was local Canaanite style. Walled towns with two-story stone, brick or wood houses usually built around a courtyard were most typical. Archaeological finds from the age of the Judges (c.1200-c.1000 b.c.e.) reveal that Israelite towns were homogeneous in layout, reflecting a democratic social structure with few extremes of poverty or wealth. Later centuries witnessed palaces and spacious homes built above and away from the masses. The first ambitious public architecture made its appearance with Solomon's *Temple which was unique in terms of its large dimensions, numerous supporting internal columns, and its utilization of cedar beams.

Hellenization introduced classical Greek architecture of which two examples have survived intact to this day: the Tomb of Zechariah and the so-called Absalom's Tomb, both in the Kidron Valley, near the walls of the Old City of Jerusalem. The peak of this period came during the reign of *Herod the

Great (37-34 b.c.e.) who blended Oriental and Hellenistic techniques in the acme of antique Jewish architecture. Little remains of his work except the *Western Wall, parts of the outer wall of the Tomb of the Patriarchs at Hebron, and impressive fortresses at Herodium near Bethlehem, and at *Masada, overlooking the Dead Sea.

With the loss of Jewish independence in 70 c.e., public Jewish architecture practically ceased, with the notable exception of the *synagogue, the importance of which increased enormously after the destruction of the Temple. The Age of Emancipation in the 19th century saw the emergence of Jewish architects, but not Jewish architecture. However, Jews made many important contributions which have had a lasting influence. The English Sephardi Jew, David Mocatta, designed a series of railway stations during the 1830s and 1840s, and in Germany, E. Jacobstahl designed several branches of the Deutsche Reichsbank. The pioneer of theater architecture was an Austrian Jew, Oscar Strand.

At the turn of the century, Alfred Messel designed the Wertheim department store in Berlin, a unique combination of stone, steel, and glass considered to be one of the most important influences on modern architecture. Throughout the 20th century, France, Russia, Italy, and Brazil have had many impressive structures built by Jewish architects. Prominent Jewish architects in the United States include Dankmar Adler, father of the American skyscraper, Victor Gruen, originator of the suburban shopping center and Max Abramovitz, designer of Philharmonic Hall in New York. Outstanding as well is Louis Kahn whose Kimball Art Museum in Fort Worth is a masterpiece of imagination, form and function.

In Israel traditional Arab village architecture, Mediterranean town planning, and French and German styles are all intermixed. Post World War I and World War II mass immigration gave rise to the *shikkun* (housing project) with its concern for practicality and little emphasis on aesthetics. However, there have been many attempts at introducing a style and working towards its formation as in Alexander Baerwald's Reali School in Haifa and Kornberg's Mount Scopus campus in Jerusalem. Post-1948 projects include institutions of higher learning such as the Hebrew Unviersity Givat Ram campus in Jerusalem, the Technion in Haifa and the Weizmann Institute at Rehovot. In addition, the Israel Museum complex in Jerusalem is outstanding, as are the Knesset building, and the memorial to J.F. *Kennedy in the hills of Jerusalem. Concert halls and theaters also exemplify Israeli architecture; among them are the Mann Auditorium in Tel-Aviv, Binyanei ha-Ummah in Jerusalem, and the Jerusalem and Haifa Theaters.

ARCHIVES is the name given to places where old records and documents are stored in an orderly manner. It is also used to denote collections of material to be used for study on specific subjects.

During biblical times archives were quite common. The earliest archives were collections of legal, political, administrative and economic documents. They were stored in rooms directly connected to the room in which current records were maintained. The archives of temples were placed in narrow rooms, inaccessible directly from the outside of the building. About the year 1500 b.c.e. private archives began to appear, and the quantity of material increased substantially. The most common type of archive during this period was the collection of the king's correspondence and documents; this is easily understood since the king was responsible for government and had the most resources to develop and maintain an archive.

There is no direct evidence that archives existed in ancient Israel. However, since writing was known, and a highly developed administrative system was in use during the period of the kings, it is not unreasonable to assume that some form of archive did exist. It is possible that because of climatic conditions the archives might have deteriorated and been destroyed.

In post-biblical times archives were also common. It is recorded that *Herod destroyed the genealogy registers to conceal his Edomite origin, and the *Sanhedrin often checked genealogy tables to determine the purity of the descent of the priests. Tax records were also maintained in Israel following the method the of Romans who were then in control. In the talmudic period written records were probably kept in depositories of the yeshivot. Also responsa, answers to religious questions, were preserved.

During the Middle Ages, when the Jews were considered a separate group, special sections in the governmental archives dealt with Jewish affairs. The longer Jews resided in a particular country, the richer its government archives are in documents relating to their history. Since Jewish life was in general subject to a system of laws and regulations, special files relating to Jews have been preserved in many government archives. The records found have

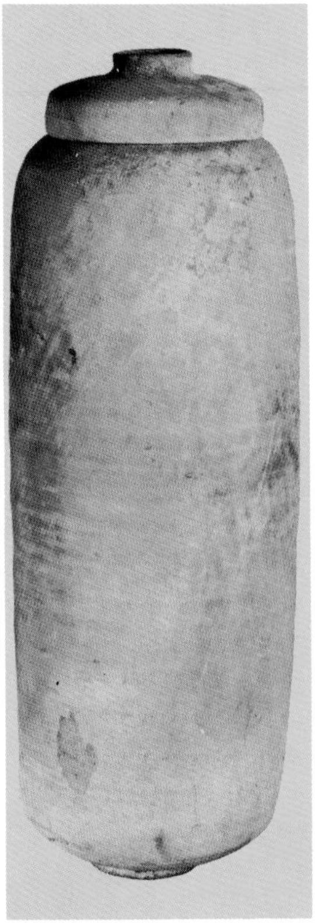

Clay jar of the type used in ancient archives to preserve important documents. This particular one contained some of the Dead Sea Scrolls.

included matters dealing with religion and education, taxation, commerce and industry, legal affairs and police reports. Many of the archives in Eastern Europe, especially Poland and Russia, were destroyed as a result of persecution, fires, and negligence.

In modern times many archives have been established by Jews to facilitate the study of subjects of interest to them. These range from Zionist archives to the *Yad Vashem archive concerning the destruction of the Jews by the Nazis. Many of these archives are in Israel, where a special law has established some public archives, and regulates their maintenance.

A special type of archive is the *Genizah,* in which unusable books or religious objects were stored. For more information on this, see **Genizah.*

1

1. An important historical archive and exhibit on the Holocaust is kept at the Ghetto Fighters' House, kibbutz Loḥamei ha-Getta'ot.
2. Members of the Moiseville (Mosesville) Jewish agricultural settlement in Argentina in the 1920s.

ARGENTINA. From old documents it appears that there were Jews in Argentina, a South American republic, in the 16th century; these were mainly *Marranos. However, they were very few in number and substantial immigration to Argentina only began in the middle of the 19th century. At first, groups of Jewish traders from Western and Central Europe came, and the first Jewish Community in Buenos Aires was founded in 1862. About twenty years later Eastern European Jews began migrating in large numbers to Argentina. The fact that Spanish is spoken in Argentina stimulated the immigration of many Spanish-speaking Sephardi Jews from Mediterranean lands. The pogroms in Russia, and Argentina's efforts to attract immigrants, led to a great influx of Jews. Indeed, Baron de Hirsch advocated creating a Jewish Homeland in Argentina and was instrumental in establishing many Jewish agricultural colonies there. In all, 240,000 Jews arrived in Argentina between 1881 and 1951. By 1970, the Jewish population had grown to an estimated 500,000. Originally the Jews lived mainly in rural colonies, but during the 1940s many moved to the towns, and Jews now play an important part in the development of industry and commerce in Argentina.

During and following World War II, Argentina no longer permitted Jewish immigration except for a small number of Jews who entered the country in 1956-57.

The Jewish community in Argentina is well organized. There are Jewish schools, some of which use Yiddish as their language of instruction, and several newspapers. A great deal of Zionist activity takes place and there is a constant flow of immigrants to Israel. Religious life is not very well organized mainly due to a lack of rabbis. In recent years, the *Conservative movement of the United States established a rabbinical college in Buenos Aires and in 1964 the *Reform movement also embarked on activities there.

Since World War II the general political situation in Argentina has not been stable and, as a result, anti-Semitic activity has increased. The overthrow of President Juan Peron in 1955 was accompanied by an upsurge of anti-Semitism, especially by movements such as Tacuara. In 1973 Peron returned after a long exile and was re-elected. The capture by Israeli agents of the Nazi war criminal Adolf *Eichmann in 1960 and his abduction from Argentina to Israel also contributed to anti-Israel and anti-Semitic feelings. Relations between the State of Israel and Argentina have always been good except for the period of the Eichmann affair.

Buenos Aires. The overwhelming majority of Argentina's Jews (approximately 380,000 out of 500,000) live in the capital city, Buenos Aires. They are organized in separate communities: those of European origin in the Associacion Mutual Israelita Argentina, and the Sephardim in four separate groups according to place of origin – North

2

Africa, Turkey and Greece, Aleppo, and Damascus. Most East European Jews and Sephardim maintain the Orthodox rite; the Conservative and Reform movements also have synagogues. However, religion does not hold a central position in Jewish life in Buenos Aires. Jewish identification is mainly nationalistic and the influence of the various Zionist parties is outstanding. Two daily papers are published in Yiddish and a large number of magazines in Spanish and Yiddish. A great number of Yiddish books are published in Buenos Aires which, after Israel, is the largest center of Yiddish in the world.

ARISTEAS, LETTER OF, is a Greek composition in the form of a letter allegedly written to his brother Philocrates by Aristeas, a Greek in the court of Ptolemy II Philadelphus (285-246 b.c.e.). The contents are as follows: On the advice of his courtiers, Demetrius of Phalerum and Aristeas, Ptolemy Philadelphus orders the sacred writings of the Jews to be translated for the library of Alexandria, Egypt. The king writes to Eleazar, the high priest in Jerusalem, requesting that expert translators be sent to him. His letter is accompanied by a precious gift for the Temple. Aristeas at the head of an Egyptian delegation goes to Jerusalem and returns with a detailed description of Judea, Jerusalem, the Temple and its services, and his talks with Eleazar. Eleazar sends Ptolemy 72 elders who are well versed in both the Mosaic Law and in the customs of Greek society. The king gives them an elaborate reception and for ten days holds banquets in their honor, in the course of which he discovers their great wisdom. They are then taken to the Island of Pharos and within 72 days they translate the Scripture into Greek. The translation, known as the *Septuagint, is approved by the king and by the representatives of the Alexandrian Jewish community, and the translators are sent back home laden with gifts.

This story, based on a legend about the Septuagint current in Alexandria by the third century b. c. e. is more a historical romance than an accurate account. The author of the Letter, who was a Jew, used this legend as a framework which he filled with certain ideas that he wished to spread among his Jewish readers. He describes the Greeks as admirers of Judaism and pleads for the establishment of closer relations between the two peoples.

There is considerable disagreement among scholars as to when the Letter was written; some date it from the late second century b. c. e.

1

2

1. The Ramat Shalom Hebrew Day School in Buenos Aires, where most Jewish schools are supported and supervised by the *Va'ad ha-Ḥinnukh,* the Jewish Education Committee.
2. Illustration of the Letter of Aristeas, showing King Ptolemy ordering his scribe to write a letter to Eleazar the high priest in Jerusalem. Byzantine, 11th century.

ARISTOBULUS I (Judah). Although he reigned for only one year, Aristobulus, King of Judea (104-103 b.c.e.) is important in the history of the Jews. His predecessor was his father, John Hyrcanus I, who had designated Aristobulus' mother to succeed him on the throne. But when John Hyrcanus died, Aristobulus immediately assumed power, threw his mother into prison and left her to die there of starvation. He imprisoned all his brothers as well, except Antigonus whom he loved. Antigonus and Aristobulus had had joint command of the army in their father's lifetime. Together, for a whole year, they had laid siege to the great city of Samaria, captured it, and then razed it to the ground.

Aristobulus was the first Hasmonean to take the title of king. He continued his father's policy of expanding the borders of Israel and captured Upper Galilee. To the Itureans who lived in the district, he gave the choice of converting to Judaism or going into exile. But tragic justice overtook Aristobulus. When Antigonus returned victorious from the wars, Aristobulus began to suspect him of wanting to

1. Chaim Arlosoroff, economist, Zionist leader, and prolific writer who published political and economic analyses, a world history of colonization and a volume of poetry.
2. Arlosoroff (2) at a meeting between Jewish and Transjordan leaders in Jerusalem, April 8, 1933. Other Jewish representatives include: Chaim Weizmann (1), Izhak Ben-Zvi (8), and Moshe Shertok (Sharett) (9).

1

become king. Aristobulus' courtiers poisoned his mind against Antigonus. When Antigonus went up to the Temple to offer prayers for his brother's welfare, for Aristobulus had fallen ill, these courtiers informed Aristobulus that Antigonus and his followers were on their way to murder him. When Antigonus arrived to visit his ailing brother, he was set upon in a dark passage and murdered. Aristobulus, filled with remorse, died soon after. His wife, *Salome Alexandra freed his brothers from prison and married one of them, Alexander *Yannai, who succeeded Aristobulus to the throne.

ARISTOTLE (fourth century b.c.e.). *Maimonides believed that Aristotle, the Greek philosopher, reached the highest degree of intellectual perfection open to man barring only the still higher degree of prophetic inspiration. Aristotle's philosophic system strongly influenced Jewish philosophers who tried to integrate it into Judaism.

Jewish Aristotelianism may be divided into two periods: from the ninth to the end of the 12th century among Jews living in the Arab world, and from the 13th century on, among Jews living in the Christian world. During the Islamic period, Jewish Aristotelianism reached its peak with Maimonides.

The second period was marked by Hebrew translations of works by Aristotle. The Aristotelian literature in Hebrew, in turn, gave rise to Hebrew commentaries and summaries. In addition, independent works in Hebrew were based on it. Samuel ibn *Tibbon and Joseph *Albo were among the famous Jewish philosophers who contributed to the Aristotelian literature.

Jewish Aristotelianism differs from the preceding types of medieval Jewish philosophy in its heightened awareness of the boundaries of faith and reason. Jewish Aristotelians held that philosophic speculations must proceed without any regard to theological doctrines. They recognized as valid only demonstrative arguments, that is to say, arguments based on the standards laid down by Aristotle.

In addition to his considerable influence upon medieval Jewish philosophy, Aristotle also appears in Jewish literary works in which history and legend are found side by side. There the theme is that all the Greek philosophers, including Aristotle, were influenced by Judaism.

2

ARLOSOROFF, CHAIM (1899-1933). The murder of Chaim Arlosoroff robbed the Jewish people of one of the most brilliant and exciting Zionist leaders in Palestine. Arlosoroff was born in Russia, but anti-Semitism forced his family to leave his birthplace and to settle in Germany, where Chaim grew up and went to school. Being very interested in economics, he studied at the University of Berlin where he received a doctorate in that subject. While he was attending the university, Arlosoroff wrote articles on Zionist matters, such as getting money to the settlers in Palestine, and planning a program of cooperation between Jews and Arabs. After finishing his studies he left Germany for Ereẓ Israel in 1924.

Arlosoroff became a leader of Mapai, the most important Jewish political party of the time, and was a close friend of the great scientist and statesman, Chaim *Weizmann. His talents were recognized early, and Arlosoroff was soon appointed head of the political department of the *Jewish Agency. At first he believed that the British would help settling Jews in Palestine, so he worked with the British government which was in charge of running that territory. Soon Arlosoroff came to feel that the British could not be trusted and that the Jews must risk angering them in order to rebuild their own homeland and save the Jews of Europe. As the terrible deeds of the Nazis against the Jews became known to him, Arlosoroff threw himself into the work of rescuing Jews. He was willing to fight the British and the Arabs in order to do that.

In 1933, in the middle of his great work as a Zionist political leader and as a writer with great influence, Chaim Arlosoroff was murdered. He was killed while walking with his wife on a beach in Tel Aviv. Even today the mystery of who killed him has not been solved. Some think that other Zionists who

1

2

3

1. **Bukhara.** Bukharan bridal gown of cotton tulle. Jewish symbols, including the *magen David* and a hand to ward off the evil eye, are embroidered on the dress.
2. **Birth.** Iraqi-Jewish amulet for a mother who has given birth to her first child, 1883.
3. **Balfour.** Israel stamp picturing Lord Balfour, issued on November 2, 1967, the 50th anniversary of the Balfour Declaration.

disagreed with his views killed him; another opinion is that two Arabs did it. His death was a terrible loss for the entire Jewish community. His memory is honored today by the many streets named after him throughout the towns of Israel and in the names of the settlements Kefar Ḥayyim, Kiryat Ḥayyim, and Kibbutz Giv'at Ḥayyim.

ARMLEDER. From 1336 until 1339, lawless groups of German peasants, intent on slaughtering Jews, swept through Alsace and Franconia. The gangs were known as Armleder on account of the leather armpiece worn by the peasants at that time.

The first band of killers, raiding Franconia, was led by a nobleman claiming that he had been called upon by an angel to kill all Jews. A new leader, calling himself "King Armleder," believed he was a prophet summoned to avenge the death of Christ. His bands destroyed 120 Jewish communities: many cities, terrified, automatically handed over their Jews to him.

The authorities did not interfere with the Armleder. In fact, when the Jews of Strasbourg were massacred, the bishop confiscated their property, and in another instance, the gangs were freed from all guilt in return for a sum of money paid to the emperor.

Eventually the general peace and security of all were threatened by the Armleder, who no longer confined their attacks to Jews. The Bishop of Strasbourg and several lords and cities came to an agreement with "King Armleder," who promised to stop the raids. Similar agreements were made in the Rhine Valley, but in Alsace the killing persisted.

ART. Is there such a thing as "Jewish art?" That question has been discussed for a long time. There are, of course, Jewish artists and it is indisputable that at every stage in their history, the Jews expressed themselves in various art forms. But is a work of art "Jewish" just because its creator is? Of great importance in this question is the attitude of the Jewish religion to art. In ancient times, art had a connection with religion; a great number of artistic works were devoted to religious worship and, obviously, the question of *idolatry is involved.

The Bible prohibits, in many places and in strong terms, the making of any image or likeness of man or beast. A religion that worships the one unseen God can tolerate no representation that might itself be worshiped. The prohibition is especially clear regarding "graven images;" and there is no doubt that at certain times the rigidity of the prohibition hampered or completely prevented the development of figurative art among the Jews.

In the Torah one "artist," Bezalel, who supervised the building of the sanctuary, is described as being capable "in all manner of workmanship, to devise curious works, to work in gold and silver and in brass, and in the cutting of stones for setting, and in the carving of wood, to make any manner of skillful work." But, in a sense, he was more a craftsman than an artist.

With the ascendancy of Greek influence, Jewish art reflected Greek style, except for the human representation common in Greek art. It is recorded that during the Roman period certain Jews did not object to having their portraits painted; on the other hand, other Jews refused to handle Roman currency bearing the figure of the emperor.

Generally, in an environment in which the worship of images played a great part, the Jews reacted strongly against this practice and suppressed representational art. In other periods, when the Jews became assimilated and the attachment to Torah was weaker, they began to share in the artistic attitudes of their neighbors, and the prejudice against representational art dwindled. However, when the Jews lived under Moslem control representational art diminished greatly since the Moslems too are opposed to graven images.

Following the fall of Jerusalem in the second century C.E. greater tolerance existed. Pious rabbis did not object to visiting baths where there was a statue of a heathen god, maintaining it was placed there for decoration only. Paintings and mosaics showing conventional figures and biblical scenes were a normal feature of decoration in synagogues in Ereẓ Israel.

During the Middle Ages, the artistic creation of *ceremonial objects for the "glorification of the *mitzvah*" became popular. The favorite articles were Torah ornaments, *Kiddush* cups, *seder* plates, Sabbath lamps, and spice boxes for the *Havdalah* service at the conclusion of the Sabbath. Embroidery also became popular and was regarded as a Jewish specialty during the Middle Ages. The illustration of books was common then; but not the books of the Bible except for the Scroll of Esther. The **Haggadah* was a favorite vehicle for artistic expression but most of the illustration reflects quite clearly the current art trends in the non-Jewish world.

In the 18th century, there were many Jewish

1

4

2

5

3

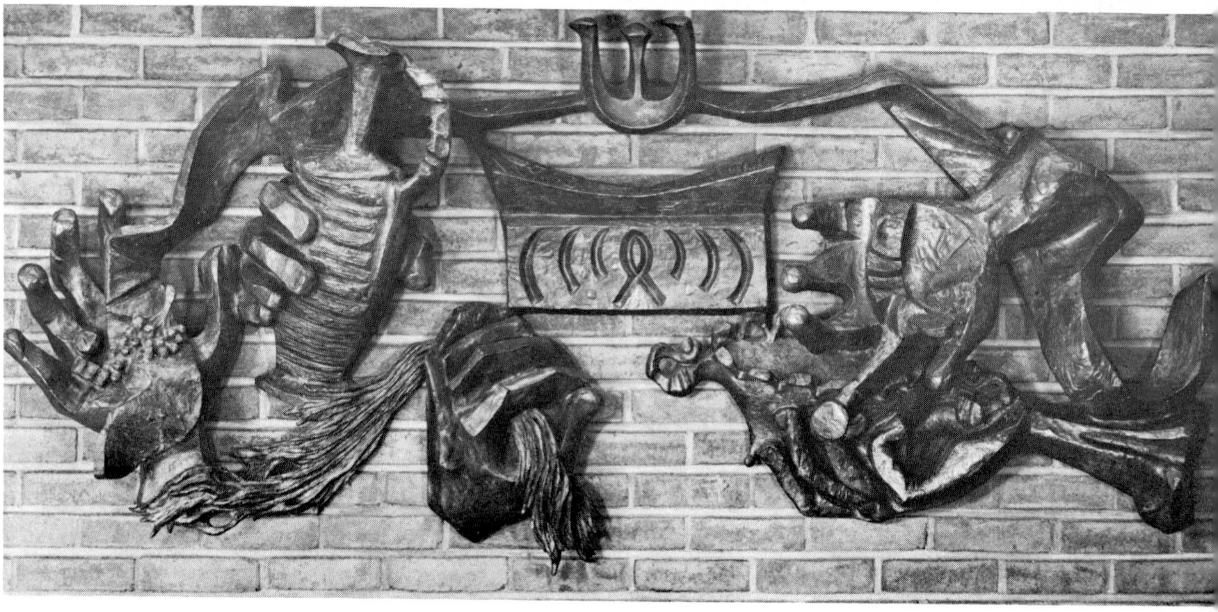

1. "Out of Bondage" by the Canadian artist Aba Bayefsky (1923-), in the Beth El Synagogue, Don Mills, Ontario.
2. White cupola of the Shrine of the Book at the Israel Museum. It houses the Dead Sea Scrolls, and the cupola is shaped after the ancient jars in which the scrolls were discovered. The Museum was jointly designed by American architects Frederick John Kiesler, (1896-1965) and Armand P. Bartos.
3. "The Offering," a seven foot cast bronze statue by the American sculptor Nathaniel Kaz (1917-). The Sculpture is in the Beth Emeth Temple in Albany, New York.
4. Welded iron gate to the Yad Vashem Memorial, Jerusalem, by David Palombo (1920-1966).
5. "Maternity" by the Dutch artist Meyer de Haan (1852-95). Oil on canvas.

1

3

1. "Orpah the Moabite." Pastel drawing by Abel Pann, Israeli painter and draftsman, 1883-1963.
2. Bronze bust of the actor Aharon Meskin, by the Israeli sculptor, Zeev Ben Zvi (1905-52).
3. Carving of a horseman in the catacombs at Bet She'arim, fourth to second century b.c.e.
4. Drawing by Ben Shahn (1898-1969), "Sacco and Vanzetti." Sacco and Vanzetti were Italian immigrants to the United States. During the industrial unrest of the 1920s they were involved in a violent strike, wrongly accused by the government, and executed.
5. Ink drawing, "Dwellings for the Feeble-minded," by Fritta (Fritz Taussig), from the concentration camp at Theresienstadt 1942-43.

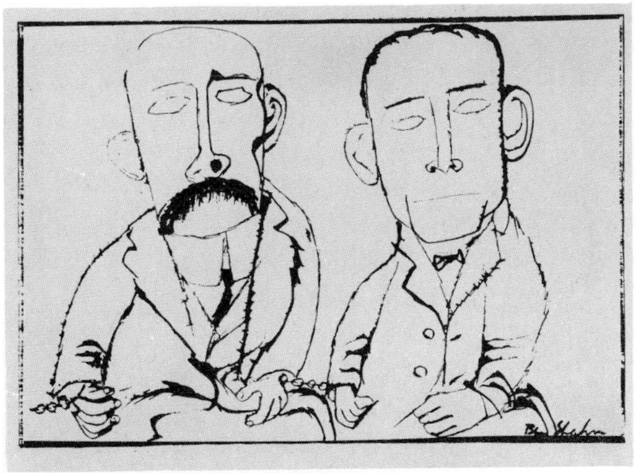
4

2

5

artists and engravers. As the subject matter became less religiously oriented, Jewish participation increased. The change continued throughout the 19th century when social restrictions became less severe. Even though the religious and social difficulties were diminishing, the uneasiness about a career in art disappeared only slowly. However, several Jewish artists distinguished themselves in this century. One of the greatest impressionists, Camille *Pissarro (1830-1903), was a Jew. A Dutchman, Jozef Israels (1824-1911), gained fame for his paintings of peasant life. Moritz *Oppenheim, a successful portrait painter, devoted much of his time to painting scenes of contemporary Jewish life. Several other Jews, including Max Liebermann (1848-1935) and Isaac Levitan (1861-1906), also distinguished themselves as artists.

With the 20th century, the world of Jewish art changed. Whereas previously Jewish artists had been few, now there was a sudden explosion of Jewish talent which left a permanent mark on artistic development. From Eastern and Western Europe, America, North Africa, and England a stream of Jewish artists appeared. Basing themselves in Paris, artists like *Modigliani, Pascin and *Chagall helped change the world of art. In sculpture Jacob *Epstein, Jacques *Lipchitz and William Zorach were significant.

The number of Jewish artists killed in concentration camps before and during World War II is not known. Many artists continued to paint while in the camps though such activity was forbidden and the materials were difficult to find. Many paintings were saved, including those by children; they reflect the emotions and spirit of the captive Jews as well as the details of camp existence. Several of these paintings are now located at the Yad Vashem Memorial in Jerusalem.

ASAPH HA-ROFE was a physician who lived in the sixth century. He is known because of a book on medicine which bears his name, *Sefer Asaph ha-Rofe,* ("The Book of Asaph, the Physician"). This work, which has never been published – it exists in 16 manuscript versions – was written by his students. Parts of it indicate that Asaph lived in northern Ereẓ Israel or in Babylonia.

Asaph apparently had many students and made them all write out a one-thousand word oath before they graduated from his class as doctors. In this oath the doctor promised to do all he could to heal the sick and to deal honestly and decently with his patients. Asaph insisted that his students be not only good doctors but also God-fearing men.

Asaph was a religious doctor and tried to harmonize science and religion. He believed that since many diseases came as punishments for sins, a patient could be cured only by praying hard, asking forgiveness and giving charity, because God was the true healer, only God could give doctors the power to use properly all the medicine they had learnt. He also taught that forbidden food was a cause of disease, while kosher food prevented it.

Asaph's fame spread to many countries and non-Jewish doctors came to him for advice. He was

1. Asaph's oath for students qualifying as physicians, based on the oath of Hippocrates.
2. Old man reciting the *Ashamnu* confession on the Day of Atonement, when prayer is accompanied by the ascetic practices of fasting and physical privation.

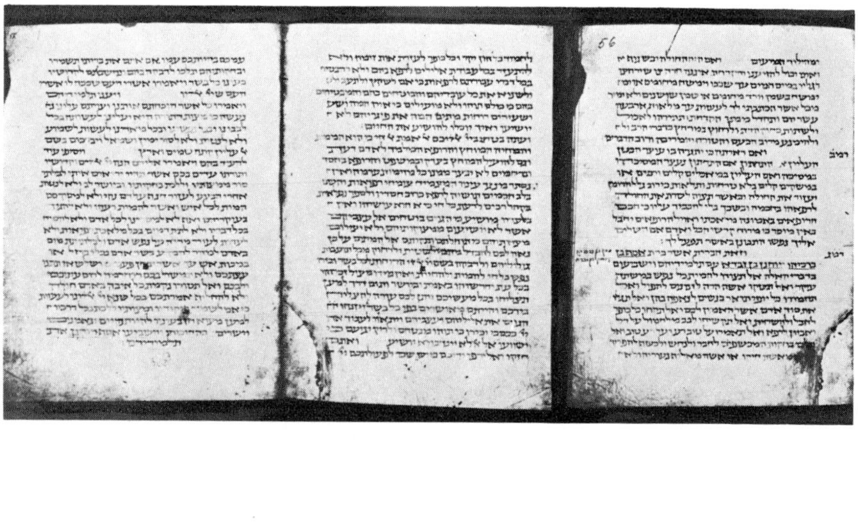
1

2

also widely quoted by later scholars. In Israel a hospital is named after him.

ASCETICISM. Could you imagine observing *Tish'ah Be-Av or the *Day of Atonement several days a week instead of one day a year? Or pledging never to drink wine or eat meat, never to marry or raise a family? Yet throughout history, many religious groups have rejected physical pleasures in this way in the hope of strengthening their religious belief or realizing a higher spiritual level. Such behavior is termed asceticism.

Why do people become ascetics? Many major religions teach that man's body and soul are separate and work against each other: the soul tries to get closer to God and to become spiritually pure, and the body, in order to satisfy its selfish desires, fights the soul. From this one could conclude that to keep his soul strong and pure, a man has to fight his own body – denying it food, comfort, and other pleasures. At this point, he adopts an "ascetic" way of life.

Asceticism has never been an important part of the Jewish faith. Judaism believes that man must serve God with his soul *and* his body. A person's soul is that part of him that loves God and His goodness and wants to be like Him, and a person's body is the physical container of his soul on earth. Nearly all the *mitzvot* which God gave are to be performed with the body. Thus the physical actions of man are sanctified. This applies to all the physical aspects of life: even sex when it is practiced in the proper framework, marriage, is in accordance with the will of God and is a *mitzvah.*

The rabbis of the Talmud considered asceticism and privation as a sin aginst the will of God who wants people to enjoy the gift of life. The great sage, Hillel, even considered taking care of and bathing the body to be a religious duty because, after all, the body was created by God.

The purpose of the fast days in the Jewish calendar, such as Tish'ah Be'Av and the Day of Atonement is mainly educational and spiritual. Tish'ah Be'Av strengthens the Jew's identification with the Jewish People by remembering the catastrophe of the destruction of the Temples. The fast of Yom Kippur comes to remind us how we have used our bodies to disobey God's will and to hurt our fellow man. Both the prophets and the rabbis stressed that mere fasting without repentance for our bad deeds is valueless.

There have always been minority groups in Jewish history who have seen value in the practice of asceticism but not as an end in itself. Asceticism must always be accompanied by the performance of the *mitzvot* and moral behavior. Most Jewish philosophers and religious authorities, however, echo the rabbis in condemning asceticism as a way of life and encouraging the proper enjoyment of earthly pleasures. *Maimonides, for example, stressed that one's body is not necessarily the enemy of one's soul. By performing God's commandments, the body can enjoy the delights of Creation in such a way as to help the soul to love God and His ways. (See also *Nazirite.)

ASHDOD is a city in the southern coastal plain of Ereẓ Israel. Presently a modern industrial city and important seaport, Ashdod is also significant because of its rich past history. In fact, archaeological excavations have revealed 22 strata which testify to continuous settlement of Ashdod dating back to the 17th century b.c.e. Among these finds are Canaanite and Israelite fortifications, a musicians' stand and a Hellenistic plant for extracting purple dye from murex, a purple shell. In the late Canaanite period, Ashdod served as an important harbor city as is shown by archaeological finds and references to its maritime trade in the archives of *Ugarit. According to biblical tradition, it was a town of the ancient Anakim ("giants"). After its conquest by the *Philistines, it became one of their five chief cities and they erected there a temple dedicated to the god Dagon. Uzziah, king of Judah, breached the fortifications of the town and built in the area.

In 734 b.c.e. the city surrendered to Assyria and in 712 b.c.e. Ashdod became the capital of an Assyrian province. Although the city was situated on the *via maris,* the trade route near the sea, it was not directly on the coast but possessed an ancient port which was called Ashdod Yam ("Ashdod-on-the-Sea"). With the

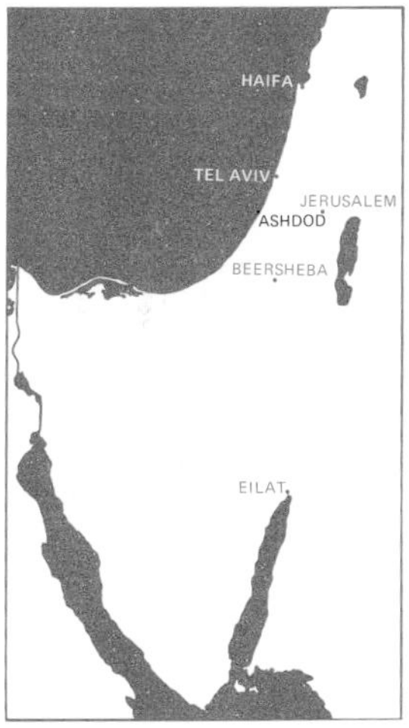

The Qumran community, an ascetic sect also known as the *yahad,* probably lived on this site at Qumran, on the northwest shore of the Dead Sea, in about the first century c.e. They endured hardship and self-sacrifice in the hopes of launching a new era of righteousness.

decline of Assyrian power, Egypt conquered the city after a siege of 29 years. In the sixth and fifth centuries b.c.e., Ashdod was the Philistine capital, so that in the days of Nehemiah, an "Ashdodite" was synonymous with a "Philistine." Nehemiah fought against Ashdod's influence which extended as far as Jerusalem.

The town continued to be a district capital in the Hellenistic period when it was known as Azotus and it served as a Greek stronghold down to the days of the Hasmoneans. Its suburbs were burnt by Jonathan and the city was captured by John Hyrcanus. Ashdod then remained in Hasmonean hands until its conquest by Rome, and later changed hands numerous times, eventually becoming the property of Herod I, who gave it to his sister Salome; she bequeathed it to Livia, the wife of Augustus Caesar, from whom it was inherited by the emperor Tiberius. From the time of the Hasmoneans until the second century c.e. Ashdod appears to have been a Jewish town. Moreover, the discovery of a synagogue at Ashdod-on-the-Sea with a Greco-Jewish inscription gives further evidence of a Jewish community there in the sixth century c.e.

1

2

1. Housing for new immigrants in Ashdod.
2. Uncovering Early Iron Age brick houses of the Philistine Period (12th century b.c.e.) in Tel Ashdod.

Gradually the city declined, and for over 1000 years it remained an unimportant village – until the modern period. During the War of Independence (1948–49), Egyptian forces entered Ashdod and advanced beyond it six miles northward to the vicinity of Jabneh. In October, 1948, the Egyptian forces were cut off in "Operation Ten Plagues" and they escaped with great difficulty; the local Arab inhabitants abandoned the place with them. The modern city was founded in 1956 four miles north of the mound of Philistine Ashdod. It received city status in 1968, and is growing into a major manufacturing center. Ashdod's population grew rapidly from 200 in 1957 to 30,000 in 1968. Town-planners envisage Ashdod as Israel's second largest port on the Mediterranean coast, and the port which was opened in 1965, has shortened transport routes in the southern half of Israel. The town plan is based on the principle of self-contained neighborhood units, each with its own social, educational, and economic services; 16 such units are provided for in the Ashdod city plan.

ASHER BEN JEḤIEL (also known as the Rosh; c. 1250-1327), talmudist. His first teachers were his father and his elder brother. He spent some time in France and then lived in Cologne and Coblenz. From there he moved to Worms, where his teacher *Meir ben Baruch of Rothenburg had been appointed rabbi in 1281. Meir esteemed his pupil, and appointed him a member of the local rabbinical court. After the imprisonment of Meir, Asher became the acknowledged leader of German Jewry and headed the unsuccessful efforts to obtain his master's release, toward which he was prepared to contribute a considerable portion of his assets.

He distinguished himself for his activities during the period the the *Rindfleisch massacres (1298), and for his decisions on matters arising from the resulting disruption of family and communal life. Fearing a similar fate to that of Meir of Rothenburg, Asher left Germany in 1303 for Barcelona, where he was welcomed with great honor by Solomon ben Abraham *Adret. In 1305 he accepted the position of rabbi in Toledo and turned down a request of the German authorities that he return to his native country, for which they were prepared to provide an imperial letter of safe-conduct and an escort of 50 soldiers.

Asher opposed the study of philosophy if it interfered with the study of Torah, and when Solomon Adret proposed a ban on the study of philosophy by anyone under the age of 25, Asher influenced the local leaders in Toledo to support this ban. He criticized those who used positions of influence at court for their own advantage, and also opposed customs which had been influenced by the Christian environment. His vast influence and moral stature enabled him to overcome the difficulties which he encountered in his activities, and his spiritual influence was acknowledged even by the Castilian queen, Maria de Molina.

The many responsa he wrote reflect both the humility that typified the German school, and the firmness and authority of one speaking in the name of the supreme political and judicial body of Spanish Jewry. For example, when the rabbi of Valencia insisted on his view in defiance of accepted practice and the opinion of Asher, the latter threatened him with capital punishment, if all the other deterrents enumerated in a letter to one of the scholars of the community should prove of no avail. Despite his reservations and doubts as to the right of the rabbis to impose capital punishment, he nonetheless permitted them to act according to the custom prevalent in Spain, and consented to sentences of mutilation, particularly in the case of informers. He is regarded as one of the outstanding halakhic authorities who put the final seal to the work of the German and French codifiers, joining to it the Spanish *halakhah.* (Further information on this may be found under *Law, Jewish.)

Virtually all the communities of Spain referred their problems to Asher, and students flocked to his yeshivah from all over Europe, and from Russia.

He was familiar with German law and Spanish common law but his knowledge of Arabic was limited to the spoken language. Having lost all his property in Germany, he lived under conditions of financial stress and his son notes that his father's assets at the time of his death were insufficient for the execution of his will. Asher nevertheless continued in Spain his ancestral custom of giving a tenth of all his income to charity.

Asher's main work is a commentary on the *Talmud modeled on that of *Alfasi. In it he sums up the decisions of the earlier codifiers and commentators. It is printed in all standard editions of the Talmud. There are also more than 1,000 of his responsa in existence, although he may well have written more.

Asher's piety and exemplary conduct are reflected in a book he wrote which includes 131 ethical sayings grouped for each of the six weekdays, in which he details rules of conduct for a Jew in his private, family, and public life, and in relation to Jews and Gentiles. He demands integrity, courtesy, and sincerity in dealings with Gentiles. *Jacob ben Asher was his son.

ASHI (known also by the honorific title of Rabbana; c. 335-427/28 c.e.) was the most celebrated Babylonian *amora* of his day. His teachers included *Rava and almost all the renowned scholars of that time. After the death of his teacher Rav Papa (371/72), he was appointed head of the yeshivah of Sura. For nearly 60 years he occupied this position. Under Ashi's leadership the yeshivah, which had declined in importance, again became an influential center of learning. At Sura, several hundred pupils and scores of distinguished veteran colleagues gathered around him. The latter were known as "the rabbis of the school of Rav Ashi"; the most outstanding was his older contemporary, Ravina.

With their cooperation, Ashi began the monumental task of editing the Babylonian *Talmud. He assembled and arranged in appropriate tractates all the vast and ramified material that the earlier *amoraim* had accumulated in the Babylonian yeshivot for more than 200 years. Ashi is credited with editing the Babylonian Talmud, since he began the work and completed the major part of it, but the task was continued after his death by the later *amoraim,* in particular by Ravina ben Huna. The significance of Ashi's work can be gauged from the tradition, quoted in the letter of *Sherira Gaon, which states that the earlier *amoraim* had a compilation of the Talmud to which each generation added its halakhic discussions and new interpretations, until Ashi – and later Ravina II – edited and gave definitive form to all the accumulated material and completed the redaction of the Talmud.

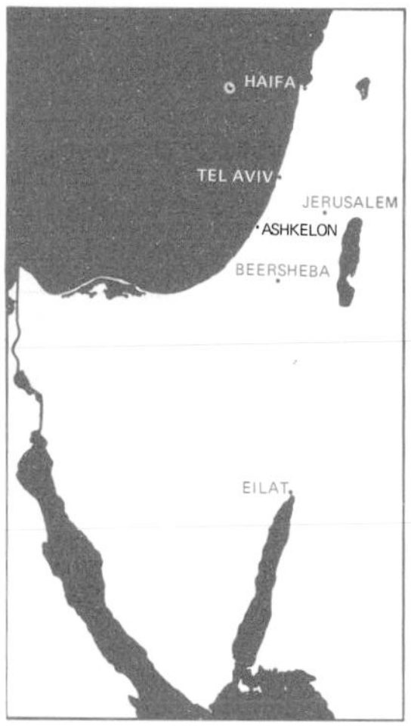

Ashi's activities and influence were not limited to the yeshivah or to his colleagues and students. Through his personality and abilities he attained a position of unusual prominence as the spokesman and leader of his generation, enjoyed the high esteem of all sections of the Jewish people, and possessed great wealth. Ashi apparently also had access to the Persian royal palace. His contemporaries held that "never since the days of Rabbi Judah ha-Nasi were learning and greatness combined in one person as they were in Rav Ashi."

Among his sayings are the following: "Everyone who is haughty will finally be humbled," and, "Any scholar who is not as hard as iron is not a scholar." His son Mar bar Rav Ashi was appointed in 454/5 head of the yeshivah. Ashi also had another son, Sama and a daughter.

ASHKELON is a city on the Mediterranean coast of Israel. A tour of the archaeological remains found in Ashkelon indicates the many peoples that in turn controlled this ancient city. Archaeological finds have included hieroglyphic writings, columns of ancient synagogues, and a statue of the Greek goddess of victory standing on a globe of the world supported by Atlas. These artifacts represent only some of the periods of Ashkelon's interesting history; it has also been under Babylonian, Crusader, Muslim and Ottoman control.

The city, then known as Asqana, is first mentioned in writings from the 20th-19th centuries b.c.e., 4000 years ago. Though the city was loyal to Egypt at that time, it is recorded that Abdihiba, the ruler of Jerusalem, complained to Pharaoh that the people of Ashkelon helped the Habiru, Egypt's enemy. It was in the 13th-century b.c.e. that an open rebellion occurred against Ramses II, and in the 12th-century b.c.e. that the Philistines took the city from the Egyptians.

There are several references in the Bible relating to Ashkelon in this period. In the Book of Judges it is mentioned that the Judeans took the city, and Ashkelon is mentioned as well in connection with the story of Samson. The Assyrians then followed, only to have the Egyptians regain control. After that Nebuchadnezzar and his Babylonian troops subdued the city. A letter in Aramaic from this period has been found; in it Adon, probably the king of Ashkelon, pleads for help, stating that the Babylonian king has reached Aphek.

The Persians who became masters of the city in the 4th-century b.c.e. were ousted by the Greeks. During the Roman period Ashkelon was considered a "free and allied city," and in the Jewish Wars (66 c.e.) the people of Ashkelon fought and defeated the Jews. In the talmudic period which followed, Jews lived in Ashkelon, as the remains of a synagogue of that period show. Talmudic sources also mention Ashkelon's orchards and a fair held there. In the Byzantine period the city was a center of paganism, whose population worshipped a fish-goddess, Derceto, whose image was a mermaid.

In the Crusader period Ashkelon was a refuge for Jews escaping from Jerusalem, and the Jewish community ransomed captives and bought ritual objects from the looted synagogues in Jerusalem. The great Jewish traveler of the 12th century, Benjamin of Tudela, described it as a "large and beautiful city." When the Muslims replaced the Christians in the 12th century the Jews moved to Jerusalem.

1. National Park at Ashkelon, with swimming area, camping grounds, and archaeological site.
2. Fragment of stone screen from the remains of a sixth-century c.e. synagogue at Ashkelon.

Modern Ashkelon is located two miles northeast of the ancient ruins. During the War of Independence the Israel army gained control of the area and shortly thereafter a Jewish development town known as Migdal-Ashkelon was founded. In 1955 Ashkelon was given city status. The city has excellent beaches, and tourism and recreation are a main source of income for its 38,000 residents. The area of ancient Ashkelon, including the archaeological finds, has been converted into a national park.

ASHKENAZI, ASHKENAZIM. The word Ashkenaz (אַשְׁכְּנַז) appears in three places in the Bible and it refers to a people and country in Asia. In rabbinic literature, however, the term took on a completely different meaning which has become accepted among Jews the world over. Ashkenaz is thus the name of the first compact area of Jewish settlement in North-West Europe which began on the banks of the River Rhine. Later the name came to refer specifically to Germany. A German Jew is thus an Ashkenazi (plural: Ashkenazim) and the German Jewish style of Hebrew pronunciation and of prayer is also called Ashkenazi. In the course of time, the term included Eastern Europe as the Jews there more or less followed the German rites and, of course, it used to describe communities anywhere in the world which were established by immigrants from Germany and Eastern Europe.

The main thrust of the term is in opposition to the term Sephardi which refers to the culture and liturgical rites of Eastern or Oriental Jews. (For more information on this see: *Sephardi, Sephardim).

Ashkenazi Jewry, perhaps because of the circumstances in which it lived, tended to concentrate on internal Jewish sources and ideas rather than try to create a synthesis with non-Jewish ideas. The *Ḥasidei Ashkenaz movement was, as its name implies, a product of this culture as was the Tosafot school of Talmud commentary. A further result of Ashkenazi Jewry's isolation from its non-Jewish surrounding was the large measure of *self-government it practiced in the Middle Ages.

The Shulḥan Arukh became accepted as the major code of Jewish Law even by Ashkenazim because Rabbi Moses Isserles wrote notes on it indicating the Ashkenazi custom when it clashed with the Sephardi. The Ashkenazi rite *siddur* and *maḥzor* have been printed since the 16th century. Until the 18th century this rite was generally followed by all Ashkenazi Jews, but since the rise of *Ḥasidism, the rite of Isaac Luria (known as *Nusaḥ Ha-Ari*) which is basically Sephardi, was accepted in ḥasidic communities. Ashkenazi scribes developed a distinctive script, and the illuminators of manuscripts a specific style. An important aspect of Ashkenazi Jewry, particularly in the Slavonic countries, was the development of the *Yiddish language which became very widespread. It is, to some degree, based on German and a very large body of literature was created in it.

The continued distinction between Ashkenazi and Sephardi has established itself in the religious life of present-day Israel where there are two chief rabbis, one Sephardi, the other Ashkenazi.

ASHKENAZI, ẒEVI HIRSCH (also known as the Ḥakham Ẓevi; 1660-1718), rabbi and halakhist. Both his father, Jacob Sak, a renowned scholar, and his maternal grandfather, Ephraim ben Jacob ha-Kohen, had escaped from Vilna to Moravia during the 1655 Cossack uprising. It was there that Ashkenazi studied under them as a youth. He wrote his first responsa in 1676, about the time he was sent to the yeshivah in Salonika to study the *Sephardi scholars' method of study. During his stay in Salonika (1676-78?) and Belgrade (1679), he adopted Sephardi customs and manners and, despite his *Ashkenazi origin, assumed the title *"ḥakham,"* the Sephardi title for a rabbi and also the name "Ashkenazi." In 1680 he returned to Ofen and continued his studies. After his wife and daughter were killed during the siege of Ofen by the Imperial army of Leopold I, Ashkenazi escaped to Sarajevo where he was appointed *ḥakham* of the Sephardi community. His parents were taken prisoner by a Brandenburg regiment after the fall of Ofen and ransomed by Jews in Berlin.

In 1707 he was appointed rabbi of the "Three Communities" of Hamburg, Wandsbeck and Altona, although he shared the position at Altona with Moses Rothenburg. It was eventually a violent controversy on a halakhic question between them that compelled him to resign his position in all three communities in 1709. Three of his responsa deal with that celebrated problem – the chicken which was allegedly found to have no heart. His decision that such a bird was *kasher* created a sensation in the rabbinic world, and was vigorously opposed by leading rabbis though supported by his son, Jacob *Emden.

In 1710, the *Ḥakham* Ẓevi became the rabbi of the Ashkenazi community in Amsterdam. There,

Silver seal of Ẓevi Hirsch ben Jacob Ashkenazi. The face of the seal shows a deer *(ẓevi) and* the letters *ḥet ẓade (ḥakham ẓevi),* all topped with a crown. The carved handle depicts the tablets of the Law, the letters *shin tet* (*shem tov* – "A good name"), supporting two lions and a crown. On the reverse side, the letters *kaf tav* (*keter Torah* – "crown of the Torah") are engraved. The crowns and letters refer to the passage in Mishnah Avot 4:13: "Rabbi Simeon said – there are three Crowns: the Crown of Torah, the Crown of Priesthood, and the Crown of Royalty – but the Crown of a good name exceeds them all."

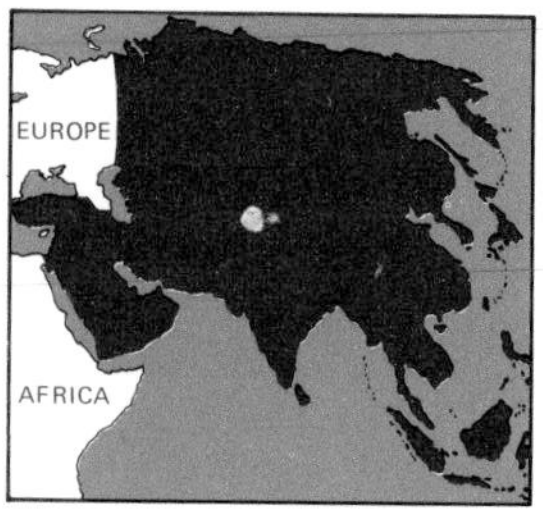

Painting of Ẓevi Hirsch Ashkenazi, framed by a listing of complimentary titles and a poem written in his honor.

Ashkenazi's relations with the Sephardi rabbi, Solomon Ayllon, were excellent. This relationship, however, deteriorated with the arrival in Amsterdam of Nehemiah Ḥayon, the emissary of *Shabbetai Ẓevi, who sought the help of the local Portuguese community in circulating his writings. Having been asked by the Portuguese elders (who did not rely on Ayllon) to rule on the matter, Ashkenazi and Moses *Ḥagiz – who was then in Amsterdam as a rabbinical emissary from Jerusalem – decided against Ḥayon and his writings and later excommunicated him. In revenge for not having been consulted, Ayllon managed to transform the issue into one of supremacy of the old Portuguese community over the newcomers' Ashkenazi one. A new commission under Ayllon was appointed and found Ḥayon's writings to be in accordance with the tradition. Upon Ashkenazi's refusal to apologize to Ḥayon, a bitter controversy took place between the Portuguese and Ashkenazi. Ashkenazi finally resigned his position in Amsterdam in 1714. After a brief stay in London (at the invitation of the Sephardi community), and a short sojourn in Emden, he proceeded to Poland and settled in Opatow. From there he was invited once more to Hamburg to take part in a complicated lawsuit. In the beginning of 1718 he was appointed rabbi of Lemberg, but he died there after a few months.

ASIA. The Jewish people originated in Asia. There the promises of God were made, and there Israel became a nation. Abraham came from Mesopotamia (modern Iraq) and Canaan, the promised land, was a bridge linking Asia with Africa, a crossroads of cultural influences from Mesopotamia, Persia, Greece, and Egypt.

The Babylonian conquest of Ereẓ Israel in the sixth century b.c.e. and the exile of the Jews to Babylonia made Jewish life more Asian. In Babylonia Judaism developed the definite form which it brought back to the Holy Land after the Exile. Even the present Hebrew alphabet was developed there. The majority of Jews remained in Mesopotamia after the first Exile. Settlement spread further in Asia, and this area, side by side with Jerusalem, became the main center of Jewish life. The Babylonian Talmud's ideas and customs became a basic element of *diaspora Judaism.

Similarly, after the Arab conquest in the seventh century c.e., all North Africa, Ereẓ Israel, Mesopotamia, and Spain looked to Damascus and the area of the Fertile Crescent as their center of government. Jewish life, through trade and migration, spread further into Asia to India and China. The Crusades (11th to 12th centuries) and the Tatar invasion (13th century) weakened Jewry in western Asia, Byzantine rule diminished it in *Asia Minor, and in the 13th century Mesopotamian Jewry declined. Numbers increased after the Expulsion from Spain (1492) when Spanish Jews and later Marranos from Portugal migrated to the Ottoman Empire and areas of Asia with Jewish centers. The Jewish population of Asia thus became largely European, and Spanish in language and religious customs. In fact the word Sephardi – which comes from the Hebrew name for Spain – came to mean Oriental. But original Asian communities remained, in *Yemen, *Iraq, *Kurdistan, and other places.

Two 19th century migrations took Jews further into Asia: from Iraq to British-ruled territories such as India and Hong Kong, and in the Russian Empire to Siberia and on to Manchuria. In the 20th century Jews have settled in Soviet Asia and there was even a Soviet attempt at a self-governing Jewish region in *Birobidzhan. Refugees from Nazi rule fled to Japanese-held territories and to China, but under the Communist regime the Chinese settlements came to an end.

After the State of Israel was established most Asian Jewry migrated there, either by choice or under pressure. Small communities still remain scattered, and Asian Jewry is only a small part of world Jewry, representing only a fraction of 1% of the total population of Asia.

Ancient Jewish settlements in Asia Minor.

ASIA MINOR is the area of Asia nearest Europe; it is also called Anatolia and roughly corresponds to modern Turkey. Jews lived there from at least the sixth century b.c.e. The biblical books of Joel and Isaiah seem to refer to it, and the Safarad mentioned by Obadiah is thought to be the town of Sardis.

Aristotle, according to a follower (c.350 b.c.e.), met there a Jew "Greek not only in speech, but also in spirit;" and in about 300 b.c.e. the Syrian ruler Antiochus III transferred 2,000 Jews from Babylonia to cities in Asia Minor. The first synagogues of the area date from this time. From then Jewish settlement spread widely and many Roman writers refer to the communities there. But our chief information comes from Josephus' *Antiquities* and the New Testament. These books describe Jewish communities throughout Asia Minor. Paul was a Jew from Asia Minor with Roman citizenship, though not all Jews there had this privilege.

Josephus tells much about the communities and the important positions many Jews held. Both Josephus and the New Testament show that many non-Jews, "God-fearers," believed in the "Supreme God," followed Jewish customs, and attended synagogues regularly – though most never became Jews.

ASSIMILATION is the process in which one cultural or national group loses its identity and becomes part of another group. Referred to Jews, assimilation means losing Jewish identity and becoming absorbed in gentile society.

Throughout Jewish history assimilation of Jews has taken place and has been motivated by many factors. In some cases Jews viewed gentile culture as superior and wished to join it. As early as 175 b.c.e., during the reign of Antiochus Epiphanes, there were Jews who wished to accept the mode of life and culture of *Hellenism. Later, in the years of early Christianity, there were Jews who gradually assimilated into the Christian way of life. In other cases, the lure of a better social or economic position led Jews to assimilate. During the Middle Ages this was sometimes the cause of *apostasy (conversion out of Judaism). At other times, persecution and *anti-Semitism compelled Jews to convert, but often only on the surface while secretly they remained Jews. (See *Marranos.)

In the middle of the 18th century, assimilation became a powerful force in Jewish life and an element of increasing importance in Jewish thought and society. Various factors combined to create this situation. The *Court Jews, their families, and social circle gradually, sometimes unnoticeably, assimilated the habits of the Christian court. The Enlightenment (*Haskalah) movement was accompanied by a certain readiness on the part of groups of Christian and Jewish intellectuals to create an "open society." The grant of civic *emancipation apparently promised that Jews could enter the emancipating society as equals if they would forgo their Jewish national identity and beliefs.

For some Jews, assimilation served as a shortcut to attaining individual advancement, as in the case of Heinrich *Heine. Later, their admiration for the modern national state, a growing appreciation of the life-style and social structure of the dominant nations, and the idea of progress combined to create the conception that the Jewish national existence was outdated. Such Jews also felt that they were guilty of intellectual and emotional dishonesty in cherishing Jewish messianic hopes. Furthermore, instead of

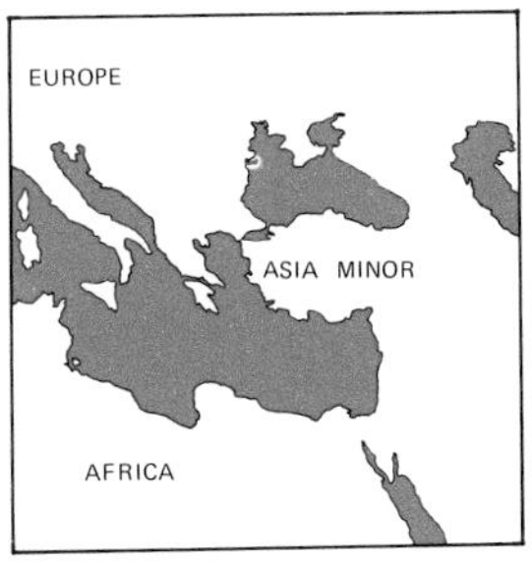

looking to Ereẓ Israel as the Jewish national homeland, Jews became imbued with nationalistic feelings for the country in which they lived. In 1848 the Jewish community of Worms formulated a program for religious reform in which they stated: "We must no longer utter prayers for the return to Palestine while we are wholeheartedly attached to the German fatherland whose fate is indissolubly our fate; all that is beloved and dear to us is contained in this fatherland. We must not mourn in sackcloth and ashes the destruction of the Temple when we long ago came into the possession of a fatherland that has become so dear to us."

Attachment to German soil, language and culture was the compelling cause of assimilation. However, during the Holocaust, the descendants of these same Jews were shocked into realizing that there was no genuine equality and security under the Germans, as even the most assimilated Jews were singled out and sent to the death camps.

United States. Assimilation in the Jewish community of the United States has been directed by several different pressures. During colonial times, there were so few Jews that they were regarded as exotics. So small a Jewish population, with fewer women than men among it, inevitably had a considerable rate of intermarriage. A recent study of Jewish marriage before 1840 has shown that at least one in seven colonial Jews and their immediate descendants married unconverted Christians; after that year, in the fourth and fifth generations of colonial Jewish families, intermarriage was so dominant that most of these families disappeared from the Jewish community. Later in American history, Jews were prompted to assimilate when the first signs of social anti-Semitism appeared and Jews were discriminated against.

However, in the period after World War II, American society became more open to Jews than any country has ever been through the whole history of the Diaspora, and this removed the need for any willed assimilation. The Holocaust and the creation of the State of Israel caused many Jews to reaffirm their Jewish identity. The rapid economic rise of the bulk of the American Jewish community into the middle and upper-middle classes during the postwar period remade the life style of American Jews, so that in many aspects Jews became part of the American establishment. This was particularly true in the realms of academic and artistic endeavor, where Jews became a dominant force during this era. It was thus no longer necessary to play down the fact of one's Jewishness. Increased efforts were made by almost every American Jewish body toward intensifying Jewish education and strengthening the connection between American Jews and Israel. The last generation of American Jews has rebuilt the institutions of Jewish communal life at an estimated cost of two billion dollars, and enormous personal energy.

The worsening of race relations in America in the 1960s, the tension between Jews and Negroes as well as the increasing influence of the *New Left among younger Jews, again posed the question of assimilation. Negro emphasis on Negro identity has evoked much more identification with Negroes among some younger Jews than with their own Jewish identity. (This subject is discussed in the article on *Negro-Jewish Relations.) The New Left has tended to see itself as part of the "Third World," and has thus sided with the Arabs against Israel. These politically active young people are not, however, numerous, and during the *Six-Day War and *Yom Kippur War, the overwhelming majority of American Jewish youth, including many left-wingers, were as involved with Israel's cause as their parents.

Nevertheless the problem of assimilation in the United States remains. Its "open society" and the educated middle class has drawn the Jew out of a ghettoized Jewish community and into the mainstream of American life, where forces of assimilation are quiet but powerful.

Soviet Union. In Russia, the Jewish population has been deprived of the last shreds of Jewish culture and forced to assimilate to Russian culture. Yet Jews cannot totally assimilate because of the Russian "passports" system in which every Soviet citizen is obliged to have an identity card on which nationality is marked. For the Jews, no matter how acculturated they have become, their nationality remains Jewish. This strange phenomenon has produced a type of "Marrano" atmosphere among much of Soviet Jewry. They have a profound emotional attachment to the State of Israel and attempt to study the Hebrew language and Jewish history. The exuberant mass gatherings of Jewish youth around the synagogues, especially on the Simḥat Torah festival in Moscow and Leningrad, have become a demonstration of their identification with the Jewish people and with Israel, and of their protest against the forced assimilation which tries to deprive them of their dignity as sons of a historic nation.

1

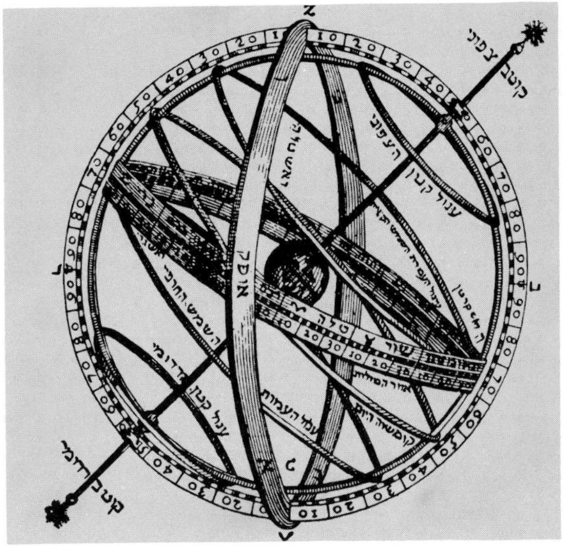

2

1. An astronomer holding an astrolabe, as shown in an illustration from Maimonides' *Guide of the Perplexed.* Maimonides and his 12th-century contemporaries tried to prove the existence of God through the study of astronomy.
2. An astrolabe as illustrated in *Ma'aseh Tuviyyah,* a work on the natural sciences by the physician Tobias Cohn, printed in Venice, 1707-08.

ASTROLABE. In early times this scientific instrument was used to determine the position of the heavenly bodies; the Hebrew name is מִשְׁטַר הַכּוֹכָבִים ("rule of the planets"). Its other name, מֹאזְנֵי הַחוֹזִים ("seer's scales"), shows that it was also used by astrologers, who made predictions about people's fortunes based on the position of the stars.

The simple astrolabe had a suspended disk, with degrees marked on the circumference and a movable pointer at the center. It was devised by the ancient Greeks, and was developed in the Middle Ages by Arab scientists, astronomers and astrologers. Surviving early models inscribed only in Hebrew show that Jews were also active in this work, and it was they who transmitted the invention to Christian Spain. In fact, the first treatise on the astrolabe in Arabic, *The Art of the Astrolabe and its Use,* was written by the Jewish Mesopotamian scientist Māshā'allāh about the year 800. When Abraham ibn Ezra, the biblical scholar, came to write his original treatise on the astrolabe in the early twelfth century, he complained of how difficult it was to find Hebrew translations for some of the technical terms required. Another Spanish Jew, Isaac (Don Zag) ibn Sid, helped draw up the astronomical tables known as the Alfonsine tables (1272) which for some centuries were used with an improved kind of astrolabe.

At the outset of the age of discovery, toward the end of the 15th century, John II of Portugal appointed a commission to find some way of putting the astrolabe to nautical use. One of its Jewish members was the royal physician Joseph Vecinho. Ocean navigation was now fully possible for the first time, and in fact until the 18th century sailors used some form of this device in preference to the sextant.

In Jewish tradition the gentile prophet Balaam was considered to have been an astronomer, and some miniature Bible illustrations represent him as holding an astrolabe in his hand.

ASTROLOGY is the study of the supposed influence of the stars, planets and other celestial bodies on human events, and predictions based on this study. Even today many newspapers have regular astrological sections forecasting what will happen to their readers in the forthcoming week, based on which "sign of the zodiac" they were born under.

In ancient times and in the Middle Ages, the study of astrology was taken very seriously indeed. In the Bible itself there is no explicit reference to astrology but some of the terms, such as diviner and soothsayer, have some connection with it. The prophets were aware of the practices of stargazers among the Babylonians and other peoples, but made

1. Wheel of the zodiac, with astrological signs for the Hebrew months. From the mosaic floor of the sixth-century Bet Alfa synagogue.
2. Illustration from a 13th-century German *maḥzor* showing a goat drawing water – a combination of the zodiac signs for Capricorn (goat) and Aquarius (water carrier).

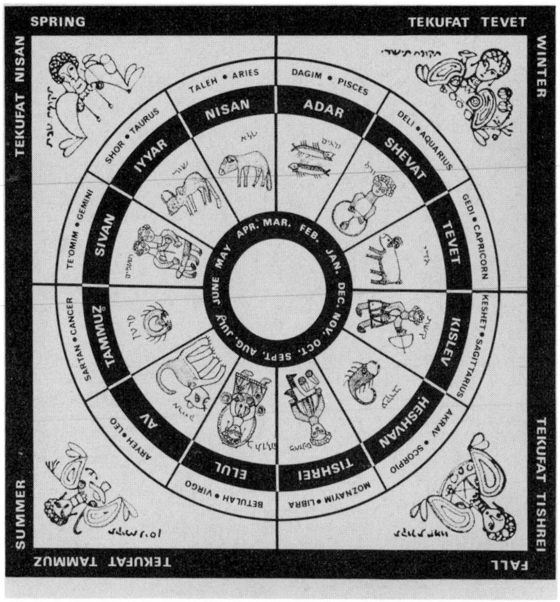

1

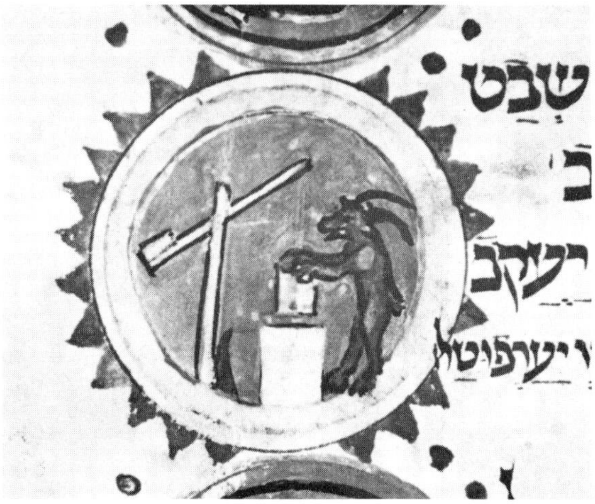

2

fun of them. The Book of *Jubilees depicts the patriarch Abraham as overcoming the beliefs of the astrologers and another post-biblical work, the first Book of Enoch, includes astrology as one of the sins of men.

However, it seems that the sages of the Talmud did believe in astrology although some taught that the People of Israel's fate is beyond the influence of the stars and dependent only on their own behavior. Some of the rabbis believed that the constellation *(mazzal)* under which one is born influences one's nature but does not entirely limit *free will. Mar Samuel, who was also an expert in *astronomy, worked out several rules of health and agriculture based on astrological principles.

In the Middle Ages, many Jewish scholars believed in astrology and compiled books on that "science." Abraham *ibn Ezra's reputation as an astrologer spread beyond Jewish circles and in his commentary on the Bible he discusses astrological matters at great length. *Judah Halevi and Ḥasdai *Crescas were skeptical as to whether human life can be influenced by the movement of celestial bodies and *Maimonides considered astrology to be "mere foolery." He also criticizes the Jews of antiquity severely for their superstitious faith in astrology.

Several Jewish astrologers (as well as astronomers) served in various royal courts in Southern and Western Europe. Their work was to formulate astrological predictions for their royal employers.

In modern Jewish religious life there are only very few vestiges of astrological beliefs. Some folk-customs derive from them but their astrological significance has been entirely forgotten. Perhaps the most outstanding is the congratulation: *Mazal tov,* which is commonly translated as "good luck" but really means "may you have a good constellation or star for this event."

ASTRONOMY.

When I see Your heavens, the work of Your fingers, the moon and the stars which You have established – what is man that You remember him, and the son of man that You take account of him?

In these words (Psalms 8:4-5) King David described the spiritual experience of beholding the heavens and the celestial bodies. The impact of this manifestation of the Creator's greatness must impress the beholder with his own smallness and insignificance. The classical Hebrew term for astronomy – *tekhunah* – is based on the word used in the above verse referring to God's *establishment* of the universe.

According to the *aggadah,* even the Patriarch Abraham was interested in astronomy and a legend has it that when he went to Egypt he taught its wise men and magicians the sciences of mathematics and astronomy. Later, in the period of the Mishnah and Talmud, many of the great sages were outstanding astronomers. Rabbi Joshua ben Ḥananiah calculated the orbit of a comet which appears once every seventy years and Mar Samuel said of himself: "The pathways of the heavens are as clear to me as the pathways of Nehardea (his home town)." He was so expert in the motions of the moon that he was given an additional name: Mar Samuel *Yarḥina'ah,* which

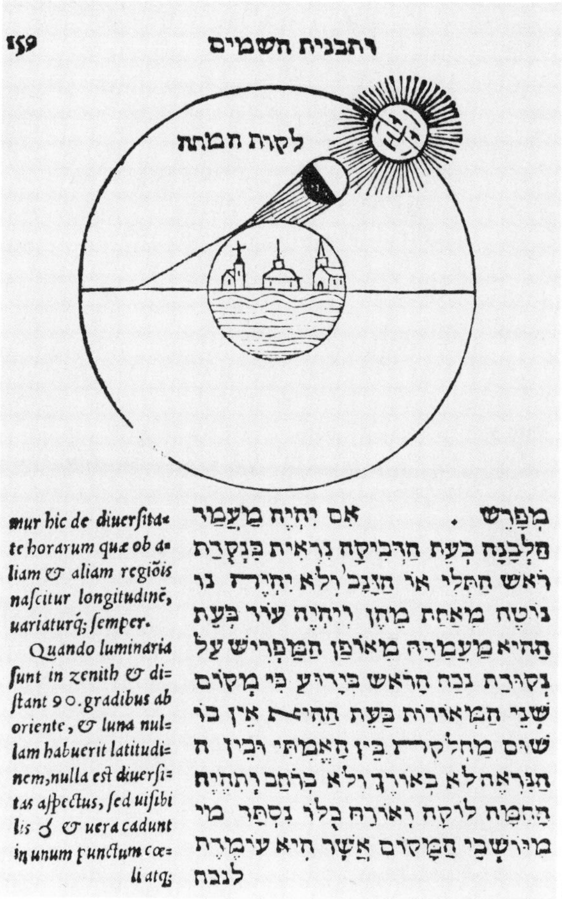

1

can be loosely translated as "moon watcher."

Astronomy was very important for the rabbis of the Talmud since the Jewish month – and thus the festivals – is fixed according to the cycles of the moon. Knowledge of astronomy was considered to be among the "secrets of the Torah" and not to be passed on to persons not well-versed in Torah. For more information on this subject see *Calendar. Although the earth is usually described as a disk, there is no doubt that the rabbis knew that the earth is a sphere. They were also expert in working out the solar and lunar cycles. Figures are given for the cycles of Jupiter, Saturn, Venus and Mars; the first two are entirely accurate but the latter two are wrong and were challenged in very early times.

In the Middle Ages Jews were very active in the study of astronomy. Their principal contribution was in the calculation of the Hebrew calendar, in the translation of astronomical works from Arabic into Hebrew and other languages, and in the compilation of astronomical tables for scientific and navigational purposes. Most of these tables were compiled by Jews. One of the important Jewish astronomers who wrote in Hebrew was Abraham bar Ḥiyya (died c. 1136) whose work influenced generations of astronomers. Besides astronomical tables and traslations of Arabic works into Latin, he wrote two important books on the subject. A good part of his work was translated into Latin and this had an influence on general astronomy. It should be remembered that in ancient times astronomy was often connected with *astrology.

The greatest medieval Jewish astronomer was undoubtedly Levi ben Gershom (1288-1344) who was also an outstanding talmudist, philosopher and Bible commentator. One historian of astronomy numbers him among the forerunners of Copernicus in that he pioneered new methods of research from which he evolved his own original system of astronomy. Another Jewish astronomer, Abraham *Zacuto created the astronomical tables which Christopher *Columbus used on his voyages.

3

2

Astronomy even found its way into Jewish religious poetry. Solomon ibn *Gabirol, in his major poem *Keter Malkhut,* described the structure of the universe according to Aristotle and Ptolemy.

Besides studying astronomy, Jews in the Middle Ages also invented astronomical instruments. These included improved versions of the *astrolabe, quadrants, and a device for measuring the height of the sun and the stars.

In modern times, from the 18th century onwards, Jews have been very active in the study of astronomy. Nowadays astronomy is connected with many other disciplines, particularly astrophysics, and great contributions have been made by Jewish scientists.

1. An eclipse of the sun, illustrated and explained by Abraham bar Ḥiyya, a great Jewish astronomer who wrote in Hebrew during the Middle Ages.
2. Mural painting of Abraham Zacuto giving his astronomical tables to explorer Vasco da Gama on the latter's departure from Lisbon in 1497.
3. The "Jacob's staff," an instrument used by astronomers and navigators, invented by Levi ben Gershom in the 14th century.

ATHALIAH. When Athaliah, daughter of *Ahab and Jezebel, married Jehoram, prince of Judah, the Northern and Southern kingdoms of Israel and Judah were temporarily allied. However, although she left her home in the kingdom of Israel to live in Judah, she did not leave her idolatrous habits behind her. Instead she immediately became unpopular by introducing the worship of Baal to Jerusalem. She continued to worship the idol even after her husband died and when her son, Ahaziah, took over the throne.

After a one-year reign, Ahaziah, who was ruling Judah, the Southern Kingdom, was murdered by *Jehu, the ruler of the Northern Kingdom. Immediately, Athaliah the queen-mother seized the throne, and set out to murder all possible rivals in the royal family including Ahaziah's children.

Jehoiada the high priest was horrified when he heard Athaliah's orders. He quickly sent his wife, who was the dead Ahaziah's sister, to try to save some of her nephews from their grandmother's hands. She managed to smuggle out Ahaziah's youngest son Joash and hid him for six years. Then Jehoiada, as high priest, arranged to have Joash crowned at the Temple as the true king.

When Athaliah was told of what was happening at the Temple she ran to the scene, calling out "Treason!" but she was promptly led to the "horses' gate" where she was killed. Athaliah's death was not mourned by the people, who saw her as a worshiper of Baal, a usurper of the throne and a murderer of the royal Davidic line.

The Amalia Hotel in Athens, 19th July 1973. Inside a gunman who has unsuccessfully tried to force his way into the El Al offices in Athens is holding hostages. Outside a Greek sharpshooter stands at the ready.

ATHENS. "An Athenian came to Jerusalem." So write the Talmud and Midrash in several places, indicating the frequent contact between Palestine and Athens. These relations go as far back as the beginning of the sixth century b.c.e., a period in which Athens was an economic giant in the Mediterranean area.

Concrete information about a Jewish community in Athens is available from the beginning of the first century c.e. Many Jewish writers of that time (such as *Philo and *Josephus) studied Athenian culture and literature, by which they were impressed.

After the Turkish conquest of Athens (1458) Muhammad II, The Conqueror, granted Athenians the right to prohibit Jews from living in Athens. However, several people fleeing from Spain arrived in Athens after 1492, and in 1705 a French traveler found 15 to 20 Jewish families living there. After 1834 a small Jewish community was organized. The Jewish population in the city increased from 60 in 1878 to 250 in 1887, and just before World War II, there were 3,000 Jews in Athens.

During World War II a total of 1,500 Jews from Athens, many having moved from Salonika, were sent to concentration camps. After the War, 4,500 to 5,000 Jews from surrounding countries reassembled in Greece – however, many emigrated to Israel, leaving only 2,850 Jews in Athens in 1968.

ATTAR, ḤAYYIM (1696-1743), was a rabbi and kabbalist. Born in Salé, Morocco, he settled in Meknes after the death of his great-uncle in order to manage his business. There he studied and taught, but the deterioration of the economic and political situation in Morocco and his belief that redemption was imminent induced him to leave for Ereẓ Israel.

He set out together with his closest disciples, and reached Leghorn, Italy, in 1739. There Attar's saintly nature soon earned him an eager audience. His home in Leghorn became a center for students who gathered to study under him, and there he preached

1

2

1. **Animals.** Even animals listened unafraid to the sweet music that King David played on his harp. Decorative first-word panel of a psalm from the *Rothschild Miscellany,* now in the British Museum, London.

2. **Burial.** "Jewish Funeral." An 18th century oil painting by an anonymous Italian artist.

1. **Bezalel.** Israel stamp issued on April 29, 1957 to mark the 50th anniversary of the Bezalel Museum in Jerusalem.
2. **Burial.** "Funeral" by Wilhelm Wachtel, 1914, from the En Harod Art Museum. This museum is the first art museum of the kibbutz movement and collects work of Diaspora artists from all periods.
3. **Candles.** Sabbath lamp by Abraham de Oliviera, 1734. It is forbidden to kindle fire on the Sabbath, and this hanging lamp with its two pools of oil could burn safely throughout the Sabbath.

1

3

2

to large audiences, urging them to repent. He sent proclamations to Jewish communities throughout Italy, urging immigration to Ereẓ Israel. Learning about the epidemics in Ereẓ Israel, some of his disciples became hesitant about making the journey to the Holy Land, but Ḥayyim declared: "It is immaterial to me who comes and who remains; he who has ideals will immigrate and inherit the Land."

In 1741, Attar with a group of 30, including Jews from Morocco and young rabbis from Italy, set sail from Leghorn. The group reached Acre in the late summer. Hearing of the epidemics raging in Jaffa and Jerusalem, Attar decided to establish a temporary yeshivah in Acre which continued for nearly a year. He then decided to move to Peki'in, attributing the deaths of two of his disciples to the fact that Acre, according to the Talmud, was not within the historic boundaries of Ereẓ Israel. During a visit to Tiberias, Ḥayyim *Abulafia urged him to reestablish his school there, but when the epidemic subsided, the group set out for Jerusalem. There Attar established the Midrash Keneset Israel Yeshivah, which had one division for advanced and one for young scholars.

He died approximately a year after settling in Jerusalem, and was buried on the Mount of Olives. The highway which was bulldozed through the ancient cemetery, when the area was in Jordanian hands, deviates from its planned course and makes a detour around the grave of Ḥayyim Attar.

AUERBACH, ARNOLD JACOB ("Red"; 1917-) is a U.S. basketball coach whose professional teams registered 1,037 victories, a record unsurpassed by any other coach, and were champions of the National Basketball Association nine times. Auerbach attended George Washington University and played varsity basketball from 1938 to 1940. In 1946, he became a coach in the professional Basketball Association of America. In 1950 he took over the last place Boston Celtics in the renamed National Basketball Association. He rebuilt the team and in 1957 won his first league title. The Celtics won consecutive N.B.A. championships from 1959 to 1966. A fiery, demonstrative individual, he railed at and occasionally fought referees, owners, coaches, players and fans. When he retired, he helped select as his replacement Bill Russell, the first negro coach in professional basketball. Auerbach was the author of *Basketball for the Player, the Fan and the Coach* (1953), and, with co-author Paul Sann, *Winning the Hard Way* (1966).

1

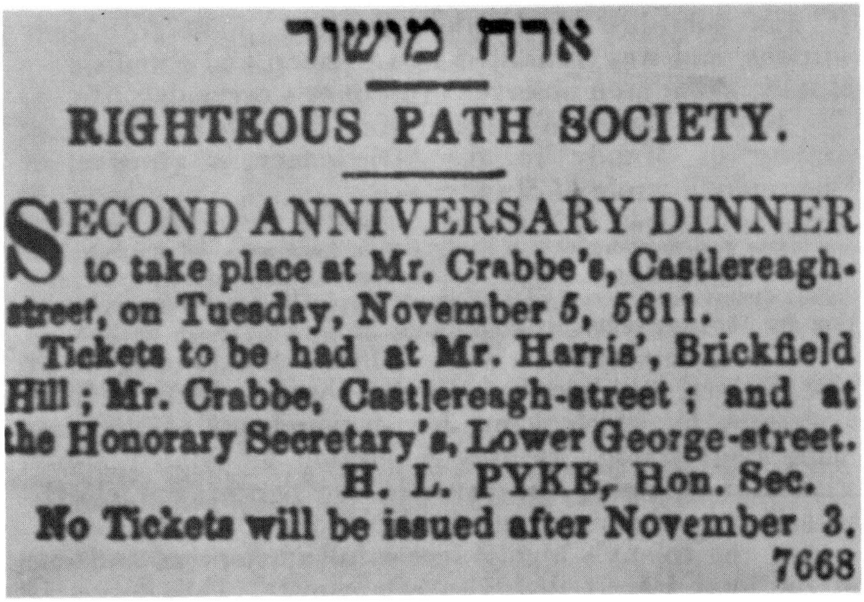
ארח מישור

RIGHTEOUS PATH SOCIETY.

SECOND ANNIVERSARY DINNER to take place at Mr. Crabbe's, Castlereagh-street, on Tuesday, November 5, 5611.

Tickets to be had at Mr. Harris', Brickfield Hill; Mr. Crabbe, Castlereagh-street; and at the Honorary Secretary's, Lower George-street.

H. L. PYKE, Hon. Sec.

No Tickets will be issued after November 3.

7668

AUSTRALIA AND NEW ZEALAND. Bound in shackles, the first six Jews to arrive in Australia came as convicts from England in 1788. They were joined by free settlers, who set up the country's first *minyan* and burial society in 1817. Step by step this remote outpost of Judaism continued to organize its religious life, despite the lack of rabbis and teachers, and the practical difficulties of religious observance. Outback families often traveled hundreds of miles to take part in religious services, or to have a child circumcised, and in 1830 a member of London's rabbinical court made the six-month voyage to Australia especially in order to arrange the colony's first Jewish divorce. The sense of distance and loneliness has been perpetuated in the names that characterize many of the pioneering synagogues, such as "The Congregation of the Remnant of Israel." The first synagogue in Sydney was constructed in 1844, and organized communities were established likewise in Melbourne (1841), Hobart (1845), Launceston (1846), Adelaide (1848), Brisbane (1865) and Perth (1892).

These tiny pioneering communities were bolstered by several waves of immigration – in the 1850s with the gold rush; from 1881 to 1911 there was an influx of Jews fleeing from the pogroms of Eastern Europe; in the 1930s there were German refugees; and after World War II thousands of *displaced persons who had survived the Holocaust in Europe sought to rehabilitate their lives in the furthest haven available.

The early settlers made a considerable impact on

2

1. An advertisement in an Australian newspaper of 1851 announcing the second anniversary dinner of the Righteous Path Society, a Jewish philanthropic organization. This was the first use of Hebrew type in a general newspaper in Australia.
2. Arnold "Red" Auerbach, the American basketball coach.

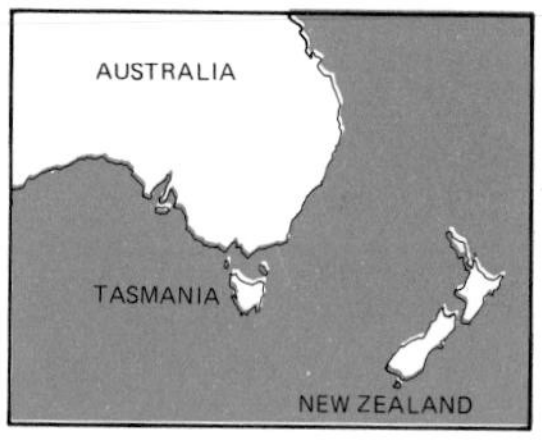

the development of the colony, and it became traditional for Jews who occupied the highest positions in the land to remain active members of their local congregations. Examples are Sir Benjamin Benjamin (1836-1905), during whose term of office as lord mayor of Melbourne the catering of all official municipal banquets was strictly kosher; Sir Archie Michaelis (born 1889), who was speaker of the Victorian state parliament and president of his suburban synagogue; Sir Isaac *Isaacs; and General Sir John *Monash.

As early as the mid-19th century, the Jewish communities maintained their own day schools. Assimilation nevertheless was favored by many circumstances. In addition to the difficulties of personnel and distance mentioned above, the shortage of Jewish women – to be expected in a frontier society – led to a high rate of intermarriage. (In 1881 there were only 78 women to every 100 men.) Furthermore, Jews were not forced to live cloistered lives. Indeed in the 1920s, Australian Jewry was in danger of losing its identity and becoming fully assimilated into the liberal surrounding society. The Zionist Federation was not founded until 1927; there was no united communal organization or representative voice; and community affairs were largely in the hands of the Australian-born segment who were wary of the very notion of Jewish distinctiveness.

In the 1950s, a great influx of European refugees rejuvenated Australia's communal life. The country now has a dozen day schools, some 50 synagogues, and scores of organizations covering the whole range of communal activities. Feeling for Israel is strong, and tourism and *aliyah* are substantial. Assimilation, however, remains a grave problem, particularly in the outlying centers: Perth (3,000 Jews), Brisbane (1,500), Adelaide (1,100) and Hobart (230). The total Jewish population of Australia is in excess of 70,000, or 0.5% of the total population.

Australia and Israel have for the most part maintained cordial relations, both in the diplomatic and in the commercial fields.

Melbourne. The vigor of this community is the product of a constructive clash of attitudes between two main types of Jewish migrants: the English and German settlers of the 19th century, and the 20th century refugees from Eastern Europe, who spoke Yiddish, had an Orthodox background, and were strongly Zionist, and who favored forthright attitudes to issues such as anti-Semitism and separate Jewish day schools. In 1948 Mount Scopus College, the first Jewish day school in Australia, was established despite the opposition of many Australian-born Jews, whose children now form a large proportion of the enrolment of over 2,000. In 1955 a group of Lubavicher Ḥasidim established the Yeshivah College, some of whose graduates formed the nucleus of Australia's first full-time tertiary rabbinical college. In addition to other schools, there are dozens of educational, religious, Zionist, cultural, sporting, welfare and students' organizations.

There have been frequent, yet minor, instances of anti-Semitism. With the continuing immigration, the Jewish population of Melbourne more than doubled between 1947 and 1974, when it exceeded 35,000, or 50% of Australian Jewry.

Sydney. The story of Australia's oldest Jewish community (founded 1832) is that of the country at large, as outlined above. Evidence of its early prosperity may still be seen in the impressive Great Synagogue, which was opened in 1878, and which houses a Judaica Library of 7,000 volumes.

Different sources of prewar migration – Western Europe and Britain – produced this city's different reactions to the challenge of assimilation. In 1933 Sydney had four congregations, and 19 in 1970. Enrolment in the three day schools, however, was only 650 in 1971. In addition there is a part-time

International soccer match at the Ramat Gan Stadium between Australia and Israel, 1969.

yeshivah with some 70 students, and a number of part-time Hebrew schools, mostly attached to synagogues. Prominent among Sydney's Jewish social services is the Wolper Jewish Hospital. In 1974 the Jewish population of Sydney exceeded 29,000, or 40% of the total Jewish population of Australia.

Other Communities. The pioneering Jewish families left a respected name in the outlying country districts. However, several Jewish communities that sprang up in the wake of the gold rush of 1851 have all but disappeared. Thus the gilt grandeur of the synagogue of Ballarat is unvisited now, except by a handful of stalwarts, and many shopfronts display the unmistakably Jewish names of the greatgrandparents of the present non-Jewish occupants.

In 1913 a dozen migrants founded a culturally self-sufficient farming community at Shepparton, which maintained a wooden synagogue, a *mikveh,* and a migrant hostel, and which retained a *shoḥet*-cum-*melamed* who bicycled his way to outlying homesteads. As with the bulk of the small communities, the majority of the local settlers moved to Melbourne in the face of the difficulties of providing adequate Jewish education.

New Zealand. Jewish traders from Sydney first settled in New Zealand in 1829, but despite the gold rushes of the 1860s, the Jewish population (now 4,000) has never risen beyond 0.2% of the general population. There has always been a highly restrictive government policy on the immigration of non-Britishers, but the few European refugees who were admitted made every attempt to counter the high rate of assimilation, particularly through intermarriage. Many Jews have held prominent positions in government and professional life, notably Sir Julius *Vogel, who was twice premier of New Zealand. There are friendly relations between New Zealand and Israel.

AUSTRIA. "The Bloodstained Land" *(Ereẓ ha-Damim)* was the name given to Austria by the Jews in the 15th century. Jews probably first came to Austria with the Roman legions; by the 13th century, Austria was a center of Jewish learning and leadership for the German lands. Jews held important positions, administering the taxes and the mints, and were active in trade. But there was much hostility, and during the Middle Ages there were several instances of *blood libels and charges of *desecration of the Host, and wholesale massacres of the Jews. In the 15th century Jewish settlement of Austria continued and its customs were influential in other countries. For example, the ceremony of *Semikhah* (rabbinical *ordination) was partly determined by Austrian customs.

Jews were expelled from various parts of Austria periodically and many anti-Jewish laws were passed. Turkish Jews came to Austria in the 18th century and were treated better than the Austrian Jews; in 1736 Diego d'Aguilar founded the Turkish community in *Vienna.

Joseph II (1780-90) was much more tolerant of the Jews than previous rulers and issued the *Toleranzpatent* in 1782. In the 19th century (December 21, 1867) all discrimination on the basis of religion was outlawed in Austria and Jewish assimilation increased. But anti-Semitism reappeared in the late 19th century. In fact, it was in this period that Theodor *Herzl, a native of Vienna, reacted to the anti-Semitism shown in the *Dreyfus case, with his dream of a Jewish state. Another famous Austrian Jew was Sigmund *Freud.

One of the largest and most terrible of concentration camps, Mauthausen, was in Austria.

Stained glass window in the Leopoldschurch in Vienna, built in 1330. It depicts a disputation between Jews (wearing Jewish hats) and Christians.

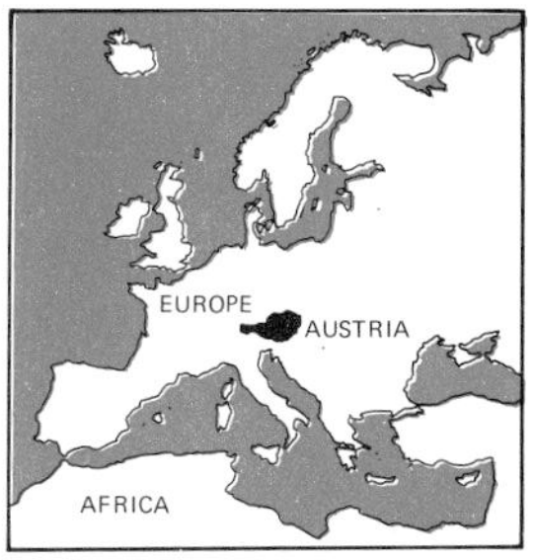

The number of Austrian Jewish victims of the Holocaust is estimated at 70,000. A large part in the campaigns to exterminate European Jewry was played by Austrian Nazis, including *Eichmann, Globocnik, and *Hitler himself.

After World War II, some Jews resettled in Austrian towns, the large majority, as in the past, in Vienna – but in 1968 nearly 65% of Austrian Jewry were aged 50 and over. Austria's payment of compensation to victims of Nazi aggression was considered inadequate, but relations between Austria and Israel were quite friendly; there was much trade between them and Austria's stand at the U.N. was favorable. Austria became a waystation for European Jewry on its way to Israel. However, its submission in 1973 to Arab terrorist demands to close the main Jewish transit center for Russian Jews on the way to Israel had a dampening effect on Austro-Israel relations.

Autographs of famous Jews.

Abraham ben Moses ben Maimon

Moses Isserles

Cyrus Adler

Samuel David Luzzatto

Shmuel Yosef Agnon

Rufus Isaacs

Adolphe Crémieux

Mayer Amschel Rothschild

Stephen S. Wise

Abraham Mapu

The first Jew to become chancellor of Austria was Bruno Kreisky. He joined the Socialist Workers Youth Association at the age of 15, and after the Fascist seizure of power in 1934, was active in the underground Socialist Party. Following his arrest in 1935, he spent nearly two years in prison, and after the Nazi Anschluss (annexation of Austria) in 1938, emigrated to Sweden. At the conclusion of World War II, Kreisky returned to Austria where he occupied a succession of important diplomatic and political positions, until in the general election of 1970 he became chancellor.

AUTOGRAPHS. After 30 years of collecting Hebrew manuscripts and manuscripts of Jewish content in other languages, the Hebrew writer, Avraham Sharon (Schwadron), succeeded in establishing a universal Jewish collection consisting of over 2,900 autographs of about 1,950 prominent personalities of Jewish origin. This collection approximately covers the period from 1480 to the present. In 1927 it was presented as a gift to the Jewish National and University Library in Jerusalem, which then proceeded to open an autograph and portrait section. The collection represents a valuable source for Jewish graphology, especially of the Hebrew script, and contains documents whose contents are of great significance for Jewish cultural history. Today the collection contains more than 12,000 autographs and 7,000 portraits.

The scientific value of a Jewish autograph collection is that it provides for the identification of manuscripts whose authors are unknown, as well as of forgeries. Special difficulties were encountered in locating the autographs of Jewish personalities of Eastern Europe, particularly those whose activities were restricted to the Jewish sphere. Very often people were reluctant to part with such autographs because they believed that a letter of a great rabbi or *ẓaddik* had the power to ward off evil, and often such a document would be buried with its owner. Autographs of the early Jewish socialists and revolutionaries in Eastern Europe are also very rare, as they were frequently destroyed, either out of fear of the police, or by the police itself. Older manuscripts originating in Eastern Europe, insofar as they have come to light, are usually in a poor condition. In the West, on the other hand, the systematic collection of autographs and the trade in them have tended to ensure their retention and proper preservation.

AUTOPSIES AND DISSECTION. Respect for the dead, and the utmost reverence for the human body after death are enjoined by both Jewish law and custom. Mutilation of the body, whether for anatomical dissection or for postmortem examination, would appear to violate the respect due to the dead, and is consequently to be forbidden. Reverence for the corpse must yield, however, to the superior value of life and its preservation. In fact, the duty of saving and maintaining life (see *Life and Afterlife) overrides all but three commandments of the Torah. Hence, the question of the permissibility of the dissection of human bodies for the study of medicine, and of autopsies for the purpose of establishing the cause of death and for the development of medical research involves these two principles. For while any tampering with the corpse is prohibited, it can be argued that as a result of dissections and autopsies the lives of others can be saved or prolonged.

In the Bible there seem to be two clear instances of the dissection of the body of a dead person: the embalming of Jacob and of his son Joseph (Genesis 50:2-3, 26). According to all evidence the process of embalming as practiced by the ancient Egyptians consisted of disemboweling the body and filling it with certain chemicals.

In the Talmud there are two references to the possibility of autopsies. It was not until the 18th century, however, when human bodies began to be used for medical research as a regular practice, that the permissibility of autopsies for medical research and saving lives became a practical question of *halakhah.* A query addressed from London to Ezekiel *Landau of Prague, inquired as to the possibility of performing an autopsy on the body of a Jew, in order to reveal the cause of death and thus find a cure for others suffering from the same disease. The questioner gave reasons for permitting this. Landau dismissed his arguments but conceded that, should there be at the time of death, in the same hospital, another patient suffering from the same symptoms, so that the autopsy could immediately help, it could be permitted on the grounds of *pikku'aḥ nefesh* (the saving of human life). Although limited, this was the first clear, recorded ruling permitting autopsies in the interest of the living, and all later discussions on the subject have used it as their starting point.

The problem became an acute and practical one with the establishment of the Medical School of the Hebrew University in Jerusalem. It was obvious that bodies would have to be made available for the study of anatomy and that the cause of medical research would necessitate autopsies. Chief Rabbi A.I. *Kook, usually liberal in his approach, entirely forbade the use of Jewish bodies for such purposes, but in 1944 his successor, Rabbi I.H. *Herzog reached an agreement with the Hadassah Hospital, permitting autopsies in the following cases: (1) When the civil law demanded it in cases of crime and accidental death; (2) To establish the cause of death when it was doubtful; (3) In order to save lives; and (4) In cases of hereditary disease. The authority to perform such autopsies was made conditional upon the signatures of three doctors. All organs dissected were to be handed over for burial after the necessary examinations had been performed. The agreement was the basis for the Law of Anatomy and Pathology passed by Israel's Knesset in 1953.

In 1965, following allegations of widespread abuse of the safeguards contained in the Law of Anatomy and Pathology, certain Orthodox circles in Israel agitated to have the law amended by reverting to the strictly limited permission given by Ezekiel Landau. A ruling to this effect was issued under the signatures of the two chief rabbis and the heads of yeshivot.

Although the objections that apply to autopsies also apply to dissection for the purpose of anatomical study, enough people bequeath their bodies for this purpose so that religious opposition has been confined largely to autopsies, despite the fact that the halakhic permission for such bequests is doubtful. Similarly most rabbinical authorities permit autopsies in the case of violent or accidental death or where crime is suspected. Most of those who oppose autopsies make an exception in the case of corneal transplants which restore sight to a blind person. In this specific instance one rabbi stated that the deceased would consider it an honor for his eye to be used for such a purpose. This permissibility of bone banks, and banks of other organs, is less likely in view of the prescription of Jewish law that all mortal remains must ultimately be buried.

AVOT (literally "Fathers") is the name of a tractate in the *Nezikin* section of the Mishnah (see *Talmud). It is commonly known as *Pirkei Avot,* "the Chapters of the Fathers" and in English as "the Ethics of the Fathers." The Fathers referred to are the great sages of the Mishnah period which ended at the beginning of the third century c.e. As a tractate it is quite different from all the other tractates since it is not occupied at all with ritual or legal matters but solely with the chain of tradition and ethical maxims.

Avot starts with the transmission of Torah (which presumably means both the written Torah and the Oral Law) from Moses down to the great masters of the Mishnah. This establishes the authenticity of what the sages taught and is followed by sayings of the *tannaim,* as the Mishnaic scholars were known. Each statement seems to be the philosophy in a nutshell of the particular rabbi who made it. The maxims cover a wealth of subjects varying from the purely religious to the social – the duty of man to God and of man to his fellow man. For example, regarding man's duty to God, Antigonos of Socho used to teach: "Be not like servants who minister to their master upon the condition of receiving a reward, but be like servants who minister to their master without the condition of receiving a reward; and let the fear of Heaven be upon you." Concerning man's duty to his fellow man, Shammai taught: "Say little and do much, and receive all men with a cheerful countenance." And this is the advice of Hillel, his contemporary: "In a place where there are no men, strive to be a man."

There are six chapters in *Avot*, but the last was not in the original Mishnah; it is an addition. The tractate is very well known since it has become customary among Ashkenazim to recite a chapter of it at the Sabbath afternoon service from the Sabbath after Passover until Rosh Ha-Shanah, thus reading it three times. The Sephardi custom is to recite a chapter on each of the six Sabbaths between Passover and Shavu'ot. Because of these weekly readings, *Avot* appears in most editions of the prayer book.

Rabbi Ḥayyim Joseph David Azulai (Ḥida), 18th century scholar and kabbalist.

AZULAI, ḤAYYIM JOSEPH DAVID (1724-1806). Few people become famous for one specialty and fewer still become expert in more than one. But Azulai utilized his many skills to distinguish himself in four areas. All were related to Jewish life, and each required that special talent that he possessed.

In an active life of more than 80 years, Azulai was a leading scholar of *halakhah*, Kabbalah and bibliography, and a representative of Jewish interests. Regarded by the Jewry of the Ottoman Empire and of Italy as the most learned man of his generation, he combined a religious and mystical yearning with an unending intellectual curiosity. In addition, he possessed a critical mind, an ability to write and an enormous capacity for hard work. (He is commonly known as "the Ḥida," an acronym made up of the Hebrew initials of his name.)

Ḥayyim Joseph David Azulai

Azulai was born in Jerusalem to a prominent family of rabbis and kabbalists. A restless man, he made many voyages abroad as a representative of communities in Ereẓ Israel. He collected money for their academies and their scholars, especially for Hebron and its yeshivah. Between 1753 and 1778 he travelled to Italy, Germany, Holland, France and England as their *shali'aḥ* or representative.

He won many friends and admirers in the places he visited, not only because of his concerned involvement in their communal activities, but also because of his dynamic personality and striking appearance.

In 1778 he settled in Leghorn, Italy, where every year he gave a scholarly talk. The streets were crowded with people who came to listen and many who just wanted a glimpse of him. He devoted his last years to writing, study and research, and to discussions with other scholars, Jewish and non-Jewish.

Many stories have been told of the wonders the versatile Azulai performed. Pilgrimages to his tomb in Leghorn were made until 1960, when his remains were moved to Jerusalem.

BA'AL SHEM TOV (Israel ben Eliezer, c. 1700-1760). The Ba'al Shem Tov, as Israel ben Eliezer is generally known, was the founder of the movement known as *Ḥasidism. Ba'al Shem Tov is a descriptive title which means the "Good Master of the Name" (for the "Master of the Good Name"), and the "Name" refers to the Name of God. Thus the bearer of the title was a person who was able to invoke the Name of God for the purpose of healing the sick or in other worthy causes. In the case of Israel ben Eliezer, the title is usually abbreviated to its initial letters and he is known as the Besht.

The Ba'al Shem Tov was born to poor and elderly parents in a small town in Podolia, which is a region in the Ukraine. He was orphaned as a child and later eked out a living as an assistant in a *ḥeder* and as a watchman at a synagogue. Constantly studying and preparing himself for his mission, he presented himself as a simpleton and ignoramus although a few people did become aware of his spiritual stature. In his 20s, Israel moved with his wife to the Carpathian Mountains where he worked first as a clay digger and later helped his wife to run an inn. According to ḥasidic tradition, he revealed himself as a healer on his 36th birthday. He immediately attracted a group of disciples. This was the beginning of Ḥasidism.

Although the few literary sources about the Besht were mainly composed after his death, and much of what we know about him comes from oral tradition, some aspects are undeniably authentic and stand out.

The Ba'al Shem Tov taught an unending love for people, particularly Jews. For him, learning and scholarship was not the sole criteria of piety but rather a love of God and joy in serving Him. He did not agree to the sterile, aristocratic scholarship which saw the unlearned as being an inferior type of human being. He believed that the common folk are just as precious in the eyes of God as the important people in the community. He drew a great deal from the *Kabbalah, the mystic teachings of Judaism, and particularly stressed the importance of *devekut,* true concentration in prayer.

The Besht's teachings had an electrifying effect on the Jewish masses who had suffered so much in the preceding years from pogroms and anti-Semitism. It gave them the lift they so much needed. As could be expected, the teachings hardly endeared him to the communal leaders who were also afraid of a new type of false messianism after the style of *Shabbetai Ẓevi. Thus a great deal of opposition arose but very many students flocked to him and these now became the leaders of Ḥasidism.

The Besht also taught the doctrine of the **ẓaddik* which later took on many different forms in the ḥasidic movement. This doctrine is that there are superior people whose spiritual qualities are greater than the normal and that these individuals can do a great deal – mainly by prayer – to help others. On the other hand, every man can commune with God even in the most humdrum activities of daily life if he performs those activities in the right frame of mind.

Israel ben Eliezer, the Ba'al Shem Tov, left an indelible effect on Judaism and Jewish life.

Israel Post Office stamp issued in 1960 to commemorate the bicentenary of the death of the Ba'al Shem Tov. The stamp pictures the *bet ha-midrash* of the Ba'al Shem Tov in Medzibezh, Podolia.

BABEL, TOWER OF. Most of you are probably familiar with the story of the world's first skyscraper, the Tower of Babel. The building of the tower is described in Genesis 11:1-9, and it is given as the reason for the existence of many languages and the dispersion of mankind over all the earth.

The Bible tells us how, when all men still spoke one language, it was decided to build "a city, and a tower with its top in the sky." The city was to be built in Shin'ar, later known as Babylonia, corresponding to modern-day Iraq. The purpose was to enable the people to make a name for themselves and avoid being scattered over the face of the earth. The unfinished tower was called Babel, because God

Israel ben Eliezer Ba'al Shem Tov

1

2

1. A 12th century mosaic of the Tower of Babel in the Palatine Chapel in Palermo.
2. An impression of the walled city of Babylon as it was in the seventh-sixth centuries b.c.e., the Neo-Babylonian period. On the left is the seven-storied temple of Marduk, and on the right is the palace complex.

mixed up (Hebrew *balal*) man's language.

Although the Bible makes it clear that building the city and the tower displeased God, nowhere does it state what exactly the sin was. Many of the talmudic rabbis hold that the tower was built for the purpose of idol worship. Some are of the opinion that the builders wanted to wage war against God. Some say they did not believe God's promise that there would be no more floods, and they built the tower to prevent the skies from caving in again.

According to some modern commentators, the building of the tower was an example of man's extreme pride in his own ability. The building became such an obsession that, according to the Midrash, when a builder fell off the tower to his death, the other builders paid no attention, but when a brick fell, they would cry: "When shall another come in its place?" According to this interpretation, every generation has its own Tower of Babel, when it begins to idolize its technology. The moral of the story is thus as applicable today as it was thousands of years ago.

BABI YAR is a ravine on the outskirts of *Kiev which has come to symbolize Jewish martyrdom at the hands of the Nazis in the Soviet Union. On September 29-30, 1941, according to an official German report, 33,771 Jews were machine-gunned there. At the end of 778 days of Nazi rule in Kiev, the ravine had become a mass grave for over 100,000 persons, the majority of whom were Jews. In spite of German efforts in August 1943 to erase all traces of the mass burial through massive incineration, the evidence could not be suppressed and after the war the Soviet public at large learned of the martyrdom. Preparations were made for a monument at Babi Yar as a memorial to the victims of Nazi genocide. But the project was allowed to lapse in the anti-Semitic campaign of the Soviet government.

Intellectuals, however, refused to be silent. Most impressive was the poem *Babi Yar* written by Yevgeni Yevtushenko. With its open attack upon anti-Semitism and its implied denunciation of those who rejected Jewish martyrdom, the poem exerted a profound impact on Soviet youth as well as upon world public opinion. Dmitri Shostakovich set the lines to music in his 13th Symphony, performed for the first time in December 1962.

In 1966, the Architects Club in Kiev held a public exhibit of more than 200 projects and some 30 large-scale detailed plans for a memorial to Babi Yar. Not one of the inscriptions in the proposed plans mentioned that most of the victims had been Jewish.

BABYLONIA. In West Asia, along the Euphrates River, where we today find Iraq, the ancient state Babylonia was once located. Akkadian scribes said that the name Babylonia came from *bāb-ilim,* the gate of the gods, but in Genesis we find that the name comes from the Hebrew root *balal,* which means to confuse. It was in Babylonia that man first revolted against God by building the Tower of *Babel, and from Ur of the Chaldees (a city in Babyonia) came Abraham, the first Jew.

From more than two thousand years before the start of the Common Era, the Babylonian Empire went through many changes of rulers and dynasties. In 612 b.c.e. *Nebuchadnezzar became the ruler of Babylonia and shortly afterwards, in 586 b.c.e., conquered Judea, destroying the Temple and exiling the Jews to Babylonia. These exiles formed a large Jewish community who yearned for their homeland; as we read in Psalm 137: "By the rivers of Babylon we sat and cried, remembering Zion . . . How shall we sing the Lord's song in a foreign land? If I forget thee, O Jerusalem, let my right hand forget her cunning."

In 538 b.c.e. King Cyrus of Persia conquered Babylonia and in 516 permitted the Jews to return to Palestine. Nevertheless many remained in Babylonia, and certain towns such as Nehardea and Maḥoza were populated entirely by Jews. Under the Persians, Jews attained positions of privilege and responsibility, for example *Ezra, who was a scribe for the Persian government, and *Nehemiah who was a cupbearer in the court. A council of elders governed the Jewish community, and an *exilarch *(resh galuta)* was appointed to be the king's representative.

By the beginning of the 3rd century, Babylonia had become the main center of Jewish studies. Academies of learning were founded by *Samuel at Nehardea, and by *Rav at Sura. Later, a great academy at Pumbedita replaced that of Nehardea. These academies produced many of Judaism's greatest sages, whose discussions constitute much of the Babylonian *Talmud. The Jews of Babylonia always kept in close contact with those still in Ereẓ Israel, and after the decline of the Palestinian academies, Babylonia became the spiritual center for all Jewry, and so remained until the 11th century.

Persecutions in the fifth century led to a Jewish revolt. In 468 half the Jewish population was slaughtered, synagogues were destroyed, and children forcibly delivered to the gentile priesthood. No wonder this year was referred to in the Talmud as "the year of the destruction of the world." Such persecutions continued until the Arab conquest of Babylonia in the 7th century, at which time the history of *Iraq began. **Babylon**, the capital city of ancient Babylonia, is called by Isaiah "the glory of kingdoms." Over the years the city was destroyed, rebuilt, then destroyed and rebuilt once again. When the Neo-Babylonian Empire was built at the expense of the Assyrian Empire, Babylon was made the capital of the new Empire, and underwent a vast program of public building and fortification. In excavations of Babylon, two palaces of King Nebuchadnezzar have been uncovered. One of them is assumed to be the location of the Hanging Gardens of Babylon, considered in ancient times to have been amongst the Seven Wonders of the World.

BADGE, JEWISH. It was in the Muslim lands that Jews were first forced to wear a distinctive sign. In the eighth century Caliph Omar II decreed that every non-Muslim was to wear a distinguishing mark. In ninth-century Sicily, for example, Christians had to mark their doors and their clothes with a swine made of cloth, while the Jews were compelled to affix a similar sign in the form of a donkey.

In medieval drawings from Christian countries, one can always tell which characters are Jews by the pointed hat, later known as the "Jewish hat."

1. A transport of women and children arrives at the concentration camp at Auschwitz. All are wearing the compulsory yellow star which the Nazis designated as a distinctive badge.
2. Hammurapi was the sixth king of Babylon and ruled the country between 1792 and 1750 b.c.e. During this time, he developed the code of Hammurapi, a code of law. The illustration shows him receiving the laws from the sun-god.

2

1

Disturbed by the fact that Jews were mixing too freely with non-Jews, the archbishops of the Fourth Lateran Council of 1215 compelled Jews to wear some distinguishing garment, in order to remove "the crime of such a sinful mixture."

In early thirteenth-century England, wealthy Jews and even entire communities paid to be freed from this "Badge of Shame," as it was sometimes called. In 1275, however, Edward I ordered that a piece of yellow taffeta in the shape of the Tablets of the Law, six fingers long and three broad, was to be worn above the heart by every Jew over the age of seven years. This sign can be seen in surviving caricatures and portraits of medieval English Jews.

Non-Jewish Frenchmen found their system more profitable. Anyone finding a Jew whose garment was unmarked, was rewarded by being given the garment. King Philip the Fair had the royal tax collectors sell the compulsory badges at a profit.

The Jews of Spain did not submit quietly to the insult of the "Badge of Shame." When in 1218 some of them threatened to leave the country in protest, Pope Honorius III abolished the regulation. When it was renewed, the King of Castile from 1263 punished disobedient Jews by a fine or a lashing. Interestingly, this king was known as Alfonso X the Wise.

In 14th-century Rome, informers were rewarded by being given half the fine payable by Jewish men who did not wear the compulsory red cape and Jewesses who did not wear the red apron. These informers were given added encouragement by local preachers.

Badges gradually disappeared throughout Europe in the course of the eighteenth century, though in the Papal States in Italy the rule was renewed as late as 1793. When the armies of the French Revolution entered Italy in 1796-97 and the law was finally abolished there too, it seemed to the world that the "Badge of Shame" was only an evil memory of the past. Indeed, it was to commemorate the yellow badge or hat that Theodor Herzl chose this color for the cover of the first Zionist periodical *Die Welt.*

In 1938, however, the evil memory was revived with a vengeance, when the Nazis compelled Jewish shopkeepers to display the words "Jewish business" in their windows. Nazi-occupied countries forced Jews to wear various badges, usually yellow, inscribed with *J* or *Jude* (meaning "Jew"), or with the Shield (Star) of David. This symbol had never been used in the Middle Ages for the Jewish Badge. These signs were also stamped on Jews' passports and ration cards.

When the Nazis occupied Holland, Dutch non-Jews, in order to show their sympathy with the Jewish citizens, wore a replica of the badge, which was inscribed: "Jews and non-Jews stand united in their struggle." In Denmark the badge was never introduced, because of the courageous resistance of King Christian X, who threatened to wear it himself. In other Nazi-occupied countries, a Jew faced the choice of concealing the sign and then being deported to a concentration camp, or of wearing the sign and becoming an easy prey to his enemies. The badge thus served the purpose for which it was designed (see also *Anti-Semitism).

BADHAN is the Hebrew word for the merrymaker or rhymester who entertained guests, especially at weddings. The Talmud mentions professional jesters who cheered the melancholy or who amused bride and groom. Jewish traveling singers, called *badhanim* or *leizanim* ("jesters") are mentioned in medieval rabbinic literature; they seem to have appeared as professional entertainers at weddings and at Hanukkah and Purim celebrations, much after the pattern of the medieval troubadours and ballad singers. The merrymaking of these *badhanim,* who were also the forerunners of Jewish theatrical art, consisted not only of folksongs and comic stories but also of skillful puns on scriptural verses and talmudical passages, which required a certain amount

1

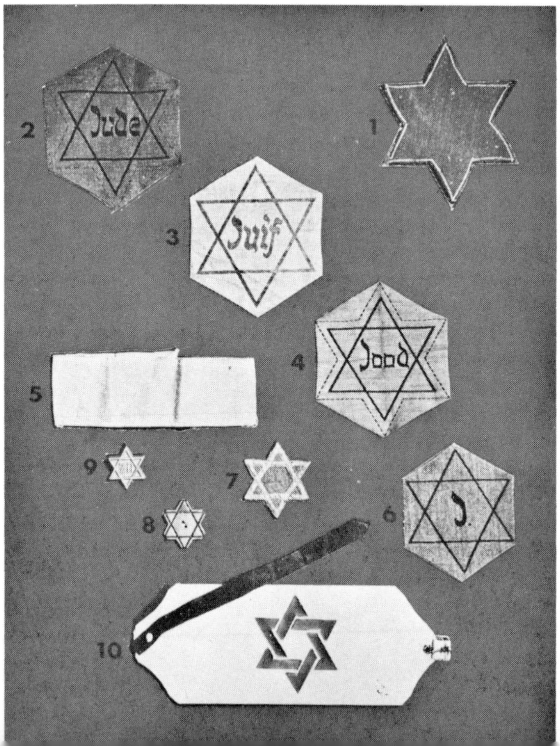

2

1. An "illegal" immigrant to Erez Israel from Europe. He is still wearing his badge.
2. Jewish badges decreed by the Nazis during their occupation of Europe during the Second World War:
1. Yellow star – worn in Lithuania, Hungary, part of Greece, part of Poland and Bulgaria; 2. black on yellow – worn in Germany, Alsace and Bohemia-Moravia;
3. black on yellow – worn in France; 4. black on yellow – worn in Holland; 5. yellow armband – worn in part of Greece, Serbia, Belgrade and Sofia; 6. black on yellow – worn in Belgium; 7. blue star on yellow background – worn in Slovakia; 8. black on yellow – worn in Bulgaria; 9. yellow star worn in Slovakia; 10. blue star on white armband worn in part of Poland, and in East and Upper Silesia.

of Jewish learning. As a result, the rabbinical authorities protested against the *badḥanim* who seemed to make jokes about scriptural verses and holy words. And the rabbis stated: "Happy the man who abstains from such."

In Eastern Europe the *badḥanim* acted as professional wedding jesters. The *Chmielnicki persecutions (1648-49), and the rabbinical opposition to unbridled merrymaking, even at weddings, led the *badḥanim* to introduce a new style of entertainment – the *forshpil* – in which the *badḥan* addressed the bride with a rhymed plea for her to repent before her wedding, while the women performed the ceremony of *bedeken,* i.e., covering the bride with the veil before proceeding to the *ḥuppah,* or marriage canopy. In the case of orphans, the *badḥan's* rhymes invoked the memory of the departed parents and injected a sad note. Later, at the wedding feast, the *badḥan* entertained the guests with music and with jests that contained personal references to the important guests and participants. In the course of time the literary style of the *badḥan* developed into a sort of Hebrew and Yiddish folk poetry. In more recent times, except in circles in Israel and the Diaspora where traditional European folkways are still preserved, the institution of the *badḥan* has been replaced by more modern forms of entertainment.

BAGHDAD. From 1947 to 1951 the Jewish population of Baghdad, the capital of Iraq, dropped from 77,000 to 5,000. By 1968 the population had been further reduced to 2,000 Jews. A city that for 2,500 years was a center of Jewish learning and life is now recognized only as a threat to Jews.

Baghdad became the largest Jewish community in *Babylonia prior to 1,000 C.E. It served also as the seat of the *exilarch, the head of the Jewish community outside Ereẓ Israel. The great yeshivot of Pumbedita and Sura had moved to Baghdad in the 9th century; when *Benjamin of Tudela visited in 1170, he noted a population of 40,000 Jews, 28 synagogues and ten yeshivot.

The Muslims controlled Baghdad prior to the 9th century. In the 13th century the Mongols gained control and permitted the Jews more freedom than the Muslims had done. In the early 17th century Pedro Teixeria, a Portuguese Marrano explorer, found 25,000 houses in Baghdad, 250 of them belonging to Jews. The Turks took control in 1638, and many restrictions which had been imposed by the Persians were removed. In the 19th century the Turkish rule became worse for the Jews. During British control (1917-1929), the situation changed for the better, but with an independent Arab Iraq, life for Jews in Baghdad worsened sharply, and when Israel was established, the overwhelming majority of Baghdad's Jews immigrated there.

BAHA'I. Originating out of the mystic Persian Bābī movement, Bahā'īsm is a world religion centered in Israel and stressing truth, equality and unity of all peoples.

The first Bāb (person who is a "gate" to divine truth) was the Persian Sayyid Ali Muhammed, the founder of the Bābī sect. However, when he declared himself Bāb, he was accused of heresy, arrested and shot in 1850. His successor, Bahā'Allah, founder of the newer Bahā'ī faith, came to Israel in 1868 where he turned the faith into a universal religion. His tomb near Acre is a shrine regarded by the Bahā'īs as the holiest place in the world. His son moved to Haifa where he erected the golden-domed Bahā'ī Temple on Mount Carmel, and arranged to have the body of Sayyid Ali Muhammed, the first Bāb, buried there.

Bahā'īs reside all over the world, in as many as 11,000 localities. However, the spiritual and administrative center of the Bahā'ī World Faith is in the Universal House of Justice in Haifa, which is directed by nine members known as the Hands of the Cause.

This rally held in Israel in January, 1969, was in protest against the hanging of nine Jews on charges of espionage in Baghdad.

Bahā'īsm is favorably disposed to Zionism since the Jewish return to Israel was foretold in the writings of Bahā'Allah. Accordingly, in June 1948, their leader wrote to Ben-Gurion expressing loyalty and best wishes to the State of Israel.

BAK, ISRAEL AND NISAN. Israel Bak (1797-1874) and his son Nisan played an important part in the cultural and religious life of the Jews of 19th century Palestine. They came from Berdichev, in the Ukraine, in 1831 and settled in Safed, in northern Ereẓ Israel where they opened a printing press. They were renewing the tradition of the People of the Book, since Hebrew books had not been printed in Ereẓ Israel for two centuries. Israel Bak also began to work the land, and his was the first Jewish farm in Palestine in modern times.

The Baks' press was destroyed during the peasant uprising against Muhammad Ali in 1834, and again when the Druze revolted in 1838. The Bak family moved to Jerusalem where in 1841 they established the first Jewish printing press. For 22 years it was the only one in Jerusalem. They printed 130 books, a significant cultural contribution, and edited and published *Ḥavaẓẓelet* (1863), the second Hebrew newspaper in Ereẓ Israel.

Nisan Bak (1815-1889) assisted and later succeeded his father both as printer and as leader of the ḥasidic community. As a result of their efforts, a central synagogue for Ḥasidim, Tiferet Israel, was built in the Old City of Jerusalem. It became known as "Nisan Bak's Synagogue." The Arab Legion destroyed it in 1948 during the *War of Independence. The facade with its intricate stone carving can still be seen.

Nisan Bak sold the press in 1883, and was able to devote himself entirely to community affairs. He initiated several building projects in Jerusalem, one bearing his name – Battei Nisan Bak. He helped influence the Turkish government to modify its decrees against the Jewish settlement in Palestine, and was a pioneer of the *Haskalah in Jerusalem. With others, Nisan founded the Ezrat Niddaḥim Society in 1884 which established the Yemenite quarter in Jerusalem and fought the missionary movement.

BALAAM, a gentile soothsayer/magician from Aram, was understandably shocked to hear his donkey talking. Balak, King of Moab, was equally shocked when Balaam, ordered to curse the Children of Israel, blessed them instead (Numbers 22-24).

The Children of Israel were camped in Moab on their way from Egypt to the Promised Land. Worried by their presence, Balak summoned Balaam to curse them. God told Balaam not to go, but Balak again sent for him. After obtaining God's permission, Balaam set out for Moab on his donkey. The donkey saw an angel blocking the way before Balaam did, and stood still. Only after the donkey complained to her master for hitting her were Balaam's eyes opened, and he too saw the angel. He then realized that he had no choice but to do and say exactly what God wanted.

1

2

1. The Bahā'ī Temple in Williamette, Illinois.
2. "Nisan Bak's Synagogue" or the Tiferet Israel synagogue in the Old City of Jerusalem. It was dedicated in 1865.

Therefore, twice when he stood on a lofty summit overlooking the camp of the People of Israel in the plain below, instead of the curse that Balak expected, Balaam blessed the nation, predicting its victory over Edom and Moab. "Third time lucky," thought Balak, and so it was – but for Israel, not Moab. Balaam, seeing Israel's tents arranged in such a way that each family was assured of its privacy, praised the nation he had come to curse, with the words: "How goodly are thy tents, O Jacob, thy dwelling places, O Israel! "

Balaam then returned home, and was eventually slain in the battle between Israel and Midian.

BALFOUR, ARTHUR JAMES, EARL OF (1848-1930). Lord Balfour, who was a British statesman, first began to take an interest in the Jewish question in 1902-1903, when Theodor *Herzl spoke with Joseph Chamberlain, the British colonial secretary and with Lord Lansdowne, the foreign secretary, about a homeland for the Jews. Lord Balfour was prime minister at that time.

He listened sympathetically to both Theodor Herzl and Chaim *Weizmann. The latter met Balfour in 1906, and spoke to him about the need to build a Jewish homeland on the soil of what was then Palestine. Lord Balfour's interest in Zionism grew more intense during World War I, when he became foreign secretary.

The meetings with Weizmann eventually led to the *Balfour Declaration, which he signed in 1917. This was England's declaration of approval that "a national home for the Jewish people" be built in Palestine. In 1925 Balfour accepted an invitation to open the Hebrew University on Mount Scopus in Jerusalem. He made the then difficult journey to Jerusalem at the age of 77, in the company of his niece and her husband, who served as Balfour's private secretary. Another niece, Blanche *Dugdale, worked closely with Chaim Weizmann.

Lord Balfour's *Speeches on Zionism* (1928) was translated into Hebrew. Jerusalem, Haifa, and Tel Aviv have streets named after him. There is also a Balfour Forest at Ginnegar and a moshav, Balfouriyyah, which was founded in 1922 in the Jezreel Valley in Israel.

BALFOUR DECLARATION, a letter dated November 2, 1917, in which the British government declared that it would support the desire of the Zionist movement "for the establishment in Palestine of a national home for the Jewish people." The letter was addressed to Lord Rothschild by Arthur James Balfour, who was then the British foreign secretary.

Palestine at the time was part of the Ottoman (Turkish) Empire. World War I was in progress, and Turkey had joined Britain's enemies. Chaim *Weizmann, an important figure in the World Zionist Movement and later Israel's first president, was convinced that Great Britain and the Zionists were natural allies. In the first place, both wanted to see Palestine separated from the Turkish Empire. Secondly, it had been suggested that if Britain were to promise to help the Zionists after the war, this would rally the support of world Jewry behind Britain instead of France, which was also interested in having an influence in Palestine after the War. And if Britain did not act promptly, the Germans might even make such a declaration first.

Weizmann and other Zionist leaders such as Nahum Sokolow worked hard to persuade senior British cabinet ministers that the British government should make such a declaration. Just at that time, the government entrusted Weizmann with a particularly challenging task in chemical research on the production of acetone, which was vital for the British

1

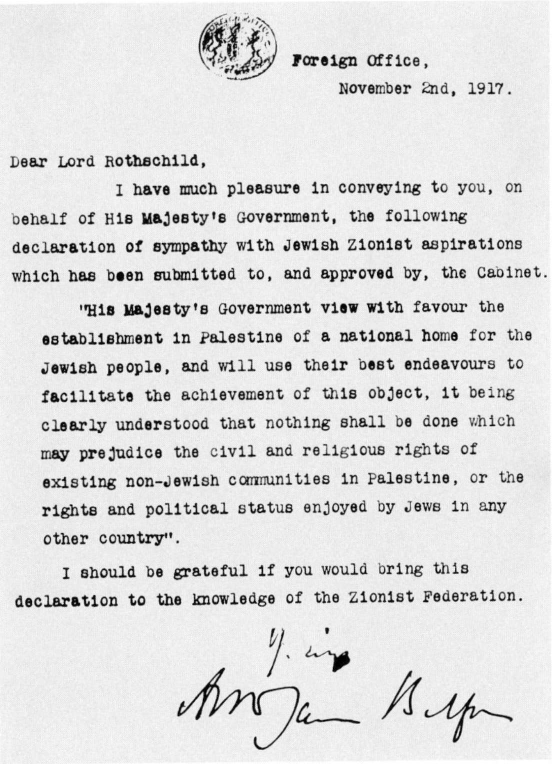

Foreign Office,
November 2nd, 1917.

Dear Lord Rothschild,

I have much pleasure in conveying to you, on behalf of His Majesty's Government, the following declaration of sympathy with Jewish Zionist aspirations which has been submitted to, and approved by, the Cabinet.

"His Majesty's Government view with favour the establishment in Palestine of a national home for the Jewish people, and will use their best endeavours to facilitate the achievement of this object, it being clearly understood that nothing shall be done which may prejudice the civil and religious rights of existing non-Jewish communities in Palestine, or the rights and political status enjoyed by Jews in any other country".

I should be grateful if you would bring this declaration to the knowledge of the Zionist Federation.

Y. sincerely
Arthur James Balfour

1. The Balfour Declaration, now in the British Museum in London.
2. 3. Back and front of a medal made by Paul Vincze and issued by the Government of Israel in 1967 to commemorate the Jubilee of the Balfour Declaration.

2

3

war effort. Through his success in this, Weizmann came in further contact with Lloyd George (minister of munitions and later prime minister) and with Balfour (first lord of the admiralty, then foreign secretary). His services were much appreciated. Weizmann, however, requested nothing for himself, but something for his people.

The very idea of a declaration of this nature was violently opposed by certain members of the Board of Deputies of British Jews and the Anglo-Jewish Association, but most especially by Edwin Montagu, a Jewish member of the government. Under their influence the warm goodwill of the intended declaration was considerably toned down. Some of these Jews were afraid that their loyalty to England would be doubted. King George V himself certainly did not think so. Indeed, he personally assured Weizmann that he was pleased his government could help bring about the Bible's promise of Israel's return to its ancestral land.

News of Balfour's letter brought joy to Jewish communities throughout the world. Copies of the Declaration were showered from airplanes over Jewish townships in Germany, Austria and Poland, and on the shores of the Black Sea. 200,000 Jews rallied at Odessa, Russia, bearing banners inscribed "Land and Freedom in Ereẓ Israel!" (Their enthusiasm was soon silenced when the Communists came to power in the same year.) The Declaration was compared to the Persian King Cyrus' permission to the exiled Jewish captives in the sixth century b.c.e. to return to Jerusalem to rebuild the Temple.

These high hopes, however, were soon shattered. The bitter struggle to have the British government honor its promises as set out in the Balfour Declaration, instead of obstructing the homecoming of Jewish refugees from lands of war and persecution, lasted throughout the entire 30 years of British rule in Palestine, known as the British Mandate.

BALTIMORE, the largest city in the state of Maryland, U.S., had 106,000 Jews living there in 1968. Founded in 1729, Baltimore began to attract Jewish settlers in large numbers only by the beginning of the 19th century.

The first Jewish settlers, who were of German and Dutch origin, were mainly poor peddlers and small storekeepers. Many of them eventually became leading merchants and clothing manufacturers, and today their descendants are mostly professionals. The second group of settlers were of East European origin, and they were somewhat disliked by the original German-Jewish settlers. Despite this, the East European immigrants continued to come and the number of Jews in Baltimore increased from about 10,000 in 1880 to about 65,000 in 1924. They worked in garment sweatshops that were owned by the well-to-do German Jews, and they lived in overcrowded houses in East Baltimore, Eventually the East European migrants also opened businesses of their own.

The first synagogue was established in 1830 by German and Dutch Jews. By 1860, several more had been founded to serve the growing community of 8,000 and with the influx of the East European settlers, many more synagogues were built. By 1960 there were 50 synagogues.

Until 1921, the German and East European Jews had two separate charity organizations. In 1921 the two combined into the Associated Jewish Charities, which in the 1960s was also concerned with recreational and educational activities.

The first Hebrew school, which opened in 1842, was directed by a synagogue. Today, over 90% of

Impressive Oheb Shalom synagogue in Baltimore, Maryland.

Jewish school children in Baltimore attend Jewish schools. There are several afternoon and Sunday schools, three Jewish day schools (which over 15% of Jewish children of school age attend) and two colleges: the Baltimore Hebrew College and the New Israel Rabbinical College.

Baltimore is an important center of Zionist activity, and funds were collected there for Palestine as early as 1847. Henrietta *Szold, the founder of Hadassah and the Youth Aliyah movement, and a native Baltimorean, began her Zionist activities there. The largest single Jewish organization is Hadassah, with over 6,300 members

BANISHMENT is a form of punishment which was widely imposed throughout the ancient world. India, the Greek cities, the Roman republic, and the Teutonic peoples all used this practice to rid themselves of undesirables, ranging from criminals to political agitators who threatened the safety of the state and the authority of its rulers. Bereft of his property and prohibited from ever returning home, the victim was reduced to the level of an outcast, a permanent stranger or wanderer in foreign lands.

Bible Times. In ancient Israel, too, banishment was not unknown, although it appears almost exclusively as a form of divine punishment. Adam was expelled from the Garden of Eden and Cain was doomed to be a wanderer, hidden from the presence of God. Two notable cases in the Bible are the banishment by Solomon of Abiathar the high priest to his family estate in Anathoth, and the banishment of *Amos from the Northern Kingdom of Israel. Collective banishment, or exile, was considered the ultimate punishment that could be meted out to the entire people for acts of defiance against God. The only form of banishment still in existence in biblical society was that imposed on a man guilty of manslaughter or involuntary homicide, for whom *Cities of Refuge were provided. It has been conjectured that banishment was not otherwise sanctioned as a punishment because residence abroad was viewed as something that cut the victim off entirely from God and even forced him to worship idols. For this reason too, exile was dreaded and deemed to have horrendous consequences.

Second Temple and Talmud Periods. Banishment was resorted to by the Romans as part of their repressive policies. Thus Archelaus the son of Herod I was banished by the Romans to Vienne in Gaul and probably remained there until he died. The *Pharisees seem also to have exercised this power. Josephus states that when they were in power they banished and brought back whomsoever they chose. The gravity of the punishment was that victims were also considered banished from the Divine Presence. On the verse, "For they have driven me out this day I should not cleave to the inheritance of the Lord," the Talmud comments that "he who lives outside the Land of Israel is regarded as worshiping idols," and this sentiment is reflected in the words of the *Musaf* prayer for festivals: "But on account of our sins we were banished from our land and removed far from our country, and we are unable to appear and prostrate ourselves before Thee and to fulfill our obligations."

Middle Ages to 18th Century. In the Middle Ages banishment continued to be one of the punishments imposed on offenders in communities having a measure of *self-government. Hence it was imposed most frequently in Spain and Poland and Lithuania, although also occasionally elsewhere. A distinction was drawn between banishment of the offender from the city or the realm, as between banishment for a limited period and for life. The Spanish kingdoms, especially at the height of Jewish autonomy in the 13th century, recognized the right of the communal organizations to banish recalcitrants or exclude new members. James I of Aragon (1213-76) gave the communities the right to punish offenders by fine, ban, flagellation, or expulsion. Privileges accorded to the Barcelona community in 1241 and 1272 empowered the communal elders "to eject or expel [recalcitrant members] from the Jewish quarter or the entire city." A similar ordinance for Calatayud Jewry empowered the community in 1229 to expel two individuals of bad repute. In the 1280s the community of Alagon banished six butchers from the city for four years and excommunicated all members who ate meat purchased from them. Offenses for which banishment was imposed included murder for which there was only one witness, or when no witness was available but where hearsay was convincing, and attack on a victim who dies after a lapse of a certain time. In Spain in particular banishment was meted out to informers. Rabbi Menaḥem of Merseburg (early 14th century) banished a man for two or three years for viciously beating his wife. Prostitution and adultery were punished by life banishment by the communal regulations of Prague of 1612. Forfeiture of domiciliary rights throughout

Lithuania was applied by the Council of Lithuania to thieves, receivers, and forgers, and could be broadened also to any persons engaged in suspicious or prohibited dealings, infringing ethics, or disturbing the peace of the community. Since the whole community was liable to make good a claim by a gentile for money he had lent to a defaulting Jewish debor, in Lithuania the Jew wishing to borrow from a gentile had first to obtain permission from the *av bet din.* A borrower who failed to do so could be banished, and his right of domicile forfeited. The Lithuanian Council also withdrew the right of domicile from and imposed banishment on a person provoking a gentile by quarrels or blows. Banishment was frequently applied in the Sephardi community of Hamburg, its governing body being empowered by the Hamburg senate to expel from the community any of its members infringing morals or engaged in dishonest business dealings, among other offenses. The offender thus sentenced was served with a writ from the beadle. If he proved unable to travel for lack of funds, the community lent his relatives money to defray the expenses of the journey. Sometimes the offender was sent abroad, mainly to Amsterdam, and if his conduct subsequently improved was permitted to return. For more information see also *Self-government.

BANKING AND BANKERS. Economic life in ancient times was mainly based on agriculture. Although money was occasionally used, barter was the common form of commercial activity. In such an agrarian system, lending was part of the assistance a man owed his neighbor and thus the Bible absolutely prohibits taking or giving interest on loans. For more information about this see *Moneylending and Usury.

With the development of the economy of ancient Israel, there was a corresponding growth in the need for credit and for a system of banking. In ancient Babylonia which was in a sense the center of the civilized world, there was a highly developed system of banking, and in their exile there the Jews came into contact with it. In the Talmud there is ample evidence that banking was practiced and methods were invented to enable merchants to do business without contravening the biblical laws against usury.

From the late eighth century, with the rapid development of city life and commerce in the

1

2

1. Monetary scrip issued by the anti-Zionist religious Neturei Karta sect of Jerusalem to avoid the use of Israel currency, c. 1948.
2. Bank note issued by Hart's Bank, run by the Hart family in Trois Rivieres, Canada in the 19th century. They remained active in Jewish affairs while amassing a fortune and playing an important role in Canadian economic development.

caliphate of Baghdad and the transition of many Jews from agricultural village life to the cities, some upper-class Jews entered the banking business. In medieval Europe the Christian Church did not want Christians to engage in moneylending and also limited the occupations that Jews were allowed to follow. The result was that a number of Jews were forced into banking. Another factor was that because of persecutions and expulsions Jews were afraid of accumulating possessions that could not be easily transported, and money was the most portable.

The position of *Court Jew also involved a great deal of banking; in fact the most important function of the Court Jew was to provide adequate credit for his ruler. Thus, throughout the Middle Ages, Jews can be said to have been active in banking, although some countries in some periods forbade Jews to engage in it, in order to leave the Christian bankers without competition.

Modern Jewish banking begins in the 19th century with the rise of the House of *Rothschild. Originally based in Frankfort, the Rothschild banks spread to Vienna, Naples, Paris and London: it was Rothschild credit which "bought" the Suez canal for England. Even until recent times, their banks did not operate on Saturdays. Other Jewish banks were active in Europe and the United States at the beginning of the century. However, most of these banks were merchant banks and not the ordinary kind of banks where people have checking accounts. In this latter field Jews have hardly been active at all, except in the State of Israel where all the regular banks are Jewish.

BARAZANI, ASENATH (1590?-1670?). There have been many great women in Jewish history. In biblical times Sarah, Rebekah, Rachel, Leah, Miriam, Deborah, and Ruth all played important roles and in Talmud times Rabbi *Akiva's wife Rachel, and Rabbi *Meir's wife Beruryah were outstanding for their self-sacrifice and understanding. Asenath Barazani, scholar, community leader and yeshivah head is another of the great women of history.

Her father Samuel, a distinguished scholar and leader of Kurdistan Jewry, was considered a saint by many of his community. He raised his daughter in an atmosphere of learning. Asenath wrote of her upbringing: "Never in my life did I step outside my home. I was the daughter of the king of Israel . . . I was raised by scholars; I was pampered by my late father. He taught me no art or craft other than heavenly matters . . . . ".

When her husband Jacob died, Asenath was well prepared to succeed him as chief teacher of Torah in Kurdistan. An expert in Jewish literature, she headed the Mosul yeshivah which attracted students from many communities. As yeshivah head she was a community leader, well respected for her work as well as for her opinions. The rabbis of the time referred to her with great respect and called her *"tanna'it"* (lady *tanna*), thus esteeming her as a talmudic authority. Tales were told of her greatness and the miracles she performed. She is also said to have studied Kabbalah and to have written a commentary on the Book of Proverbs. Her descendants continued the tradition of learning and community leadership.

BARCELONA, principal port and commercial center of north-eastern Spain, was one of the oldest Jewish communities in Spain. Ninth, tenth and 11th century references are found to Jewish affairs and legal rights.

The 11th century Jews were artisans and merchants. Gradually they entered the service of the Barcelonian counts and, by the 12th century, served as financiers, advisers, and diplomats. But Christian anti-Jewish propaganda grew in Barcelona and, in 1263, a public disputation was held in which Naḥmanides was forced to confront the apostate Pablo Christiani before James I of Aragon. For more information on this see *Disputations and *Naḥmanides.

Forced to turn to commerce and moneylending, the Barcelona Jews obtained from James a constitution granting them autonomy in religious, social, and monetary affairs. Foremost in Spain in scholarship, wealth and esteem, their 1327 constitution enlarged their jurisdiction to the entire northeastern region.

Restriction of Jewish trade, the 1348 plague losses, and Christian persecutions in 1393 slowly destroyed the Barcelona Jewish community during the 14th and 15th centuries. Only the converted Jews (*Marranos) remained and enjoyed prosperity. The 1486 introduction of the *Inquisition by Ferdinand doomed even these.

Moroccan and Turkish Jews resettled in Barcelona in the 20th century. Greeks, Poles and Rumanians followed after World War II, and in 1933, German immigration began. By 1968, the community numbered 3,000 and was the best organized in Spain with a community center, talmud torah, old age home and youth camps. Franco's meeting in 1965 with the leaders of the Barcelona Jewish community was the first meeting between a Spanish head of state and Jewish leaders since 1492.

BAR GIORA, SIMEON, was one of the heroes of a Jewish revolt against the Romans (66-70 c.e.). That was the revolt which resulted in the destruction of the Second Temple. He was famous for his daring and outstanding bravery and the Romans thought he was the most important Jewish leader in that war. First

Detail from the *Barcelona Haggadah,* hand-drawn in the 14th century. It is assumed to have originated in Barcelona because the coat of arms of that city appears in various places throughout the book.

becoming famous in the battle of Beth Horon, when the Roman governor Cestius Gallus (66 c.e.) was routed, he became one of the leaders of the war party. He ravaged Idumea, captured Hebron and advanced on Jerusalem.

The war party was opposed by the Zealot party, which was led by John of Giscala, the rival of Bar Giora. John of Giscala terrorized Jerusalem, until its citizens turned to Bar Giora and let him into the city. The two men and their factions fought each other until the very arrival of Titus, with the Roman army, at the city walls. Bar Giora fought bravely against the Romans but Jewish military strength had been undermined by the previous battles among the Jews themselves. Those battles had also destroyed the stores of food which would have enabled the people to bear a long siege.

Because of the disunity among the Jews and the lack of supplies, the Romans were finally able to capture Jerusalem. Simeon tried to escape through an underground tunnel, but found that there was no way out. So, dressed in white and covered with a purple cloak, he appeared suddenly in front of the Roman soldiers. Awestruck, the soldiers summoned their general who had Bar Giora bound and taken to Rome. There he was led in chains in the triumphal march of Vespasian and Titus, and then executed. It is possible that many of his men had thought that Simeon Bar Giora was the messiah, so greatly was he admired.

1. Meir Bar-Ilan, central figure in the Zionist religious movement.
2. Library of Bar-Ilan University, Ramat Gan.

1

BAR-ILAN, MEIR (1880-1949), leader of religious Zionism. Bar-Ilan was born in *Volozhin, Russia, the son of Rabbi Naphtali Ẓevi Judah Berlin, who was the head of the famous yeshivah there. Meir later Hebraized his name. As a young man he joined the *Mizrachi movement, representing it at the Seventh Zionist Congress (1905) at which, unlike the majority of Mizrachi delegates, he voted against the *Uganda Scheme. In 1911 he was appointed secretary of the world Mizrachi movement, working in Berlin; it was he who coined the Mizrachi slogan *"Ereẓ Yisrael le-am Yisrael al pi Torat Yisrael"* ("The land of Israel for the people of Israel according to the Torah of Israel"). He moved to the United States in 1915, served as president of the U.S. Mizrachi, and from 1925 was a member of the Board of Directors of the *Jewish National Fund. In 1926 Bar-Ilan settled in Jerusalem where he played a leading role in the life of the Jewish community. He was a leading opponent of the Palestine partition plan in 1937, and of the British White Paper of 1939, and advocated civil disobedience and complete noncooperation of the Jewish population with the British authorities. After the establishment of the State of Israel, he organized a committee of scholars to examine the legal problems of the new state in the light of Jewish law. He also founded an institute for the publication of a new complete edition of the Talmud. Bar-Ilan University near Tel Aviv, founded by the American Mizrachi movement, is named in his honor, as is the Meir Forest in the Hebron hills, and the moshav Bet Meir near Jerusalem.

His older brother, Ḥayyim Berlin (1832-1912) was also a famous rabbi. He served in several Russian towns and in 1906 settled in Jerusalem where he was appointed Chief Rabbi in 1909. A yeshivah in New York is named after him.

2

BAR KOKHBA. Sixty years after the destruction of the Second Temple (132-135 c.e.), the Romans still occupied Palestine and oppressed the Jews. It seemed useless for tiny Israel to revolt against the mighty Roman Empire, but led by one astonishing man, Simeon Bar Kokhba, it did. Israel not only revolted, but gained a series of stunning victories, to the point where the huge Roman army was completely routed and driven out of the country. Bar Kokhba became the head of the Jewish State, with the title of Nasi – Prince.

He was a stern man, strong of body, mind and will. He had the force necessary to unite and inspire the nation in its supreme effort to gain independence and rebuild the Temple. So impressive was he, that Rabbi Akiva, the greatest sage of his day, acclaimed

Bar Kokhba as the Messiah. But although Jerusalem was again in Jewish hands, there was no time to rebuild the Temple or refortify the city. Bar Kokhba was busy recruiting his army and training his soldiers. He knew that the Romans would return with the strength of the whole Roman Empire behind them. Bar Kokhba selected a corps of elite soldiers, each one of whom had to prove his bravery by cutting off a finger. When the rabbis objected to this self-mutilation, the test of strength was changed; each man had to uproot a cedar tree while riding past it. Bar Kokhba was so self-confident that he became arrogant even to the extent that when he went to battle he asked God neither to help nor hinder, but let things take their normal course. The Roman Emperor, Hadrian, brought Julius Severus, the leading Roman general of his day, all the way from Britain to take command of the campaign. Legions from all parts of the Roman empire were sent to put down one of the fiercest revolts the empire had yet experienced. Severus did not fight pitched battles with the Jews, but a drawn-out war of attrition, gradually taking town after town and fortress after fortress until he succeeded in encircling Bar Kokhba and besieging him in the fortress town of Bethar which guards the western approaches to Jerusalem. Bethar fell after a long siege.

The rabbis relate that Bethar was impregnable and was taken by treachery. In Bethar there lived a holy man, Eleazar of Modi'in. A Samaritan found his way into the besieged city and whispered in the saintly man's ear. The populace, suspicious of the Samaritan's actions, took Eleazar to Bar Kokhba who angrily wanted to know what the Samaritan had told him. When Eleazar did not reply, Bar Kokhba became impatient and pushed him away. Eleazar fell and died. Immediately thereafter the city was taken and a terrible massacre ensued. Tradition has it that the blood flowed into the valley and thence to the sea. Bethar fell on the ninth of Av, the same date as the destruction of the First and Second Temples. Bar Kokhba himself, it is related, did not die by human hands. The Romans found his body strangled by a huge serpent. The Roman victory had been won at tremendous cost. So many Romans died that when Hadrian informed the Senate of the victory over the Jews, he omitted the customary salutation "I and my army are well."

The name Bar Kokhba, which means "son of a star" is a clear reference to the Messiah. The Jews saw him as the symbol of the new age, who would free them of the foreign yoke and herald the Kingdom of God and the rebuilt Temple. But when he was defeated they called him Bar Koziva – "son of lies." His real name has recently been found in letters discovered in caves on the shore of the Dead Sea. Here he is called Simeon Bar Koseva, Nasi of Israel. The letters also prove that the revolt lasted some four years, a mighty effort by a tiny nation against the then ruler of the world.

Looking out from one of the caves near the Dead Sea, where excavations recently uncovered letters and implements from the time of the Bar Kokhba revolt.

BAR-LEV, HAIM (1924-   ), rose from the rank of private to become eighth chief of staff of the Israel Defense Forces.

Bar-Lev arrived in Palestine from Yugoslavia in 1939. In 1942 he completed the course at the Mikveh Israel agricultural school, and began his military career. During the struggle against the British *Mandate regime, he served with the underground commandos, the *Palmaḥ, and was in charge of blowing up the Allenby Bridge over the Jordan river near Jericho. During the *War of Independence (1948-49), though only 25, he served successively as commander of the Eighth Battalion in Negev Brigade, commander of a mechanized battalion, and brigade operations officer.

In 1956, after attending Senior Officers' School in England, Bar-Lev became director of training at General Headquarters. He led an armored brigade in the *Sinai Campaign of 1956, and was commanding officer of the Armored Corps from 1957-61. Bar-Lev studied administration and economics at Columbia University in New York, and continued his studies in Paris in 1966. However, he was recalled a year later

1

1. General Haim Bar-Lev, eighth chief of staff of the Israel Defense Forces. In 1972 he was appointed Minister for Commerce and Industry.
2. Bar mitzvah boy praying at the Western Wall in Jerusalem. He is wearing a *tallit* (prayer shawl) and strapped to his head and left arm are *tefillin.*

and appointed deputy chief of staff just before the *Six-Day War (1967). On January 1, 1968, he became chief of staff.

Following his retirement from the army, Bar-Lev joined the Cabinet in 1972 as Minister of Commerce. He was again recalled to active duty during the *Yom Kippur War (1973) to become special adviser to the Chief of Staff, David Elazar.

BAR MITZVAH, BAT MITZVAH. Bar Mitzvah, meaning "son of the commandment," and bat mitzvah, meaning "daughter of the commandment," is the name given to the stage when a boy or girl reaches legal maturity as a Jew. The boy receives this status at the age of 13 years plus one day; the girl at 12 years plus one day.

Upon reaching this age a Jew must keep all the commandments and is considered an adult. The father of the bar mitzvah is no longer responsible for the child's deeds. He and she are now considered old enough to keep a fast day, to be responsible for any vow that they might make, and to exercise self-control. Since Jewish children are educated to keep the *mitzvot* even before bar mitzvah, the most visible sign of that stage for a boy is the tefillin he then puts on every day, the fact that he is counted to make up the *minyan* required for prayer, and the fact that he can ⅽe called to the Torah.

The bar mitzvah is called up to read the Torah in the synagogue on the first Sabbath after his 13th birthday according to the Jewish calendar. In Germany, those boys who could, and had pleasant voices, conducted parts or all of the service. In some communities the boy reads the whole portion of the Torah for that week but in most he is called to *maftir* and reads the *haftarah.*

On a Sabbath when a bar mitzvah is celebrated, the morning service in synagogue has a more festive air. Members of the boy's family are also called to the Torah reading, and a special sermon is delivered by the rabbi, stressing the boy's new responsibility and privileges. After that the boy is given a gift – usually a prayer book – by the community. A festive meal is usually held and the bar mitzvah boy gives a speech.

Bat mitzvah celebrations were introduced in France and Italy, and adopted in other countries. In Israel, the girl's father and brothers are called to the Torah, a special sermon is

2

preached, and the girl is presented with a gift, – usually a prayer book. In some congregations a collective bat mitzvah is held.

BARON, SALO (1895-   ), historian, was born in Galicia and taken to Vienna early in World War I. He studied at the university there and was ordained by the Jewish Theological Seminary in Vienna in 1920. Baron taught history at the Jewish Teachers College in Vienna during the years 1919-26. He went to the United States to teach at the Jewish Institute of Religion in New York and remained at the Institute from 1927 till 1930. From 1930 to 1963 he taught at Columbia University, and served as director of the Center of Israel and Jewish Studies at Columbia from 1950 to 1968. Baron was the first member of an American history faculty to teach Jewish studies. The many departments of Judaic Studies that now exist in universities throughout the United States owe much to his example, and a substantial number of his former students are among their leading professors.

Using his exceptional range of talents in many languages and disciplines, Baron undertook the largest work of Jewish history in the contemporary period, *A Social and Religious History* of the Jews, comprising 14 volumes.

BARUCH, BERNARD (1870-1965), stock analyst, self-styled "speculator" and statesman, was born in Camden, South Carolina. By 1902, by means of his fanancial wizardry and careful market research into raw materials such as gold, copper, sulfur, and rubber, he had amassed a fortune of over three million dollars.

Baruch first entered public life in 1916. Then, as a result of his knowledge of the raw materials market, President Wilson appointed him to the advisory commission of the Council of National Defense. During World War I he served as chairman of the War Industries Board with power to virtually mobilize the American wartime economy. During World War II President Franklin Roosevelt named him chairman of a committee to report on the rubber shortage and to plan a solution. In 1943 he became adviser to War Mobilization Director James Byrnes, and in 1946 he was named the U.S. representative to the United Nations Atomic Energy Commission. No Zionist, he opposed the establishment of any state on the basis of religion, and looked upon himself always as first an American and then a Jew.

Bernard Baruch, American public figure. Baruch's father Simon, emigrated to the United States from Prussia in 1855. The family became prominent: Simon and one of his sons, Herman, were well-known doctors; Hartwig, the eldest son, was a Broadway actor, and Bernard amassed a personal fortune and rose to great importance within the administration of the United States.

BASHEVIS SINGER, ISAAC (1904-), Yiddish novelist, critic, and journalist. The younger brother of the Yiddish novelist I.J. Singer, Bashevis was born into a rabbinical family in Leoncin, Poland. He grew up in Warsaw where he made his career until his emigration to America in 1935. His education was traditional, although the rabbinical seminary he attended also taught secular subjects and modern Hebrew. His home on poor and teeming Krochmalna Street where his father held a *bet din* (rabbinic law court), the old-world tradition, and his brother's example as a secular Yiddish writer were all of the greatest importance to Bashevis' artistic and moral development.

Bashevis published short stories in several journals (often under the pseudonym Bashevis, derived from his mother's name, Bath Sheba) and was recognized early in his literary career.

He has written dozens of short stories and several full length novels, as well as a major autobiographical work. After he moved to the United States his books started to appear in English translation and at the present time he writes in Yiddish, though the work appears only in English.

Bashevis uses a great deal of *Kabbalah in his stories, which are frequently populated with demons and imps. But above all he is a marvelously interesting storyteller, no matter where he may be leading his expectant, and often puzzled, reader.

BASLE (Basel, Bâle), Swiss city. The earliest information on a Jewish community dates from the beginning of the 13th century when Basle was still a German free city. The medieval Jewish cemetery was discovered in recent years and the remains were transferred in 1938 to the present Jewish cemetery. In the Middle Ages the Basle Jews were free to acquire and sell real estate. They engaged in commerce and moneylending, sometimes providing loans to the bishops of Basle. During the *Black Death they were accused of poisoning the wells; the members of the city council attempted to defend them, but finally yielded to the guilds who demonstrated before the town hall. Six hundred Jews, with the rabbi at their head, were burned at the stake; 140 children were forcibly baptized. Thus ended the first Jewish community in Basle – on January 16, 1349.

The second half of the 14th century was a period of prosperous growth despite restrictions imposed by the Church. However, in 1397, the slander of well poisoning was renewed. The Jews fled in panic and the community again came to an end. In 1434 a Church Council held in Basle introduced compulsory attendance of Jews at conversionist sermons. For four centuries there was no Jewish community in Basle. At the end of the 16th century, however, Basle became a center for Hebrew printing. The printing houses were owned by Christians, but they had to have recourse to Jewish proof readers for whom they obtained residence permits. After the granting of *emancipation to the Jews of Switzerland in 1866 Jews were able to return and settle in Basle. A synagogue was consecrated in 1868.

The first Zionist Congress was held in Basle in 1897 where the "Basle Program" was adopted and other Zionist Congresses were subsequently held there. During World War II Basle served as a temporary refuge for many Jewish refugees, most of whom left after the war. The second largest Jewish community in Switzerland, Basle had 2,291 Jews in 1960 and 838 Jewish families in 1969.

BAT KOL (Hebrew בַּת קוֹל ; literally "daughter of a voice") is a heavenly or divine voice which revealed God's will, choice, or judgment to man. For example, before the death of Moses, a heavenly voice proclaimed that God Himself would attend to his burial. When a Roman officer sacrificed his life, so that Rabban Gamaliel II would be spared, a *bat kol* declared: "This high officer is destined to enter into the World to Come."

With the cessation of prophecy, the *bat kol* remained the sole means of communication between God and man. In most instances, where reference is made to a *bat kol,* it is to an external voice which is heard by the recipient of the message.

The authority granted to a *bat kol* in determining the Law is discussed in two different talmudic passages. In one instance, after three years of controversy between Bet Shammai and Bet Hillel, the sages accepted a *bat kol's* pronouncement that "the words of both are the words of the living God, but the *halakhah* is in agreement with the rulings of Bet Hillel." In another instance, Rabbi Joshua explained that the Torah "is not in heaven" and therefore no attention is given to a "heavenly voice" and it is rather the majority of the sages who determine the *halakhah.*

BEARDS AND SHAVING. One can see from ancient monuments that Babylonians and Persians had curly and groomed beards, whereas Egyptians were mostly clean-shaven, except for their pharaohs, who wore braided beards extending from the chin only. However, in Leviticus 19:27 and 21:5, the Israelites were forbidden to destroy the "corners" of the beard, possibly to make them different from other peoples or because shaving certain parts of the face formed part of pagan rites which the Bible opposed. In the Bible shaving of the head and beard is a sign of mourning and humiliation. Priests were not allowed to shave the "edges" of their beards and were allowed only to trim their hair.

In talmudic times, the beard was regarded as "the adornment of a man's face." A young priest could not bless the people until he had grown his first beard. Since God had given man his beard to distinguish him from woman, the rabbis forbade shaving as contrary to nature.

In the Middle Ages, whereas Jews in Islamic countries grew their beards long, those in Christian Europe were permitted by their rabbis to clip them with scissors; however, a clean-shaven man could not be a *ḥazzan.* The Kabbalah maintained that the hair of the head and beard had a spiritual quality and, as

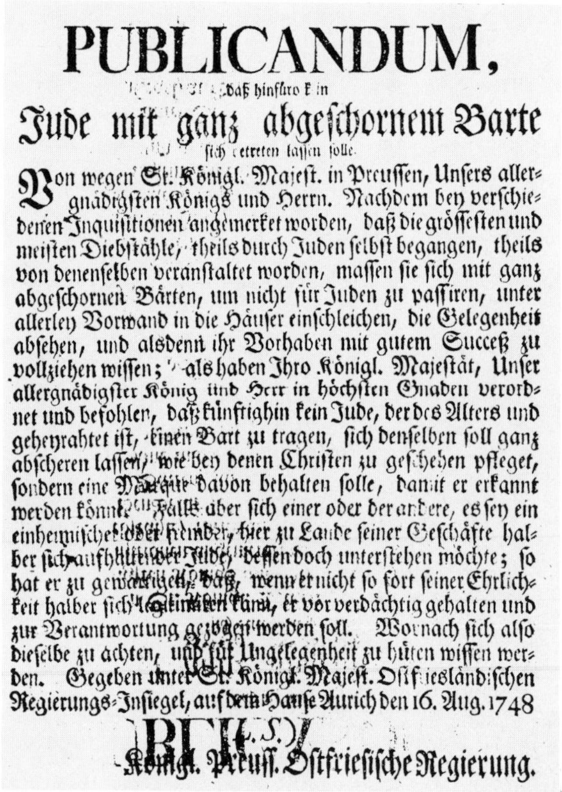
PUBLICANDUM,

daß hinführo kein

Jude mit ganz abgeschornem Barte

sich betreten lassen solle.

Von wegen Sr. Königl. Majest. in Preussen, Unsers allergnädigsten Königs und Herrn. Nachdem bey verschiedenen Inquisitionen angemerket worden, daß die grössesten und meisten Diebstähle, theils durch Juden selbst begangen, theils von denenselben veranstaltet worden, massen sie sich mit ganz abgeschornen Bärten, um nicht für Juden zu passiren, unter allerley Vorwand in die Häuser einschleichen, die Gelegenheit absehen, und alsdenn ihr Vorhaben mit gutem Succeß zu vollziehen wissen; als haben Ihro Königl. Majestät, Unser allergnädigster König und Herr in höchsten Gnaden verordnet und befohlen, daß künftighin kein Jude, der des Alters und geheyrahtet ist, einen Bart zu tragen, sich denselben soll ganz abscheren lassen, wie bey denen Christen zu geschehen pfleget, sondern eine [illegible] davon behalten solle, damit er erkannt werden könne. Falls aber sich einer oder der andere, es sey ein einheimischer oder fremder, hier zu Lande seiner Geschäfte halber sich aufhaltender Jude, dessen doch unterstehen möchte; so hat er zu gewärtigen, daß, wenn er nicht so fort seiner Ehrlichkeit halber sich legitimiren kann, er vor verdächtig gehalten und zur Verantwortung gezogen werden soll. Wornach sich also dieselbe zu achten, und für Ungelegenheit zu hüten wissen werden. Gegeben unter Sr. Königl. Majest. Ostfriesländischen Regierungs-Insiegel, auf dem Hause Aurich den 16. Aug. 1748

[illegible] (L. S.)

Königl. Preuss. Ostfriesische Regierung.

Royal decree of Frederick II of Prussia, issued in 1748, prohibiting Jews from shaving their beards. Prussians were generally clean-shaven, and Frederick wished the Jews to be easily distinguishable from them.

this way of thinking spread to Eastern Europe, the rabbis gradually forbade even trimming the beard.

Halakhah forbids only the removal of the hair with a single-edged razor and then only for five parts of the face; but doubts concerning the definition of these parts led to a total prohibition, although chemical agents, scissors, or the electric razor with two edges are allowed. Strictly observant Jews do not shave during *ḥol ha-moed* (the intermediate days of Passover and Sukkot), nor during the **Omer* period or the Three Weeks of semi-mourning between the Fast of *Tammuz and *Tish'ah Be'Av. To have a haircut (and, for some, to trim the beard) in honor of the Sabbath and the festivals is regarded as a pious duty.

Several European rulers (such as *Nicholas I of Russia and, later, the Nazis) made Jews cut off their beards and sidelocks. Others (like Marie Theresa of Austria) made them grow beards so that their Christian neighbors could recognize them as foreigners. Nowadays this is not such a reliable way to distinguish between Jews and gentiles. The vast majority of Jews today do not wear beards, which are mainly to be seen among the followers of *Ḥasidism, in certain yeshivah circles in Israel and abroad, and among many rabbis.

BEDOUIN are the nomadic tribesmen of the deserts of the Middle East. They are generally Muslims and are considered to be the purest of the Arab stock.

The penetration of Bedouin into Palestine began more than 13 centuries ago and continued intermittently until the late 19th century. They occupied the uninhabited regions of the arid Negev, the Ḥuleh Valley marshlands, the coastal sand dunes, and the rocky hill country of Judea. In 1948 there were 80,000 Bedouin in Israel, 60,000 of whom lived in the Negev. Organized in tribal clans, they engaged mainly in sheep-rearing and desert agriculture, but frequent droughts led to wanderings and raids on villages and settlements. Tribal courts, staffed by sheikhs, maintained law, but in the 1950s the Bedouin increasingly turned to regular Israel courts, so that by 1962, tribal courts were abolished.

The Israel Government opened clinics and schools for the Bedouin and sought to introduce new economic opportunities. Tents gave way to housing projects, and sheep- and camel-herders began to work as building and agricultural laborers. Villages in the north and in the Negev encouraged permanent settlement, and thus the number of nomadic Bedouin was greatly reduced (from 80,000 in 1948 to 36,000 in 1970).

After the Six-Day War (1967) the Bedouin of the Judea and Samaria regions and of the Sinai, numbering some 75,000 in total, began to enjoy some employment opportunities and social benefits in Israel. The expansion of manganese mines and oil plants in Sinai brought employment to the Bedouin of the areas and some heads of tribes even own cars in which to take the laborers to work. In addition, the Israel government employs these Bedouin in various relief projects.

Many Bedouin serve in Israel's Defense Forces and some have distinguished themselves in action.

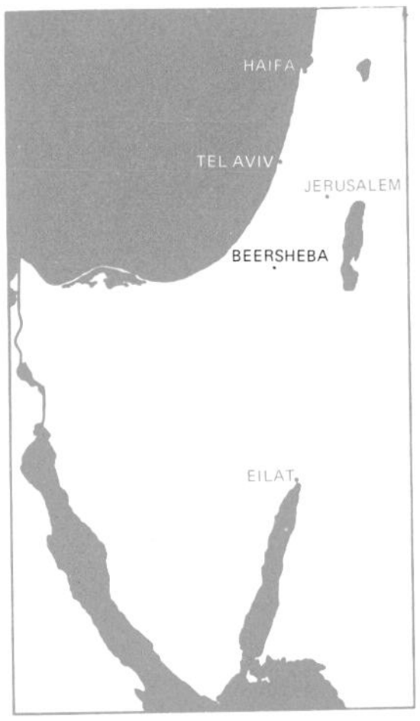

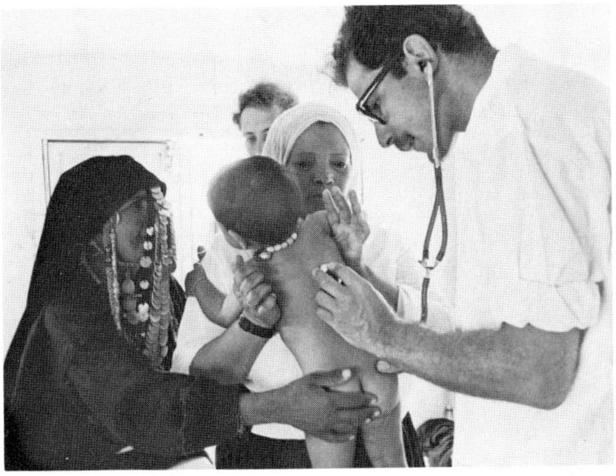
An Israeli doctor, assisted by a Bedouin nurse, examines a Bedouin child in a mobile clinic in northern Sinai, 1969.

BEERSHEBA. Until the days of David and Solomon, "from Dan to Beersheba" was the customary designation for the entire area of the Land of Israel, Beersheba being regarded as the extreme southern point of the country. According to the Bible, Abraham and Isaac dug wells at Beersheba and also formed alliances there with Abimelech, King of the Philistines. The origin of the name Beersheba is explained by the wells and by the seven ewes which Abraham set aside as a sign of the alliance (in Hebrew, *be'er* well; *sheva,* oath or seven).

After the Israelite conquest, Beersheba became a city of the tribe of Simeon and was later incorporated into the tribe of Judah. The biblical town of Beersheba is found at Tell al-Sab (Tell Beersheba), two and a half miles northeast of the new town, where remains from the Iron Age to the Roman period have been found in excavations.

Abandoned in the Arab period, Beersheba was not resettled again until 1900, when the Turkish government set up an administrative district in

1. A Jewish beggar and child. Etching by E.M. Lilien (1874-1925).
2. Beersheba, Israel's southern metropolis, busy with industries and scientific, academic and cultural institutions. Today the population of Beersheba is largely Jewish, and the minaret of the mosque in the foreground of the picture dates from before the War of Independence.

1

Southern Palestine and built an urban settlement in this purely nomadic region. In World War I, the town was the scene of many heavy losses to the British army; thus Beersheba has a British War Cemetery of about 1,300 graves. After the war, when its strategic role ended, Beersheba's population dwindled and in 1931 the number of Jews had decreased to 11.

During the *War of Independence in 1948, the invading Egyptian army made Beersheba its headquarters for the Negev. When the town was taken by Israel forces in the same year, it was totally abandoned by its inhabitants, but early in 1949 Jewish settlers, mostly new immigrants, began to settle it once more. From 1951 large new suburbs were built, extending mainly to the north and northwest, while to the east a large industrial area sprang up.

Today's Beersheba is the capital of Israel's Southern District, and a hub of communications linking up with the main roads and railroads. A pumping station of the Eilat-Haifa oil pipeline is located there, and its largest industries (ceramics, sanitary ware, chemicals, etc.) exploit Negev minerals. The city has several academic, scientific, and cultural institutions, among them the Negev Hospital, the Municipal Museum, the University of the Negev (now renamed Ben-Gurion University), and the Negev Institute for Arid Zone Research. In addition, Beersheba serves as a market center for the Negev Bedouin, a sight which delights tourists and brings back the flavor of the old nomadic town to a new and bustling city.

2

BEGGING AND BEGGARS. Although the Bible is concerned with the poor and the needy, there is hardly a reference to begging or to beggars, and there is, in fact, no biblical Hebrew word for it. The needs of the poor were provided by various laws of charity. Possible references are contained in the assurances that whereas the children of the righteous will not have to "seek bread," the children of the wicked man will, after his untimely death, be vagabonds "and seek their bread out of desolate places" (Psalms 37:25; 109:10).

In the Talmud. During the talmudic period, however, the itinerant beggar who went from house to house figured with some prominence. The Mishnah deals with the rights of the beggar who "goes from place to place" and who had sometimes to be provided with lodging for the night. It was regarded as immodest for women to beg, with the result that the Mishnah lays it down that if a man left insufficient means for his children, the daughters should remain at home and the sons go from door to door. The rabbis are critical of those beggars who used to feign such afflictions as "blindness, swollen belly, and shrunken leg" in order to arouse the compassion of the charitable. Nevertheless one rabbi takes a charitable view of those impostors, pleading that they perform the useful function of exercising the charitable instincts of the people. Nor was the cheerful impudent beggar unknown, as the following story in the Talmud indicates: "A beggar once came to Rava who asked him: 'What do your meals usually consist of?' 'Plump chicken and matured wine,' answered the beggar. 'Do you not consider this a burden on the community?' asked Rava. The beggar retorted: 'I do not take from them – I take what God provides.' At that moment appeared Rava's sister, who had not seen him for 13 years, bringing him a fat chicken and matured wine. 'Just what I told you!' said the beggar."

Communal Aid. Two factors tended to keep begging within bounds. The one was the delicate custom of sending food to the poor in order to spare their feelings, and the other was the highly organized system of collection for and distribution to the poor through the official charity funds. Although some rabbis ruled that a beggar forfeited his rights to organized charity, one of the outstanding authorities showed a great measure of human understanding when he wrote that although "the poor are everywhere supported from the communal chest, if they wish in addition to beg from door to door they may do so, and each man should give according to his understanding and desire." In Cracow, however, in 1595 and in the Spanish and Portuguese congregation in London in the second half of the 17th century, begging was completely outlawed.

This admirable system of organized relief for the poor from the community chest seems almost to have eliminated beggars until the 17th century. A notable literary description of the English Jewish beggar is Israel Zangwill's *King of the Schnorrers.*

It would seem that an increase in the number of Jewish beggars took place in the 17th century as an aftermath of the *Chmielnicki pogroms, when hundreds of Polish communities were destroyed and thousands of penniless and destitute Jews roamed over Europe. From this time dated *"shnorrer,"* the accepted Yiddish term for a beggar, which became a characteristic feature of Jewish life. Sometimes the *shnorrers* openly collected for themselves, at other times for a poor bride's dower, or to restore a house which had been burnt down in one of the many conflagrations of wood-built houses. If the 18th century has been styled "a century of beggary" as a whole, it certainly applies to the impoverished Jewish communities of Central and Eastern Europe up to the dawn of the modern period.

In Israel. Beggary, which was rife in Ereẓ Israel before the establishment of the State of Israel, has been largely eliminated in the streets, as a result of the increased activities of the Ministry of Social Welfare. It is still, however, a feature of the synagogues during the morning services. The beggars consist of two groups, genuine beggars, and collectors for the old-fashioned yeshivot who are to some extent encouraged by the authorities of the yeshivah, not only as a source of income but in addition as affording the worshipers an opportunity of combining prayer with charity. A similar sentiment is held toward beggars in cemeteries. Despite objections that they disturb worshipers, opinion among the Orthodox is opposed to their removal.

Related subjects are discussed under the following headings: *Charity; *Ḥalukkah;* *Hospitality; *Poverty.

BEGIN, MENAḤEM (1913-) is an Israel statesman, once the commander of the *Irgun Ẓeva'i Le'ummi (I.Ẓ.L.). Begin was born and educated in Brest-Litovsk. He graduated in law from Warsaw University. Although he never met Vladimir *Jabotinsky, Begin was inspired by his belief in Jewish legionism and joined the *Betar movement, becoming a member of its leadership in Poland in 1931, and head of the movement in that country in 1938. During the Palestine riots of 1936-38, Begin organized a mass demonstration near the British Embassy in Warsaw and was imprisoned by the Polish police. When the Germans occupied Warsaw, Begin escaped to Vilna, where he was arrested by the Soviet authorities and sentenced to eight years hard labor in the Arctic region. Because he was a Polish citizen, Begin was released at the end of 1941, and arrived in Palestine in 1942 with a Polish contingent formed in the U.S.S.R.

Menaḥem Begin, Israel statesman, and the commander of the Irgun Ẓeva'i Le'ummi during the years before the creation of the State of Israel.

Toward the end of 1943, after being released from the Polish ranks, Begin became commander of I.Ẓ.L., declared "armed warfare" against the Mandatory government at the beginning of 1944, and led a determined underground struggle against the British. In turn, the British offered large rewards for his arrest, but he managed to hide from them by disguising himself as a bearded rabbi in Tel Aviv and by enlisting the cooperation of his numerous admirers.

After the establishment of the State, Begin's leadership of the I.Ẓ.L. was often in conflict with the Ben-Gurion government, but he did his best to avoid violent chashes between the two factions. He was on board the I.Ẓ.L. ship **Altalena* when it approached Tel Aviv with a consignment of arms during the Arab-Israel ceasefire of June 1948. When the Israel government ordered the ship stopped, he preferred to allow it to be blown up rather than to start a civil war between the I.Ẓ.L. and the government.

In 1948, Begin founded the Ḥerut party and became its leader. He led the party's protest campaign against the reparations agreement with West Germany in 1952. He was instrumental in establishing the Gaḥal faction in the Knesset in 1965. In May, 1967, on the eve of the Six-Day War, Begin was named minister without portfolio in the Government of National Unity. However, he and his Gaḥal colleagues left the government in 1970, when the majority accepted the U.S. initiative for peace talks with the Arabs, because they felt that Israel's security was not served by that policy.

BEILIS, MENAḤEM MENDEL (1874-1934) was the victim of a *blood libel charge in Russia in 1911. On March 20, 1911, the mutilated body of Andrei Yushchinsky, a 12-year-old boy, was discovered in a cave on the outskirts of Kiev. The monarchist rightist

1. Menaḥem Mendel Beilis, victim of a 1911 blood libel charge. He was held in prison for two years until his acquittal. He is seen here on his way to Kiev to stand trial in 1913.
2. March in support of Israel during the Six-Day War, June 1967, in Brussels.

1

press immediately launched a vicious anti-Jewish campaign, accusing the Jews of using human blood for ritual purposes. Although the police investigation had traced the murder to a gang of thieves associated with a woman, Vera Cheberiak, notorious for criminal dealings, the chief district attorney of Kiev disregarded the police information and instead looked for a Jew on whom to blame the crime.

In July 1911, a lamplighter testified that on the day Yushchinsky disappeared, he had seen him on the premises of the brick kiln owned by a Jew. On the strength of this testimony, Mendel Beilis, the superintendent of the brick kiln, was arrested on July 21, 1911, and sent to prison.

The case attracted universal attention. Protests and addresses by liberal-minded men were published all over the world, affirming that the blood libel was baseless. The trial took place in Kiev in 1913. The lamplighter and his wife, on whose testimony the indictment of Beilis rested, when questioned by the presiding judge, answered, "We know nothing at all." They confessed that both had been confused by the secret police and made to answer questions they did not comprehend. Two Russian professors of high standing, Troitsky and Kokovtzoff spoke on behalf of the defense in praise of Jewish values and exposed the falsity of the notion of ritual murder. The jury, composed of simple Russian peasants, unanimously declared Beilis "not guilty."

Beilis left Russia with his family for Ereẓ Israel, and in 1920 he settled in the United States. Bernard Malamud's novel *The Fixer* is based on the Beilis case.

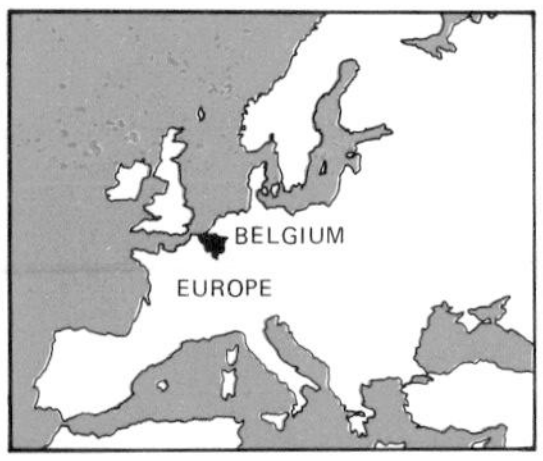

BELGIUM, a small kingdom in Western Europe, has been a kind and tolerant friend to the Jews from the time she gained her independence in 1831 until the present day. Although we have evidence that Jews lived in Belgium as early as the year 1200, those communities disappeared due to expulsions and massacres, so that the real history of Belgian Jewry begins with Belgium's independence in 1831. At this time, the Jewish religion received official recognition and was guaranteed freedom. Belgium's tolerance encouraged the influx of many Jews from Central and Eastern Europe, and thus the Belgian Jewish community grew, its two main population centers becoming Brussels and Antwerp.

The discovery of diamond mines in Africa in the early 20th century was a turning point for Antwerp's Jewry. The diamond trade became central to the community and Jewish enterprise made Antwerp the capital of the industry in Europe. Antwerp's Jewish population grew rapidly, many of its members being immigrants from Eastern Europe whose ties with traditional Judaism were very strong and who succeeded in building an extremely well-organized Jewish community, a bulwark of European Judaism.

By the time of the Nazi invasion in 1940, there were between 90,000 and 110,000 Jews living in Belgium, approximately 55,000 of them in Antwerp, which as Belgium's largest Jewish community, suffered the heaviest losses during the *Holocaust. The Nazis issued numerous edicts barring Jews from professional life, paralyzing their religious and economic life, ordering them to wear the yellow *badge and finally deporting them to *concentration and extermination camps. However, these Nazi atrocities met with resistance and protest on the part of the Belgians, whose "illegal" press and underground resistance worked in cooperation with the Jewish resistance movements to develop a vast, well-organized network of activity for hiding Jews. Due to these efforts, an estimated 3,000 children and 10,000 adults were saved in Belgium, this being a relatively high proportion compared to that of other occupied countries. When more money was needed to sustain those in hiding, millions of francs were

2

contributed by numerous non-Jewish organizations, and large sums of money were secretly obtained from the Belgian government in exile.

The aftermath of the war saw a large decrease in Belgium's Jewish community. However, official statistics are unavailable since the Belgian Constitution does not allow any mention of religion on documents of civil status. In the years following the war, the Jewish population remaining in Belgium continued to decrease considerably and in 1970 was estimated at 40,000. As in the past, the Belgian government's relations with the Jewish community remain favorable. Not only does Belgian law recognize the Jewish religion but it also guarantees public Jewish worship and provides the salaries of recognized rabbis, cantors and religious teachers, in addition to subsidizing Jewish day schools.

Antwerp's Jewish community continues to be closely knit and an important center of Orthodoxy in Western Europe. Its congregations provide numerous community services and control religious day schools in which 90% of Antwerp's Jewish children receive their education.

Among the first countries to establish diplomatic relations with Israel in 1949, Belgium has since been Israel's friend. During the *Six-Day War and *Yom Kippur War non-Jews walked side by side with Jews in public demonstrations of solidarity with Israel, and the Belgian press as a whole supported Israel's point of view.

BELIEF. In the Bible there are no articles of faith or dogmas in which the Jew is commanded to believe. Belief in God's existence and infinite ability is taken for granted and is the basis of the Bible. This is the importance of the story of the Exodus from Egypt; the Children of Israel witnessed God's wonders and passed on the record of their own personal experience to their descendants. The biblical word *emunah* (and its other forms) which is often translated as "belief" really means "trust" or "confidence," which is something quite different.

There is no catechism (i.e., a creed of belief) even in the Talmud. Although the rabbis did enumerate those ideas which a person must believe in order to merit "a portion in the World to Come" they did not compile a list of the fundamental dogmas of Judaism. In discussions throughout the Talmud and midrashic literature there is material on the subject and this material was the basis for later developments.

As the Jews came into contact more and more with Muslim and Christian religious philosophy during the Middle Ages, the need was felt for a definitive statement of those beliefs that make a Jew a Jew. This need had not been felt before because a person's Jewishness was natural and not exposed to external challenge. The medieval Jewish philosophers gave a great deal of thought to formulating articles of faith and disagreed among themselves as to how many there should be. Some even opposed any such formulation on the grounds that every *mitzvah* is an article of faith.

One of the first formulations was that of Ḥananel ben Ḥushi'el who was an important Babylonian scholar of the 11th century. He saw, as basic to the Jewish religion, the following four principles: (1) belief in God; (2) belief in the prophets; (3) belief in the World to Come; and (4) belief in the coming of the Messiah. The *Karaites (a Jewish sect) also took an interest in dogma and one of their leading theologians of the 12th century, Judah Hadassi, listed ten articles of faith: (1) God's unity and wisdom; (2) God's eternity and unlikeness to any other being; (3) He is the Creator of the world; (4) Moses and the other prophets were sent by God; (5) the Torah is true; (6) the Jews are obliged to study Hebrew in order to understand the Torah fully; (7) Jerusalem was chosen by God as the eternal dwelling place of

THE THIRTEEN CREEDS.

I.

I BELIEVE with a firm and perfect faith, that God is the creator of all things: that he doth guide and support all creatures; that he alone has made every thing; and that he still acts, and will act during the whole eternity.

II.

I believe, with a firm and perfect faith, that God is one, there is no unity like his; he alone hath been, is, and shall be eternally, our God.

III.

I believe, with a firm and perfect faith, that God is not corporeal, he cannot have any material properties, and no corporeal essence can be compared with him.

שלשה ע״ר

עקרים

א

אני מאמין באמונה שלימה שהבורא יתברך שמו הוא מנהיג ובורא לכל הברואים והוא לבדו עשה ועושה ויעשה לכל המעשים :

ב

אני מאמין באמונה שלימה שהבורא יתברך שמו הוא יחיד ואין יחידות כמוהו בשום פנים והוא לבדו אלהינו היה הוה ויהיה :

ג

אני מאמין באמונה שלמה שהבורא יתברך שמו אינו גוף ולא ישיגוהו משיגי הגוף ואין לו שום דמיון כלל :

אני

The first English translation of Maimonides' Thirteen Articles of Faith by B. Meyers and A. Alexander, in a prayerbook printed in London in 1770.

His glory; (8) the dead will be resurrected; (9) there will be a divine judgment; and (10) God will mete out reward and punishment.

Perhaps the most famous of the various formulations of dogmas is the Thirteen Principles of Faith of *Maimonides. Originally written in Arabic, this creed is the basis of the *Yigdal* hymn (see *Prayer) which is part of the daily service and is usually recited at the conclusion of the Friday evening synagogue service. The 13 fundamentals are: (1) The existence of God, which is perfect; (2) God is "one" in every sense of the word; (3) God has no body or physical attributes; (4) God is eternal; (5) God alone must be worshiped; (6) the prophecy of the Bible is true; (7) Moses was greater than any other prophet; (8) the entire Torah was given to Moses; (9) the Torah will never be superseded or abrogated; (10) God knows the actions of men; (11) God rewards and punishes; (12) the Messiah will ultimately come; and (13) the dead will be resurrected. These principles have also been put in the form of a creed in which each begins with the words "I believe with perfect faith that . . . ;" the creed is printed in most prayerbooks. Joseph *Albo reduced the number of dogmas to three.

In post-medieval times, interest in dogmas on the part of Jewish philosophers waned. Moses *Mendelssohn rejected belief as a requirement of Judaism and claimed that performance of the *mitzvot* is the sole criterion. Samson Raphael *Hirsch, who was perhaps the most powerful spokesman of the Orthodox creed, claimed that "the catechism of the Jew is his calendar."

1

2

1. Official emblem of the Belorussian Soviet Republic in the early 1920s. For some time the slogan, "Workers of the World, Unite!" was inscribed in Yiddish, in addition to Belorussian, Russian and Polish.
2. Members of the Jewish collective farm "Emes" in Belorussia, c. 1928.

BELORUSSIA. Located in the northwestern region of *Russia, Belorussia is part of *Lithuania (Lita), its Jews being considered "Litvaks." Between the 14th and 18th centuries it was part of Poland-Lithuania, and from the partition of *Poland (1772-95) until the Revolution of 1917, it was part of the northwestern region of Russia. Under Soviet rule Belorussia became a political entity, known as the Belorussia Soviet Socialist Republic, which is its present name.

Jewish merchants apparently first visited Belorussia as early as the 1400s, and played an important role in developing the area, particularly those Jews from *Brest-Litovsk who were wealthy merchants and large-scale farmers. However, the Christian community continually opposed permanent Jewish settlement, and in one area, it was not until 1630 that the Christians granted the Jews permission to build a synagogue.

Nevertheless, the Jewish communities in Belorussia grew, the largest ones being *Minsk and *Pinsk. Although the majority of Belorussia's Jews were extremely poor, culturally the Jewish community was rich and flourishing. In general, the Jewish community was influenced by the *Mitnaggedim* (opponents of *Ḥasidism) who predominated in the north and west of the region. Most of the celebrated Lithuanian yeshivot were in Belorussia, those of *Volozhin and Mir among others. Ḥasidism penetrated Belorussia from the south and two of the fathers of Ḥasidism, Menaḥem Mendel of Vitebsk and Shneur Zalman of Lyady, were active there. In fact, Belorussia was the cradle of *Ḥabad Ḥasidism.

By the mid-19th century *Haskalah came to Belorussia and towards the end of the century, *Zionism also began to spread among the Jews of the area. Self-defense organizations to protect the Jews during the wave of pogroms of the early 20th century were established by the Labor Zionists in every town.

The Revolution of 1917 initiated the breakup of traditional Jewish social and spiritual life in Belorussia. It became a battlefield between the Red Army and the Polish Army, and the Jewish communities suffered severely from attacks by the Polish Army when Jews were killed indiscriminately on charges of spying. After the treaty of 1921, Belorussia was divided between the Soviet Union and Poland, and during the first years of Soviet rule the Jews of Belorussia found themselves in an exceptional situation: they were accepted by the peasant population, and Yiddish was actually encouraged. However, with the consolidation of the Soviet regime, the Jewish religion began to be discouraged and persecuted. *Ḥadarim* and yeshivot were closed down and synagogues turned to secular uses. Still, Jews maintained yeshivot secretly and fought courageously for the right to publish siddurim and Jewish calendars. Underground Zionist youth movements such as *He-Ḥalutz and *Ha-Shomer ha-Ẓair, continued to defy the Soviet anti-Zionist campaigns.

On the other hand, in the western part of Belorussia which was under Polish rule from 1920 to 1939, Jewish culture was able to develop naturally. *Ḥadarim* and yeshivot flourished and the Zionist movement was well-organized. *Vilna, Brest-Litovsk, Bialystok, and *Warsaw were the major Jewish centers. However, in 1939, western Belorussia was annexed by the Soviet Union and its Jews suffered the same fate as those in other regions under Soviet rule.

In 1941 the Nazis invaded Belorussia and the Jews of the area were caught in the persecutions of the *Holocaust.

BELZ. If your grandparents are from Belz, you may have once heard them quietly humming a Yiddish song which lovingly refers to their hometown as "*mein shtetaleh* Belz." Today Belz is in the Ukrainian Sovet Socialist Republic; between the World Wars it was in Poland. Jewish settlement in Belz dates from the beginning of the 16th century, but only 300 years later did it become famous – as the center of Galician Ḥasidism. The *rebbes* of the Roke'aḥ dynasty officiated as rabbis of the Belz community. The founder of the dynasty, Rabbi Shalim Roke'aḥ (1779-1855) was appointed rabbi of Belz, and was recognized as a *ẓaddik* by the thousands of Ḥasidim who flocked to study under him in his splendid *bet midrash.* His successors continued to attract disciples, and by 1921 the 2,100 Jews of Belz made up exactly one half of the total population of the town.

The young man on the left is the Belzer *rebbe,* Issachar Dov, at the Western Wall, 1970. The old man is his father-in-law, Ḥayyim Meir Hager, the *rebbe* of Vizhnitz.

One of Rabbi Shalom's successors as Belzer *rebbe,* Rabbi Aaron (1880-1957), was a diminutive figure who lived an ascetic life, and was fearlessly active in communal affairs; 33 members of his family were murdered during World War II, while he was repeatedly confined in ghettos and deported. He managed to reach Ereẓ Israel in 1944, where he established yeshivot and *battei midrash.* His home in Tel Aviv became the new center for the followers of Belz Ḥasidism throughout the world, and his grave in Jerusalem has become a place of pilgrimage on the anniversary of his death.

He was succeeded by his very young nephew, Rabbi Issachar Dov (born 1948), who established a *bet midrash* in Jerusalem.

Though the dynasty of Belz Ḥasidism thus survived, the township of Belz suffered a cruel fate. In February 1942 during the Nazi occupation, about 1,000 Jews from Belz were deported to death camps. In May 1942 an additional 1,540 were deported. Those remaining were hunted down and deported in September of that year.

All that is left now of the bustling lifestyle of prewar Belz is a sprinkling of Jews clustered around one synagogue – and a nostalgic melody still hummed by its ageing survivors around the world.

BEN-ASHER, MOSES AND AARON. The most important book in Judaism is, of course, the Bible. Therefore it is crucial to have an exact, established text. The Hebrew language is made up of consonants and vowels – the books of the Bible were originally written without the vowels and so some words can be read in different fashions. Also, the Torah (as well as parts of the rest of the Bible) is read in the synagogue with a special melody which is marked on the words by what is known as cantillation marks. These too were not in the original text. All these aspects of the Bible were established by people known as masoretes (for more information see *Masorah). Two of the most important of these were a father and son, Moses and Aaron Ben-Asher, who lived in the second half of the ninth century and the first half of the tenth.

The Hebrew Bible as we know it is the work of the Ben-Ashers as far as the vocalization and other signs are concerned. The important codex, as a pointed Bible is called, is known as the *Keter.* In the colophon at the end of that book it is stated that Aaron Ben-Asher vocalized and pointed it. *Maimonides considered it to be the most perfect of all the versions. A manuscript of parts of the Bible has been discovered which Moses Ben-Asher pointed. From the colophon of that we learn that it was written in Tiberias in 896 c.e. Aaron Ben-Asher also wrote a sort of grammar book in which he gives the laws for vocalization, pointing and related matters.

On the basis of literary evidence, it was once thought that the Ben-Ashers were *Karaites. Recently this has been disproved. Unfortunately, nothing is known about their personal lives.

BENE-BERAK, an important industrial area in Israel with a predominantly Orthodox population, is located several miles north of a biblical city of the same name, which was included in the territory of the tribe of Dan (Joshua 19:45). After the destruction of the Second Temple in 70 c.e., Bene-Berak became a center of Jewish learning when Rabbi *Akiva established his academy there. A famous night-long *seder* held in Bene-Berak by Rabbi Akiva and his colleagues is described in the Passover **Haggadah.* Bene-Berak was known for its fertile orchards and vineyards, and was described in the Talmud by the biblical phrase, "a land flowing with milk and honey."

The modern Bene-Berak is situated just three miles from Tel Aviv, which has now grown to join it. With its thousands of yeshivah students wearing their characteristic black hats and carrying outsize volumes

1

2

1. Ben Asher's system of pointing the text of the Bible was not unopposed. His contemporary, Ben Naphtali, differed from him on about 850 minor points, and the illustration shows a page from the *Lisbon Bible* (1482/3) which lists the disputed points.
2. The *Bet Knesset* of the Ponevezh yeshivah in Bene-Berak at the opening of a month of *kallah* (or special study). To the right of the picture is the famous Ark of the Law which was originally in an Italian synagogue.

of the Talmud, Bene-Berak is the yeshivah equivalent of a university city. It was established in 1924 by a group of 13 Orthodox families from Warsaw, Poland, who engaged mostly in farming; by 1974 its population exceeded 75,000. It grew so rapidly because of its closeness to Tel Aviv and its mainly Orthodox population and way of life. Thus on the Sabbath and festivals, all roads are closed to traffic, so that there is a complete public observance of Jewish law. There are more than 200 synagogues, many of them centers of ḥasidic *rebbes* and their followers, some of whom live in closed neighborhoods, such as Zikhron Meir, Vizhnitz and Satmar. In addition, there are many yeshivot in Bene-Berak, the best known being the Ponevezh Yeshivah with its magnificent gilt Ark of the Law which was transferred from a disused Renaissance synagogue in Italy.

Side by side with its religious way of life, Bene-Berak is a thoroughly modern and industrialized area. In 1974 it had over 170 factories and workshops for food preserves, cigarettes, wool textiles and other products.

BENEDICTIONS. Very many of the prayers in the **Jewish liturgy** are in the form of benedictions. In Hebrew this is known as בְּרָכָה *(berakhah:* pl. *berakhot)* from the root meaning to bless. Thus the benediction is a way to bless God. Some scholars point out the similarity with another Hebrew word meaning "knee" and suggest that our usage comes from the act of "bending the knee," i.e., bowing down. From this it would appear that "praise" is a better translation than "bless."

The blessing formula was created in very ancient times and even occurs, in various forms, in the Bible. The rabbis of the Talmud considered benedictions to be very important and felt that a person should recite at least one hundred a day. Blessings should not be pronounced in vain since they contain the name of God and "you shall not take the name of the Lord your God in vain."

Every blessing opens with the words "Blessed art Thou, O Lord" *(Barukh Attah Adonai).* When the benediction is recited by itself or when it is at the beginning of a series, the words "our God, King of the Universe" *(Eloheinu Melekh ha-Olam)* are added. There are three different forms of blessings. The first is a short blessing, such as the blessing over bread: "Blessed art Thou, O Lord our God, King of the Universe, who brings forth bread from the earth" *(Barukh Attah Adonai Eloheinu Melekh ha-Olam, ha-moẓi leḥem min ha-areẓ).* The second type is a long blessing, e.g., the first benediction of the *Grace after Meals, in which a concluding blessing is recited at the end of the prayer: "Blessed art Thou O Lord, who feedest all." The third type of blessing forms part of a series. The second section of the Grace after Meals, for example, begins with the words "We thank thee," and ends with the blessing "Blessed art Thou O Lord, for the land and the food." The **Amidah* consists of a series of blessings, and the **Shema* is preceded and followed by benedictions.

*Maimonides divided the blessings into three types – those that are recited before enjoying a pleasure (such as food); those that are recited for the performance of a religious duty (such as hearing the *shofar*); and those which are thanksgiving and praise (such as Grace after Meals).

Blessings are recited before the performance of a *mitzvah,* including the commandments of rabbinic origin, such as the lighting of candles on the Sabbath or on Ḥanukkah. When a *mitzvah* is performed for the first time in the year, the *She-Heḥeyanu* benediction is also added, "who has kept us alive and preserved us and enabled us to reach this season."

There are blessings for various occasions such as on hearing good news, on hearing bad news, on seeing the first blossoms on a tree, and on smelling fragrant plants – and many others can be found in the Prayer Book.

In the Talmud there are two opinions about the form of benedictions. One says that every benediction must have the name of God *(Adonai)* and the other that every benediction must also mention the attribute of God's kingship *(Melekh ha-Olam).* Although nowadays all benedictions are recited in Hebrew, it is clear from the Talmud that a blessing recited in another language is also valid as long as it is formulated according to the rules.

Amen. When a person hears a benediction recited he must respond *Amen* אָמֵן. This response shows that the hearer identifies himself and agrees with the benediction. According to some opinions the word *Amen* is made up of the initial letters of אֵל מֶלֶךְ נֶאֱמָן *(El Melekh Ne'eman;* "God, the faithful King"). When a person responds *Amen* to a benediction it is as though he also recited the benediction; thus a person who does not know the necessary benediction can answer *Amen* and fulfill the requirement. At festive meals, for example, only the leader of the participants recites the *ha-moẓi,* and if the assembled

1

2

1. Illustrations for the blessings recited before eating fruit (above) and vegetables (below). They appear in an illuminated manuscript of the Grace after Meals and other benedictions, which was made in Nikolsburg in 1728.
2. Symbol of the Benei Akiva youth movement, used as an official postage cancellation during the world conference of the movement held at Mikveh Israel, 1958.

guests respond *Amen* they do not have to recite it themselves.

Interestingly, the word *Amen* has a unique history. The scholars who in the third century b.c.e. produced the first translation of the Bible – the Greek *Septuagint – encountered a serious problem: Greek simply had no word meaning *Amen.* They therefore adopted the Hebrew word. When Jerome faced a similar problem in producing his Latin translation in 400 c.e., he too adopted the Hebrew word *Amen.* In this way, over the centuries, this ancient Hebrew word has found its way into every one of the 1,200 languages into which the Hebrew Bible has been translated.

BENEI AKIVA. The two Tablets of the Law, a sheaf of corn, a sickle and olive leaves, together make up the badge of Benei Akiva, the youth movement of Ha-Poel ha-Mizrachi, a religious Zionist organization, and represent its ideology. The Tablets stand for the Torah: Benei Akiva is a religious movement. The agricultural motifs represent the ideals of pioneering and working the land of Ereẓ Israel. Benei Akiva teaches its members that to live full Jewish lives, they must be religious and must live in Israel, ideally on a kibbutz, building up the land.

Benei Akiva, named after Rabbi *Akiva, was founded in Jerusalem in 1929. Since then in accordance with its teachings, the work of the movement has been to bring religious youth together, to encourage *aliyah,* to set up religious kibbutzim and moshavim, and to establish yeshivot for boys and religious schools for girls. After the Six-Day War, Benei Akiva members made up the first group to settle within the walls of the Old City of Jerusalem, where they opened up a new yeshivah.

In Israel alone the movement has some 160 branches, about half of which are in newly-established settlements, with over 25,000 members. In addition, there are over 20,000 members in 60 Diaspora cities. They likewise attend weekly meetings, seminars, camps and functions, all directed towards the realization of the twin ideals of Torah and *avodah* (or pioneering labor) which are reflected on the movement's badge, and which are represented in Israel by the yeshivah and the kibbutz respectively.

BENEI MOSHE ("Sons of Moses") was a secret order of *Ḥibbat Zion founded in Russia in 1889 to ensure personal dedication to the spiritual renaissance of the Jewish people and the return to Ereẓ Israel. Benei Moshe, founded on the seventh of Adar, the traditional birth date of Moses, was active in Russia and Ereẓ Israel until 1897.

1. **Bedouin.** Boy of the Jabaliyya tribe, one of the Bedouin tribes which wander through the Sinai desert.
2. **Agriculture.** School children in Arad, in the south of Israel, 1969. They are planting trees in celebration of Tu bi-Shevat, the New Year for trees.
3. **Agriculture.** Soldier opening the valve of an irrigation pipe at a new *Naḥal* (army) settlement in the Aravah, Ein Ḥaẓevah, 1964.

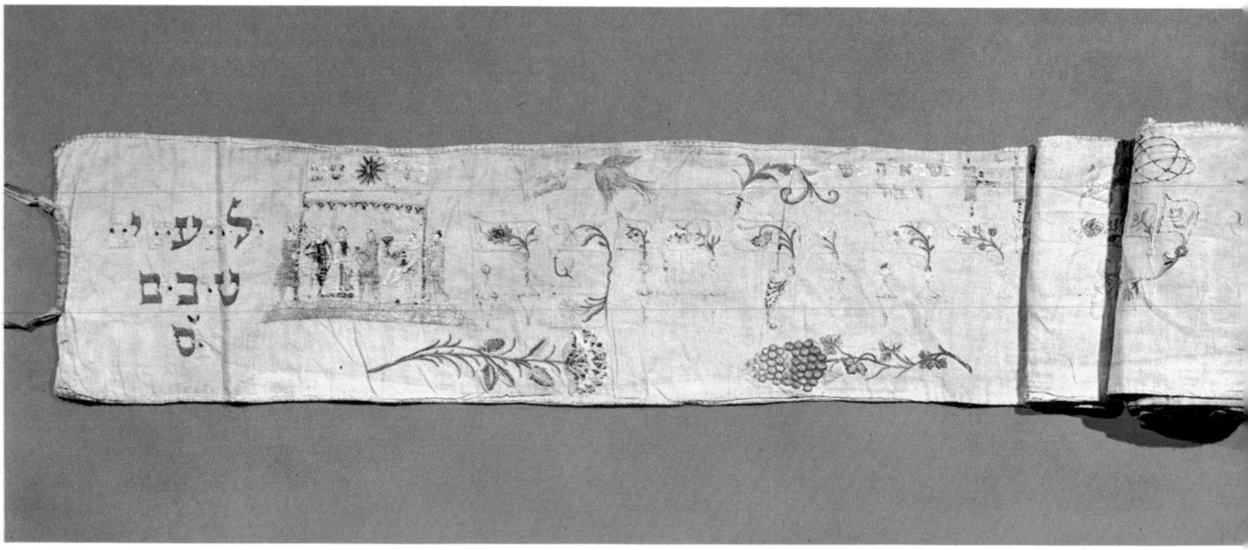

1

2

1. **Birth.** Linen wrapper for *Sefer Torah* made from a circumcision diaper and embroidered in silk thread with the name and date of birth of the baby.

2. **Aaron.** "This is the *menorah* and Aaron pouring oil into the lamps." A full page illustration of Aaron, the high priest, performing his duties in a 13th century French manuscript written by Benjamin the Scribe. The manuscript is a collection of biblical, historical, ritual and legal treatises.

Benei Moshe chapters consisted of at least five members, who called each other "brother," and were headed by leaders and advisers. A member was initiated in a ceremony in which he vowed to adhere faithfully to the statutes. The language used was Hebrew, and knowledge of Hebrew was a prerequisite for membership. The minimal eligibility age was 20. Despite its very small membership (about 160), the order exerted considerable influence on the Ḥibbat Zion movement, whose leaders were, in fact, members of Benei Moshe.

Benei Moshe's practical achievements were in the field of modern Hebrew education in Ereẓ Israel and elsewhere, in helping to found the settlement *Reḥovot, and in the establishment of Hebrew publishing.

BENE ISRAEL, a Jewish community in India, claim that their ancestors fled Ereẓ Israel when they were persecuted by the Greeks (175-163 b.c.e.), during the events of Ḥanukkah. According to the Bene Israel tradition, their ancestors were shipwrecked in the Indian Ocean and 14 survivors were cast ashore on the Konkan coast, about 26 miles south of Bombay, where they and their descendants remained for centuries, isolated and unknown to other Jewish communities. According to other theories, the Bene Israel are either descendants of Yemenite Jews or of the Babylonian-Persian Diaspora.

Because of their isolation, the Bene Israel forgot much of the Hebrew language, prayers, and ceremonies, and adopted the names, customs, and dress of their Hindu neighbors, and their language, Marathi, as their mother tongue; however, they continued to observe circumcision, dietary laws, the Sabbath and some fasts and festivals, and recited the *Shema.* Many of them were oil-pressers, and they became known to their neighbors as *Shanwar Telis,* which means "the Sabbath-observing oilmen."

In the 18th century, some of the Bene Israel moved to Bombay, where they discovered there were other Jewish groups in India, and were introduced to the ways of traditional Judaism. They refused Herzl's invitation to participate in the First Zionist Congress in 1897, explaining that they were waiting for "the Divine Hand" to bring them back to Zion.

The occupations of the members of the community varied. Some were military men, others were civil servants, merchants, artisans, farmers and professionals, and one became mayor of the city of Bombay in 1937-38. In 1969 there were about 13,000 Bene Israel in India, but the number has been declining because of emigration to England and Israel. From the establishment of the State of Israel until 1969, over 12,000 Bene Israel emigrated there. There were some rabbis in Israel who were not sure as to whether the Bene Israel were real Jews but the official rabbinate and the majority of rabbinical authorities decided that they were authentic Jews, and that all Jewish law applies to them. At first there were some difficulties in their absorption into Israel society, but these have now been overcome; a good number of the Bene Israel work in Israel's aircraft industry.

Bene Israel in Bombay, November 1936, at a reception for the folklorist and Hebrew translator, Dr. Immanuel Olsvanger.

BEN-GURION, DAVID (1886-1973). Both admirers and opponents, Jews and non-Jews, regard Ben-Gurion as foremost among the founding fathers of modern Israel. Ben-Gurion was the first prime minister and defense minister of Israel and an outstanding leader of the pioneering labor movement in Ereẓ Israel. An energetic and committed Zionist, he headed the struggle for Jewish independence in Palestine.

Ben-Gurion was born in 1886 in Plonsk (then in Russian Poland) where his father, Avigdor Gruen, was a fervent Zionist. Ben-Gurion's mother died when he was 11 years old. He was educated in a modernized Hebrew-language *ḥeder,* and studied secular subjects with private tutors. At the age of 14 he was among the founders of a Zionist youth group, "Ezra." He joined the Po'alei Zion movement in 1903, traveling and speaking on its behalf. During the revolution of 1905-06 he was arrested twice but released at the intervention of his father. In 1906 Ben-Gurion settled in Ereẓ Israel, working in the orange groves of Petaḥ Tikvah and the wine cellars of Rishon le-Zion.

After a few years of activity in Zionist movements in Palestine, Ben-Gurion joined a group of young Zionists and Po'alei Zion who went to study at Turkish universities. Their object was to establish close ties with the educated ruling circles in Turkey and join in their political struggle in the hope that, in return for their support, Turkey would permit the development of Ereẓ Israel as a center of the Jewish people. However, with the advent of the anti-Zionist persecutions by the Turkish administration, both he and Izhak *Ben-Zvi were arrested and accused of conspiring against Ottoman rule. Exiled to Egypt in March 1915, they later proceeded to New York, where their main efforts were directed to the establishment of the He-Ḥalutz organization, preparing young Jews for settlement in Palestine. In 1917 Ben-Gurion married Paula Munweis (born in Minsk, Russia, 1892), a nurse in New York, and an active member of Po'alei Zion. She was a devoted wife until her death in 1968.

After the *Balfour Declaration Ben-Gurion was among the first in the United States to call for the formation of Jewish battalions to liberate Palestine. Volunteering for the British Army in May 1918, he reached Egypt in August as a soldier in the Jewish Legion, and from there proceeded to Palestine where he began working towards a united labor movement and a Jewish socialist society based on the collective principles of the *kibbutz. In 1921, he was elected secretary-general of the newly-formed *Histadrut (labor organization) which he and Berl *Katznelson headed for nearly 14 years.

In the 1930s, Ben-Gurion turned his efforts to Zionist activities and in 1935, became chairman of the *Jewish Agency executive. From 1935 to 1948, both he and Chaim *Weizmann directed all Zionist affairs.

1. David Ben-Gurion at his home, kibbutz Sde Boker, in December 1954.
2. David Ben-Gurion with President Chaim Weizmann (center), and Israel's first chief of staff, Ya'akov Dori (right) at a military ceremony in 1949.

1

2

Toward the Founding of the Jewish State. The British proposal for the *partition of Palestine into an Arab and a Jewish state was accepted by Ben-Gurion in the belief that even a small Jewish state would be a powerful instrument for the realization of Zionism. However, shortly afterwards the British government abandoned the partition plan and in 1939 issued the declaration of a new anti-Zionist policy (the White Paper of 1939) which restricted *aliyah* and Jewish rights to acquire land. Ben-Gurion condemned the White Paper and called for active resistance. He proposed the intensification of *"illegal" immigration, involving incidents with British coastal guards, and settlement of land in areas prohibited to Jews.

After World War II Ben-Gurion led the political struggle against the British and authorized the sabotage activities of the Hebrew Resistance Movement (Tenu'at ha-Meri ha-Ivri). Encouraging "illegal" immigration, he visited the camps of Jewish survivors in Germany, and at their conference in 1946 he declared: "We shall not rest until every one of you who so desires joins us in the land of Israel in building a Jewish state." In the months immediately following the war he ordered the *Haganah leaders to begin acquiring large quantities of arms in preparation for the contingency of an armed clash with the Arabs.

When the *War of Independence broke out in December 1947, Ben-Gurion headed the defense effort, organizing the raising of financial support, the acquisition of arms, the recruiting of military experts, and the preparation of operational plans. During the course of the war he molded the character and structure of the Israel Army, which was officially formed in May 1948. His military and political decisions played a central role in all the fateful events of the war that determined the borders of the state: the conquest of the northern Negev, the retreat from Sinai and the occupation of Eilat.

In the spring of 1948, despite great pressure from the U.S. government and the doubts of many of his colleagues, Ben-Gurion insisted upon the establishment of the Jewish state immediately at the termination of the British Mandate. On May 14, 1948, he proclaimed the rebirth of the independent Jewish nation. He became prime-minister and minister of defense of the provisional government, continuing in these posts after the election to the first Knesset in 1949. In December 1949, he declared Jerusalem the capital of Israel.

Ben-Gurion devoted most of his efforts to

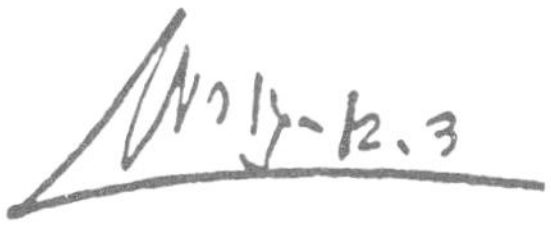

David Ben-Gurion

strengthening the army and to winning the support of the world powers for Israel's struggle. He had a formative influence on the emergent character of the State of Israel, making the ingathering of the exiles a supreme principle, and placing the advancement of science and research a central factor in the development of the country and its people.

In December 1953 Ben-Gurion announced his resignation from the government. After many years of political work he felt he needed a rest from the tensions of high office. By joining the new non-party kibbutz Sedeh Boker in the heart of the Negev, he wished to set an example of personal pioneering, particularly in the Negev, which he regarded as foremost in importance for the future of Israel. However, in February 1955, Ben-Gurion was recalled to serve as minister of defense in the government headed by Moshe Sharett.

After the elections in November 1955, Ben-Gurion again assumed the twofold functions of prime minister and minister of defense. In his search for allies, he established close relations with France, and in October 1956 Ben-Gurion went there for a secret meeting with the representatives of the French and British governments, at which concerted military action against Egypt was planned (see *Sinai Campaign).

After the Sinai Campaign, Ben-Gurion's efforts were directed at consolidating Israel's international position. During 1960-62 Ben-Gurion traveled to the United States, Western Europe, Burma, and the Scandinavian countries. During this period he met with Chancellor Adenauer (1960) and with President Kennedy (1961) in New York and with President de Gaulle in Paris (June 1960).

In September 1960 the government and the country were shaken by the "Lavon Affair," a controversy involving national security and intelligence. Ben-Gurion took a firm and uncompromising stand on the issue and in January 1961, he demanded that his party (Mapai) choose between himself and Lavon. Mapai chose Ben-Gurion, but in June 1963 he resigned from the government, recommending Levi *Eshkol as his successor. He again retired to Sedeh Boker and devoted himself to writing the history of the rebirth of Israel. It seemed as if Ben-Gurion's public career had come to an end. But in the spring of 1964, he returned to the public arena by again raising the question of the "Lavon Affair" and demanding a judicial inquiry, as well as attacking Levi Eshkol and other members of the government. This time Mapai decided against Ben-Gurion and as a result, Ben-Gurion organized his followers in an independent list, the Israel Workers List (Reshimat Po'alei Israel, or Rafi).

Rafi rejoined the government on the eve of the Six-Day War (June 1967) and, shortly after the war, joined with Mapai and Aḥdut ha-Avodah to form the reunited Israel Labor Party (Mifleget ha-Avodah). However, Ben-Gurion did not participate in the negotiations and did not join the new party. He continued his demand for a renewed inquiry into the "Lavon Affair" which he regarded as a moral fight for truth and justice. He remained a solitary figure, whose preeminent and single-minded role in the establishment and building of the state assured him a unique position in public life and in the affection of the people. In 1970, he resigned from the Knesset.

Ben-Gurion's personality embodied great spiritual forces and tremendous willpower. As an orator, publicist, and forceful debater, he strove to strengthen both the labor movement in Ereẓ Israel and the Zionist movement and to build the foundations of the State of Israel.

BENJAMIN OF TUDELA. In the second half of the 12th century, a man from Tudela in Northern Spain, began an incredible journey. For approximately ten years he traveled throughout the Mediterranean area, writing notes about the people and places he saw on his travels from Spain to the Indian Ocean. His *Sefer ha-Massa'ot* (Book of Travels) has made it possible for the 20th-century reader to understand life in this region during medieval times.

It is believed that Benjamin was a gem merchant, but little is known about his personal life since he hardly wrote anything about himself. Rather, he was particularly interested in the life of the Jews in the various communities he visited. In each place he recorded the number of Jews, the leading scholars of each community, and the economic conditions of the people. He found Jews working as dyers in Brindisi, Italy, as silkweavers in Thebes, Greece, tanners in Constantinople, and glassworkers in Aleppo and Tyre, Syria. He was particularly interested in Jewish learning, and his account of the intellectual life in Provence, France, is significant, as is his characterization of the organization of synagogue life in Egypt. He also traveled throughout Palestine, giving a detailed description of the holy places he encountered. These descriptions of Palestine during the Crusader period were more objective and precise than those of the Christian pilgrims at this time and therefore make his Book of Travels an important source of information.

The travels of Benjamin also provide us with valuable knowledge about the non-Jewish world. Of Baghdad he wrote an account longer than that of any other city on his itinerary and described the court of the caliph and the charitable organizations in the city, as well as the surviving talmudic academies.

In addition, his writings on non-Jewish subjects are vivid and sometimes impressive historical accounts. Among these are his reports on the constant fighting between the Italian republics of Genoa and Pisa, the landing of the Crusaders in South Italy, the palaces and pageants of Constantinople, and the wealth and weaknesses of the Byzantine Empire. Furthermore, from the conversations during his journey he learned and wrote much about places which he had not visited, and he is said to have been the first European to mention China by its present name.

Benjamin's work has been translated into almost every European language and is used as a primary source-book by all historians researching the medieval period.

A fragment from the 'Praise of the Fathers of Old' by Ben Sira. This scroll was found at Masada and dates from the first century c.e.

BEN SIRA is the name of a Hebrew sage and scribe who lived in the second century b.c.e. and who wrote the book, Wisdom of Ben Sira, also known as Ecclesiasticus. His full name is given as Simeon ben Jesua ben Eleazar ben Sira, and his book is a work of the *Apocrypha, and deals with the love of wisdom and the praise of wise men.

Similar to the book of *Proverbs with its wise sayings, the Wisdom of Ben Sira teaches man virtue and good deeds, and guides him in his conduct toward all men. It stresses, as does the book of Proverbs, that the fear of the Lord is the beginning and the end of all wisdom.

For the rabbis of the early talmudic period the work had an importance almost equal to that of the book of Proverbs. Its sayings, quoted either in Ben Sira's name or anonymously, are cited in the Talmud. In fact, these quotations are often introduced with the phrase "as it is written," which is ordinarily reserved for biblical verses. Nevertheless, the Wisdom of Ben Sira was not included in the canon of the 24 books of the Bible, and at one point in the talmudic period some *amoraim* even forbade it to be read. However, the book did find its way into the *Septuagint, the Greek translation of the Bible, as well as into the Christian Bible. Furthermore, several of Ben Sira's maxims are to be found in other books of the Apocrypha and in the New Testament, as well as in the writings of early medieval Jewish scholars. Ben Sira's influence on ancient Hebrew prayers and *piyyutim* is particularly great.

In 1896, Solomon Schechter discovered among the **Genizah* fragments in Cairo a page of the original Hebrew work. During the next four years, Schechter and other scholars found many other fragments from various manuscripts, comprising about two-thirds of the entire book. Later, some pieces of the Hebrew original were discovered in Qumran Cave II near the Dead Sea, and in 1964 Yigael Yadin discovered some fragments at *Masada which indicate that the manuscript of the *Genizah* represents substantially the original Hebrew version of the book.

BEN-YEHUDA, ELIEZER (1858-1922) is considered to be the father of modern Hebrew and was one of the first active Zionist leaders. Believing that a living Hebrew, spoken by the people in its own land, was necessary for the rebirth of the nation, Ben-Yehuda fought untiringly for this goal. Furthermore, he believed that the Jewish people must establish a community in Ereẓ Israel to serve as a focal point for Jews in the Diaspora in order to save them from assimilation. As he wrote in the preface to his dictionary: "In those days it was as if the heavens had suddenly opened, and a clear incandescent light flashed before my eyes, and a mighty inner voice sounded in my ears: the renascence of Israel on its ancestral soil."

Born in Lithuania in 1858 as Eliezer Yiẓḥak Perelman, he changed his name to Ben-Yehuda when he went to live in Palestine. On the way to Ereẓ Israel in 1881, Ben-Yehuda married his childhood acquaintance, Deborah Jonas, and when they arrived in Jaffa, Ben-Yehuda told her that they would speak only Hebrew together. They thus established the first Hebrew-speaking home in Palestine and their son, Ben-Zion (later called Ithamar Ben-Avi) became the first child in modern times to learn Hebrew as his native language.

To further his goal of spreading the *Hebrew language, Ben-Yehuda wished to begin with the Orthodox Jews of Jerusalem who knew written Hebrew and would be able to learn the spoken tongue quickly. He adopted Orthodox customs, grew a beard and earlocks and prevailed upon his wife to wear a *sheytl* (wig) in order to be accepted by the Orthodox community. However, he soon quarreled with them as they realized that he introduced Hebrew not as a holy tongue but rather for political and national purposes. Subsequently, Ben-Yehuda's own attitude became very anti-religious and he registered as a national Jew "without religion."

In the years which followed, Ben-Yehuda accepted a teaching position as the Jerusalem Alliance School which became the first school where some courses were taught in Hebrew, due to his insistence that the Hebrew language be used for teaching Jewish subjects. At the same time Ben-Yehuda started a weekly newspaper first called *Ha-Ẓevi,* and then *Ha-Or.* It told the Jewish community what was happening throughout the settlement and enriched the Hebrew language by coining new words and adapting words from foreign languages.

In 1891 Ben-Yehuda's wife died and about six months later he married her younger sister who adopted the Hebrew name Ḥemdah. Her strong anti-religious attitude further intensified Ben-Yehuda's, and together they fought against the **ḥalukkah* system, the Orthodox system of charity distribution. The extreme Orthodox Jews were angered by this attitude and found a pretext for revenge in a line Ḥemdah wrote for the newspaper: "Let us gather strength and go forward." They interpreted this to the Turkish authorities as meaning: "Let us gather an army and proceed against the East." Consequently, Ben-Yehuda was charged with conspiracy to revolt and was sentenced to a year's imprisonment. Many Jews throughout the world were outraged; his sentence was appealed and he was released.

Portrait of Eliezer Ben-Yehuda, father of the modern Hebrew language.

Ben-Yehuda then continued his work in reviving the Hebrew language. He presided over the Va'ad ha-Lashan which was the forerunner of the Academy of the Hebrew Language, and worked 18 hours a day on a Hebrew dictionary. In 1910 he began to publish his *Complete Dictionary of Ancient and Modern Hebrew,* volume by volume, and after his death his widow and son Ehud continued its publication which was completed in 1959 (17 volumes). The dictionary attempts to include all the Hebrew words used in the different periods and developmental stages of the language. This dictionary, as well as Ben-Yehuda's newspaper are the achievements which helped to make Hebrew the modern living language of Israel, and which enabled Ben-Yehuda to realize his dream: the revival of the Hebrew language as a spoken tongue after more than two thousand years.

BEN-ZVI, IZHAK (1884-1963), second president of Israel, is also remembered as the founder and leader of Zionist Socialism, a pioneer in the Zionist labor movement and a leader of Jewish self-defense, both

1. The President, Izhak Ben-Zvi, and his wife, Rachel, arriving at Bangui, the capital of the Central African Republic, in 1962. They are being greeted by national assembly officials of the Republic.

Izhak Ben-Zvi

in Russia and in Ereẓ Israel. He also made important contributions to Jewish historiography by researching ancient and remote Jewish communities. His personal modesty and empathy for all the communities and sects of the country endeared him to the citizens of Israel.

Born in the Ukraine in 1884, Ben-Zvi was active in Jewish self-defense in his home town and later helped to form the Po'alei Zion party. His family was imprisoned in 1906 when police found weapons belonging to Ben-Zvi's self-defense organization hidden in their home, but Ben-Zvi managed to escape to Vilna, where he continued his activities with Po'alei Zion.

He settled in Israel in 1907 and founded *Ha-Shomer in 1909 with the help of Rachel Yanait whom he married in 1918. She also helped him to found the first Hebrew Socialist periodical *Aḥdut* ("Unity"). However, with the persecution of Jews by the Ottoman governor during World War I, *Aḥdut* was closed down and Ben-Zvi together with David *Ben-Gurion was imprisoned and eventually deported. Both made their way to New York where they founded the *He-Halutz movement of America and initiated a volunteer movement for Jewish battalions in the U.S. Among the first volunteers, they returned to Palestine in the Jewish Legion of the British Royal Fusiliers, and later joined the *Haganah.

A prolific journalist, Ben-Zvi wrote extensively for many newspapers, and in addition published many scholarly works about Jewish communities and sects (such as the Samaritans, Karaites, and Shabbateans). He headed the Institute for the Study of Oriental Jewish Communities in the Middle East, which he founded in 1948, and which was renamed the Ben-Zvi Institute in 1952.

Upon the death of President Chaim *Weizmann in 1952, Ben-Zvi was elected president, and while in office continued his research and writings. He served for two five-year terms and died in office at the beginning of his third term in 1963. After his death, the Yad Izhak Ben-Zvi memorial institute was founded and became dedicated to publishing Ben-Zvi's complete works and to continuing his interest in researching Jewish communities.

BERDICHEV is the typical Jewish town depicted in Russian and Jewish literature and folklore, particularly in the writings of *Mendele Mokher Seforim and *Shalom Aleichem. Located in the Ukraine, Berdichev became an important center of Volhynian *Ḥasidism in the last quarter of the 18th century. As the town grew, a number of noted scholars served as its rabbis, the most famous of whom was *Levi Isaac of Berdichev.

By the middle of the 19th century, Berdichev had grown into the second largest Jewish community in Russia, having a population of 46,683 and containing numerous synagogues and *battei midrash.* During this period, Berdichev was also a center for the *maskilim* who began to spread the idea of *Haskalah through the town, and who met with strong opposition by the Ḥasidim. Nevertheless, due to their efforts, the first public school in Berdichev giving instruction in Russian was opened in 1850.

However, in the latter half of the 19th century the town of Berdichev began to suffer economic hardship. As a result, the wealthier *maskilim* left for the larger cities, while the remaining majority of the Jewish population was so poor that a large number of children were even unable to attend *ḥeder.* According to the 1897 census, only 58% of Jewish males and 32% of Jewish females were able to read or write any language.

In early 1919, the Jews in Berdichev became victims of a pogrom perpetrated by the Ukrainian army, and later, under the Soviet government, most of the synagogues were closed. Yiddish continued to receive official acknowledgment and Yiddish schools were opened in Berdichev. In 1924, a government law court was established there, the first in the

Ukraine to conduct its affairs in Yiddish. However, in the mid-1930s all Jewish cultural activities there were suspended with the approach of World War II.

During the *Holocaust, early in July 1941, the Nazis established an extermination unit in Berdichev. Immediately afterward wholesale massacres began and a *ghetto was set up in the city. It was destroyed on October 5, 1941, after all the inhabitants were murdered. One report states that there were about 6,000 Jews in Berdichev after the war as compared with over 30,000 before the war.

Under Soviet rule, *mazzah* baking was prohibited in the early 1960s, but it was resumed after a few years. In 1970 there were an estimated 15,000 Jews in Berdichev with a synagogue, a cantor, and a ritual slaughterer for poultry. The cemetery was reported to be neglected but the Jews had erected a fence around the grave of Levi Isaac of Berdichev.

BERIḤAH. For many thousands of Jews, the defeat of Hitler and liberation from the concentration camps was not the end of their difficult times. Not wishing to remain in Eastern Europe among the memories of the Holocaust, they tried to escape to other parts of Europe or to Ereẓ Israel. Had it not been for the work of the Beriḥah, they would never have reached their destination.

Beriḥah, "flight" in Hebrew, was the name of an underground organization which moved Jews from Eastern Europe into Central and Southern Europe between 1940 and 1948. As the final destination was to be immigration to Palestine, the spontaneous mass movement of Jewish survivors from Europe to Ereẓ Israel also took this name.

In December 1944, a group of former Jewish *partisans and leaders of various Zionist groups met in Lublin to discuss moving the Jewish survivors of the War to Ereẓ Israel. A month later they were joined by the survivors of the Warsaw Ghetto fighters under Yiẓḥak Cukierman, and they founded the Beriḥah organization, with Abba Kovner as its leader.

When the first group was moved to Rumania in the middle of January, 1945, the mass flight had begun. Trains of the International Red Cross were used to transport people from Poland to Rumania; to get people to Ereẓ Israel, stations on the way to Italy (from which they would go to Palestine) were organized in Hungary and Yugoslavia. Soon Jews were being smuggled into Italy from Germany and Austria. Soldiers of the *Jewish Brigade Group and other units assisted in this operation, and the American Jewish Joint Distribution Committee provided funds for food and clothing for the refugees.

Jewish survivors were smuggled through American-held territories; forged Red Cross documents were made to enable people to travel freely; Soviet and Polish truck drivers were bribed to smuggle people to a transit station. Through these and other means, the Beriḥah was able, in only four years, to smuggle out of Eastern Europe 80% of the 250,000 Jews who were fleeing toward Palestine. Many of these people and the leaders of the Beriḥah fought to open the gates of Palestine and to establish the State of Israel.

Survivors of Hitler's Holocaust on their way to Ereẓ Israel across the mountains, helped by the Beriḥah, 1945.

BERLIN. The history of Jews in Berlin is a story of taxes and restrictions. From the first mention of Jews in a letter from the Berlin local council on October 20, 1295 (forbidding wool merchants to supply Jews with wool yarn) until the present, Jewish life in Germany's largest city has not been easy.

Early restrictions included limitation of residence permits, and taxation in return for protection. Jewish storekeepers were permitted to sell only certain products and land ownership was forbidden. In 1510 Jews were accused of crimes against the Catholic Church – 111 Jews were arrested, and 51 sentenced to death. Of these, 38 were burned at the stake.

Under the proclamation of March 11, 1812, citizenship was finally granted to Jews. Restrictions on their residence rights in the state as well as the special taxes they had to pay began to be lifted. These were not entirely removed until 1860 when civic equality was finally attained. Jews began to enter the political and social life of Berlin. The *Reform movement continued to grow. There were increasing instances of intermarriage and conversion, yet there was a backlash of hostility and anti-Semitism. Communal life continued to flourish, however, because of a constant flow of immigration from Russia and Poland.

1

2

1. Grenadierstrasse in the Jewish quarter of Berlin. Drawn by the caricaturist Karl Arnold in *Simplicissimus,* 1921.
2. A lithograph of the actress, Sarah Bernhardt, done in 1879.

The Jewish population of Berlin increased greatly. In 1812 there were 3,292 Jews and in 1890 the number had risen to 108,044. In 1925 there were 172,672 Jews living in Berlin, comprising 30% of German Jewry. Following the period of *Nazism that number was reduced to 6,000 in 1945.

At the beginning of Nazi rule, severe economic and social restrictions were placed on Jews, and many lost their jobs. Jews were forced to wear a yellow star (see Jewish *Badge), and large numbers of them were sent to concentration camps.

In 1970 there were in Berlin 5,577 Jews (4,080 of them over the age of 41), with a low birthrate and many mixed marriages.

BERNHARDT, SARAH (1844-1923), was born Rosine Bernard, and is still considered by some experts to have been the greatest actress in history. She was the eldest of three illegitimate daughters born to Judith Van Hard, a Dutch-Jewish music teacher. When Sarah was ten years old she was sent to the convent of Versailles and baptized. However, she remained proud of her Jewish heritage. She made her debut at the Comédie Francaise in 1862 as Iphigénie in Racine's *Iphigénie en Aulide.* She acted at the Odéon from 1866 to 1872, and achieved popular acclaim in Coppée's *Le Passant* as the page Zanetto, her first male role. Returning to the Comédie Francaise, she became one of the greatest interpreters of Racine, playing *Andromaque* in 1873 and *Phèdre* in 1874. Temperament and impatience with authority ended her career at the Comédie in 1879. She embarked on a series of tours abroad and drew crowds wherever she appeared. In 1899 she took over a large Paris theater, renamed it The Sarah Bernhardt, and directed it until her death. Here she presented *Hamlet* and herself played the title role. A neglected knee injury resulted in complications, and in 1914 she was obliged to have her right leg amputated. She continued to appear in roles which permitted her to sit.

The "Divine Sarah," as she was called by Victor Hugo, died while at work on a film.

BERNSTEIN, LEONARD (1918-) a U.S. composer and conductor, studied composition, piano and conducting. In 1943 he was appointed assistant conductor of the New York Philharmonic. He attracted national attention by performing brilliantly when called upon to conduct a difficult program at short notice. In 1958 he was appointed music director and conductor of the N.Y. Philharmonic, the first American-born musician to occupy this post.

He retired in 1969 to devote himself to composing. Among his symphonic works are the *Jeremiah Symphony,* with a vocal solo in Hebrew; *The Age of Anxiety,* utilizing jazz rhythms; *Kaddish* (in Hebrew), an oratorio for narrator, chorus, and orchestra, which he conducted for the first time in Tel Aviv in 1963; and *Chichester Psalms* (also in Hebrew), for chorus and orchestra (1965). Bernstein had his greatest popular triumph with *West Side Story* (1957), which owed much of its success on both stage and screen to his dynamic music. He is a brilliant lecturer on music and produced an exceptionally popular series of young people's concerts. They were broadcast on television and reached a wide audience, being rebroadcast in Israel too.

Bernstein was closely associated with Israel from 1947, when he conducted his first concerts there. After the establishment of the State he was instrumental in creating the Koussevitzky music collection at the National Library in Jerusalem. Over the years he has made guest appearances with the Israel Philharmonic Orchestra, both in Israel and on its tours abroad.

BERTINORO, OBADIAH (c. 1450 - before 1516) was a rabbi and commentator on the Mishnah, whose family had come from the town of Bertinero in northern Italy. In 1485 he left his home to settle in Ereẓ Israel, and travelled via Rome to Naples, where he stayed for four months. In 1487 he reached Palermo, where he preached every Sabbath during his three-month stay. He was asked to become rabbi there but refused, and sailed to Egypt, where he arrived early in 1488.

He went on to Cairo where he was received with great honor. There too, he was asked to remain, but refused. He continued his journey through Gaza, Hebron and Bethlehem. In Jerusalem, where he arrived just before Passover in 1488, he was warmly welcomed by Rabbi Colombano who had also come from Italy. Bertinoro became the spiritual leader of Jerusalem Jewry, and united the divided community. He started regular courses of study and preached twice a month in Hebrew. He also collected funds from Italy to support the poor.

He completed his commentary on the Mishnah in Jerusalem. It was published in Venice in 1549, and has become as standard a commentary on the Mishnah as Rashi's is on the Talmud. Clearly written, it is based on Rashi and on Maimonides. Bertinoro's writings on Rashi's commentary on the Pentateuch were published in 1810. He is buried on the Mount of Olives.

BET ALFA is in the eastern Jezreel Valley at the foot of Mount Gilboa in Israel. It may be the site of the town of Hilfa, which is mentioned in the Talmud. The foundations of an ancient synagogue were discovered near there in 1929 by explorations done on behalf of the Hebrew University. The synagogue, measuring 46 x 92 feet, included a courtyard, hall,

The mosaic floor of the synagogue at Bet Alfa. The central panel shows the signs of the zodiac, the section at the front of the picture tells the story of the binding of Isaac, and the far panel is the lion with a seven-branched *menorah.* The mosaic dates from the sixth century b.c.e.

two side aisles and a women's gallery. It faced south toward Jerusalem. A small cavity in the floor probably served as a *genizah;* above it was an Ark for scrolls of the Law. The whole floor of the building is paved with mosaics.

Two inscriptions were found at the entrance to the hall. One, in Aramaic, states that the mosaics were made during the reign of Emperor Justin (518-527). The other, in Greek, gives the names of those who made the mosaics, Marianos and his son Ḥanina. There are three mosaic panels in the center of the hall. The first shows the **Akedah,* the binding of Isaac on the altar. The second mosaic represents the signs of the *Zodiac. The third depicts a synagogue ark with a gabled roof and an "eternal light" suspended from its top. On either side is a lion with a seven-branched *menorah.* Above the *menorah* and between the lions are pictured ritual items such as *lulavim* (palm branches), *etrogim* (citrons), and incense holders. Curtains adorned it on either side.

The designs are simple and strong. In these mosaics, the artists took great care to make each scene expressive. The mosaics of Bet Alfa are striking in their coloring and style, and are among the finest examples of Jewish art in the Byzantine period.

A kibbutz was founded at Bet Alfa in 1922.

BETAR is a Zionist youth movement which was founded in 1923 in Eastern Europe, with the aim of giving youth a Zionist education, teaching them the Hebrew language and culture, and instructing them in methods of self-defense. The name of the movement is the abbreviation of Berit Trumpeldor, in memory of Joseph *Trumpeldor, whose life exemplified the ideas of Jewish self-defense and pioneering. The students and young workers who founded the movement declared themselves a "part of the Jewish Legion to be established in Ereẓ Israel," and dedicated themselves to the oath: "I devote my life to the rebirth of the Jewish State, with a Jewish majority on both sides of the Jordan." Believing in the ideal of *aliyah* to Ereẓ Israel, by any means, legal or "illegal," they organized a farm for the agricultural training of pioneer settlers in Palestine.

While the first Betar immigrants to Palestine (1925-29) joined the *Histadrut (a Zionist labor organization) and the *Haganah, Betar entered into ideological conflict with the Zionist-Socialist movement; a conflict which sometimes broke out into physical clashes on the streets of Tel Aviv. Accordingly, Betar broke away from the Zionist-Socialist movement, joining the Union of Zionist Revisionists, and in 1931, broke away from the Haganah and formed the *Irgun Ẓeva'i Le'ummi as a separate underground organization.

Outside of Ereẓ Israel, the first world conference of Betar took place in 1931 and Vladimir *Jabotinsky, a believer in Jewish "legionism" and military power, was elected president of the movement. Defense training was proclaimed the most important duty of every member, and courses were given in street fighting, boxing, handling small arms, and military tactics. In addition, a central naval school of Betar was established in Italy in 1934 to train cadets, a school for training sailors in Latvia in 1935-39, and flying courses were eventually given by the Irgun Ẓeva'i Le'ummi.

In the late 1930s Betar aided *"illegal" immigration to Palestine and saved thousands of Jews who otherwise could not have entered the country because of the British restrictions. In 1938, Betar had a world membership of 90,000 but during World War II most of its European members were killed. With the loss of European Jewry, Israel became the center of the movement, which in the late 1960s numbered about 8,000 members, of whom 4,500 were in Israel in a total of 74 branches. Betar also established 12 cooperative and collective settlements in Israel and in addition set up sports centers.

BETH JACOB is the name of a network of religious schools for girls organized in Poland in the post-World War I era with the aid of Agudat Israel, an Orthodox organization whose schools for boys were to be found in every community. While the boys' schools were of the old traditional type, the newly formed schools for girls combined Jewish traditional studies and vocational training.

The first school was founded in Cracow in 1917 by Sara Schnirer. The school in Cracow had an enrolment of only 30 pupils, but the success of this early venture in imparting religious Jewish studies, some secular learning, and vocational training led to the formation of a large number of schools in a number of countries. By 1929 there were 147 such schools in Poland, and 20 schools in Lithuania, Latvia, and Austria. The Beth Jacob school system included teachers' training institutes founded in 1931 and post-graduate courses (1933).

With the invasion of Austria, Poland, Lithuania and Latvia by the Nazis and subsequently by the

Russians, the activities of the Beth Jacob schools were discontinued. At the end of World War II Beth Jacob schools were opened in Israel, England, Switzerland, Belgium, France, Uruguay, Argentina, and the United States. In Israel there are 92 schools, and about 15 in other countries. In the U.S. the Beth Jacob National Council was organized in 1943. By 1947 there were eight schools under their supervision. In 1951 two teacher-training schools were established and in the late 1950s two high schools and a teachers' seminary were founded.

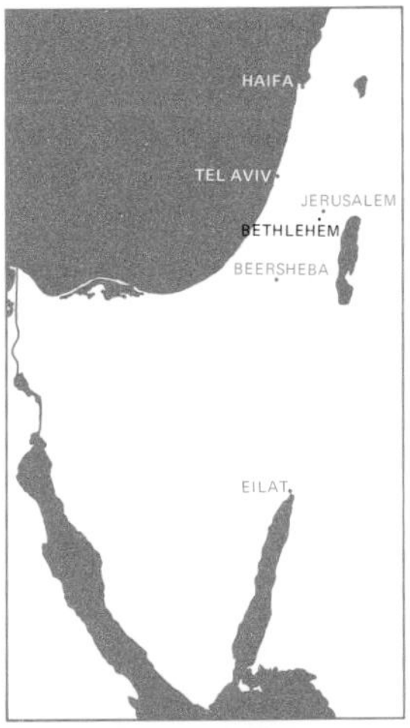

BETHLEHEM. The city of Bethlehem, located five miles south of Jerusalem, has been the setting for many events and personalities significant to both the Jewish and Christian religions. According to Jewish tradition, it is in the vicinity of Bethlehem that the matriarch *Rachel is buried, and accordingly, this site has been the focus of Jewish pilgrimages throughout the ages.

During the period of the Judges, Bethlehem was one of the chief towns of the tribe of Judah, and was the scene of the story of *Ruth and Boaz as related in the Book of Ruth. Ruth's great-grandson, *David, was born in Bethlehem and it was there that the prophet Samuel anointed him king.

After the destruction of the Temple when *Gedaliah ben Ahikam served as governor of Judea, Bethlehem was again significant; it was the town from which Gedaliah's assassins came. After the Babylonian exile ended in 516 b.c.e., the exiles from Bethlehem returned to their city and Jewish settlement continued there until the time of *Bar Kokhba. In 135 c.e., a Roman garrison was stationed there to root out the remnants of Bar Kokhba's army, and from that time, a gentile population resided there.

According to Christian tradition, *Jesus was born in Bethlehem. On the reported spot, Helena the mother of the Emperor Constantine built a church, which was destroyed during the Samaritan uprising in 529 c.e., but later rebuilt by Justinian in the form that it has kept to the present time. In fact, because the paintings portray people in Oriental costume, the Persians are said to have spared the building when they captured Bethlehem in 614. During the Arab conquest, Bethlehem suffered no damage, and during the Crusades its Church of the Nativity was the place where two crusader kings, Baldwin I and II, were crowned. In the years which followed, when Bethlehem fell under the rule of the Mamluks and the Turks, the Christians continually reduced the size of the entrance to the church for security reasons, so that by now it is just a low and narrow opening.

Today's Bethlehem has numerous Christian buildings and is a main attraction for Christian pilgrims, particularly on Christmas when a special Mass is recited.

Whereas from 1948 Bethlehem was under Jordanian control and not accessible to Jewish pilgrims, after the Six-Day War in 1967 Bethlehem once again became part of Israel, and Rachel's tomb has become the center for an unending stream of visitors.

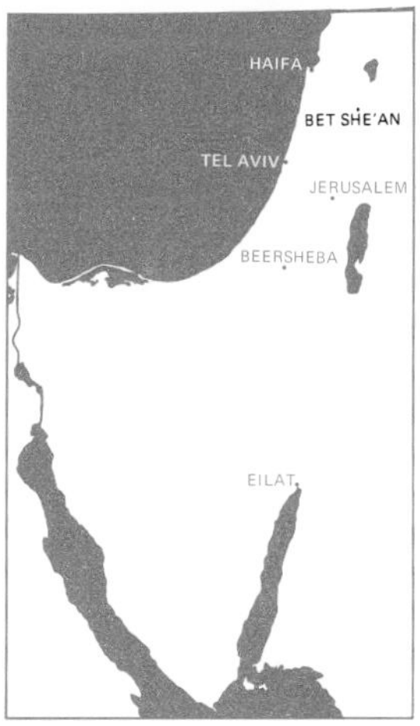

BET SHE'AN is a city with a very long history. It is situated on a main crossroads about 25 miles southeast of Tiberias and is 390 feet below sea level. The excavations of Tel Bet She'an proved the importance of the place as a station for caravans and a center of

2

1. The tomb of Rachel in Bethlehem, where Jews come to pray.
2. A view of the town center of Bet She'an from the west. The mountains of Jordan are seen in the background.

Egyptian rule probably as early as the 15th century b.c.e. An Egyptian basalt stone found there, dating from the late 14th century b.c.e., has an inscription which mentions the Habiru (thought by some to be the ancient Hebrews), who disturbed the peace and undermined government authority in the region.

The valley of Bet She'an was the portion of the tribe of Issachar, but the tribe of Manasseh extended its settlements to this territory. During Saul's reign the city was in the hands of the Philistines, but in the time of Solomon it was again under Jewish rule. The wall, the gate, and the style of stone-cutting in the hill belong to the Solomonic period.

By the first century b.c.e., many Jews lived in Bet She'an. During the Hasmonean period Bet She'an became an important administrative center, and Alexander *Yannai built ramparts around the city. In 63 b.c.e. Pompey revived the Greek way of life, and the city became the capital of a group of ten Greek cities called the Decapolis Alliance. When the Jewish War broke out in 66 c.e., 13,000 Jews were murdered in Bet She'an. A beautiful Roman theater, built in 200 c.e., can still be seen.

During the mishnaic and talmudic periods Bet She'an was inhabited by Jews. They made fine linen and grew field crops and olives. Bet She'an was then a world center for making and exporting textiles. An excavated synagogue, dating from the fourth century, had a beautiful mosaic floor of geometrical design. The synagogue was burned down in 624.

From the beginning of the 20th century, Jews started to resettle in the area. Some 12,000 people live there, despite the shelling that has taken place from time to time from beyond the Jordan River.

1. Bruno Bettelheim, American educational psychologist.
2. Carved *menorah,* a Jewish symbol which appears frequently in the decoration of the catacombs in Bet She'arim.

1

2

BET SHE'ARIM was an ancient city in the Lower Galilee, near the modern town of Kiryat Tivon on the Nazareth-Haifa road. Although settlement at Bet She'arim apparently started in Bible times, the city is first mentioned at the end of the Second Temple period. During talmudic times, important scholars lived there. Bet She'arim reached great prosperity in the late second century when Rabbi *Judah ha-Nasi went to live there and made it the seat of the Sanhedrin. From the beginning of the following century, it became the central burial place for Jews of Ereẓ Israel and the Diaspora. The city was destroyed by Romans during the suppression of the Jewish revolt in 352 c.e. However, a small settlement continued there during the Byzantine period.

The city of Bet She'arim extended over the summit of a hill – an area of 25 acres, 450 feet above sea level. It was surrounded by a wall, two sections of which have been discovered. Remains of large buildings, including a large synagogue, have been found, as well as a glassmaking shop and about 1,200 bronze coins struck in the first half of the fourth century. An oil press used mainly in the Byzantine period was found nearby. Rock-cut catacombs that were prepared to provide burial places for sale to people outside Bet She'arim were found in all these areas.

The soft limestone rock of the area was easily carved, and many simple decorations were found on the walls of the burial chambers. Most favored were religious symbols and ritual objects, especially the seven-branched *menorah and the Ark of the Law, with columns and steps. Also the *shofar, lulav, etrog* and an incense shovel of the Temple were depicted. Heavy ornamental stone doors were decorated to imitate wooden doors, complete with panels, nailheads and knockers. Among others, many rabbis and sages were buried in these chambers. Two-hundred and fifty epitaphs in Greek, Hebrew and Aramaic were found, and one of them reads: "He who is buried here (is) Simeon, son of Johanan, and on oath, whoever shall open upon him shall die of an evil end."

BETTELHEIM, BRUNO (1903-) is a U.S. psychologist and educator who helped build one of the world's most successful institutions for the treatment of emotionally disturbed children. Autistic children who responded to nothing (not even blinking when sand was in their eyes) have been helped to live much more normal lives while residing at the Sonia Shankman Orthogenic School that Bruno

Bettelheim heads. Disturbed children live and study there and often stay for as long as eight years. In order to compare child rearing methods in Israel kibbutzim with his own methods, Bettelheim wrote *The Children of the Dream* (1969).

Bruno Bettelheim was born in Vienna and studied art at the University there. In 1938 he was sent to Dachau concentration camp and then to Buchenwald. He was released in 1939 and permitted to go to the United States where he wrote about those experiences in the *Informed Heart* (1960). He observed that Hitler wanted to destroy all human personality and claimed that he maintained some of his own humanity in the camps only by studying others psychologically. He was harshly critical of the Jews for not revolting against Nazi terror. It has been pointed out, however, that this criticism was based on limited evidence.

His life's work with emotionally disturbed children was greatly influenced by his experiences in the Nazi camps.

BEZALEL, son of Uri of the tribe of Judah, was an expert in metal work, stonecutting, and woodcarving, and chief of the artisans who were employed both in the construction of the *Tabernacle and in designing the priests' vestments. He was assisted by Oholiab of the tribe of Dan, who was an expert craftsman and embroiderer.

Bezalel's construction of the Tabernacle and its equipment followed the plan that God had detailed Moses on Mount Sinai. He was chosen for the task because he was endowed with "a divine spirit of skill, ability, and knowledge." Bezalel's name which means "in the shadow (or under the protection) of God" further implies that he was divinely inspired.

1

In the *aggadah* we are told that though God had appointed Bezalel as the architect of the Tabernacle, He nevertheless commanded Moses to obtain the approval of the Children of Israel for the appointment, in order to teach that no leader should be appointed without the consent of the people. At the side of Bezalel, who belonged to the aristocratic tribe of Judah, worked Oholiab, of the lowliest tribe, that of Dan, to show that before God "the great and the lowly are equal."

Named after Bezalel the artisan is the Bezalel Academy of Arts and Design in Jerusalem and the Bezalel Art Museum which is part of the school. Both were founded in 1906 by the sculptor Boris *Schatz. His son Bezalel grew up (like his biblical namesake) to be an artist in his own right.

BIALIK, ḤAYYIM NAḤMAN (1873-1934), the greatest Hebrew poet of modern times, was also an essayist, storywriter, translator and editor who exercised a profound influence on modern Jewish culture. Bialik was born in the village of Radi, near Zhitomir (Volhynia). His father, who came of scholarly stock, had come down in life through his impracticality in his business affairs. For his father as well as his mother, this was a second marriage, both having been widowed previously. Despite his family's dire economic circumstances, some of Bialik's best poems recall and idealize the enchanted hours which he spent as a child romping in the secret shade of the forest. Other poems recall loneliness and parental neglect.

When Bialik was six, his parents moved to Zhitomir in search of a livelihood and his father was reduced to keeping a saloon on the outskirts of town. Shortly thereafter, in 1880, his father died and the destitute widow entrusted her son to the care of his well-to-do paternal grandfather. For ten years the gifted, mischievous Ḥayyim Naḥman was raised by this stern, pious old man. At first he was instructed by teachers in the traditional *ḥeder*, but later, from the age of 13, he pursued his studies alone.

Convinced by a journalistic report that the yeshivah of *Volozhin in Lithuania would offer him an introduction to the humanities as well as a continuation of his talmudic studies, Bialik persuaded his grandfather to permit him to study there. In fact, however, the curriculum of the yeshivah enabled him to immerse himself only in the scholarly virtues of talmudic studies. But in the end modernist doubts triumphed over traditionalist

1. Bezalel and Oholiab building the Tabernacle. Woodcut from the *Koborgor Bible,* Nuremburg, 1483.
2. Ḥayyim Naḥman Bialik, Hebrew poet.

2

certainties. Bialik began to withdraw from the life of the school and lived in the world of poetry, reading Russian verse and European literature. While still in the yeshivah Bialik joined a secret Orthodox Zionist student society, Neẓaḥ Israel, which attempted to blend Jewish nationalism and enlightenment with a firm adherence to tradition. In this period Bialik was influenced by the teachings of *Aḥad Ha-Am's spiritual Zionism.

In the summer of 1891 Bialik left the yeshivah for Odessa, the center of modern Jewish culture, in southern Russia. He was attracted by the literary circle that formed around Aḥad Ha-Am, and harbored the dream that in Odessa he would be able to prepare himself for entry to the modern Orthodox rabbinical seminary in Berlin. Penniless and alone, he earned a livelihood for a while by giving Hebrew lessons, while continuing to study Russian literature and German grammar. At first the shy youth did not become involved in the literary life of the city but his first poem, a song longing for Zion, was favorably received by the critics.

When Bialik learned, early in 1892, that the yeshivah of Volozhin had been closed, he cut short his stay in the company of the writers of Odessa, and hurried home in order to spare his dying grandfather the knowledge that he had forsaken his religious studies. On returning home he found that his older brother too was dying. The atmosphere at home embodied for him the despair and squalor of Jewish life in the Diaspora.

In 1893, after the death of his brother and grandfather, Bialik married Manya Averbuch, and for the next three years joined her father in the timber trade in Korostyshev, near Kiev. During the long and lonely stretches in the forest, he read very widely. In business, however, he failed, and in 1897 Bialik found a position as a teacher in Sosnowiec, near the Prussian border. But the pettiness of provincial life depressed him, and in 1900 Bialik finally succeeded in finding a teaching position in Odessa, where he lived until 1921, except for a year's stay in Warsaw (1904), where he served as literary editor of a Hebrew journal. Together with three other writers he founded the Moriah Publishing House which produced textbooks for the modern Jewish school. Throughout these years Bialik's reputation grew, and when his first volume of poems appeared in 1901, he was hailed as "the poet of the national renaissance."

Soon after, in 1903, the Kishinev pogroms deeply shocked the whole civilized world. After interviewing survivors of the atrocity, Bialik wrote *"Al ha-Sheḥitah"* ("On the Slaughter," 1903) in which he calls on heaven either to exercise immediate justice and, if not, to destroy the world, spurning mere vengeance with the famous lines:

Cursed is he who says 'Revenge!'
Vengeance for the blood of a small child
Satan has not yet created.

Later he wrote *"Be-Ir ha-Haregah"* ("In the City of Slaughter," 1904), a searing denunciation of the people's meek submission to the massacre, in which he is bitter at the absence of justice, and struck by the indifference of nature: "The sun shone, the acacia blossomed, and the slaughterer slaughtered."

After three years in Berlin, Bialik settled in Tel Aviv in 1924 where he spent the rest of his life. He died in Vienna where he had gone for medical treatment.

Bialik was a very learned man in Jewish subjects and, together with Yehoshua Ḥana Rawnitzki, he compiled an anthology of the *aggadah* (*Sefer ha-Aggadah,* 1908-11) which is still a standard text in Israel's schools. He was very active in public affairs had traveled all over the world in the cause of Zionism and the Hebrew language. In his later years he took an increasingly positive attitude towards Judaism and initiated the popular *Oneg Shabbat,* a Sabbath study project.

Bialik's literary career was a turning point in modern Hebrew literature. He had a thorough command of Hebrew and the ability to fully utilize the resources of the language. To a large degree he anticipated the Hebrew spoken in modern Israel and influenced it a great deal. Very many of his poems have been set to music and are still very popular, particularly the poems he wrote for children. In Israel, he is considered to be the national poet and his position is much the same as that of Shakespeare in English-speaking countries.

BIBLE. The Jewish people is known as the "People of the Book." That "Book" is the Bible, because the Bible tells the story of the origins and early history of the Jews, and secondly, because for the Jews the Bible is the most sacred text there is.

NAMES

In the Talmud the Bible is known as *Mikra,* which is a noun formed from the verb *kara* meaning "to read." The commonly used Hebrew name for the Bible, however, is *Tanakh.* This word is formed from the initial letters of the Hebrew names of the three parts of the Bible: *Torah* (the first five Books), *Nevi'im* (The Prophets) and *Ketuvim* (The Writings, or Hagiographa). The English name, "Bible," is from the Greek meaning "book," and the other accepted English name, "Scriptures" (or Holy Scriptures), is from the Latin and means "writings." Christians often refer to the Hebrew Bible as the Old Testament

בראשית ברא
אלהים את
השמים ואת
הארץ: והארץ
היתה תהו ובהו
וחשך על פני
תהום ורוח אלהים מרחפת על פני
המים: ויאמר אלהים יהי אור ויהי אור:
וירא אלהים את האור כי טוב ויבדל
אלהים בין האור ובין החשך: ויקרא
אלהים לאור יום ולחשך קרא לילה
ויהי ערב ויהי בקר יום אחד:

The first page of the Bible, which relates the story of the Creation. This Pentateuch was printed in Faro, Portugal, in 1487 for Don Samuel Gacon.

to distinguish it from the Christian New Testament; that name is obviously unacceptable to Jews because they have no newer work which supersedes the Bible.

THE CANON

The first of the three sections of the Bible is called the Torah meaning "teaching." It contains five Books and is therefore also known as the *Ḥummash*, or *Ḥamishah Ḥumshei Torah,* which means the Five Books (or Fifths) of the Torah. In English it is also sometimes called the Law, and also the Pentateuch, which is Greek for "Five Books." This section of the Bible tells the story of the Jewish people to the death of Moses.

The second section contains the subsequent history of the Jewish people as well as the writings of the Prophets. Because of the crucial role the prophets played, this section is called *Nevi'im* or Prophets. It contains 21 separate books, but according to the Jewish tradition both Books of Samuel are considered to be one, as are both Books of Kings. Furthermore, the 12 "minor" prophets are also counted as one Book. Thus the number is eight.

The third and final section is mainly a collection of various writings dealing with piety and wisdom, although it does contain some Books of a historical nature. The Hebrew name for this section is *Ketuvim,* which means "writings." It is also known by the Greek name, Hagiographa, which means Holy Writings. *Ketuvim* contains 13 separate Books, but traditionally Ezra and Nehemiah go together, as do the two Books of Chronicles; thus the total comes to 11.

All in all, there are 39 separate books in the Bible or, according to the traditional arrangement, 24.

The word Canon indicates the authoritative list of the books of the Bible. The term has mainly negative connotations because it indicates which books are not to be included. Many of the excluded books are in the *Apocrypha and the Pseudepigrapha. The canon of the various sections of the Bible was fixed by the rabbis of the Talmud on the basis of the holiness of the various books as they knew them. The process of canonization extended over a long period of time, though unfortunately there is no exact evidence as to the details.

The Torah was certainly the first section to be fixed. According to tradition, the whole Torah was written by Moses and by his death was complete. The critical view is that parts of the Torah were written in different periods and that it was finally edited and canonized during the Babylonian exile, that is, before 444 b.c.e.

The rabbis regarded Haggai, Zechariah and Malachi as the last of the prophets, the "divine spirit" having ceased in Israel with their deaths. The *Nevi'im* section seems to have been finally determined by 323 b.c.e. With regard to the *Ketuvim* the situation is quite different. There are even differences of opinion in the Talmud as to which books should be included. It seems, therefore, that this section was not crystallized until well into the second century c.e.

TORAH

The Torah tells the story of the People of Israel until the death of Moses and the entry into the Promised Land. It also contains the laws that God commanded the Jews. The five books of the Torah are known in Hebrew by their first word, or the first key word. The books are *Bereshit* (or Genesis), *Shemot*

1

2

1. Recent Polish stamp showing Adam and Eve standing by the Tree of Knowledge of Good and Evil.
2. "Moses slaying the Egyptian," from an 18th century *Haggadah*, the service for the first two nights of Passover.

(Exodus), *Va-Yikra* (Leviticus), *Be-Midbar* (Numbers), and *Devarim* (Deuteronomy).

THE FIVE BOOKS

Bereshit gives an account of the *Creation of the World (hence the name Genesis) and the early history of mankind. It continues with the story of the Patriarchs *Abraham, *Isaac and *Jacob and tells how *Joseph was sold into slavery in Egypt and later brought his brothers and father there. The Book closes with the Children of Israel in Egypt and the death of Joseph.

Shemot tells the story of the Jews in Egypt; how they were oppressed and enslaved by a pharaoh "who knew not Joseph." It continues with the account of *Moses' birth and his selection by God to lead the Children of Israel out of Egypt. After the ten *plagues, it tells of the Exodus from Egypt and the crossing of the Red Sea. The climax of the Book is undoubtedly the *Revelation at Mount *Sinai when the Jews heard the *Ten Commandments (or at least the first two) from God Himself, and received various parts of the Torah. The narrative continues with the story of the *Golden Calf, while the rest of *Shemot* is taken up with a description of the priests' vestments and an account of the making and erection of the *Tabernacle. Scattered through the Book are various laws which include ritual, criminal, and civil legislation.

Va-Yikra, the third of the five books is an independent unit as far as its theme is concerned. This is indicated by its alternative Hebrew name, *Torat Kohanim,* or Teachings of the Priests. This Book is concerned with the whole system of sacrifices in the Tabernacle (which was later transferred to the *Temple); it gives an account of the inaugural service at the Tabernacle including the installation of the priests; it continues with the laws of ritual *purity and impurity; and the last section deals with the *dietary laws of the permitted and forbidden foods, the *festivals and the *Sabbatical and Jubilee years.

The keynote of *Va-Yikra* is holiness, a holiness which applies to the ordinary Jew as much as to the priests. Indeed, one memorable verse reads: "The Lord spoke to Moses, saying: 'Speak to the whole Israelite community and say unto them: You shall be holy, for I, the Lord your God, am holy,' " and among the laws immediately following this statement comes the commandment: "Love your neighbor as yourself." Clearly, the holiness is not just that of the Tabernacle and the sacrifice, but that of everyday life. Accordingly, the ancient Jewish custom is for children to start their study of Bible with this book, *Va-Yikra.*

Be-Midbar is the fourth Book of the Torah. The word means "in the wilderness" and indeed the Book tells the further story of the Jews' 40 years wandering in the wilderness before they entered the Promised Land. In the Talmud this Book is also known as the *Ḥummash ha-Pekudim,* the "*Ḥummash* of the Census" since the Book records the counting of the Children of Israel. It is from this that the English name Numbers derives.

Besides the censuses, the Book tells of the departure from Mount Sinai and the preparations of the Children of Israel for their entry into the Land of Canaan. Because the people were influenced by the negative report brought back by the 12 spies (except *Joshua and Caleb) and started to complain, God decreed that they would have to remain in the wilderness for 40 years, corresponding to the 40 days the spies spent in Ereẓ Israel, and that they all (again except Joshua and Caleb) would die in the wilderness and not merit entering the Promised Land. *Be-Midbar* also records other instances of rebellion against God and Moses, the most serious being the rebellion of *Korah and his followers. Besides these historical records the Book also contains many laws on a wide range of subjects including the *Sabbath, **Tefillin*, **Tallit*, the *Red Heifer, *Cities of Refuge, and *inheritance. Some of the military campaigns against various peoples who blocked the Jews' passage are also described.

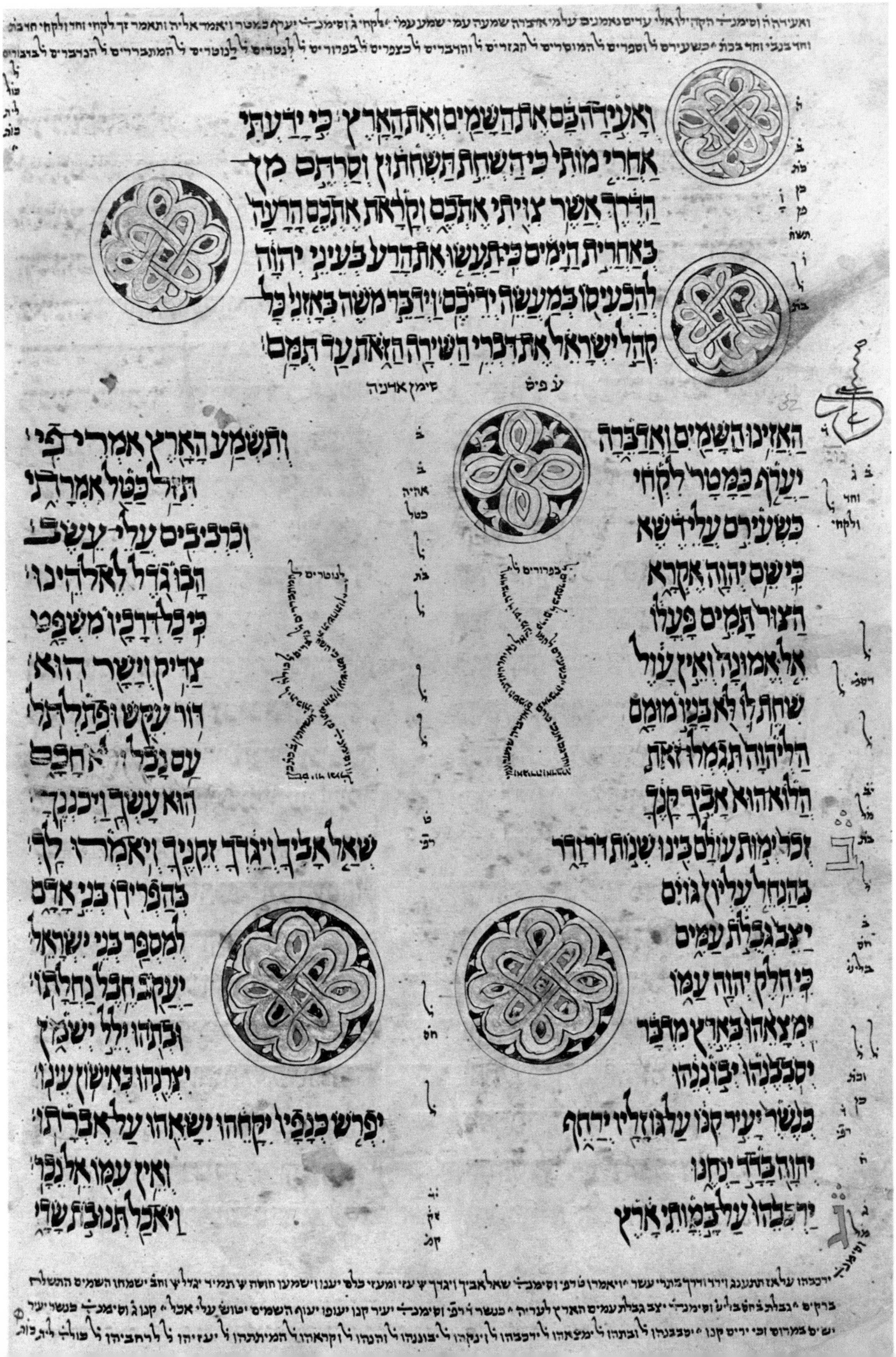

ואעידה בם את השמים ואת הארץ כי ידעתי
אחרי מותי כי השחת תשחתון וסרתם מן
הדרך אשר צויתי אתכם וקראת אתכם הרעה
באחרית הימים כי תעשו את הרע בעיני יהוה
להכעיסו במעשה ידיכם וידבר משה באזני כל
קהל ישראל את דברי השירה הזאת עד תמם

האזינו השמים ואדברה ותשמע הארץ אמרי פי
יערף כמטר לקחי תזל כטל אמרתי
כשעירם עלי דשא וכרביבים עלי עשב
כי שם יהוה אקרא הבו גדל לאלהינו
הצור תמים פעלו כי כל דרכיו משפט
אל אמונה ואין עול צדיק וישר הוא
שחת לו לא בניו מומם דור עקש ופתלתל
הליהוה תגמלו זאת עם נבל ולא חכם
הלוא הוא אביך קנך הוא עשך ויכננך
זכר ימות עולם בינו שנות דור ודור שאל אביך ויגדך זקניך ויאמרו לך
בהנחל עליון גוים בהפרידו בני אדם
יצב גבלת עמים למספר בני ישראל
כי חלק יהוה עמו יעקב חבל נחלתו
ימצאהו בארץ מדבר ובתהו ילל ישמן
יסבבנהו יבוננהו יצרנהו כאישון עינו
כנשר יעיר קנו על גוזליו ירחף יפרש כנפיו יקחהו ישאהו על אברתו
יהוה בדד ינחנו ואין עמו אל נכר
ירכבהו על במותי ארץ ויאכל תנובת שדי

Bible. Page from a 15th century Yemenite Bible. This is the Song of Moses (Deuteronomy 32:1-43), which Moses recited before he died. He called on heaven and earth to be witnesses to his instructions to the Israelites to follow the way of God. The prose section is written in a single column at the top of the page and the poetic section is in two ornamental columns. Between the columns and at the sides is the *masorah,* the traditions for correct spelling, writing and reading of the Hebrew Bible. At the top and bottom of the page there is a commentary on the passage.

Bible. Full-page frontispiece to the *Schocken Bible,* written in south Germany by Ḥayyim the Scribe, in about 1300. The first word of the Bible and of the Book of Genesis, *Bereshit* ("In the beginning . . ."), is written in the center of the page, and the 45 circles depict incidents from the Book of Genesis.

Reading from right to left, the top row illustrates the story of Adam and Eve in the Garden of Eden; Cain slaying Abel; Noah and his ark; and the Tower of Babel. The next row of pictures shows the destruction of Sodom and Gomorrah; the sacrifice of Isaac; Esau; and Jacob's dream. Row three: Joseph's dream and his sale into captivity. The four circles around the initial-word are of Joseph's experiences in Egypt in the house of Potiphar and his interpretations of dreams. In the sixth row Joseph is a powerful man in Egypt, and is reunited with his brothers, and (in the first circles of the seventh row) with his father. Then begins the story of the slavery in Egypt, the birth of Moses and (eighth row) the Exodus from Egypt. The last row shows the drowning of the pursuing Egyptian army; the Revelation at Mt. Sinai; the spies returning from Canaan, and the punishment of the rebel Korah. Finally, Balaam mounted on his ass is confronted by the angel with the fiery sword.

Devarim is the last Book of the Torah. In Jewish sources this Book is also known as *Mishneh Torah* which means the "Repetition of the Torah"; from this idea comes the English name, Deuteronomy, from the Latin meaning the Repeated Law.

Devarim is, in fact, Moses' farewell address to the Jewish people before his death and their entry into Canaan. The discourse contains a brief summary of the whole journey since Egypt and highlights some of the outstanding incidents. The Book also includes a repetition of the Ten Commandments in nearly the same form as in *Shemot,* and many of the laws in the preceding four Books are also given again.

Aware that he was soon to die, Moses made an impassioned plea to the Jews to keep the covenant that God had made with them. This is recorded towards the end of *Devarim.* He commands the priests to read the Torah publicly every seven years. This is followed by the dramatic Song of Moses, which opens:

Give ear, O heavens, let me speak,
Let the earth hear the words I utter!

as though Moses is calling the very heavens and earth to bear witness to his plea to the People of Israel. In poetic language he again reviews Israel's history and calls on them to remain faithful. Turning to the tribes of Israel one by one, Moses evokes God's blessing on each of them. The Book closes with an account of Moses' death on Mount Nebo in Transjordan, overlooking the Promised Land.

AUTHORSHIP OF THE TORAH

According to the Jewish tradition, the whole Torah was written by Moses at God's command. This includes even the last eight verses which record the death of Moses and the mourning for him. The Talmud explains that Moses wrote these verses "in tears." The existing text of the Torah scroll which is read in the synagogue is exactly the same as the Torah that Moses wrote. For information on the Torah scroll and the reading of the Torah, see *Torah.

NEVI'IM

The second section of the Bible, *Nevi'im,* is made up of two sub-sections: the Former Prophets and the Latter Prophets. The Former Prophets comprise Joshua, Judges, *Samuel (two Books) and Kings (two Books). In the Latter Prophets are included the Books of *Isaiah, *Jeremiah and *Ezekiel, and the twelve so-called Minor Prophets: *Hosea, Joel, *Amos, Obadiah, *Jonah, Micah, Nahum, *Habakkuk, Zephaniah, Haggai, *Zechariah, and Malachi. Although the second sub-section is called Latter Prophets, many of the prophets included in it were active during the period recorded in the Book of Kings. Moreover, the description "Minor Prophets" which is given to 12 of the books refers more to their size than to their stature.

THE FORMER PROPHETS

These Books are historical rather than prophetic in nature. They relate the history of Israel from the time of its entry into the Land of Canaan in the 13th century b.c.e. until the destruction of the First Temple in 586 b.c.e. Nevertheless these Books are considered books of prophets, firstly because their authors were divinely inspired, and secondly because they are more than histories of Israel: they also record the Covenant between God and Israel, and they stress that only by continued and faithful adherence to that Covenant can Israel hope to survive.

Joshua, the first Book of the Former Prophets relates the conquest of Canaan and its early settlement from the death of Moses until the death of Joshua. The first two sections of the Book tell of the conquest of the Land of Canaan and the division of the land among the tribes, including the establishment of cities of refuge under the control of the Levites. The final chapters record the negotiations with the two-and-a-half tribes of Israelites who remained east of the Jordan, and the covenant at Shechem between them and the other tribes. This covenant is the appropriate conclusion to the Book of Joshua and the zenith of Joshua's accomplishments. As one scholar puts it: "The victor in battle against the Canaanites, and the judge of disputes among the tribes, is also the man who, in the dawn of Israel's existence, set it upon the firm foundation of its history by uniting it about a new sanctuary of the Lord in the heart of the land." For more details on the life and achievements of Joshua, see the article by that name.

The Book of Judges is named for the series of charismatic leaders of the period between the death of Joshua and the institution of monarchy in ancient Israel, that is, from about 1200 to about 1000 b.c.e. These Judges were not judges in the legal sense, but heroes upon whom "rested the spirit of God" and who led single tribes or groups of tribes in military campaigns to free Israel from periodic foreign oppression. The rule of each judge was temporary and in no case did these leaders receive the allegiance of all the tribes. Only in the case of *Deborah is there any hint of a judicial function among the activities of a Judge-savior.

The events of the first chapter of Judges took place after the death of Joshua. Israel had had a long series of impressive victories, but several areas of the land were yet to be conquered. Whereas the initial stage of conquest was carried out by all Israel in a united camp under one leader, Joshua, the mopping-up operations were left to the individual tribes. The text relates the capture of several cities that had escaped their unified onslaught. The many archaeological discoveries of the present century corroborate the account given in the Book of Judges of the conquest of Israel. Archaeological evidence has shown that a major onslaught did take place in the 13th century b.c.e. The cities of Bethel, Debir and Lachish were violently destroyed in this period, and the settlements built on their ruins were typically Israelite. Archaeology seems to verify the descriptions of the Book of Judges of continual fighting, with peaceful periods alternating with times of crisis.

The Book of Judges is not just a history book; it gives what could be called a philosophy of Jewish history. Israel repeatedly sinned by worshiping false gods, and God punished them by subjecting them to foreign oppressors. Realizing their sin and its consequences, the people repented of their idolatry and prayed to the Lord for deliverance. God sent a Judge to rescue the people from the hands of their oppressors, and a quiet period followed. After the death of the Judge the people lapsed into idolatry and the cycle began again. The Book of Judges further records the activities of all the individual Judges. Details of the careers of the most prominent ones may be found in the articles on *Ehud; *Deborah; *Gideon; *Jephthah; and *Samson.

The final sections of the Book have no obvious connection with the preceding chapters and are characterized by the recurring phrase "in those days there was no king in Israel, each man doing what was right in his own eyes." It would seem that these sections were intended to illustrate the dangers of irregular tribal rule which could only be remedied by the crowning of a king. The next two Books set out how this need for central authority was filled.

Samuel I and II are two continuous Books, chiefly concerned with the establishment of the monarchy in Israel and the succession of rulers in the early united monarchy of the nation. It is abundantly clear, however, that the chief interest is not in giving an historical account but to establish the national religious significance of the monarchy for Israel. The king of Israel was chosen by God rather than by the nation and was anointed with holy oil by God's prophet. For more information on the idea of monarchy, see *Kingship.

The first Book of Samuel starts with an account of the birth and boyhood of *Samuel, and his becoming the prophet of Israel. In Samuel's old age the people called for a king rather than face the prospect of Samuel's corrupt sons becoming his successors. Saul was chosen, but when he failed to destroy all the Amalekites, Israel's bitter enemies, as God had commanded, Samuel announced his rejection by God. David was chosen by God to take his place, and the story of the conflict between *Saul and *David and of David's ultimate victory makes up the greater part of both the Books of Samuel, which end with David ruling over a unified Israel.

The Book of Kings starts with the accession of *Solomon, David's son, and his successor to the throne of Israel. It continues with an account of the building of the Temple in Jerusalem. As long as Solomon did God's will, he and his kingdom prospered. Toward the end of his reign, however, he married foreign wives who introduced idolatry into Israel.

Rehoboam inherited the throne from Solomon his father and went to Shechem to be crowned. Jeroboam, a warrior who had served as a high official under Solomon, came to Shechem with a deputation

The destruction of Pharaoh and his army as they cross the Red Sea in pursuit of the Children of Israel. A 16th-century painting on wood by Lucas Cranach the Elder.

of elders to ask Rehoboam to lighten the burden of taxes which his father Solomon had imposed on Israel. Rehoboam answered haughtily: "My father made your yoke heavy, but I will add to your yoke; my father chastised you with whips, but I will chastise you with scorpions." As a result of his policy, all the tribes except Judah and Benjamin broke away and formed the Northern Kingdom, which was known as Israel. Rehoboam's Southern Kingdom was known as Judah.

Jeroboam ruled over the ten tribes and set up two calves of gold in Beth-el and Dan, saying: "Behold thy gods, O Israel." He also changed the dates of the various festivals to widen the rift between his ten tribes and the Southern Kingdom of Judah.

The Book of Kings continues with the history of the two sister states, Judah and Israel. The former was always ruled by descendants of David but in the latter, the kings were often overthrown – and usually murdered. The new dynasties which were then established did not usually last long. The two states were often at war but occasionally they made treaties and the ruling houses joined in marriage.

The two prophets, *Elijah and *Elisha, dominate a large part of Kings. Elijah waged an unrelenting campaign against idolatry, particularly against the Ba'al worship which *Ahab's wife, Jezebel, introduced into Israel.

Kings II closes with an account of the destruction of the two kingdoms. The Northern Kingdom was destroyed in 722 b.c.e. by Shalmaneser, king of Assyria. All the inhabitants were driven into exile and thenceforth are known as the *Ten Lost Tribes. The Southern Kingdom, Judah, was conquered in 586 b.c.e. by *Nebuchadnezzar, king of Babylon, who destroyed the Temple in Jerusalem on the Ninth of Av. A great part of the population was taken into captivity to Babylon. The story of their return, 70 years later, is taken up in the Book of Ezra.

THE LATTER PROPHETS

These Books are largely the poetic orations of the prophets Isaiah, Jeremiah and Ezekiel, and of the twelve prophets named above.

Isaiah contains prophecies which cover the period from 740 b.c.e. to c. 540 b.c.e., from the year of the death of King Uzziah until the return of the Babylonian exiles to Jerusalem. His career began at a time of growing prosperity that brought the people comfort and luxury. Material growth was accompanied by the territorial expansion of the kingdom of Judah, achieved by military power

ויהי אחרי
מות משה
עבד

Opening page of the Book of Joshua from the *Lisbon Bible,* Lisbon, 1482. The wide decorative border is typical of the Portuguese school of manuscript illumination.

cultivated by King Uzziah. Isaiah, however, rejected human schemes and wisdom as the means to work out the destiny of Israel, and advised instead a total reliance on God.

To the people around him, the economic and political situation had never seemed brighter. A national sense of complacent self-satisfaction and pride could hardly be avoided. Isaiah, however, saw that wealth had been purchased at the price of virtue, and corruption was rife in high places. The guilty were acquitted in exchange for bribes, and the innocent were denied justice. The fatherless went undefended, and the mansions of the rich contained the spoils of the poor. The aristocratic women of Jerusalem especially served the prophet as a target for his denunciations and predictions of doom. Foreign trade apparently brought with it idolatrous religious practices and superstitions, so that Isaiah charged that "Everyone worships the work of his own hands." Hypocrisy, especially in regard to the sacrifices in the Temple, infuriated Isaiah. What good are sacrifices if the penitent continues to oppress the weak and the helpless?

A recurrent theme in his writings is the coming of God in His fierce anger to punish Israel and the

Lo let that night be solitary
& let no joyful voice come therein
Let the Day perish wherein I was Born
And they sat down with him upon the ground seven days & seven nights & none spake a word unto him for they saw that his grief was very great

"Job Cursing the Day that he was Born" by William Blake, 1825.

nations. Yet the divine wrath is but an instrument with which to humble the arrogant and punish the evildoers. Once this anger has accomplished its purpose, God will show His graciousness and mercy to the holy seed that will remain when the work of destructive purification has been fulfilled.

In addition to the concrete historical hope of the survival of a remnant of Israel in his own period, the prophet tells of the *End of Days, when the whole world will be transformed, and the Messiah will rule. Isaiah showed an ardent faith in Jerusalem as the inviolable city of God and proclaimed it as the future site of the universal acceptance of the God of Israel by the nations, who will no longer wage war: "They shall not hurt nor destroy in all My holy mountain; for the earth shall be full of the knowledge of the Lord, as the waters cover the sea" (Isaiah 11:9).

Jeremiah lived to see the dramatic events from the break-up of the Assyrian Empire to the fall of the Kingdom of Judah in 586 b.c.e. brought about by the Babylonian Empire. He was deeply concerned by the march of events and every act of that tragic drama is reflected in his book. Jeremiah can, to some degree, be considered the Prophet of Doom since he is almost completely taken up with the impending disaster. His words and deeds can be related to known events to a degree impossible with other prophets. Jeremiah did not want to be a prophet and his deeply personal poems, the so-called confessions, express his reactions towards his fate and reveal his temptations and his wrestling with God. Nevertheless the Divine compulsion was laid upon him, overruling his objections, and Jeremiah was God's prophet as long as he lived.

Profoundly shocked at the idolatry prevalent in Judah, Jeremiah thundered against it, and warned of its dire consequences. He urged submission to God on His terms, expressed in the covenantal law. The Covenant required that Israel should acknowledge no other god than the God of Israel. Jeremiah warned of God's judgment which would fall upon the unrepentant people of Judah. He spoke in particular of the foe from the north, Babylonia, and the surrender of Jerusalem to the Babylonians in 597 b.c.e. confirmed his warnings. He regarded the Babylonian army as an instrument in the Divine hands for carrying out a merited punishment on the guilty nation and its leaders.

***Ezekiel** was the only prophet to prophesy outside the Land of Israel. Ezekiel saw the entire history of Israel as one continuous breach of the Covenant, for which the destruction of the Temple was the just and predicted punishment. From the prophet's call until the start of Jerusalem's siege the prophecies are condemnatory. During the siege years and briefly thereafter the prophecies condemn Israel's neighbors who were involved in Judah's revolt but failed to support her. However, although the Book of Ezekiel starts on a note of doom, it continues with consolation, and the news of Jerusalem's fall is followed by consolatory prophecies of its restoration. Ezekiel is transported in a vision to the future Jerusalem and describes the future Temple in detail. He also gives a blueprint for the reorganization of the priesthood and the allocation of the Land of Israel to the respective tribes. Among the most striking prophecies in the Bible is Ezekiel's vision in Babylonia, of the valley of dry bones which become miraculously reconstructed and come to life. Such a message must have been of great encouragement to the depressed exiles of Judah.

***Hosea** heads the group of the Twelve Prophets. He prophesied during the time of the First Temple, when the Jews still lived in their own land. Hosea's fiery denunciation of the unfaithfulness of Israel towards their God and his predictions of the terrible punishments in store for his people were couched in stinging terms which lashed at his contemporaries. But at the end, Hosea called for repentance: "Take with you words and return unto the Lord," and predicted that Israel and God would be reconciled and Israel would flourish once again.

Joel begins with a vivid description of an invasion of locusts which was a punishment on Israel and continues with a searing picture of the calamities which will befall the nations which have shed Israel's blood and exiled her survivors: "For great is the day of the Lord and very terrible, and who can abide it?" (Joel 2:11). An opportunity for salvation would be given Israel by their merciful God: "Turn to Me with all your heart, and with fasting, and with weeping, and with lamentation" (2:12). Repentance will bring forgiveness and the Lord will turn His terrible wrath on the exilers of His people and the plunderers of His Temple: "Egypt shall be a desolation, and Edom shall be a desolate wilderness, for the violence against the children of Judah." Joel's final prophecy is the most comforting of all: in the Messianic age "Judah shall be inhabited forever, and Jerusalem from generation to generation . . . and the Lord dwells in Zion."

***Amos**, a herdsman of Judah, went to the Northern Kingdom of Samaria to warn its people of impending punishment from God because of their sins. Amos especially decried the ill-treatment of the poor by the rich; ritual observance isolated from moral behavior is denounced as a mockery to God who demands righteousness and justice, not sacrifices. The Book of Amos reveals God's role in human history, since all that happens is due to Him: "Shall evil befall a city and the Lord hath not done it" (Amos 3:6). Amos ends with a description of the Golden Age when God and His people would be reconciled: "And I will return the captivity of My people Israel, and they shall build the waste cities and inhabit them; and they shall plant vineyards and drink the wine thereof . . . " (9:14).

***Obadiah** is the shortest Book in the Bible. It is but one chapter with one theme: the downfall of Edom, Israel's most bitter enemy. Because of the close blood relationship with Israel, since Jacob and Esau the fathers of the two nations were brothers, Edom's unreasoning hatred is that much more despicable: "For the violence done to your brother Jacob shame shall cover you . . . You should not have gazed on the day of your brother . . . the day of his disaster . . . " (Obadiah 1:11,12).

***Jonah** is known for the incident involving the whale, or large fish, but that episode is secondary to the lesson the Book comes to teach. Jonah learned through bitter experience that non-Jews are also God's creatures and one must not begrudge them God's love and forgiveness. Also to be learned is the fact that true repentance is accepted by God and earns His pardon for almost any sin. Because of its theme of sin, repentance, and forgiveness the Book of Jonah is read every Day of Atonement at the *Minḥah* service.

Micah directed his prophecy against the rich who lived in ill-gotten spendor at the expense of the poor. He warned them that God would forsake His people and that the inevitable results of the corruption of Judah would follow: the ravaging of Judah by its enemies, the destruction of Jerusalem and the Temple, and exile. Micah stated God's demands simply: justice tempered with mercy. Micah's verses of consolation are beautiful in their vision of the glorious future of Zion: "For out of Zion shall go forth the law, and the word of the Lord from Jerusalem . . . . And they [the nations] shall beat their swords into plowshares, and their spears into pruning-hooks; nation shall not lift up sword against nation, neither shall they learn war any more. But they shall sit every man under his vine and under his fig-tree; and none shall make them afraid . . . " (Micah 4:5).

Nahum is the only prophet who did not condemn Israel at all; he pictured the downfall of Assyria and brought comfort to Judah with his assurance that its ruthless oppressor would soon perish. Nahum's message was most welcome; he prophesied the destruction of all the nations that oppressed Israel. The first chapter describes God and His attributes: "The Lord is a jealous and avenging God, the Lord reserves wrath for His enemies . . . "; it proclaims

God's anger against those who anger Him and compassion for those who have faith in Him. In the second chapter we are given a vivid picture of the defeat of Nineveh and the joy this brought to Judah. The third chapter is a continuation of the second, giving the reason for Nineveh's ruin: the merciless treatment it accorded to all peoples it conquered: " "All that hear the report of you, clap their hands over you (in joy); for upon whom has not your wickedness passed continually?"

Habakkuk dwells on the sins of the oppressors of Israel which are of such magnitude that they make the sins of Israel seem minor in comparison. He challenged God for allowing the merciless Chaldeans (or Babylonians) to conquer Israel, and struggled with the problem of the existence and success of evil in the world. God answered Habakkuk: "The righteous shall live by his faith." The temporary victory of evil should not cause a man's faith to falter because, in the end, justice will triumph.

Zephaniah described the great day of the Lord when all sinners would be punished. The terror of the scene is forcefully portrayed and its horror can be fully felt. He warned that only righteousness and humility could possibly save one from God's anger. The Philistines, Moab, Assyria, Cush and Ammon were all to feel the strong arm of God upon them. Judah too would not escape punishment. But after undergoing purification through suffering, the knowledge of the Lord would spread among the nations, and Israel would take its rightful exalted position among them: "For I will make you to be a name and a praise among all the peoples of the earth . . . " (Zephaniah 3:20).

Haggai wrote about the period of the restoration of the Second Temple which started in 538 b.c.e. with the reign of King Cyrus of Persia, who allowed the Jews to return to Judah and rebuild the Temple in Jerusalem. They were beset by enemies who disrupted the holy work, and disillusionment spread among them. Haggai came with a message of encouragement, infusing the people with renewed vigor and zeal in their task of building the Second Temple, promising that "the glory of this latter house shall be greater than that of the former" (Haggai 2:9). According to the Talmud, Haggai lived to feel the strong arm of God upon them. Judah too just reward for one who had worked so hard to have it built.

Zechariah continued in the same task as Haggai; he too encouraged the Jews to rebuild the Temple. Zechariah reminded Israel that before God returned to the Temple the people must return to God through righteousness, justice, and mercy: "Return to Me, says the Lord of hosts, and I will return to you." The nation's future security would be guaranteed, "Not by might, nor by power, but by My spirit, says the Lord of Hosts" (4:6), and Israel would flourish once again. Zechariah prophesied of the Golden Age of the Messiah when God's Kingdom would be established on earth.

Malachi. The ecstasy of rebuilding the holy Temple passed and the Jews fell into disreputable ways once again. Intermarriage was common, as was divorce, and morals were weak. Malachi was faced with the task of awakening the people from their religious lethargy and bringing them back to God. He denounced their neglect of the Temple service and compared this unfavorably with the non-Jews who brought abundant offerings to God. Malachi announced the coming of the Day of Judgment which would remove the sinners from the nation and thus clear the way for the Messianic Age: "Behold I will send you Elijah the prophet before the coming of the great and terrible day of the Lord. And he shall turn the heart of the fathers to the children and the heart of the children to their fathers; lest I come and smite the land with utter destruction."

AUTHORSHIP OF THE PROPHETIC BOOKS

According to rabbinic tradition, Joshua wrote most of the Book of Joshua; the sections recording his death and subsequent events were added by other writers. The same tradition has it that the prophet Samuel wrote the Book bearing his name as well as the Book of Judges and the Book of Ruth (see below under *Ketuvim*); Jeremiah wrote his own Book and the Book of Kings; King Hezekiah and his colleagues committed the Book of Isaiah to writing; and Ezekiel and the Twelve Prophets were committed to writing by the Great Assembly, an institution that existed some time after Ezra. The critical view sees the Book of Isaiah as being the work of at least two separate prophets, one of whom lived in Babylonia after the destruction of the Temple.

KETUVIM

The last section of the Bible is *Ketuvim* which includes twelve Books: Psalms, Proverbs, Job, Song of Songs, Ruth, Lamentations, Ecclesiastes, Esther, Daniel, Ezra, Nehemiah, and Chronicles I and II. The Hebrew name *Ketuvim,* which means "writings," emphasizes the difference between these Books and the section called Prophets. Basically the prophesies were oral speeches which the prophet delivered to Israel; only later were they written down. *Ketuvim*, on the other hand, are literary works which were meant to be written. Another characteristic of the *Ketuvim* is that each Book is a separate entity which can be read by itself with no reference to other Books, unlike the Prophets who, to be understood, must each be placed in the correct historical context.

The Book of *Psalms is usually considered the first of the *Ketuvim*. It is a collection of religious psálms, prayers, and poems which can be understood on many levels. According to Jewish tradition, the Psalms were composed by a variety of people, and King David wrote the bulk of them. The Psalms sing of God's role in nature and His control over the fate of every individual as well as over nations. The Psalms reflect the emotions and thoughts of a God-fearing man in all types of situations, ranging from ecstasy to despair. Love of God and trust in Him pervade the whole Book.

***Proverbs** is one of the three "wisdom books" representing the affirmative element in wisdom in contrast to the questioning tone of Job and Ecclesiastes. Proverbs is a teacher's dream; it cultivates the mind and trains the student in ethical principles by the use of proverbs, warnings, sayings of the sages, and riddles or puzzling questions. The basic theme of the book is summed up in the motto which begins and ends the introduction: "The fear of the Lord is the beginning of knowledge." According to tradition, King Solomon wrote this Book when he was middle-aged.

The Book of *Job is the story of one man, Job, and his acceptance of the sufferings God brings upon him and his family. But the problem of the final meaning and message of the book has over the centuries aroused a wide variety of responses. To some sages of the Talmud and Midrash, Job is to be regarded as one of the few truly God-fearing men of the Bible, the most pious non-Jew who ever lived. To others he was a blasphemer. This fascinating Book which has aroused so much controversy over its meaning is discussed more fully in its own article. The Talmud states that Moses wrote the Book of Job, and records a difference of opinion as to whether Job ever really existed, or whether the story is a parable.

THE FIVE SCROLLS

Within the general heading *Ketuvim* there is a subdivision of five books called the *Megillot* or Scrolls. They are: Song of Songs, Ruth, Lamentations, Ecclesiastes and Esther. These are known as *megillot* because they are read publicly in the synagogue from handwritten scrolls.

The *Song of Songs is read on the Sabbath of Passover. The Book is a song of love which the rabbis interpreted as being a poetic expression of the love between God and Israel. King Solomon is said to have composed this Book in his youth, though one tradition attributes its commitment to writing to King Hezekiah. There is a separate article on *Song of Songs.

The Book of *Ruth which is read on *Shavuot, tells the story of Ruth, a young Moabitess who embraced Judaism. She refused to stay behind in the land of Moab when her mother-in-law returned to Israel: "Where you go I shall go . . . Your people will be my people, and your God my God." The Book of Ruth was written by the prophet Samuel.

***Lamentations**, which was written by Jeremiah, is read on *Tish'ah be-Av (the ninth day of Av), the day of the destruction of the two Temples. The agony of the author and his overwhelming sorrow can be felt throughout the Book. Yet the feeling is expressed that the horrors which befell Israel were justified by the sins of the nation against God.

***Ecclesiastes** is a book full of despair because of all the evil prevalent in the world, and all the wickedness perpetrated by man against his fellow man. Solomon is said to have written Ecclesiastes in his old age when he reached the conclusion that all that occurs under the sun is decided by God and has a reason, but man with his limited vision cannot comprehend the logic and justice of certain events. Another tradition has it that King Hezekiah committed Ecclesiastes to writing. This Scroll is read during *Sukkot.

The Book of Esther is read on *Purim from a parchment scroll. It is the exciting account of a hairbreadth escape of the Jews from annihilation. The story is set in Shushan, the capital of Persia, during the reign of Ahasuerus. The villain is Haman, the hero Mordecai, and the beautiful heroine is Esther. The authorship of Esther is attributed to the Great Assembly; for details of the story see *Purim. Esther is the last of the Five Scrolls.

The Book of *Daniel is named for a man whose fortunes and predictions are the subject of the book. Brought from Judah to Babylon by Nebuchadnezzar when that Babylonian king conquered Judah, Daniel and his three friends Hananiah, Mishael and Azariah came to occupy important positions as administrators of the whole province of Babylon after Daniel was able to successfully interpret the King's dream. This

Book is also attributed to the Great Assembly. The story of Daniel's trial in the lion's den and the rest of the Book of Daniel are discussed in the separate article on *Daniel.

***Ezra and *Nehemiah** were two personalities who dominated the period covered by the Books of those names. The Book of Ezra focuses on the period highlighted by the return of the exiles from Babylon to Judah (following the defeat of Babylonia by the Persians) and the rebuilding of the Second Temple, which became a political as well as a religious center. Nehemiah was cupbearer to the Persian King Artaxerxes, a very important position. He was granted permission to leave Persia in order to rebuild Jerusalem. He was governor there for 12 years, returned to Persia, and then was permitted to return to Jerusalem for a second term of duty. Nehemiah completed rebuilding the walls of Jerusalem, reorganized a viable force for the protection of Judah, and attended to its religious interests.

Chronicles is the last book of the Bible. The Hebrew name *Divrei ha-Yamim* means "the events of the times," since it is a brief description of the history of Israel from the time of David until the destruction of the Kingdom of Judah in the sixth century b.c.e., during the reign of Zedekiah. A lengthy introduction, mainly comprised of lists detailing the descent of the Children of Israel from Adam, serves as a background, and at the end, an excerpt is given from the Edict of Cyrus, which allowed the Jews to return home.

In the history of the people, the author stresses several points, above all the tie between Israel and their God. This tie exists not in consequence of any deed but in and of itself. The tie is mutual: the people serve their God, and God watches over and provides for His people. Like the tie between the people and their God, the tie between Israel and its land is described as a phenomenon existing in its own right without the need for assurances, explanations and reasons. The Book of Chronicles comprises two parts, and according to tradition was mainly written by Ezra.

THE LANGUAGE OF THE BIBLE

The books of the Bible were originally written in the Hebrew language with the exception of two words in Genesis (31:47), a single verse in Jeremiah (10:11), and sections of Daniel (2:46-7:28) and Ezra (4:8-6:18; 7:12-26), all of which are in Aramaic. Two words in the Song of Songs are Greek. All in all there are 23,100 verses in the Bible, divided into 929 chapters. The text of the printed Bible consists of three distinct elements. These are the consonants, the vowel symbols, and the musical notations for the chanting or melodic recitation of the text as part of the synagogue service. (Further details on this may be found in the article on *Torah). The vowel symbols and the musical notations were developed by the masoretes (see *Masorah) while the history of the consonantal text, with which this section is exclusively concerned, is of great antiquity and complexity. Besides the actual consonants there are also various markings, known as diacritical points.

The very idea of recognizing certain books as belonging to a fixed canon carries with it an attitude of reverence for the text and fosters care and accuracy in its transmission. From the generation of the destruction of the Temple, for the first time there was one stabilized official text with binding and unimpeachable authority. No further developments of any significance took place in the consonantal text of the Hebrew Bible during the 600 years that elapsed between the latest manuscripts from the period of the Mishnah (200 c.e.) and the earliest medieval ones (c. ninth century c.e.). None of the

Carpet page from a Yemenite Bible, San'a 1469. It is decorated with both floral and geometric designs.

medieval manuscripts, and not even the thousands of Bible fragments from the ancient Cairo **Genizah* represent a variance from the received text.

PRINTING

The story of the printing of the Hebrew Bible begins with the 1477 edition of the Psalms, most probably produced at Bologna. The Bologna Pentateuch of 1482 by Abraham ben Ḥayyim di Tentori set the pattern for many future editions, culminating in the Bomberg Rabbinic Bibles of the next century. The firm of Joshua Solomon Soncino printed its first complete Bible, the *Soncino Bible, in 1488. The Brescia Bible produced in 1495 by Gershom Soncino was a pocket edition specifically produced for the persecuted Jews who, perpetually moving from place to place, found it difficult to carry the huge and costly folio Bible.

In the 16th century, Daniel *Bomberg, a Christian merchant of Amsterdam, published the first Great Rabbinic Bible in Venice. It contained Targums and commentaries (see below). Here, for the first time in Hebrew, Samuel and Kings were each divided into two books. The second edition (1524/5) was the product of a partnership between Bomberg and Jacob ben Ḥayyim ibn Adonijah, the text of which became the standard masoretic text and has continued as such for 400 years. While all the above-mentioned editions appeared in Italy, Spain and Portugal also had their own printing presses.

The story of modern times begins with Seligmann Baer (Germany, 1825-1897) who published the Hebrew Bible in single volumes with notes. Baer strictly followed the Masorah.

Bibles containing the original Hebrew text together with the important ancient translations arranged in parallel columns are called polyglots, which means "many-tongued." They were at one time important in ascertaining correct readings or meanings of the text. The oldest one in print is the Complutensian Polyglot (1514-17).

TRANSLATIONS

Aramaic. In Talmud times a special reader used to translate the Torah into Aramaic, which was then the commonly spoken language, as it was being read in the synagogue. The Torah reader would stop after each verse (or after each three verses) so as to permit the translator to recite the Aramaic version, or Targum. The Targums are not always literal translations of the corresponding Hebrew text; they are often intermingled with various paraphrases, and supplements based on the **aggadah.*

The formal recognition of a written Targum belongs to the post-talmudic period, no earlier than the fifth century c.e. The official Targum to the Torah is known as Targum Onkelos, after a celebrated proselyte who is said to have composed it under the guidance of Rabbi Eliezer and Rabbi Joshua. His Targum is the most literal of the Aramaic translations of the Torah, and to this day many Orthodox Jews still observe the custom of going over the weekly portion of the Torah privately on the eve of the Sabbath, verse by verse in Hebrew, Targum, and Hebrew again.

There are several other Targumim such as Targum Jonathan and Targum Yerushalmi, which did not attain the status of Targum Onkelos.

Greek. The Greek version of the Bible, known as the Septuagint (Latin for: "seventy"), owes its name to a story related in the ancient Letter of *Aristeas. According to this account, 72 scholars summoned to Alexandria from Jerusalem by Ptolemy II Philadelphus early in the third century b.c.e. achieved a perfect Greek translation of the Pentateuch with all the finished versions being identical as a result of divine inspiration, though each of the translations had been done independently.

Latin. Jerome (c. 345-420), a leading biblical scholar and secretary to Pope Damascus I, was in charge of the official Latin translation of the Bible. Jerome's translation of the Bible in conjunction with his revision of the New Testament and the Old Latin text of the *Apocrypha became the standard Latin translation, commonly called the Vulgate.

Judeo-Persian. As Maimonides attests, a Persian translation of the Pentateuch was in existence centuries before Muhammad (seventh century c.e.), while some time later the Pentateuch appeared in a Judeo-Persian translation.

Judeo-Tatar. The Bible translations into Judeo-Tatar originated among the *Karaites of the Crimea, Russia.

Judeo-Romance Languages. During the Middle Ages, there were Jewish translations of the entire Bible in the Romance languages (such as French and Italian), and in the Jewish dialects based on them. They appear to have a common source – a traditional version of the Bible in Low Latin, which the Jews in Imperial Rome used in the synagogue and for the purposes of study.

Ladino (Judeo-Spanish). Judeo-Spanish translations of the Bible dating from the 13th to the 15th centuries were among the earliest Castilian versions of the Bible. These early works were written in Latin characters. After the Spanish expulsion in 1492 Ladino versions of the Bible were mainly printed in Hebrew characters for the use of Jewish refugees in the Sephardi Diaspora.

Yiddish. The oldest Yiddish versions of the Bible stem from the scholarly work of German rabbis in the 13th century. From the 14th century onward, prose translations of various biblical books were specifically designed for the unlearned and for women, in view of the widespread ignorance of Hebrew.

English. The first comprehensive English translation of the Bible was produced late in the 14th century; it is connected with the Christian group known as the Lollards. William Tyndale (16th century), is however considered the father of the Bible of the English-speaking world. His translation was the basis of the Great Bible of 1539. The Bishops' Bible (1568) was fathered by Archbishop Parker and formed the basis of the Authorized Version of 1611. This Authorized Version, otherwise known as the King James Bible, immediately achieved a preeminent position throughout the English-speaking world, which it has retained.

There have been several Anglo-Jewish versions of the Bible. After several early attempts by individual Jews and Jewish organizations in the 18th and 19th centuries, the Jewish Publication Society of America in 1917 published a complete translation of the Bible. This has remained the "standard" English translation for Jews. In 1962 the same organization published a new English translation of the Torah, and the rest of the Bible was in preparation.

Other Modern Languages into which the Bible has been translated include German (with several Jewish versions), Dutch, Danish, Norwegian, Icelandic, Swedish, Finnish, Italian, Spanish, Portuguese, Catalan, French and Provençal, Romansh, Rumanian, Hungarian, Slavonic, and Arabic. In fact the Bible has been translated more than any other major literary work, and in part or as a whole has appeared in almost all the languages and dialects of the world, and not only in the older languages such as Syriac, Coptic and Armenian. The more exotic translations include versions of the Scriptures in Chinese, Japanese, and American Indian dialects. John Eliot produced the earliest Amerindian Bible for the Massachusetts Indians in 1663, and by 1830 parts of the Bible had been translated and printed in the Creek and Cherokee languages of the "Five Civilized Tribes," using the alphabet devised by the Cherokee chief Sequovah.

BIBLE COMMENTARY

Talmudic Literature. The voluminous body of talmudic literature – the *Oral Law – is essentially a compilation of hermeneutic, interpretative and analytic explanations of the Bible, which is the Written Law. According to rabbinic tradition, Moses not only received the Written Law on Mount Sinai, but also the definitive explanation of the meaning hidden in the Torah's compact literary style. This interpretation is incorporated in the *Talmud. An important body of explanatory works is the *Midrash literature.

Medieval Scholarship. From the time of the *geonim* for about 1,000 years, studying the Bible and explaining it was one of the main activities of Jewish scholars. Some of the commentators attempted to give a straightforward explanation often based on the rules of grammar; others gave a more elaborate explanation, seeking out new and deeper meanings in the text. This preoccupation with Bible commentary was not restricted to one age or one place; wherever the Jews lived they worked at it. On the page of the Rabbinic Bible (see above) are printed the commentaries of *Rashi, Abraham *ibn Ezra, and *Naḥmanides, but there are innumerable other commentaries.

Modern Exegesis (which means textual interpretation) started in the 18th century with the rise of the Haskalah movement. The modern commentators attempted to interpret the Bible in the light of all the modern knowledge available – historical, archaeological and linguistic. Often the interpretation was reflected in the translations they produced, because translation cannot be isolated from interpretation. Many modern exegetes are critical of the Bible; that is, they do not see it as the indisputable word of God but rather as a literary composition compiled over many generations. Viewing the Bible as a human work obviously affects the way it is studied and interpreted, and the critical scholars often assign various parts of the same Book to different periods and even "correct" what they consider to be mistaken texts. Many non-Jews have worked and still work in the field of Bible scholarship. One of them, Julius Wellhausen (1844-1918), reconstituted Israel's history on the basis of his theories. For many years his was considered the classical approach, but later on as new evidence continually became available, his theories were largely disproved. There can be no doubt that the theology of many of the Christian Bible critics influenced their method of study and the conclusions they reached.

Bible criticism is divided into two categories: Higher Criticism, which means the study of the Books (or parts of them) with regard to when, where and by whom they were written, and Lower Criticism, which is the close study of the actual texts with a view to reconstructing their allegedly original form. One great Jewish scholar has stated that "Higher Criticism" is just another name for Higher anti-Semitism.

RELIGIOUS IMPACT

The Bible is holy to Jews because it represents the Word of God. This is particularly true of the Torah which is, so to speak, God's direct statement. The *halakhah,* or Jewish law, which is the authoritative guide for a Jew's life, is mainly based on the Torah; so obviously study of the Torah as well as the rest of the Bible is one of the prime religious duties.

There is evidence of the important part the Bible played in the Jewish consciousness from very early times. The creation of the Septuagint (see above, under Translations) in the reign of Ptolemy Philadelphus (283-245 b.c.e.) means that there must have been qualified translators in Egypt at that time. Alexandrian scholars also began to interpret the Bible in the middle of the second century b.c.e. There can, of course, be no doubt about the importance of the Bible in Talmud times, a few centuries later. The whole system of Judaism and Jewish law is based on a minute examination of every letter in the Bible. The rabbis of the Talmud were intensely aware of the fact that the Torah, in particular, is the revealed word of God and treated it with the reverence and devotion due to it. The custom of reading the Torah publicly is very, very ancient – originating with Ezra in the fifth-fourth centuries b.c.e. At some later date a reading from the *Nevi'im* was added; this corresponding passage from the Prophets is known as the *Haftorah.* To ensure that the assembled congregation understood the reading it too was translated into the vernacular which was then Aramaic (see above, under Translations).

In the liturgy, readings from the Bible play a prominent role. The **Shema* as well as the Song of Moses after the crossing of the Red Sea are central to the daily morning service, and the prayers are studded with various selections from the Book of Psalms as well as verses from other Books.

During the Middle Ages the masoretes completed the work of finalizing the vowel signs and melodic markings (for more on this see *Masorah). From then on, the Bible became the example of perfect Hebrew which the poets and philosophers of the Middle Ages tried so hard to emulate. From the 16th century the study of the Bible as such was neglected; but it was still studied indirectly through the study of Talmud, which continually discusses it. In modern times, particularly since the rise of the *Haskalah movement, there has been intensified interest in the Bible as an independent text. In the State of Israel one of the highlights of the Independence Day celebrations is the Bible Quiz in which competitors from all over the country participate. Every few years an international quiz is held.

במדבר קעט

תם ונשלם ספר ויקרא תהלה לאל גבור ונורא

במדבר

First page of the commentary of Gersonides (1288-1344) to the Book of Numbers *(Be-midbar)* printed by Daniel Bomberg in Venice, 1546. The word *"Be-midbar"* is contained in an ornate border.

For Christians the Bible (or the Old Testament as they know it) is also a holy Book, though they do not feel bound by its laws. For them the supreme authority is the New Testament. Throughout the ages Christians have made attempts to interpret the Bible in accordance with their specific religious beliefs. The

Muslims also consider the Bible to be holy but believe that its authority was superseded by the Koran. Many biblical stories are repeated in the Koran, though often in a garbled form.

In the Arts. The stories of the Bible have been an unending source of inspiration for novelists, poets, painters and musicians. Innumerable stories and poems have been written on biblical themes, often with the author using his imagination to embellish the facts recorded in the Bible. Most of the world's great painters and sculptors have taken biblical incidents as their themes. Two outstanding examples are *Rembrandt and *Michelangelo. Scores of oratoria as well as other musical forms have been composed to biblical texts. Of course, the Bible itself has often been decorated and illustrated. For more on that subject see *Illuminated Manuscripts.

BIOGRAPHIES AND AUTOBIOGRAPHIES. We live today in a culture in which relatively insignificant personalities are honored by biographies; we find it common that those who are not so honored compensate by writing their own life stories. It is hard to believe that until the Middle Ages biographies of great Jewish personalities had not been written. With the exception of the book of *Nehemiah which is autobiographical in nature, and the biography of *Saadiah Gaon, which was written by his sons, autobiographies and biographies were completely unknown to Jews before the Middle Ages.

The reason for this phenomenon was that the historians of the ancient and medieval periods were more interested in events than in people. Mainly concerned with the transmission of the Torah, these historians tended to simply list scholars and rabbis in chronological order, briefly describing the achievements of each, while details of their lives, birthplaces, families, travels and deaths were only mentioned in passing.

While actual biographies were not written during medieval times, historians would include certain biographical facts about the actions and character of a personality with the intention of teaching a moral and describing his model behavior. This ethical and educational approach made almost all Hebrew writings of that time heroic, legendary tales rather than authentic biographies. In each case little historical data was given.

Often biographical accounts were written to present one man's position in a religious conflict. The biography of *Anan, the founder of the *Karaite sect, is an example of a personality about whom dramatically different biographies were written; his enemies described him as a villain, while his followers glorified him as a hero.

During the medieval and Renaissance periods, autobiographies sometimes resulted from the need for self-scrutiny, and more often emerged from letters, introductions to books, apologies and personal diaries. Usually, however, the writer focused his attention on historical events and the part he played in them, more than on his own personal life. *Maimonides, describing his life in his letters, gives an account of his daily working schedule and of certain aspects of his life, while Isaac *Abrabanel's introductions to his biblical commentaries reflect the catastrophes that befell European Jewry in his time.

Probably the best developed autobiography written in Hebrew during the Middle Ages is *Ḥayyei Yehudah* ("The Life of Judah") by Leone (Judah Aryeh) *Modena. In his book Modena honestly describes his addiction to card-playing, which repeatedly threw him into debt. He carefully details the tragic fate of his three sons. Modena also wrote about his various illnesses as well as his dreams, visions and astrological beliefs.

From letters of other writers similar autobiographies were reconstructed, as in the case of Moses Ḥayyim *Luzzatto. In ḥasidic literature sketches by various rabbis described their spiritual development, for example, *Naḥman of Bratslav. Kabbalists often described their visions and the development of their mystical insight. Memoirs and diaries, such as the diary of Anne *Frank, may be considered unconscious autobiographies, since they were originally not intended for publication but, nonetheless, contain valuable autobiographic information.

In the 19th and 20th centuries real biographies began to appear. Among the first was Isaac Euchel's *Toledot Rambeman* on Moses *Mendelssohn. Biographical sketches of the great rabbis were written, among them a life of Rashi. Since then biographies have been written about many significant figures in Jewish history. In recent years some biographies of ḥasidic rabbis have been written on a historical basis. Biographies of all the great figures of the medieval *Ḥasidei Ashkenaz have also been written. From the end of the 19th century autobiographies have become increasingly common, and among them are those of J.L. *Gordon, Ḥ.N. *Bialik and Chaim *Weizmann.

BIOLOGY is the study of living organisms, both plant and animal, their activities, their function and their environment. The two main disciplines within biology are botany, the study of plants; and zoology, the study of animals, including man.

Problems relating to biology are raised in various passages in the Bible, particularly in the account of the *Creation of the world. The laws of ritual *purity and impurity, the parables taken from nature and the accounts of God's providence over His creatures all involve biology. The rabbis of the Talmud were exceedingly interested in all aspects of biology and in the Talmud there is a wide range of views and descriptions of plant and animal life; some of these opinions are derived from the rabbis own observations and experience, others from the folklore of ancient peoples and others from Greek and Roman science. Accordingly, some of the information is mistaken but an amazingly high proportion is correct.

Although the rabbis believed that everything is reproduced from its own species, which was originally created during the six days of creation, the rabbis – like the ancient scientists – did believe in spontaneous generation, i.e., the creation of certain types of insects from the soil or other matter. The miraculous tales about Joshua ben Ḥanania, however, that he was able to create animals from plants were rejected as being cases of conjuring. The rabbis did know that all animals, including fish, reproduce sexually and were very interested in what is called embryology, the study of the animal before it is born. Their views on the periods of gestation of various domesticated animals was quite accurate, but for wild animals their figures were unrealistic. They believed that the gestation period for a snake is seven years, whereas in fact it is several months including the laying of its eggs and their hatching. With regard to the time that elapses between the blossoming and the ripening of fruit of various trees, their figures were reasonably accurate.

The sages of the Talmud were also interested in heredity. The fact that parents transmit some of their characteristics to their children was known in antiquity, but the laws of heredity were formulated only in 1865 by Gregor Mendel. However, one Israel scholar, Prof. Judah Felix, has suggested an ingenious interpretation of the story of Jacob and Laban's sheep which is found in Genesis 30: 31-43; 31:7-12. According to this theory, Jacob utilized a knowledge of genetics in order to ensure that the flock of sheep and goats would bear a high proportion of speckled and striped offspring. The general attitude of the rabbis on the question of heredity and genetics was the same view developed by the philosophers and naturalists of Greece and Rome. Although the sages believed that a clear division exists between the contributions of the father and the mother to the formation of the child, they also realized that each of the parents' characteristics influence the whole child.

In the Talmud there is also considerable material on the question of grafting trees of different types to obtain hybrids. The information recorded on this subject, however, is more in the nature of agricultural folklore than science. A belief was also current that different animal species could crossbreed to produce some rather peculiar offspring.

No matter what the state of science at that time, the ancient rabbis were keenly aware of the complexity of life and of the world around them. They asked penetrating questions and some of the answers they gave might seem to modern people, raised on science, completely incorrect; for that time, however, they were adequate. Above all, the sages saw in the wonders of nature the glory of God. "If all the human beings were to join together, they would be unable to create even one gnat and imbue it with a soul" is a statement made in the Talmud which still is true today as it was then.

Modern Biology. Jews apparently played no part in the renaissance of modern biology. One reason for this was the exclusion of Jews from universities. The first Jew to figure prominently in the history of biology was Marcus Eliezer Bloch (1723-1799), a physician who devoted himself to zoological research. Starting from the early 19th century, a number of Jews played important roles in the major advances in the science. Robert Remak (1815-1865) originated the terms ectoderm, endoderm, and mesoderm for the three primary layers of embryo and Ferdinand Julius Cohn of Breslau (1828-1898) has rightly been called the father of bacteriology. In the 20th century the number of Jews who have made contributions to biology has grown enormously. More than 100 Jews are members of the U.S. National Academy of Sciences and of 46 Nobel Prizes in biological sciences between 1950 and 1967, 11 recipients were Jews.

BIRDS. The first connection between birds and Judaism is found in the Bible where there are numerous descriptions, parables and allegories taken from bird life, as well as laws concerning their ritual fitness as food. To the 37 birds mentioned in the

Bible, the Talmud adds many more discussing in particular, what features make a bird "unclean," and therefore not kosher.

Referred to by the general Hebrew terms *ẓippor* and *of,* birds in the Bible are also described with regard to their characteristics: the beauty and purity of the dove, the cruelty of the eagle, the concern for its young of the griffon vulture, the desolation and destruction symbolized by the owl. Ezekiel the prophet referred to the kings of Egypt as eagles having "great wings and long pinions, full of feathers," while Isaiah compared the powerful king of Babylonia to a bird of prey who would conquer Israel. One law in the Torah specifically treating birds is that you must "let the mother go and take only the young in order that you may fare well and have a long life " (Deuteronomy 22:7). This law may have ecological significance. In Psalms 124, deliverance from the enemy is likened to a bird escaping from a trap.

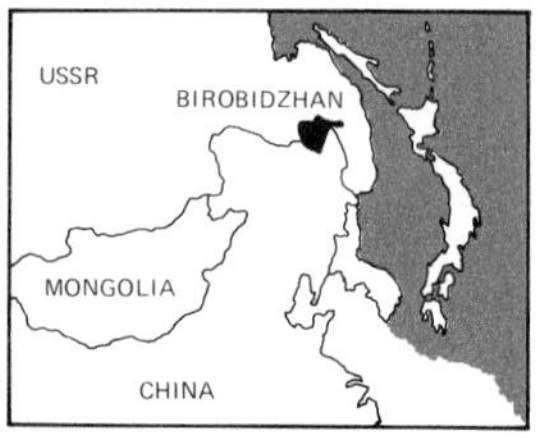

With regard to dietary laws, the Talmud declares that "there are innumerable species of clean birds," and bases its list of 24 'unclean' birds on the lists from the Torah, from the Book of Leviticus which lists 20, and the Book of Deuteronomy which lists 21. Included in these are all birds of prey (vultures, ospreys, kites, falcons, ravens, hawks etc.). Although the Bible does not list the characteristics of clean birds, the Mishnah says 'clean' birds must have a crop, a gizzard which can easily be peeled off and an extra claw. Today only birds for which there is a tradition as clean birds are considered kosher. Jews from different traditions eat different birds; for example, the pheasant of the Germans is unknown to the Turks and is therefore forbidden to them.

In the Talmud there is some uncertainty as to whether bird flesh is considered to be meat with regard to the laws of "meat and milk" (see *Dietary Laws). The final decision is that it is and therefore must be slaughtered in the proper manner (see *Sheḥitah), although in a slightly modified form. The eggs of 'unclean' birds are also forbidden since "anything which comes from an unclean thing is unclean." A fertilized egg which has a blood spot in the yolk or the albumen is also forbidden.

In Israel today there are over 350 species of birds.

A street in the city of Birobidzhan in the early 1930s.

BIROBIDZHAN. In the late 1920s the Soviet Union wanted to settle all of its Jews in Birobidzhan, a state with an area of 13,900 square miles on the border between China and the U.S.S.R. All other nationalities had their own states in the Soviet Union, but the Zionists were strongly opposed to establishing a separate Jewish community in the U.S.S.R. because it would prevent Jews from leaving for Zion.

The first Jewish settlers, who arrived in 1928, lived under extremely difficult conditions. There were heavy rains, floods, and an outbreak of disease. More than half of the original settlers left. In 1934, however, when a Jewish intellectual (Joseph Liberberg) was appointed chairman of the region and went to live there, many other Jews were encouraged to come. Jewish schools, newspapers and theaters were established, and Yiddish was taught even to non-Jews. The false trial and execution of Liberberg and others in 1937 destroyed the leadership of the community. The trials proved that however successful the "Jewish Autonomous Region" might be, it would always remain under the power of the Soviets. This appeared to prove the Zionist claim that only in Ereẓ Israel can the Jews be in control of their state.

After World War II, many homeless Jews went to Birobidzhan. By 1948 the population reached its highest level – 30,000. The Soviets, however, suppressed all Jewish activity in the region and Birobidzhan again declined. The state still exists, but only 12,000 Jews live there, isolated from the rest of the Jews in the Soviet Union. The Jewish Autonomous Region solved neither the Soviets' problem of what to do with the Jews, nor the Russian Jews' problem of how to live together in a Jewish community within the U.S.S.R.

BIRTH. There is nothing in the universe more mystifying than the act of creation, and no act of creation more mystifying than the creation of the human being. For the beginning of life is a moment both joyful and shrouded in pain. Woman's pain in childbirth was foretold in the Bible after Eve's disobedience in the Garden of Eden, when God said: "I will make most severe your pangs in childbearing. In pain shall you bear children." The Bible further mentions the pain of childbearing when *Rachel was dying in childbirth and named her son Ben-oni, "the son of my suffering." (The child was renamed Benjamin by his father.)

However, perhaps to make up for the anguish of the birth process itself, Jewish custom provides for great festivity and joy following the birth of a child. A boy is named when he is eight days old at his *circumcision ceremony, an event of great religious importance and happy celebrating. A girl is named in the synagogue on the first day following her birth on which the Torah is read. The service, usually on the Sabbath, is likewise followed by a festive meal popularly known as a *Kiddush.* It is said that he who has children brings the Day of Redemption closer.

In Halakhah: The commandment to "be fruitful and multiply" is regarded as the first *mitzvah* or commandment of the Bible, which also lays down the laws of family *purity, the details of which are to be found in the Talmud. There is a period of ritual impurity for a woman following childbirth after which, in the days of the Temple, the mother would bring a thanksgiving offering, and in addition a sin offering because in the anguish of childbirth she may have made a rash vow which she later regretted.

The Talmud teaches that the laws of the Sabbath are suspended for a woman in childbirth, which means that all work necessary for the delivery of a child may be performed on the Sabbath. Within the first three days of giving birth, the Sabbath may be violated to attend to the needs of a woman whether she demands it or not; from the third day to the seventh day only if the woman herself asks.

Because childbirth is a time of stress, it may happen that life is endangered to the point that one life may have to be sacrificed to save the other. In such case, so long as the child is as yet unborn, the mother's life must be saved before that of the child. Accordingly, Judaism which sees the preservation of life as one of the highest ideals, takes a firm view on abortion (destruction of an unborn child). Every human life, however small, is precious. Therefore, only if the pregnancy endangers the mother's life or seriously affects her health is abortion permissible. Life is a gift granted by God and may not be taken lightly.

Similarly, on the question of birth control, the traditional view is that when the mother's health would be endangered by a pregnancy, contraceptive means are permitted, but only to be used by the wife. However, the Talmud teaches that one should not limit the size of one's family, for who knows what great soul may thus be prevented from being born.

In the Aggadah. The Talmud explains that there are three partners in the creation of a human being; the father and mother who supply the physical parts, and God, Who supplies the spirit. At death, God reclaims his part, and the spirit lives on even though the body has died.

The *aggadah* describes the unborn fetus as having his arms by his sides, his head between his knees, his mouth closed; he eats from what his mother eats, drinks from what she drinks. There are no better days for a person than those days. No wonder a child cries when he is born: he has left a world of comfort and pleasure. While in his mother's womb he learns the whole Torah, but as soon as he is about to be born,

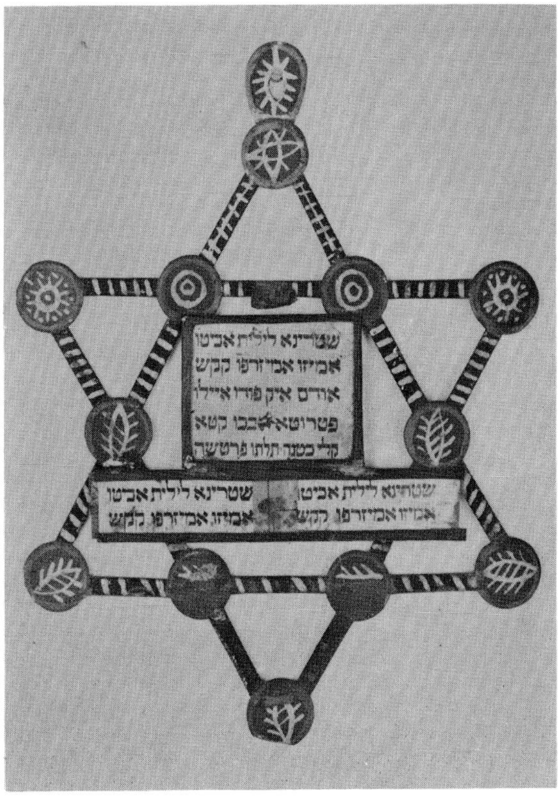

A childbirth amulet to protect mother and child from evil spirits. This 20th century amulet from North Africa is shaped as a Star of David.

an angel comes, touches him on the mouth, and the infant forgets all that he has learned. Before he is born he must take an oath that he will be a righteous person, not a wicked one.

Folklore: In various Oriental and European communities, the event of childbirth was accompanied by much exotic *folklore and superstition. In medieval times and until recently, to protect the mother and infant from evil spirits, *amulets in the shape of the palm of a hand or a seven-branched candelabrum were hung in the room. While giving birth, the mother was given the keys of the synagogue, to hold in her hand, and the band of the Torah scroll was wound around her waist. During pregnancy, to ensure that the child would be a boy, the mother pronounced his intended name every Friday.

Today most of these practices have disappeared since delivery now takes place in modern hospitals. However, the traditional customs accompanying childbirth are still very much alive. Expectant parents recite Psalms both at home and in the hospital, and in Israel, the *Western Wall is the place where family members go to pray while the child is being born.

BLACK DEATH, or bubonic plague, was a series of severe epidemics which raged from 1348 to 1350. The death toll was, by various estimates, between one-quarter and one-half of the population of Europe as well as unknown numbers in Asia and Africa. The Black Death struck some towns so suddenly that burial became impossible and the streets were littered with decaying corpses. The germ which caused the disease, *pasteurella pestis,* flourished only at certain temperatures, so that the outbreak was erratic, depending on the season or the climate of the area. The unexplained irregularity of the epidemics added to the mystery and the terror.

Faced with such horrors people reacted by going to extremes, turning either to religion or lawbreaking and savagery. In Europe, Jews died in proportionately greater numbers than Christians, not because they were more susceptible, but because they were slaughtered by their Christian neighbors. Jews were often accused of causing the plague by poisoning wells and were brutally attacked and killed. "Confessions" of well poisoning were extracted under torture and publicized.

Since it was obvious that the Jews were suffering as badly as their Christian neighbors and would hardly be poisoning their own wells, Pope Clement VI issued a bull (or decree) on September 26, 1348, which denounced the accusation of well poisoning by Jews. However, this failed to halt the violence which occurred in some areas even before the plague arrived.

In many localities fierce conflicts took place between the Jews and their attackers, and Jews tried to defend themselves. In Mainz the Jews set fire to the Jewish street and to their own homes. In Strasbourg 2,000 Jews were burned together in a mass grave dug by the Christians. A contemporary account describes their mass martyrdom: "They joyfully arrayed themselves in their prayer shawls and shrouds . . . , took each other by the hand, both men and women, and danced and leapt with their whole strength" so that they should come into God's presence with singing.

The overall result of the accusations and persecutions during the Black Death was a deterioration of the legal status of the Jews of Europe. The image of the Jew as a handy scapegoat became firmly established. The lack of any strong condemnation of anti-Semitic atrocities encouraged the commission of similar acts later on, yet the Jews were able with great vitality to reconstruct their communal and spiritual life.

BLACK JEWS IN AMERICA. The small groups of American negroes who believe in or have adopted Judaism include groups which identify with the mainstream of Jewish life as well as religious cults following a self-appointed charismatic leader with little evidence of any historical links to the Jewish religion.

Individuals professing Judaism appeared from time to time within the Black community in the American South before the Civil War. There were also small numbers of American Negroes who converted to Judaism during the post-World War II period, and joined established congregations. There are a few communities with their own rabbis and synagogues. Some black Jews are descended from the *Falashas of Ethiopia.

In the 1960s a few young black Jews began studying at Jewish institutions (generally Orthodox), but the prospect for integration with other Jews on an institutional level seemed remote. Toward the goal of greater integration, a group comprised predominantly of young adult black Jews was organized in 1965, with some significant support from white Jews, calling itself Hatza'ad Harishon

Ḥizkiyyahu Blackwell, one of the Black Jews who came to settle in Dimona and Arad, in Israel, 1970.

("the first step"). In addition to promoting contact between white and black Jews, this group has sought to enlarge Jewish educational opportunities among the black Jews.

Most black Jews, however, are members of small urban sects that originated in American cities after World War I. One type of sect was led primarily by West Indian figures interested in the total spectrum of Negro life in America who saw the sect as a politico-religious device for alleviating the general condition of the oppressed Blacks. The second, led primarily by Southern American Negroes, emphasized the more emotional and purely religious elements common to the Christian sectarian pattern predominant among American Negroes. Groups of both types have regularly appeared in urban areas, and for the most part are only faintly connected to historically recognizable Judaism. They usually consist of a few dozen individuals (mostly women) who attach themselves to a magnetic figure who generally proclaims, by means of visions, kabbalistic sources, and verbal traditions, a rediscovery of the true lost roots of the Black nation in Judaism. Their religious practices draw upon elements from both the Christian and Jewish traditions. Knowledge of Hebrew, ritual and religious sources other than the Bible itself are rudimentary. These cult groups bear such names as Bnei Israel, the Commandment Keepers, Temple of the Gospel of the Kingdom, Kohel Beth B'nai Yisrael.

No reliable statistics exist for the number of black Jewish congregations or for total membership, but estimates suggest a few dozen distinct groupings in cities such as New York, Chicago, Philadelphia, Boston, and Cincinnati, with membership between two and six thousand. Relationships with the white Jewish community are generally tenuous or non-existent.

At the end of 1969 and the beginning of 1970 several black Jewish families from Chicago arrived in Israel and settled in Dimonah, after having spent some time in Liberia. These families, however, did not succeed in integrating themselves and by 1973 most had left. Because of this negative experience, the Israel government does not encourage such migration.

It has been suggested that for many black Jews – as for many Black Muslims – a primary motivation in their religious orientation was to seek a haven from the rejection experienced at the hands of white society.

BLAKE, WILLIAM (1757-1827) mystical English poet and engraver. One of the great figures of the English romantic movement, Blake described his poems as prophecies, declaring that his model was the Bible, which he termed "the great code of art." His main biblical poems are *The Four Zoas, Milton,* and *Jerusalem,* and his other works, as well, are saturated in biblical imagery and references.

Blake was in touch with various occult circles and shared with them the belief that Britain was the cradle of the Israelite people. This explains his tendency to identify English names and places with those in the Bible, and also explains the last verse of his preface to *Milton:*

I will not cease from mental fight
Nor shall my sword sleep in my hand,
Till we have built Jerusalem
In England's green and pleasant land.

Although he knew little or no Hebrew, and was not Jewish, Blake was also influenced by ideas which can be traced to the *Kabbalah. However, strangely enough, in spite of many Judaistic ideas and currents of feeling, Blake's moral ideas are anti-Judaic, even anti-Semitic. In fact, he viewed the Law and the Commandments as an evil system, and he identified the God of Sinai with some evil being.

BLASPHEMY. "What's in a name? " the old saying goes, implying that names are not really very important. Judaism however teaches us that the name of God is so holy and important that blasphemy – misusing God's name, cursing or joking with it – is a serious sin.

Only the High Priests in the Temple were ever permitted to utter the real name of God: the punishment in the Talmud for anyone else using, and especially misusing it, is death by stoning. Even the substitute names which we use for God are so sacred that the law says that a blasphemer using these names must be whipped. According to Maimonides, blasphemy includes rubbing out God's name if it is written: the punishment for one who does so is flogging. Yet another form of blasphemy is speaking out against the king, as the king is considered God's servant on Earth.

When a Jew dies, it is customary for his relatives to make a tear in their clothing to show their sadness. In the Bible (II Kings), we read of Eliakim and others who tore their clothes when they heard blasphemy, so upset were they at the desecration of God's name. From this the Shulḥan Arukh, the code of Jewish law, tells us that whoever hears blasphemy in any language from a Jew must tear his garment as if he were in mourning. Blasphemy is a sin not only for Jews: the law forbidding blasphemy is one of the Seven Laws of Noah, applying to all mankind, Jew and non-Jew alike.

BLINDNESS. The Jewish attitude toward blindness is one of special concern, since blind people are naturally helpless in many ways, and therefore more likely to be exploited or hurt. The Torah commands: "Thou shalt not put a stumbling block before the blind," and this commandment is taken to include not only those who are actually blind, but also those who lack understanding of a particular matter. In other words, one must not trick a person who may be "blind" to what he is doing. The Bible also mentions blindness in reference to people who were blind, among them the patriarch *Isaac, as well as *Eli, the high priest, and *Samson.

Judaism regards a blind person as perfectly normal, and the only restrictions placed upon him are due to the limitations of his physical disability. At one time it was believed that a blind person should not fulfil certain religious duties such as being called up to the Torah reading, conducting the service, acting as judge or reading the Shema. However, all these opinions were later refuted, and it is now accepted that a blind man may practice Judaism like any other Jew. He cannot, however, perform those acts which specifically involve *reading* a text such as the actual reading of the Torah or Megillah since these must be read from a kosher Hebrew text and not by heart or from braille.

Because Israel is a country whose inhabitants have immigrated from all parts of the world, including many backward nations, there is a larger percentage of blind people in Israel than in other Western countries. Nevertheless, in Israel today, blind people can lead a normal life thanks to the fine educational institutions and numerous agencies and associations which aid in their job placement, training and rehabilitation. In addition they can enjoy a vast amount of literature, biblical, secular, Hebrew and foreign, which has

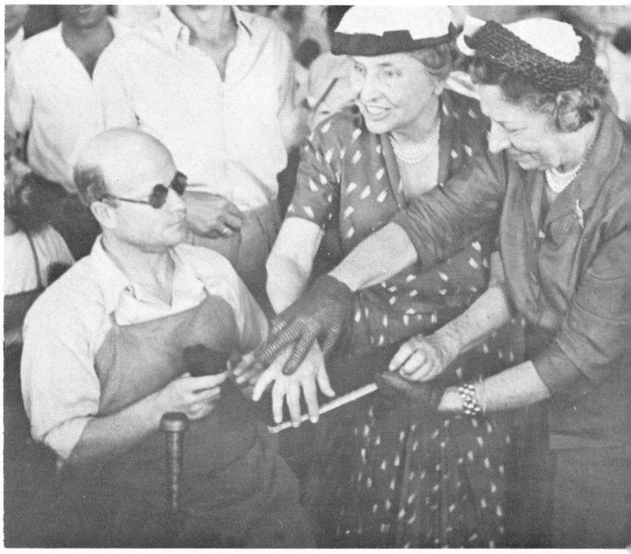

Helen Keller, an American who set an example to all handicapped people by the miraculous way she overcame both blindness and deafness, visiting Israeli facilities for the blind.

been printed in Hebrew braille. (Strangely, Hebrew braille is written from left to right, like English writing.)

Moreover, Israel has developed two machines to further aid blind people. The Transicon is a type of computer which electronically photographs printed material, and converts it into braille script. Thus, a blind man does not have to wait for a particular book to be printed in braille, but can read whatever he pleases. The second machine, the Philapbraille, is a typewriter which produces whatever is typed both in ordinary script and braille, so that the blind person typing may check his own work.

BLOOD. The absolute prohibition to consume blood is one of the few laws in the Bible that is commanded not only to Jews but to all men (Genesis 9:4). It is thus a more universal law than the Ten Commandments. The reason given for the prohibition is that "the blood is the life; and thou shalt not eat the life with the flesh" (Deuteronomy 12:23, and elsewhere).

The *dietary laws, the laws of *kashrut,* command us to drain and remove all the blood from cattle, beasts and fowl. In being prepared for food, fish are normally cut up, drained, and rinsed clean, but strictly speaking these laws do not apply to the blood of fish. However, because Jews do not like the sight of blood, this "permitted blood" is also forbidden "because of appearances." Human blood is of course forbidden, though this prohibition does not include the blood swallowed for example from one's bleeding gums.

Throughout the Bible, blood is mentioned in many connections. In Egypt, the Jews smeared blood on their doorposts so that the Angel of Death would pass over their houses during the plague of the firstborn sons. Blood was sprinkled inside the Temple and daubed on the horns of the altar as a means of purification. The ceremonies of consecrating priests and of purifying lepers also required the use of sacrificial blood. In the Mishnah, we read that the blood of animals used for sacrifices flowed from the altar into the brook of Kidron, from where it was collected and sold to gardeners as fertilizer.

Frequently mentioned in the Talmud is bloodletting, a medical treatment based on the belief that the regular removal of blood is healthy for a person. The Talmud says that a bloodletter – the person who performs the treatment – is amongst the ten services a town must have: no scholar should reside in a town where there is no bloodletter. In the ancient and medieval world at large, there were no restrictions on how often a man could be treated by having blood removed, but both the Talmud and Maimonides recommended that bloodletting be practiced in moderation.

BLOOD LIBEL. In the 13th century Emperor Frederick II published a document which stated: "There is not to be found, either in the Old or the New Testament, that the Jews are desirous of human blood." It is shocking that such a document needed to be published. Yet, for many centuries, Jews have been tortured and killed because they were accused of killing non-Jews for their blood.

The blood libel is the claim that Jews murder non-Jews, especially Christians, in order to obtain their blood for Passover or other rituals. This slanderous lie ignored the fact that the Torah expressly forbids the consumption of blood. In fact, the laws of slaughtering, soaking and salting meat for food (see *Dietary Laws) are designed to extract every drop of blood.

Many stories circulated concerning the murder of Christian children and the use of their blood by Jews. Much of the incitement came from within the Church and was encouraged by hatred of the Jews, who were different and who refused to accept Christianity. One story, dated 1255, stated "that the child (little Saint Hugh of Lincoln) was first fattened for ten days with whilte bread and milk and then . . . almost all the Jews of England were invited to the crucifixion." This story appears in Chaucer's "Prioress' Tale."

Enlightened churchmen and responsible heads of state always opposed the circulation of the blood libel. About 1240, Emperor Frederick II undertook to demonstrate that the blood libel was false.

Broadsheet by Michael Stoeritz, Prague, 1694. The woodcuts tell the story of a Jewish child who converts to Christianity of his own free will. In the first picture he is taken to a Jesuit school, and in the second he is returned to his home. After his father fails to force him to renounce his new religion, he is brutally murdered and secretly buried. The body is discovered and in the center picture it lies in state in the city square, where miraculously it blossoms. The father hangs himself in prison and his body is quartered and burned. This kind of anti-Semitic propaganda influenced the thinking of the uneducated peasants and often sparked off attacks on the Jewish communities.

Churchmen and even apostates were questioned and it was determined that the Jews were innocent. His document quotes supporting texts and adds: "There is also a strong likelihood that those to whom even the blood of a permitted animal is forbidden, cannot have a hankering after human blood. Against this accusation stand its cruelty, its unnaturalness and the sound human emotions which the Jews have also in relation to the Christians." Documents and statements such as this were not heeded, nor did the statements of Jewish scholars succeed in preventing the blood libels from shaping the image of the Jew for centuries to come.

After the 17th century, blood libel cases spread to Eastern Europe. As economic conditions in these countries deteriorated, the blood libel cases multiplied. It was used as a political weapon to attract the uneducated masses to support anti-Semitic groups. Such was the case in the *Damascus Affair (1840) in which western powers struggled for influence in the Middle East. In the late 19th and the 20th centuries, supposed experts were brought to testify against the Jews. The Nazis used the blood libel in anti-Semitic propaganda.

The blood accusation was very common in Czarist Russia. The first case supposedly occurred on Passover eve, 1799, when the body of a woman was found near a Jewish tavern. The last substantial case was the celebrated *Beilis trial (1911-1913). In the Soviet Union little mention has been made of blood libel.

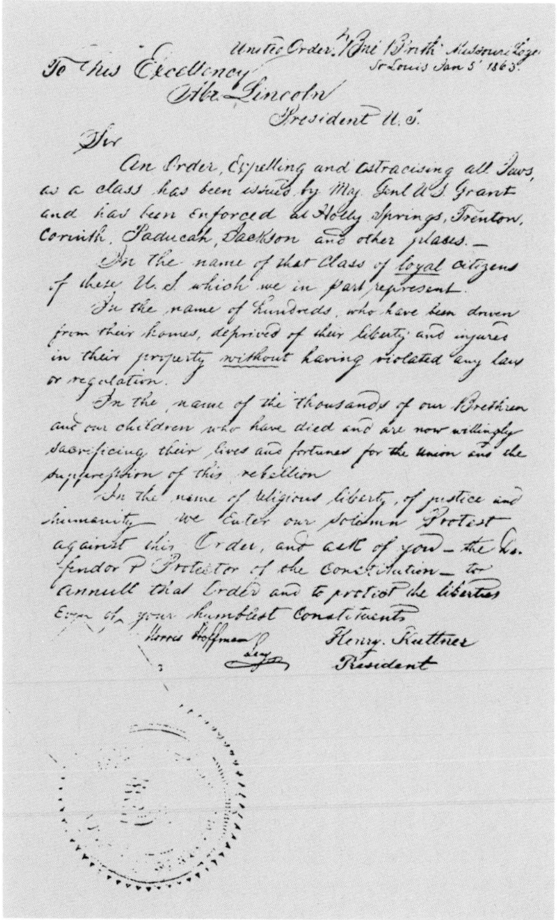

United Order B'nai B'rith Missouri Loge
St Louis Jan 5' 1863.

To His Excellency
Abr. Lincoln
President U.S.

Sir

An Order, Expelling and Ostracising all Jews, as a class has been issued by Maj. Genl U.S. Grant and has been enforced at Holly Springs, Trenton, Corinth, Paducah, Jackson and other places.—

In the name of that Class of loyal citizens of these U.S. which we in part represent.

In the name of hundreds, who have been driven from their homes, deprived of their liberty and injured in their property without having violated any law or regulation.

In the name of the thousands of our Brethren and our children who have died and are now willingly sacrificing their lives and fortunes for the Union and the suppression of this rebellion

In the name of religious liberty, of justice and humanity— we Enter our Solemn Protest against this Order, and ask of you— the Defender & Protector of the Constitution— to annull that Order and to protect the liberties Even of your humblest Constituents

Morris Hoffman
Secy

Henry Kuttner
President

Letter from the Missouri lodge of B'nai B'rith, St. Louis, sent to President Lincoln in January 1863 protesting against U.S. General Grant's anti-Semitic order. General Grant had directed the expulsion of Jews 'as a class' within 24 hours from the department of Tennessee, but President Lincoln revoked the order.

B'NAI B'RITH is the world's oldest and largest Jewish service organization, with lodges and chapters in 45 countries. In 1970 B'nai B'rith's total membership numbered approximately 500,000 Jewish men, women, and youth. There are 1,700 men's lodges, 25% of them outside North America, with a male membership of 210,000, and a U.S. budget of over $13,000,000. Its program encompasses the totality of Jewish concerns and includes many programs in the interest of the wider community. B'nai B'rith was founded on October 13, 1843, by 12 men who met in a cafe on the Lower East Side of New York to establish a new fraternal order for U.S. Jews who then numbered 15,000 souls. In 1865 the order made a substantial grant to aid cholera epidemic sufferers in Ereẓ Israel, and six years later to provide food, clothing, and medical supplies for victims of the Chicago fire. The organization established orphanages, homes for the aged, and hospitals. After 1881, when the mass immigration from Eastern Europe poured into the country, B'nai B'rith sponsored Americanization classes, trade schools, and relief programs.

B'nai B'rith Women came into being with the founding of a ladies' auxiliary chapter in San Francisco. By 1968 B'nai B'rith Women had over 1,000 chapters in 22 countries, with a membership of 135,000. Some 90% of the chapters were in North America.

When anti-Semitism in the United States increased, B'nai B'rith founded its Anti-Defamation League (ADL) in 1913 to strengthen interreligious understanding and cooperation, to improve relations between the races, and above all to protect the status and rights of Jews.

The concern of B'nai B'rith for the preservation of Jewish tradition and values was given new impetus with the establishment in 1923 of the first B'nai B'rith Hillel Foundation to serve the religious, cultural and social needs of the 400 Jewish students at the University of Illinois. The Hillel movement spread to almost 270 university campuses on six continents. Hillel also sponsors chairs of Judaic studies and faculty programs. About 300,000 Jewish students are enrolled on the campuses served by full-time Hillel Foundations and part-time Hillel Counselorships.

B'nai B'rith also sponsors a youth organization and many projects in adult education. It entirely supports the State of Israel by promoting the sale of Israel Bonds and the purchase of trees for the afforestation program.

BODY AND SOUL are among those words and ideas which people are likely to think about jointly. This pairing exists whether the relationship between the body and the soul is thought to be close or distant.

Jewish theology, as opposed to Jewish philosophy, has no clear doctrine on the relationship between body and soul. Some talmudic rabbis did not consider views on such a purely theoretical subject important; rather, they focused their interest on the practical question of the resurrection of the body (see *Life and Afterlife), and God's future judgment. Other sages did speculate on the subject.

The talmudic rabbis thought the body to be separable, in a sense, from the soul. God breathed the soul into the body of Adam (Genesis 2:7). During sleep the soul departs and receives spiritual strength from above. However, the Midrash states that body and soul are indeed closely related. The body cannot survive without the soul, nor can the soul survive without the body. The close relationship is also seen in the rabbinic understanding that the soul is a guest in the body during its stay on earth. Just as God fills the world, sees but is not seen, so the soul fills the body, sees but is not seen.

The soul is pure, the spiritual essence of man. Thus, for the Sabbath, the Holy Day of the week, God gives each man an extra soul, which departs as the Sabbath ends. The spices at *Havdalah*, at the conclusion of the Sabbath, refresh man as his additional soul departs. God put the soul into the body as His part in the creation of human life. Because it was God who originally gave man his soul, it is only for Him to take, man may not. Thus murder, suicide, mercy killings or anything which would hasten death is forbidden. Man is judged by God according to the sins which contaminate the soul, and man can purify his soul by walking in the ways of Torah. The body cannot blame the soul for sin, nor can the soul blame the body. They must be judged as one.

Medieval Jewish philosophers often compared the soul to a king and ruler of the body, but the soul was thought to be a stranger on earth, continually desiring its heavenly home. Intellectual and moral perfection were thought to compose the soul.

*Maimonides wrote in his *Mishneh Torah* that in the World to Come there are only the souls of the righteous, without bodies, serving God. (See also *Asceticism).

BOHEMIA. The history of Jews in Bohemia has been as varied as the history of Bohemia itself.

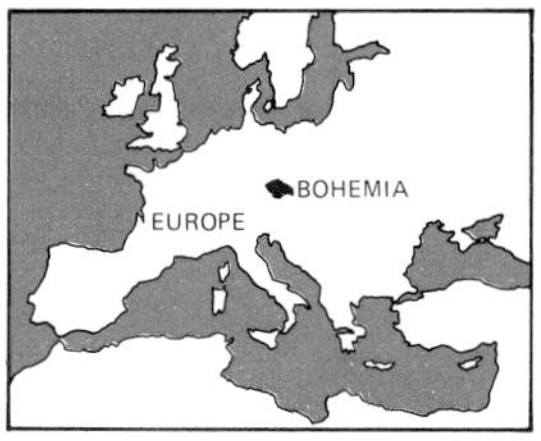

Until the 14th century, Bohemia was an independent kingdom in Central Europe. Then it became part of the Holy Roman Empire and later of Austria-Hungary. From 1918 it has been part of modern Czechoslovakia. Jewish slave traders in Bohemia are mentioned as early as the 10th century. Late in that same century, the Crusaders massacred many Jews and forcibly converted others. But in the 13th century, however, the Jewish settlement was well established and Jewish scholars were plentiful.

The 14th century brought a return of tragedy to the Jews of Bohemia. They were accused of the

Wall in the Pinkas synagogue, Prague. Behind the *menorah* are written the names of the 77,297 Jews of Bohemia and Moravia murdered by the Nazis between 1939 and 1945.

*blood libel and in 1350 the entire Jewish community of Cheb was murdered. The atrocities reached their peak in 1389 when Jews were massacred in Prague, Bohemia's largest city. It was during this tragic period that King Charles IV confirmed a number of privileges formerly issued to the Jews and in some cases afforded them protection, although their status remained that of serfs.

Although a government edict of 1501 permitted Jews to remain within Bohemia, they were in fact expelled from Pilsen in 1504 and shortly afterwards from Prague. Some few individuals were expressly permitted to remain. In 1540 the formal policy was changed and Jews were expelled from all cities under control of the King. Many of them moved to Poland or Turkey.

By 1600 one half of Bohemia's Jews lived in Prague. Conditions for Jews improved under Rudolf II (1576-1612) and the Prague Jewish community became a significant center of Judaism. Hebrew printing flourished and its scholars were numerous. Rabbi Judah Loew ben Bezalel (*Maharal) was one of the leading Torah sages of this period; David Gans was an outstanding astronomer and writer. He wrote of Bohemia, declaring, "This land is full of God's blessings." The fortunes of the Jews rose and fell according to the whim of the ruler. By 1724 about 30,000 Jews lived outside Prague in many small towns and villages. They were heavily taxed and restricted, although their communal lives were fairly autonomous.

In 1782 a law was passed which severely limited the Jews' right to *self-government. They were no longer permitted to have their own courts and Jewish schools were directed to teach in German. Synagogues could be built only with official permission and some professions were closed to Jews. Hebrew books were censored, and only Jews who had completed a German elementary school course could obtain a marriage license.

The 19th and 20th centuries were a period of assimilation. When the restrictions against Jews were annulled, they became more integrated into the surrounding society. Before 1848 most Bohemian Jews were poor, after that date they became increasingly prosperous. By the first half of the 20th century, without a strong religious community, many Jews had become indifferent to their faith. By 1930 the percentage of mixed marriages was 30%.

Anti-Semitism was especially strong among the German population of Bohemia during the 1920s and 1930s. The blood libel reappeared, and Jewish storekeepers were boycotted. World War II once again brought death and destruction to the Jews of Bohemia; almost 70,000 Bohemian Jews perished under the Nazis. Many of those who survived later emigrated to Israel.

BOMBERG, DANIEL, who died between 1549 and 1553, was one of the first and the most prominent Christian printers of Hebrew books. Bomberg left his native Antwerp as a young man and settled in Venice. Rich and well educated, and even having studied Hebrew, he developed a deep interest in books. He probably learned the art of printing from his father Cornelius. In all, nearly 200 Hebrew books were published (many for the first time) at Bomberg's printing house in Venice, which he set up on the advice of the apostate Felix Pratensis. He published editions of the Pentateuch and of the complete Hebrew Bible, both with and without commentaries, and was the first to publish the Bible *Mikra'ot Gedolot.* In order to produce this work, he had to cast great quantities of type, and engage experts as editors and proofreaders. Bomberg had to obtain special permission for his Jewish staff to be exempted from wearing the distinctively colored Jewish hat (see *Badge, Jewish).

As a result of the success of his early work, Bomberg expanded his operations. He published the

דברי הימים א

אדם

שת אנוש : קינן מהללאל ירד : חנוך מתושלח למך : נח שם חם
ה ויפת : בני יפת גמר ומגוג ומדי ויון ותבל ומשך ותירס : ובני גמר
אשכנז וריפת ותוגרמה : ובני יון אלישה ותרשישה כתים ודודנים :
בני חם כוש ומצרים פוט וכנען : ובני כוש סבא וחוילה וסבתא
י ורעמא וסבתכא ובני רעמה שבא ודדן : וכוש ילד את־נמרוד הוא
החל להיות גבור בארץ : ומצרים ילד את־לודים ואת־
ענמים ואת־להבים ואת־נפתחים : ואת־פתרסים ואת־כסלחים אשר
יצאו משם פלשתים ואת־כפתרים : וכנען ילד את־צידון בכרו
טו ואת־חת : ואת־היבוסי ואת־האמרי ואת הגרגשי : ואת־החוי ואת־
הערקי ואת־הסיני : ואת־הארודי ואת־הצמרי ואת־החמתי : בני שם
עילם ואשור וארפכשד ולוד וארם ועוץ וחול וגתר ומשך :
וארפכשד ילד את־שלח ושלח ילד את־עבר :

Title page from the Book of Chronicles, published by the Bomberg Press in Venice in 1568. The title word Adam is made up of individual wood engravings.

first complete editions of the two Talmuds (1520–23) with the approval of Pope Leo X. (Only individual tractates of the Babylonian Talmud had hitherto been published.) The pagination of Bomberg's editions of the Talmud, with commentaries, has become standard ever since. (See also *Printing, Hebrew).

BONDS, STATE OF ISRAEL. Jews who do not have the privilege of living in Israel can still share in building the country. By 1970, more than two million people in 35 countries throughout the world had invested one and a half billion dollars in State of Israel Bonds. The money has been used to develop agriculture and industry, to build new housing, tourist facilities, and electric power plants, to develop Israel's harbors and ports, and to improve living conditions for Israel's population, which has quadrupled since 1948.

The Israel Bond Organization was established in 1951 with the help of David Ben-Gurion, Eliezer Kaplan, Golda Meir and 50 American Jewish leaders. The first bonds were redeemed in 1963, 12 years after they were issued, and in 1970 the amount paid back to bondholders totaled over 700 million dollars.

Although the bonds do not yield high interest, the drive has proved successful, especially in the United States, because of the dedicated and enthusiastic effort by volunteers in synagogues, labor unions, women's groups and Zionist organizations.

BOOKS. "My son! Make your books your companions, let your cases and shelves be your pleasure grounds and gardens. Bask in their paradise, gather their fruit, pluck their roses . . . . " That Judah ibn *Tibbon should have written these words to his son is quite understandable. Essential to Jews is the learning of Torah, and since talmudic days books have played an important part in Torah study.

In ancient times all books were scrolls. Those used for holy purposes were written on animal skin; others were made from tree bark, parchment and similar materials. The Talmud and Midrash speak often of scroll-books. We read that the high priest on the Day of Atonement read from a scroll during the Temple service and then rolled it up. There is no mention in the Talmud of books with folded pages.

Though most of the books in ancient times were writings of biblical works, there were also non-biblical works, such as community and family records, and even commercial papers. Also appearing in scroll form, several of these books were found among the Dead Sea Scrolls. As with biblical works, the *scribe used only one side of the parchment. There were several writing instruments – those made of reed were most common. Black carbon ink was preferred, but the Talmud often mentions the juice of gallnuts being used.

The world "Bible" comes from a Greek word meaning books; in Hebrew the term used was *Kitvei-ha-Kodesh* ("Holy Writings"). The titles given to the early works reflected what was found within. The names of Talmudic sections, tractates, also reflects the contents: *Kiddushin* (marriage), *gittin* (divorce) are two examples. In later times titles were taken from names of the authors, contents of the books, but sometimes they had no connection with what was included within. An example of the latter is the kabbalistic masterpiece *Sefer ha-Zohar* ("Book of Splendor").

Because books were so important, they were well taken care of. In his ethical will, Judah ibn Tibbon, a translator and grammarian of the 12th century, wrote to his son: " . . . take particular care of your books. Cover the bookcases with rugs of fine quality; and preserve them from damp and mice, and from all manner of injury, for your books are your greatest treasure." Bindings were to protect as well as to beautify the book. Until the 17th century binders prepared book covers by pasting together paper pages, often using old manuscripts, cutting them and pasting them together until they achieved the desired thickness. Jewish bookbinders were found all over Europe, doing their work also for the Church and for

David Ben-Gurion addressing an Israel Bonds gathering at the Fontainebleau Hotel in Miami Beach, Florida.

1

2

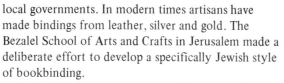

3

1. Prayerbook bound in silver, bearing the coat of arms of Isaac Mendes. It was crafted by Benjamin Levi of Portsmouth in 1746.
2. Page from the Bamburg Maḥzor, 1279. In the absence of capital letters in the Hebrew script, the initial word of a verse was often enlarged and intricately decorated in Hebrew manuscripts.
3. Bookplate designed for a pediatrician by the American artist, Solomon S. Levadi, 1933.

local governments. In modern times artisans have made bindings from leather, silver and gold. The Bezalel School of Arts and Crafts in Jerusalem made a deliberate effort to develop a specifically Jewish style of bookbinding.

In the Middle Ages a popular addition was the *hakdamah* (introduction) in which the author gives his motives for writing the book and says something about its content. Often, the *hakdamah* was also a work of literary art. *Naḥmanides wrote several excellent *hakdamot.* Abraham *ibn Ezra, in his rhymed introduction to his own Commentary on the Torah, explained the approach he used and why the form used by other commentators was insufficient. One edition of a work on morality included a four-line verse intended to convince the hesitant purchaser that his investment would be worthwhile. Indeed, it was said that a "book without a *hakdamah* is like a body without a soul." With the introduction of printing, it became customary for publishers also to write prefaces apologizing for mistakes.

In the Middle Ages book selling was a popular trade. Individual authors also sold their own books, often traveling from town to town for this purpose. When printing began in the 15th century, the book trade increased substantially. Authors continued to "push" their books. It was easier if the books had a *haskamah,* a recommendation by a scholar or rabbi. Traditionally it heaped flowery praises upon the author's head and promised the reader moral profit and intellectual delight. The *haskamah* developed into a protection of the author's rights to the book and became a shield against censorship as well. The 19th and 20th centuries saw the growth of large firms, headed by Jews, which became important publishers and booksellers of works of general interest as well as of Judaica.

Although little is known about private book collections prior to the Middle Ages, Jews have been book collectors throughout history. One of the greatest treasures of Hebrew books, Rashi's Commentary printed in 1475 was found in the collection of an Italian Catholic priest, Giovanni Bernardo de Rossi. Prominent Jewish book collectors included David Oppenheim, the rabbi of Prague, who started his library in his youth. In the late 17th century he acquired 4,500 printed works in addition to 780 manuscripts. This collection, possibly the most important private Jewish library ever assembled, is now in the Bodleian Library at Oxford University. Elkan Nathan *Adler, an English lawyer, also compiled a large collection, which included 30,000 fragments from the Cairo *Genizah.

Other outstanding collections have been acquired by the Jewish Theological Seminary library and the New York Public Library. Since the end of World War II, continuing searches directed by Professor Shlomo Shunami, have been made to acquire from German sources many irreplaceable manuscripts and books which were looted by the Nazis. Those which could be identified were returned to owners who claimed them, but most have been placed in the National Library in Jerusalem.

Books and learning are so much a part of Jewish tradition, that Jews are called "the people of the Book." Indeed, many of the violent acts of anti-Semitism throughout history were accompanied by the defacement and burning of books. The persecutors, knowing how much anguish this would cause, identified the book with the Jew. (See *Censorship). Today, all over the world, with books and paperback editions readily accessible, Jewish book collectors are common. Israel ranks second in the world in the number of books of all kinds bought per person. The Israel army issues a prayer book and a Bible to each new soldier, and has drives to collect reading material for every army base and outpost. During the Yom Kippur War of 1973, many soldiers who were university or yeshivah students brought their books with them so they could study whenever they might snatch a free moment. Tanks and bunkers held miniature libraries.

Jews have traditionally been proud of their books, but as Joseph Solomon del Medigo wrote in the 17th century: "It is not the quantity of what we read that is important, but its quality."

Chapbooks – flimsy, unbound pamphlets – were sold by chapmen (peddlers) probably as early as the 16th century. They were crudely done on cheap paper and little is known of the earliest ones. They included popular literature and *ma'aseh* books which were legends of wondrous deeds, simple ethical works and instructions for the good life, chiefly in Yiddish, by Ḥasidic rabbis. The most common chapbooks, seen to this day, are seasonal works such as the **Haggadah* for *Passover, or *kinot* for *Tishah be-Av.

Bookplates. When printed books were relatively rare and expensive, collectors had to be rich to afford them and pride in possession of books was great. To mark this pride (and to reduce the possibility of theft) many booklovers had special labels printed to be pasted inside the cover. The labels almost always included the name of the owner, and the words "ex libris" or *"mi-sifrei"* ("from the library of") and sometimes a motto. Often they were designed by artists. Bookplates soon became articles with almost as much beauty as the books themselves.

The first bookplate with Hebrew words was designed by Albrecht Durf about 1500. The first bookplate for a Jew was that made by Benjamin Levi of Portsmouth, England, for Isaac Mendes in 1746. After this many Jews followed suit and often incorporated coats-of-arms to which they were not entitled. But until the 20th century Jewish bookplates were rare. Some libraries had a separate plate for each book, and today these books are collected for their plates alone.

Jewish bookplates generally had a double motif: one obviously Jewish (Hebrew words, or a representation of the Bible, shield of David, or something of historic importance in exile) and the other reflecting the professional or other interest of the collector (medical, legal, or an object of family interest). Today, America and Israel are foremost in the field and many institutions (Jewish libraries, synagogues and community centers) have their own distinctive plates. Today many people are commissioning inexpensive bookplates in a revival of the art.

BORMANN, MARTIN (1900-), one of the most sought after Nazi leaders. He joined the Nazi Party in 1925, and rose to be one of the highest officials in it. He played an important role in planning the murder of the Jews of Europe in the *Holocaust. In 1946 Bormann was sentenced to death in absentia by the International Military Tribunal at *Nuremberg. He had been with Hitler just before the latter's death but had evidently managed to escape from the bunker. His exact whereabouts after the war remained unknown. The attorney-general of Frankfort opened a case against Bormann and a reward of 100,000 DM was posted for information leading to his arrest.

In 1973, following the examination of dental evidence, the courts officially declared that Bormann had died in 1945.

BOSTON, the capital city of Massachusetts, U.S., had a Jewish population of about 210,000 in 1970. Although Boston was founded as early as 1628, it was only in the mid-19th century that a Jewish community was organized there. This Jewish community, however, was not socially integrated into the general Boston community, which consisted of Yankees who controlled its social, cultural, and financial institutions, and Irishmen who dominated its politics. There was even an active anti-Semitic movement in the 1940s, inspired by an Irish priest.

The first Jewish community in Boston was of German origin, and it established a synagogue in 1842. This community was small and numbered only 3,000 in 1875. From the 1870s onwards, however, many East European Jews settled in Boston, so that by 1895 there were 20,000 Jews. The German Jews tended towards Reform or Conservative congregations, whereas the East European Jews established many Orthodox synagogues. In 1969 there were about 75 congregations in Boston — 20 were Orthodox, 35 Conservative, and 20 Reform. In spite of the differences in religious ideology, the entire Boston Jewish community established in 1935 the Rabbinical Association of Greater Boston (now known as the Massachusetts Board of Rabbis) which, among other activities, supervises *kashrut*.

The well-established culture of Boston influenced the Jewish community's attitude toward Jewish education and the Jews of Boston established many Hebrew congregational schools, two Jewish day schools, a college, called the Hebrew Teachers College, and the Bureau of Jewish Education, which supervises most of the Hebrew schools. Brandeis University, situated in the greater Boston area, was established by American Jewry in 1948 as a secular university, where there would be no discrimination against Jews.

Wood engraving of the first synagogue in Boston, Massachusetts, built in 1851.

THE FIRST ISRAELITISH SYNAGOGUE
IN BOSTON
"Ohebei Shalom", Friends of Peace
Erected in 1851

Although separate charities were established by the German and East European Jews, they were eventually united in 1895 into the Federation of Jewish Charities, today known as the Combined Jewish Philanthropies.

BOVE-BUKH is the name of a frequently reprinted chivalric romance of the early 16th century composed by Elijah *Levita. The book is a Yiddish adaptation of the Italian version *(Buovo d'Antona)* of the Anglo-French romance *Sir Bevis of Hampton* of the early 14th century. A crude prose version of Levita's book was published under the title *Bove Mayse* at the end of the 18th century, and this version remained a popular favorite among the Jews of East Europe. The Yiddish term *bobe mayse*, which means a fantastic or unbelievable tale, originates from the title of this book and does not mean "a grandmother's tale" as is commonly believed.

BOYCOTT. A boycott is an attempt at isolating a person or a group of persons by having no contact with him or them in any way — economic, social, or political. In history the boycott has frequently been used as a weapon against the Jews by anti-Semites.

Towards the end of the 19th century, the boycott was the basic weapon used for victimizing the Jewish communities of Europe. Austrian anti-Semites publicized the slogan "Don't buy from Jews" and Jews were not accepted in merchant guilds and trade associations. Between the two World Wars, particularly in Poland, taking away trade from the Jews was made out to be the perfect cure for poverty and unemployment. With the Nazi rise to power in Germany, a general anti-Jewish boycott was announced. Shops owned by Jews were often picketed, and sometimes destroyed. The Polish government followed the German example, and tried to drive the Jews out of Poland by strangling them economically. This "cold pogrom" as the boycott is often called, undermined the foundations of the livelihood of hundreds of thousands of Jews.

Anti-Nazi Boycott. As a protest against anti-Jewish activities by the Nazis in the 1930s, Jews held mass rallies, and from these an anti-German boycott emerged. The boycott spread throughout Poland, and developed into an organized movement. In England, the German fur business almost closed down because of the boycott. Various anti-German boycott groups formed in France, Rumania, Yugoslavia and in the U.S.A., where the American Jewish Congress created a Boycott Committee. Though anti-German boycott movements no longer exist, many Jews throughout the world still refuse on principle to buy any products made in Germany.

The Arab Boycott was initiated against the State of Israel in order to ruin Israel's economy and thus weaken its military potential. The boycott consists, first of all, of a complete boycott of Israel and Israel goods by all Arab states. The boycott also tries to dissuade foreign commercial and industrial companies from establishing business relations with Israel by threatening not to allow them to sell their products in Arab markets.

The boycott is conducted by the Central Office for the Boycott of Israel in Damascus, and by regional boycott committees in each of the Arab states. In enforcing the boycott, the Arab countries demand that all foreign companies wishing to establish business ties with an Arab state sign a certificate declaring that they are not engaged in any "boycottable offense." "Boycottable offenses" include economic ties with Israel, owning shares in an Israel corporation, producing or selling motion pictures which favorably depict Israel or Jewish history. A "Certificate of Origin," verifying that none of the components of the goods is made in Israel, must be attached to all foreign-made goods sold in Arab states. The boycott is not only anti-Israel but also anti-Jewish: Jewish firms are suspect and find it difficult to enter into business relations with Arab countries.

The Israel economy has grown in spite of the Arab boycott. When certain firms have given in to the boycott, other firms have usually taken their place. Many governments and firms have refused to supply the certificate demanded by the boycott offices and have not been excluded from Arab markets. Some large companies have decided to ignore the Arab boycott because they realize that succumbing to it will make them lose business and prestige in their own local markets, where there is often a large Jewish community. The Arabs themselves have often not fulfilled their threats when their own interests were involved.

Israel has defended itself by discontinuing trade with firms which have given in to the boycott in any way, and by convincing firms that the Arab threats are hollow.

BRAND, JOEL JENÖ (1906-1964), member of the Budapest Jewish relief committee set up during

1

2

1. Pickets outside a five-and-ten-cent store in New York, urging a boycott of Nazi goods, November 1937.
2. Joel Brand testifying at the trial of the Nazi war criminal, Adolf Eichmann, in Jerusalem, 1961.

World War II. Brand, who was born in Naszód, moved to Erfurt, Germany, with his family in 1910. Active in left-wing politics, he was arrested in 1933, but released in September 1934. He escaped to Hungary where, from 1938, he was active in a semi-clandestine organization for helping Jewish refugees, establishing contact with German Nazi agents who were then secretly working in Hungary. As a member of a Jewish committee formed in 1943, Brand met Adolf *Eichmann, upon whose orders he left for neutral Turkey in 1944, to present the Jewish Agency with a German proposition (the sincerity of which has never been established) to prevent the extermination of Hungarian Jewry in exchange for a supply of trucks and other equipment. He hoped to meet Moshe *Sharett in Turkey, but the latter was prevented by the British authorities from traveling to Turkey, and Brand, at the entreaty of Jewish Agency officials in Istanbul, continued to Palestine to conclude negotiations there. He was arrested in Aleppo, Syria, by the British, who claimed that they suspected him of being a Nazi agent, and was taken to Cairo. On October 7, 1944, he was released in Jerusalem, but Hungarian Jews from the provinces had meanwhile been deported to Auschwitz and exterminated. Brand remained in Ereẓ Israel, and after the war devoted himself singlemindedly to tracking down Nazi war criminals. Brand testified at the Eichmann trial. He died in Frankfort where he was testifying against Hermann Krumey and Otto Hunsche, two of Eichmann's chief aides.

1. Louis D. Brandeis, American jurist and the first Jew to be appointed to the U.S. Supreme Court.

Louis D. Brandeis

BRANDEIS, LOUIS DEMBITZ (1856-1941). The Supreme Court of the United States is where the rights and liberties of Americans are guarded. The nine justices in their majestic black robes are an awesome sight and it is their task to see that the constitution is protected. In 1916 the first Jew was chosen to sit on the bench of the Supreme Court. He was Louis Brandeis, born in Louisville, Kentucky, in humble surroundings, son of immigrants from Bohemia. His parents' liberal home was the scene of many discussions on questions of the day, such as equality and slavery. Young Louis developed early a deep concern for his fellow man.

After graduating Harvard Law School in 1877, he became known as one of the great lawyers of his day. He was called the "People's Advocate" because he was always ready to fight for the rights of the downtrodden, the poor and the simple worker.

One of his cases came to have a tremendous significance for Brandeis. He was invited to serve as arbitrator in a strike that broke out in the New York garment industry in 1910. Most of the employers and employees were Jewish. As Brandeis got to know them, he learned more about the Jewish people and their special way of life. For the first time he became aware of his people's hopes to have a homeland – Palestine – and became a very active Zionist.

In 1916 President Woodrow Wilson appointed him Associate Justice of the Supreme Court. There was much opposition to naming a Jew to the high court of the land, but Wilson wanted a man to represent the common people and Brandeis had proved over and over that he was indeed the "People's Advocate." After a few years he was honored and esteemed by all and called a "friend of justice and of man."

His love for Palestine continued and he was generous with gifts to help rebuild the land. A colony in Israel was named in his honor Ein ha-Shofet – Spring of the Judge.

BRATISLAVA (also known as Pressburg) is the capital city of Slovakia, Czechoslovakia; until 1918 it was in Hungary and was the chartered capital of the kings of Hungary. The first Jews may have arrived with the Roman legions and there is a tradition that

Jews were martyred there during the First Crusade. The first document to mention Jews dates from 1251. During the 14th, 15th, and 16th centuries the Jews were expelled from Bratislava several times, and various anti-Semitic regulations were made. In the 18th century the community again began to grow; in 1709 there were 189 Jews in Bratislava, and there were 722 by 1736.

The Jews pioneered the textile trade, and the yeshivah they established in the town became an important center of Jewish learning. The great authority of Rabbi Moses *Sofer made Bratislava a center of Orthodox Judaism for the whole world. At the end of the 19th century the community was divided in a fierce controversy between the Orthodox and Reform wings.

1

In 1939, a titular independent state of Slovakia was set up by the Nazis. The rise of *anti-Semitism launched a wave of terror, with attacks on the synagogues and the yeshivah. Nearly 1,000 Jewish students were expelled from the university. When World War II broke out, all Jewish shops were confiscated. Only a small fraction of the Jews survived the Nazi terror of the war.

After the war, many Jewish refugees made their way to Bratislava and it became the Jewish center of Slovakia. By 1947 there were 7,000 refugees there. In 1949 the Communist regime started to impose severe restrictions on Jewish life and many Jews emigrated to Israel. In 1969 the Jewish population of Bratislava was estimated at about 1,500.

BRAZIL. At the turn of the 16th century, *Marranos either fleeing from persecutions in Portugal or deported by the Spanish *Inquisition, formed the first Jewish settlements in Brazil, a country in South America. The immigrants fostered the sugar and tobacco industries, and developed rice and cotton plantations. At the end of the century, further activity by the Inquisition sent more Marranos to Brazil. When the Dutch conquered the Pernambuco region in 1631, Marranos returned to practicing Judaism openly. Jewish communities flourished in Itamaraca and Recife. The peace, however, was short-lived: Portugal captured Recife in 1654, and Jews were again forced to flee.

2

With the proclamation of Brazilian independence in 1822, some Marranos reverted to Judaism, and Jewish immigration from Europe began. Rio de Janeiro, Sao Paolo and Bahai (Salvador) were the locations of the main Jewish communities. Rio de Janeiro was the main Marrano center in Brazil in the 18th century. Many Marranos were sent from there to Cuba for trial,

1. A corner in the Jewish quarter of Bratislava.
2. Recife, the center of Jewish life in Brazil until the city fell to the Portuguese in January 1564. Faced with the alternatives of the Inquisition or flight, the Jewish community fled the city.

Stamp issued by the Brazilian post office in honor of the visit by President Zalman Shazar of Israel in 1966.

and it was only in the mid-nineteenth century that Jews dared to practice their religion openly in Rio de Janeiro.

After World War I many Jews came to Brazil, and there was further Jewish immigration in 1933, from Germany. Approximately 140,000 Jews live in Brazil today, most of them professionals, merchants, or land and property owners. Newspapers and periodicals are published by the Jewish communities, and there are many Jewish schools in Brazil.

Rio de Janeiro is a state and a city in the United States of Brazil. The first attempt at communal organization in Rio was made in 1846 by Jews originating from Morocco, and in 1873 a Jewish society for religious and welfare matters was founded. When Brazil was declared a republic in 1889, the number of Jews in Rio de Janeiro was estimated at 200. In 1900 there were two synagogues, one of North African immigrants, and the other of French and West European settlers. By the end of World War I the city's Jewish population was estimated at 2,000.

Many Jews immigrated to Rio de Janeiro after World War I, and established various Jewish institutions: synagogues, charities, cemeteries, medical infirmaries, Zionist organizations, libraries and schools. Today there are thirteen Jewish educational institutions in Rio de Janeiro, the majority of which are elementary schools, but some also include high schools. In 1960, there were approximately 50,000 Jews in the State of Rio de Janeiro, most of them in the city of Rio de Janeiro.

BREAD. The rabbis regarded bread as the staple diet and no meal was considered complete without it. They instituted a special benediction to be recited before eating bread made from one of the five species of cereals (wheat, rice-wheat, spelt, barley and two-row barley) grown in Ereẓ Israel. This blessing (popularly called *Ha-Moẓi*) is: "Blessed art Thou, Lord our God, King of the Universe, Who bringeth forth *(ha-moẓi)* bread out of the earth." After pronouncing this benediction, other food or beverages may be eaten without saying another blessing – except for wine and fruits, for which their particular blessings must be recited in all cases. Before the benediction over bread is said, one is obliged to wash the hands by pouring a quarter "log" (approximately 0.137 liters) of clean water over them, and drying them properly (see *Washing the Hands). After eating bread at least of the size of an olive the full *Grace after Meals has to be said.

A religious duty of Jewish women when baking is to separate a small portion of the dough about the size of an olive, as *ḥallah,* and to burn it. In Temple times the *ḥallah* portion was given to the priests. From talmudic times, it was the special duty of the housewife to bake the bread for the Sabbath. This bread, usually prepared from white flour, is also called *"ḥallah."* Two such loaves are placed on the festive Sabbath table as a symbol for the double portion of *manna which the Israelites in the wilderness received every Friday, and because of the Showbread in the Temple, which was displayed each Sabbath. The bread for Sabbath is usually braided, and of oblong shape, but for Rosh Ha-Shanah it is round. Where wine is lacking, **Kiddush* (but not *Havdalah*) may be made over bread.

As a protective measure against assimilation which might lead to intermarriage the rabbis prohibited Jews from eating food cooked by a gentile, or bread baked by a non-Jew *(pat akkum).* However, this interdiction does not apply to bread sold by a professional non-Jewish baker *(pat paltar),* if the ingredients are not otherwise forbidden by the *dietary laws.

Bread must be treated with special regard. Raw meat should not be placed on it nor spilt wine be allowed to spoil it; it should also not be thrown across the table. Providing bread for the poor was regarded as a great religious duty; the withholding of it from the hungry, a sin. Whenever the Talmud sage, Rabbi Huna, broke bread for a meal, he first opened his door and said, "Let everyone in need come and eat," as is done at the beginning of the Passover *seder.* Bread with salt was regarded as the poor man's food but sufficient for the humble student of the Torah, and it has remained a custom to sprinkle a little salt on bread partaken at the beginning of meals. In Jerusalem it is the custom to greet official guests of the City Council with bread and salt as they enter the city's limits.

BRENNER, JOSEPH ḤAYYIM, (1881-1921), Hebrew novelist. Brenner was born in the Ukraine and after studying in a yeshivah, he went to Gomel where he joined the Bund, a Jewish left-wing organization. Later he served three years in the Russian army, but at the outbreak of the Russo-Japanese war, he deserted and escaped to London.

1

There he worked in a printing shop, founded a Hebrew language periodical and became active in the Po'alei Zion, a socialist-Zionist movement. All this time he had been writing. After working as an editor in Lemberg, Poland, he emigrated to Ereẓ Israel in 1909. During World War I he became an Ottoman citizen so that the Turkish authorities would not expel him from the country. Brenner lived and worked as an editor and writer in many different towns in Ereẓ Israel. He was murdered during the Arab riots on May 2, 1921.

Brenner wrote many short stories and novels. He described the life of the Jews in Russia, the plight of the Jewish workers in England, and the state of the Jewish community in Jerusalem that lived on charity in the form of the **ḥalukkah*. He was concerned about social conditions and described his subjects negatively, no doubt hoping to arouse his readers to change things.

He translated some of the world's classic books into Hebrew and both wrote and translated in Yiddish. In his writings, Brenner made an important contribution to the development of modern Hebrew.

BREST-LITOVSK. For many generations the Jewish community of Brest-Litovsk was the most important in Lithuania. It was one of the three founding communities of the Council of Lithuania, in which Brest-Litovsk's delegate and its rabbi were for long given great honor. (For more information see *Self-Government, Jewish).

The community represented Lithuanian Jewry before the central authorities according to the following resolution: "It has thus been decided. If His Majesty the King has occasion to visit one of the three principal communities – in the event of his arrival in Grodno or . . . Pinsk, they will inform the Brest community." If the Brest community decided to give the King a gift, the Council was expected to pay for it. A resolution of 1644 further expresses the honor accorded to the Brest-Litovsk community: "As to the order of signatures of the honorable members of the Council, it has been thus decided: they shall sign in the following order: first the Council members from Brest."

The first Jews settled in Brest-Litovsk in the 14th century. Throughout the Middle Ages they shared the plight of most other Jewish communities in Eastern Europe: expulsion, unfair taxes and, all too often, pogroms and other forms of persecution. In the economic area in the 16th and 17th centuries the Jews of Brest were engaged in commerce, crafts, and agriculture. By the 20th century, most Jews were shoemakers and tailors. Brest-Litovsk was a stronghold of the *Mitnaggedim,* the opponents of *Ḥasidism.

The Holocaust brought destruction to the Jewish population of Brest-Litovsk. Of the 30,000 Jews who lived there in 1941, only about 200 survived the War. In 1970 the Jewish population of the town was estimated at 2,000. It had no synagogue, the last one having been converted into a moviehouse in 1959.

BRIBERY means giving a gift to a person, usually someone in authority to persuade him to favor the donor. A payoff to a policeman to look the other way is a bribe, and a lollipop to get a small child to sit still is a bribe in a sense. A pledge of a large donation to a campaign fund becomes a bribe if the donor expects tax favors or freedom from prosecution in return for his contribution.

The laws against bribery date back to the Bible, where the commandment is directed at judges who were urged to be impartial. The commandment not to take bribes is repeated in the Bible several times, twice with the reason given that "bribes blind the clear-sighted and upset the pleas of the just" (Exodus 23:8; Deuteronomy 16:19). This was later interpreted to mean that a corrupt judge tends to identify the interests of the donor with his own and

2

1. Joseph Ḥayyim Brenner.
2. Rabbi Ḥayyim Soloveichik, also known as Ḥayyim Brisker. In 1892 he succeeded his father as rabbi of Brest-Litovsk (Brisk) and threw himself into communal activity there. His reputation grew and his leadership in both rabbinical and lay matters was taken for granted.

is thus blind to the rights of the other party, and also that such a judge would not grow old without becoming physically blind. The donor of bribes is also blamed as a tempter or accomplice of the taker. Bribery seems to have been rather widespread in ancient times, or else the prophets would hardly have denounced it so vehemently, but it was in the nature of unethical misconduct rather than of a criminal offense. There is no penalty prescribed in the Bible for taking bribes but under talmudic law for the violation of a negative injunction where no penalty was prescribed in the Bible, the transgressor was liable to be flogged. The rule was therefore evolved that taking a bribe invalidated the judge's decision. Some talmudic judges even refused to sit in judgment over any person who had shown them the slightest courtesy, such as helping them to alight from a boat.

Bribing non-Jewish rulers, officials, and judges was regarded as necessary. In view of their bias against Jews, it is not hard to understand such an attitude. Throughout history bribes were often demanded of Jews simply for permission to practice their religion, and the bribes were not always money. Concessions and obligations were required in many places in return for religious freedom or tolerance, however limited. The *Dhimma* laws of the Muslims, the *Toleranzpatent* of Josef II of Austria (1781) are examples of official requirements such as distinctive dress, subservient behavior, and special services with which, in addition to a money tax, they bought a measure of benevolence. Unofficially, of course, and in many ways, Jews had to buy favor to survive.

In the State of Israel the taker and the donor of bribes are equally punishable. Demanding a bribe is the same as taking it, and offering or promising is the same as giving it. Even the intermediary between the donor and the taker (or the intended taker) bears the same criminal responsibility. No other evidence being normally available, the taker is a competent witness against the donor, and vice versa, and though they are accomplices their evidence need not be corroborated.

BRISCOE, ROBERT (1894-1969), Irish politician and communal leader who was the first Jewish member of the Irish Dail (parliament) and the first Jewish Lord Mayor of Dublin. He was active in the struggle for Irish independence. From 1917 to 1924 he served in the Irish Republican Army and was sent to the United States to secure financial and moral aid from Irish Americans. He sat in the Dail from 1927 to 1965. From 1928 he was a member of the Dublin Corporation (city council), serving as mayor in 1956-57 and 1961-62. Briscoe was an active supporter of the Revisionist movement and a member of the executive of the New Zionist Organization. He gave support to the activities of the *Irgun Ẓeva'i Le'ummi, which utilized his experience of clandestine paramilitary strategy in Palestine.

Robert Briscoe receiving the mayoral chain from the outgoing Lord Mayor Dockrell in June, 1961. This was the second occasion on which Briscoe was voted into office as mayor of Dublin.

BUBER, MARTIN (1878-1965), the philosopher and theologian, Zionist thinker and leader, had a profound impact on Christian as well as Jewish thinkers. The grandson of the noted Talmud and Midrash scholar, Solomon Buber, Martin Buber was deeply stirred by the religious message of Ḥasidism and considered it his duty to convey that message to the world. He wrote several books on Ḥasidism including collections of Ḥasidic tales. He was very concerned about Jewish education in Germany and, together with Franz *Rosenzweig he translated the Bible into German.

During the early Nazi period (1933-38) Buber traveled throughout Germany lecturing, teaching and encouraging his fellow Jews, and thus organized something of a spiritual resistance to the oppressions which were beginning. In 1938 he settled in Palestine and was appointed professor of social philosophy at the Hebrew University, where he taught until his retirement in 1951.

In his later years Buber remained very active in public affairs and in Jewish cultural endeavors. He was one of the founders of the College for Adult Education Teachers, established to train teachers from among the new immigrants who came to Israel. He was the first president of the Israel Academy of Sciences and Humanities. After World War II Buber lectured extensively outside Israel and became known throughout the world as one of the spiritual leaders of his generation.

Martin Buber, philosopher and theologian, Zionist thinker and leader.

The starting point of Buber's philosophy is the relation between man and the world. He identified two basic forms of relation, the I-Thou and I-It, into which all man's relations, both with other men and things in the world, can be divided. The I-Thou relation is characterized by openness and directness among other qualities; the I-It by the absence of these qualities. The I-Thou relation is one in which the parties speak to one another as equals; the I-It relation is characterized by the fact that one partner uses the other to achieve some end. I-Thou relations among men leads to the notion of God as the Eternal Thou and to the description of the relation between man and God as I-Thou. For Buber the essence of the religious life is not the holding of religious beliefs, but the way in which one meets the challenge of everyday life.

In the years before the establishment of the State of Israel, Buber proposed a joint Arab-Israel state, believing that "the Jewish people proclaims its desire to live in peace and brotherhood with the Arab people and to develop the common homeland into a republic in which both peoples will have the possibility of free development." Even after the proclamation of the State and the attack on it by the Arab countries, he still hoped and believed that Jews and Arabs would come to live in peace.

BUDAPEST, the capital of Hungary, was created in 1893 by the unification of three old towns – Buda, Obuda, and Pest. Each had Jewish communities from the Middle Ages (Buda from the 11th century) which at times played an important role in the city and in the government of the country. At other times, as in the rest of Europe, they suffered oppressive treatment, especially in the late Middle Ages.

In 1526 Hungary was conquered by the Turks who ruled for 150 years. Jews who had dispersed earlier, returned to Buda, Obuda and Pest, and although heavily taxed, profited from the tolerance of the Ottoman Empire. Jews generally preferred Turkish rule, but this ended in 1686, and Hungary again became part of the Holy Roman Empire. In that reconquest, half of the Jewish community of Buda (1,000 strong) died and the rest were expelled, the Jewish quarter was looted and the Torah scrolls were destroyed.

Jews returned in 1689. Thereafter conditions varied between toleration and expulsion. The Emperor in Vienna generally protected the community but the non-Jewish citizens frequently agitated against this policy. Even in 1848, during the Hungarian Revolution, which was supported by Jews, demands were made for their expulsion.

The situation was similar in Obuda and Pest. In the 18th century the counts of Zichy were official protectors of the Obuda community, receiving in return a "protection tax." Obuda Jews produced fine linen, for which the town gained a European reputation.

Pest was noted for Jewish scholarship. It was a

center for all Hungary. The Pest community led the struggle for Jewish civil rights throughout Hungary and Pest Jews were prominent in the revolution of 1848. Theodor *Herzl and Max *Nordau were born in Pest.

All three communities were active in social work, sponsoring hospitals, schools, orphanages, institutes for the handicapped and rabbinical seminaries. Fine synagogues graced the city. The Dohany Street synagogue, built in Moorish style by the Pest community in 1859 and still standing, was the largest in Europe, perhaps in the world, seating 3,000.

During the Holocaust period about 180,000 (50%) of Budapest's Jews died. In 1944 *Eichmann entered Hungary, which had joined the German side in 1941, and began deportations. He was forced to leave for a time by the Hungarian government, but the extremist Arrow Cross Movement seized power and systematically hunted down Jews. Eichmann returned.

Passes issued by neutral countries saved about 100,000 Jews, and a further 40,000 survived when the Russian Army arrived in 1945. Since then Hungary has had a Communist government. During the short revolutionary period in 1956, about 25,000 Jews left Budapest. In 1968 there were 70,000 Jews who ran schools, two rabbinical seminaries, various community institutions and one newspaper.

The Jewish museum in Budapest, established at the beginning of the 20th century.

BUKHARA is a Soviet region situated in Central Asia. Bukharan Jews believe they originated from the Ten Tribes who were exiled from Ereẓ Israel in the sixth century b.c.e. The names of the Bukharan Jews, as well as expressions in their language, suggest that some of them came from Persia. There is, however, no evidence as to the origin and the exact date of settlement of Jews in Bukhara, nor is there any information about them before the 13th century.

In the 13th century, when Bukhara was ruled by Tatar-Mongolians, the Jewish community endured much suffering and became impoverished. During the 14th century, however, its situation improved. At the end of the 16th century, when Bukhara became an important Islamic center, Jews were forced to live in a special quarter, and to wear a badge to distinguish them from the Muslims. In the middle of the 18th century, the Muslims began to compel them to convert to Islam. During the second half of the 19th century, certain parts of Bukhara were conquered by the Russians, who did not impose any special restrictions on the Jews, and many Bukharan Jews from Muslim areas, where the situation of the Jews was still difficult, migrated to the Russian-dominated areas. These immigrants included forced converts *(anusim)*, who returned to Judaism once they were under Russian rule. In 1920 the Communist Red Army conquered all of Bukhara and established it as part of the Soviet Socialist Republic of Uzbekistan.

The emigration of Bukharan Jews to Palestine began in 1868. Some of the emigrants were wealthy Jews who wanted to make Jerusalem a spiritual center for their community. In 1892 they founded the Bukharan quarter in Jerusalem. This quarter still exists and is famous for its colorful synagogue. The children of the original founders remained in Jerusalem to study while their parents returned to Bukhara to conduct their business affairs. During World War I many Bukharan Jews lost their wealth as a result of the war and the revolutions, and they returned to Palestine impoverished.

Most Bukharan Jews were poorly educated until the beginning of the 19th century, when schools were opened for their children. Unlike their treatment of Russian-European Jews, the Soviet authorities gave religious freedom to Bukharan Jews who, therefore, remained one of the most religious groups among Soviet Jewry. In 1970 there were approximately 12,000 Jews in Bukhara, of whom a great number took advantage of the Soviet government's relaxation of its emigration laws and moved to Israel.

BULGARIA. Jewish settlement in Bulgaria, located along the Black Sea, is as old as the Common Era itself. Jewish communities are known to have existed in different periods through the centuries, and Judaism left its mark on the doctrines and practices of the early Bulgarian Christians. In the 15th and 16th centuries, the Bulgarian Jewish population was reinforced by Hungarian, Bavarian, and Spanish Jewish immigrants. As a result of the influx, the Jewish community in Bulgaria split into three – Romaniots (that is, those Bulgarian Jews who pray according to the Byzantine Jewish rite), Ashkenazim and Sephardim.

In 1934, the Jewish population numbered 50,000. From the time of the first Zionist Congress, Bulgarian Jewry identified closely with Jewish ideals, and the Zionist movement dominated all Jewish communal organization.

During and after World War II, Bulgarian Jews suffered a great deal. Their basic rights were restricted by anti-Jewish legislation, their property confiscated, and hard labor was imposed upon them. In 1943, a formal agreement was signed for the deportation of 20,000 Bulgarian Jews. Prior to this, the Bulgarian government had surrendered all Bulgarian Jews living in German-occupied areas into the hands of the Nazis.

All anti-Jewish legislation was abolished in 1944 and afterwards, when the Soviet army entered the country and the Communist Party dominated the Bulgarian government, organized Jewish life was reestablished. Jewish communist leaders announced that Bulgarian Jews had nothing to do with international Jewish organizations – the Jews were to be nothing more than Bulgarians of Jewish origin. Nevertheless, most of the Jews remained faithful to the Zionist idea and between 1949 and 1951, almost 45,000 Jews left Bulgaria for Israel.

Only 7,000 Jews were left in Bulgaria after the mass exodus. Organized Jewish life has declined steadily and today there are no rabbis and no religious schools in Bulgaria. The government of the country disapproves of ties between Bulgarian Jews and other Jewish communities, but the Jews of Bulgaria live free from persecution.

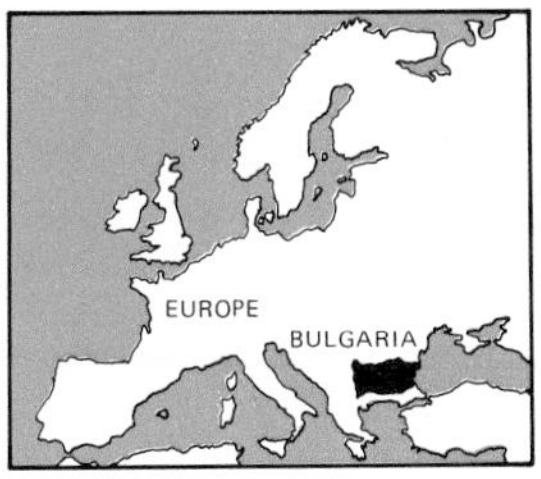

BURIAL.

In The Bible. Decent burial was regarded to be of great importance in ancient Israel, as in the rest of the ancient Near East. Abraham's purchase of the cave at Machpelah as a family tomb (Genesis 23) and the subsequent measures taken by later patriarchs to ensure that they would be buried there occupy a prominent place in the patriarchal narratives. Biblical biographies ordinarily end with the statement that a man died, and an account of his burial reflects the value assigned to proper interment. To bury an unidentified corpse was considered to be so great a good deed that even the high priest was required to do it although it involved him in becoming ritually unclean.

There is no explicit biblical evidence as to how soon after death burial took place, but it is likely that

2

1. Bulgarian Maccabi youth organization celebrating 'Shekel Day' c. 1935.
2. A stone coffin, or sarcophagus, at Bet She'arim. This is known as the shell sarcophagus because of the distinctive carving both on the lid and on the sides of the coffin.

it was within a day after death. This was dictated by the climate and by the fact that the Israelites did not enbalm the dead (Jacob and Joseph were embalmed following Egyptian custom).

In Post-Biblical Times. Rabbinic legend stressed the antiquity of burial by relating that Adam and Eve learned the art of burial from a raven which showed them how to dispose of the body of their dead son Abel by scratching away at a spot in the earth where it had interred one of its own kin. Maimonides ruled that even if the deceased had not wanted to be buried, his heirs must bury him. The Talmud rules that the burial of gentiles is also a religious duty.

In talmudic times, burial took place in caves, hewn tombs, sarcophagi, and catacombs; and a secondary burial, i.e., a re-interment of the remains sometimes took place about one year after the original burial. Jewish custom insists on prompt burial as a matter of respect for the dead, a consideration of particular relevance in hot climates. The precedents set by the prompt burials of Sarah (Genesis 23) and of Rachel (Genesis 35:19) are reinforced by the Torah's express command that even the body of a man who had been hanged shall not remain upon the tree all night, but "you most bury him the same day" (Deuteronomy 21:23). Some delays in burial are, however, justified: "Honor of the dead" demands that the proper preparation for a coffin and shrouds be made, and that the relatives and friends pay their last respects. Certain delays are unavoidable. Funerals may not take place on the Sabbath or on the Day of Atonement; and although the rabbis at one time permitted funerals on the first day of a festival, provided that certain functions were performed by gentiles, and regarded the second day of festivals "as a weekday as far as the dead are concerned," some modern communities prefer postponement. Where there are two interments at the same time, respect demands that the burial of a scholar precedes that of an *am ha-arez* ("average citizen"), and that of a woman always precedes that of a man.

The duty of burial is an obligation of the deceased's heir but if they cannot or do not perform it, the whole community is responsible. In talmudic times, the communal fraternal societies for the burial of the dead evolved out of an appreciation of this duty. In many communities, even till modern times, acceptance into the **ḥevra kaddisha* (as the society is known) is considered to be an honor and only mature, respected men and women are initiated.

One of the functions of the *ḥevra kaddisha* is the *Tohorah* rite. This is washing the corpse and

Les ASSISTANS jettent de la terre sur le CORPS .

1

2

1. Copperplate engraving by Bernard Picart, 1723, showing members of a *ḥevra kaddisha* assisting at a burial.
2. Absalom's tomb in the Kidron Valley, Jerusalem. The tomb dates from the first century c.e.

preparing it for burial. In ancient times various cosmetics were used but these have been largely discontinued. The corpse is dressed in simple white shrouds and, as a rule, wrapped in the **tallit* he wore during his lifetime. The *tallit* is, however, invalidated by having one of the *ẓiẓit* removed.

Coffins were unknown in biblical times. The corpse was laid, face upwards, on a bier and brought to his grave. The custom of burying important people in coffins developed only later. Rabbi Judah ha-Nasi, however, ordered that holes be drilled in his coffin so that the earth touch his body. This custom is always followed where coffins are used and in countries outside Ereẓ Israel it is also customary to put earth from Ereẓ Israel in the coffin.

In ancient times a form of coffin was the ossuary

Entrance to the Tombs of the Sanhedrin in Jerusalem, first century c.e. Inside the cave are 70 burial places, and thus the tombs have become known as the Tombs of the Sanhedrin.

which was a small chest in which the bones of the deceased were placed after the flesh had decayed. In various places in Israel, such as *Bet She'arim, stone coffins, known as sarcophagi (singular sarcophagus) have also been found. Many were elaborately carved, some with non-Jewish motifs. In the Middle Ages there was no general rule as to whether burial should be in a coffin. In Spain the coffin was not used, while in France it was, and was commonly made from the table that had witnessed the hospitality of the deceased. Coffins were also used in Eastern Europe and often rabbis' coffins were made from the desks at which they had studied. In the 16th century the idea grew that it was meritorious to be buried in direct contact with the earth – "For dust you are, and to dust you shall return" (Genesis 3:19) – and interment without a coffin became the rule for strictly Orthodox Jews. In countries where the secular authorities insisted on the use of a coffin, their bottoms were either made of loose boards or holes were drilled into them.

In the Western world even Orthodox Jews nowadays use coffins in compliance with the law of the land but they are usually made plain and of cheap wood. In Israel, burial is without a coffin except for soldiers who are buried in plain wooden boxes.

Cemetery. Although nowadays burial always takes place in a cemetery, this was not always so. In biblical times the practice was to bury the dead in family sepulchers which might have been in natural caves or man-made buildings. In Talmud times, the custom developed of setting aside special places to bury the dead. This was primarily to keep the graves out of town since they can be a source of ritual impurity, particularly for the *kohanim* (priests). (For more on this see *Purity and Impurity, Ritual.) The cemetery, therefore, has no intrinsic holiness and is not "hallowed ground." However, great care has always been taken to keep the cemetery in the best possible order out of respect for the dead and sensitivity to the mourners. No activity showing disrespect for the dead, such as animals grazing there, was allowed. Further, anything that shamed the dead, such as eating and drinking or wearing *tallit* or **tefillin* or reading from the Torah, is also forbidden because the dead cannot do these things.

In some places, such as Rome and other Italian towns, as well as Sardinia, Jews in the Middle Ages buried their dead in catacombs. These were deep subterranean tunnels. Several such catacombs have been discovered, many of them richly decorated with Jewish motifs.

It is customary to visit the cemetery on the anniversary of a loved one's death, as well as during the month of Elul, preceding the High Holy Days. Cemeteries are usually owned by the community and some people reserve space next to their relatives. *Kohanim* are always buried in the first rows since their relatives, also *kohanim,* may not enter the cemetery and so can see their loved ones' graves from outside. Apostates and suicides were at one time buried in a separate section of the cemetery but this law is usually not followed.

The custom of decorating graves with flowers is strongly opposed by some Orthodox rabbis on the ground that it is a "gentile custom." Neither Conservative nor Reform Judaism, however, objects and it is also common practice in Israel, particularly in military cemeteries.

Tombstones. The first tombstone mentioned in the Bible is the monument the patriarch Jacob set up over the grave of Rachel. From other parts of the

The painted tombs at Maresha, northwest of Hebron. The tomb is composed of underground halls with long rows of cells which contained the corpses. It dates from the third-second centuries b.c.e., the Hellenistic period.

Bible and in talmudic times, it seems that such monuments were set up for important people. Later the custom developed of erecting some sort of marker on the grave, most probably to be able to locate it easily, and so that *kohanim* should avoid it. Still later people started to inscribe epitaphs on the gravestones, recording the name of the person buried there, his dates and some biblical verse and statement in his praise. Some of the epitaphs described the function and position of the deceased and some, from early periods, have been found in Greek.

At the present day it is the universal custom to erect tombstones and a special order of service exists for the consecration of the tombstone. This usually consists of readings from the Book of Psalms, a memorial prayer and the *Kaddish.* In Israel the custom is to consecrate the tombstone on the 30th day after burial, while in the Diaspora the custom is to do it after 12 months. In Israel the tombstone is a stone slab lying flat on the grave, which is also the custom among Sephardim. Ashkenazim outside Israel usually use an upright headstone.

Funerals. Escorting the dead to his last resting place is considered a great *mitzvah* "the fruit of which a man enjoys in this world while the stock remains for him in the world to come." It justifies even an interruption in the study of the Torah and is called "the true kindness" since one can expect no reciprocation of any sort. The minimum duty is to rise as the funeral cortege passes, and accompany it for four paces." "One who sees a funeral procession and does not escort it," states the Talmud, mocks the dead and blasphemes his Maker." Only if the hearse passes a bridal cortege is the bride given preference; to honor the living is considered greater than to honor the dead.

The more elaborate ancient funeral rituals have either disappeared or been modernized. The recital of psalms in the home still precedes the burial act; however, the custom of having musicians, torchbearers, and barefooted professional mourners in the funeral procession has been discontinued.

The funeral service, now often conducted in the vernacular, varies according to the age of the deceased. Only two men and one woman participate at the funeral of children who die before they reach the age of 30 days, although children who have learned to walk and thus are already known to many people are escorted as adults. In such and normal cases, the coffin is carried on the shoulders of the pallbearers into the cemetery prayer hall where the *Zidduk ha-Din* ("acknowledgment of the Divine judgment") beginning with the affirmation, "The Rock, His work is perfect, for all His ways are judgment," is recited. In some communities, this prayer is recited after the coffin has been lowered into the grave. In the cemetery while the coffin is being borne to the grave, it is customary to halt at least three times and recite Psalm 91. In talmudic times, seven stops were made for lamentations symbolizing the seven times that the word *hevel* (vanity) occurs in Ecclesiastes 1:2, corresponding to the days of the creation of the world. Some Sephardi rites have the custom of seven *hakkafot* ("circumambulations") at the grave.

When the coffin is lowered into the grave, those present say, "May he (or she) come to his (or her) place in peace;" they then fill in the grave. As they leave, they throw grass and earth behind them in the direction of the grave, while saying, "Remember (God) that we are of dust." Prior to leaving the cemetery they wash their hands. In the cemetery prayer hall or at the graveside, Psalm 91 and the *Kaddish* are recited by the mourners. The participants at the funeral then recite "May the Almighty comfort you among the other mourners for Zion and Jerusalem" as they stand in two rows between which the mourners pass.

The precise order of the funeral varies from place to place and from community to community. Many of the customs among the Sephardi Jews are close to those of talmudic times than Ashkenazi customs.
Reform Jewish Practice. Certain burial practices are unique to Reform Jews (mainly in the U.S.). Embalming and delay of burial for a day or two are permitted if necessary to wait for the arrival of relatives from a distant city (sometimes funerals are delayed even without this reason). Reform Jews are usually buried in ordinary clothes, without earth in the coffin. Reform rabbis generally permit cremation, although it is still rare among Jews. (See also *Death and Mourning; *Life and Afterlife).

BURNING BUSH. "Now Moses was keeping the flock of Jethro his father-in-law, the priest of Midian; and he led the flock to the farthest end of the wilderness, and came to the mountain of God, unto Horeb. And the Angel of the Lord appeared unto him in a flame of fire out of the midst of a bush; and he looked, and, behold, the bush burned with fire, but the bush was not consumed. And Moses said: 'I will turn aside now, and see this great sight, why the bush is not burnt.' And when the Lord saw that he turned aside to see, God called unto him out of the midst of the bush, and said: 'Moses, Moses.' And he said: 'Here am I.' And He said: 'Draw not nigh hither; put off thy shoes from off thy feet, for the place whereon thou standest is holy ground'" (Exodus 3:1-5).

When the Holy One, blessed be He, revealed himself to Moses, why did He do so in a bramble bush (Hebrew *seneh*)? Was it to show that there is no place too humble for the Divine Presence to dwell in? We read in the Talmud: "O *seneh,* it is not because you are the tallest of the trees that the Holy One, blessed be He, caused His Divine Presence to rest upon you, but because you are the lowliest of all the trees."

In the *Midrash Rabbah,* the rabbis observed that just as you can put your hand into a thorny bramble easily, and it gets scratched when you pull it out, so Israel went down to Egypt unnoticed but came out with great signs and wonders. Another comparison that the Sages drew between the people of Israel and the Burning Bush was the following: "Just as the *seneh* flourishes wherever there is life-giving water, so Israel flourishes only by virtue of the Torah which is called water."

If you live in Israel, you may find that the firm that insures your parents' property against damage by fire is called the *Seneh* Insurance Co., because "the *seneh* burned with fire, but the *seneh* was not consumed."

"The Burning Bush," at St. Catherine's Monastery in Sinai. Christian tradition believes this to be the original burning bush of the Bible.

BUSTANAI BEN ḤANINAI **(c. 618-670).** In *Babylonia the Jewish community enjoyed a great measure of *self-government. The leader of the Jews was called the *exilarch. According to legend, toward the end of the Persian rule in Babylonia the king decreed that all the descendants of the house of David be exterminated, including the exilarch Ḥaninai, whose wife was pregnant at the time. Later the king had a dream in which he saw himself hewing fruit trees in a grove *(bustan).* Before the last tree was felled a venerable old man appeared before him and struck him on the forehead. On the advice of his courtiers the king consulted a Jewish sage concerning the meaning of this dream. The sage, who was Ḥaninai's father-in-law, interpreted that the old man represented King David trying to prevent the extermination of his descendants. The king then summoned Ḥaninai's widow to court and supplied her with all her needs. When she bore a son, she named him Bustanai in memory of the king's dream.

When Bustanai grew up, he appeared in court before the king and the wisdom he displayed on that occasion amazed all who were present. Thereafter the king honored him and appointed him exilarch, to the great satisfaction of the Jews. After the Arabs

Byzantine church at Shivta in the Negev.

conquered Babylonia, Caliph Omar confirmed Bustanai as exilarch; he gave Izdundad, one of the captive daughters of Chosroes II, king of Persia, to Bustanai in marriage, while the caliph himself married her sister, thereby giving de facto recognition to Bustanai as one of the successors of the kings of Persia. This legendary story throws light upon the course of events after the death of Bustanai. The Persian princess bore Bustanai three sons. When Bustanai died, however, his other sons by his Jewish wives sought to treat their brothers by the Persian princess as slaves, because their mother had not been converted to Judaism. The scholars of the yeshivot, however, decided in favor of Izdundad, and her relatives, who held high offices in the government, also decided in her favor; her eldest son even married a daughter of an important rabbi.

BUXTORF, JOHANNES (1564-1629) was a Christian who became professor of Hebrew at the University of Basle, Switzerland. He compiled an edition of the Hebrew Bible with its most important commentaries. For this purpose he employed two Jewish scholars for whom he had to get special residence permits because otherwise Jews were not allowed to live in Basle. Buxtorf had the greatest respect for the Jewish traditions about the Bible and maintained an active correspondence with Jewish scholars throughout the world.

His son, Johannes II (1599-1664) followed in his father's footsteps and succeeded him in the Chair of Hebrew at Basle. Johannes II also believed in the authenticity of the Jewish traditions and defended them in a fierce controversy with another Christian Hebraist, Ludovicus Capelus. Johannes' view was officially adopted by the Swiss Church. He also translated Jewish classical texts, including *Maimonides' *Guide of the Perplexed.*

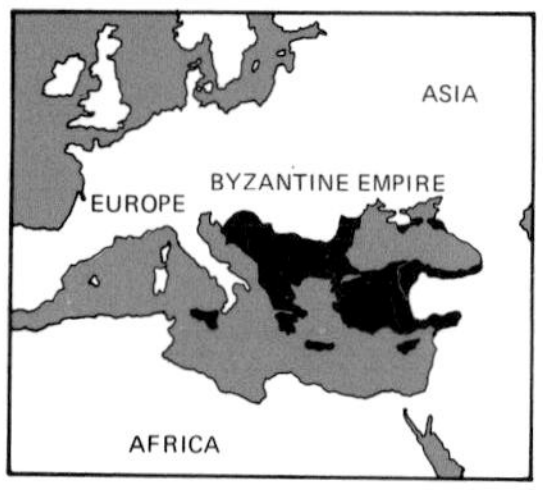

BYZANTINE EMPIRE. This was the continuation of the Roman Empire after Constantine transferred his capital to the East in the year 330. The Byzantine world covered Asia Minor and the Near East, including Ereẓ Israel, which had been conquered by Rome. Christianity gradually became the 'established' religion. All emperors after Constantine except *Julian the Apostate professed Christianity.

Judaism in Roman law was a 'permitted religion,' and Jews enjoyed freedom of worship and civic rights. Officially they kept this status. But the Church, itself just freed from persecution, soon forced restrictions and humiliations on Jewry. It became a crime to become a Jew and equally to hinder Jews becoming Christian. Intermarriage was illegal. Christian Byzantium became fanatically anti-Jewish and preachers denounced Jewish religion and practices, accusing Jews of all evil. Much of this, after it had died down in the empire, influenced ideas in medieval Europe and thus the growth of Western anti-Semitism.

Under Julian, who despised the Church and tried to restore the old culture and religion, Jews gained imperial support. Julian promised to rebuild the Temple in Jerusalem, but his death prevented this. Justinian (sixth century) restricted Jewry even more. Jewish communities nevertheless increased throughout the Byzantine empire and prospered internally, especially in the provinces and even in the capital, though subject to restrictions in law and outbreaks of prejudice. Jews sometimes had political influence, and were in demand as physicians of the nobility and even the imperial family.

The Jewish tradition, which developed in the empire centered on Constantinople (now Istanbul), became known as the Romaniot tradition – Greek in language and Byzantine in culture. (All Byzantines considered and called themselves Romans, hence the name). Scholarship and literature were highly developed, especially in southern Italy in the ninth to 11th centuries. The Fourth *Crusade in 1204, disrupted the Byzantine Empire and the Ottoman Turks gradually conquered what was left, taking the capital, Constantinople, in 1453. The western half of the old Roman Empire had fallen away over the centuries until by the early Middle Ages it was a separate, unconnected society. The Semitic world, including Ereẓ Israel, was conquered by the Muslim Arabs in the seventh century. When Constantinople fell to the Turks the Byzantine Empire was merely a relic of the past, the last link with the mighty 'world' empire of Rome. The conquest of 1453 was the end of a legend and an age.

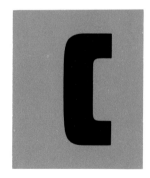

CAESAREA, a city on the Mediterranean coast south of Haifa, was originally known as Straton's Tower. It was an ancient town and was named after Straton, who ruled Sidon in Lebanon during the fourth century b.c.e. The Hasmonean king, Alexander Yannai, captured it in 104 b.c.e. and incorporated it into the Hasmonean kingdom. However, it did not remain under Jewish rule for very long. The city was captured by the Roman commander Pompey and later fell under the rule of Cleopatra. Caesarea came under Jewish rule again only when the emperor Augustus returned it to *Herod, who greatly enlarged the city and renamed it Caesarea in honor of the emperor (in approximately 13 b.c.e.). Herod surrounded the city with a wall and built a deep sea harbor, and although the population of Caesarea was half gentile and half Jewish, Herod favored the non-Jewish inhabitants and encouraged the city to become a leading center of Hellenistic culture. Later it became the seat of the Roman procurators who ruled Ereẓ Israel.

It was in Caesarea that the clashes between the Jewish and the gentile population sparked the Jewish revolt against Rome in 66 c.e. which ended in the destruction of the Temple. During the war, when Vespasian arrived to subdue the country and conquer Jerusalem, he made Caesarea his headquarters, and when he became emperor, raised it to the status of a Roman colony. Some 60 years later, when the Bar Kokhba revolt broke out (131-135 c.e.), the Roman general Severus also made Caesarea his headquarters. After the revolt was suppressed, Rabbi *Akiva and other sages were martyred in the city.

During the third century c.e. Caesarea became a center of Christian learning and at the same time, one of the great talmudic centers in Ereẓ Israel. The Jerusalem Talmud speaks frequently of "the sages of Caesarea," and reference is also made to a synagogue there where the prayers were recited in Greek.

When the Byzantines divided Ereẓ Israel into provinces (358-429 c.e.), Caesarea became the capital of the first province (Palaestina Prima) and reached its greatest extent; it was surrounded by a semi-circular wall and was served by two aqueducts. In 640 c.e. it was the last city in the country to fall to the Arabs.

Under Crusader rule, the town again rose to importance. It was splendidly reconstructed with strong fortifications, a new harbor and a beautiful cathedral. However, the Crusaders' presence affected the Jewish community adversely so that by 1170 only 20 Jews remained there.

Today Caesarea has become a central tourist attraction with modern hotels and the only golf course in Israel. But the past is still an integral part of the city since there are relics from practically every period of its history. The remains of towers, temples and fortresses as well as statues, mosaics and hundreds of inscriptions are being constantly uncovered in excavations and are helping archaeologists to investigate Caesarea's rich and picturesque past. In fact, the impressive Roman theater has been reconstructed and is used for special concerts and musical recitals.

1

2

1. The old Roman amphitheater at Caesarea has been restored and is used today. In this picture, the musicians Leonard Rose, Isaac Stern and Eugene Istomin play at the 1961 Israel Festival concert.
2. Sunset over the ancient harbor of Caesarea. The harbor was built by Herod at the end of the first century b.c.e.

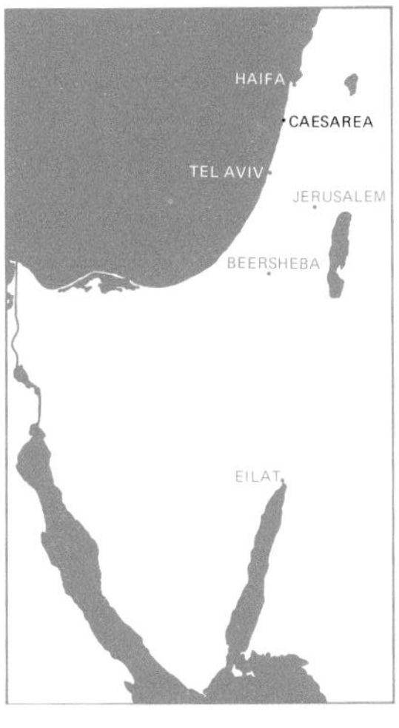

CAIN AND ABEL. The story of Cain and Abel, the characters in the world's first murder, is a complex one that has inspired controversy and works of creative imagination. The most obvious explanation for the murder itself is jealousy. Abel the shepherd and Cain the farmer each brought an offering to God from the fruits of his labor. Abel's sacrifice was accepted by God but Cain's offering was rejected. The explanation for this lies in the descriptions of the two offerings. Whereas Cain's offering is described simply as "of the fruits of the soil," Abel is recorded as having brought "of the choicest of the firstlings of his flock." Cain, in his overpowering jealousy, killed his brother.

For this act he was doubly punished. Cain, the farmer, was to be denied the fruits of the soil and was to become a ceaseless wanderer on earth. However, to allay Cain's expressed fear of being killed by any who might come across him, God placed a protective mark upon him, and he then settled in "the land of Nod."

According to the Midrash, Cain was not only the "first murderer" but also the first person to show ingratitude. Abel, who was far stronger than Cain, overcame him in the struggle, but being moved to compassion by his brother's plea for mercy, released his hold upon him, only to be slain himself.

Yet Cain has never been viewed as completely evil, and his complex nature has inspired many interpretations. The best-known is the romantic epic poem *Cain* by Lord Byron, in which God's benevolence is challenged. More traditional interpretations which depict Cain as a villain include William Blake's *The Ghost of Abel.*

CAIRO. Old Cairo was known as Fostat. It was built in 641 c.e. by 'Amr ibn al-'As, the Arab conqueror of Egypt. As the capital of Muslim Egypt, it quickly grew into a large and prosperous city to which came immigrants from all parts of the Arab Empire.

Jews were there from the beginning of the dispersion, and in the 10th century many more arrived from Mesopotamia. Two communities developed, the Mesopotamian and the Palestinian. There was also a large community of *Karaites, for whom Cairo has always been a major center.

New Cairo, built in the 10th century to the north of Fostat, immediately attracted many Jews and it became the religious and cultural center for all Egyptian Jews. Fostat and new Cairo were the homes of distinguished rabbis and scholars, among them the great *Maimonides. A synagogue storeroom full of

1

2

1. Cain killing Abel. From the Duke of Alba's Castilian Bible, 1433.
2. Cairo's oldest synagogue. In the storeroom of this synagogue the "Genizah" documents were found.

important, ancient documents and manuscripts was discovered there in the 19th century. (See *Genizah). Fostat began to decline, especially after the Crusader period when the Egyptians burned it to prevent its capture. It was rebuilt, but never achieved its former distinction.

Jews were generally well-treated and prospered under their early Muslim rulers, but under the Mamluks, from 1250 to the Turkish conquest of 1517, they were often persecuted. So were the Egyptian Christians, the Copts. At first, under Turkish rule, the situation improved but not for long. Arab historians describe how the Turkish sultan Baybars (1233-77) once gathered all Christians and Jews together and threatened to burn them alive unless they paid a large ransom. This they did over many years. Often synagogues and churches were closed and non-Muslims were subjected to persecution. But although fanatical outbreaks were common, the Jewish community continued to exist.

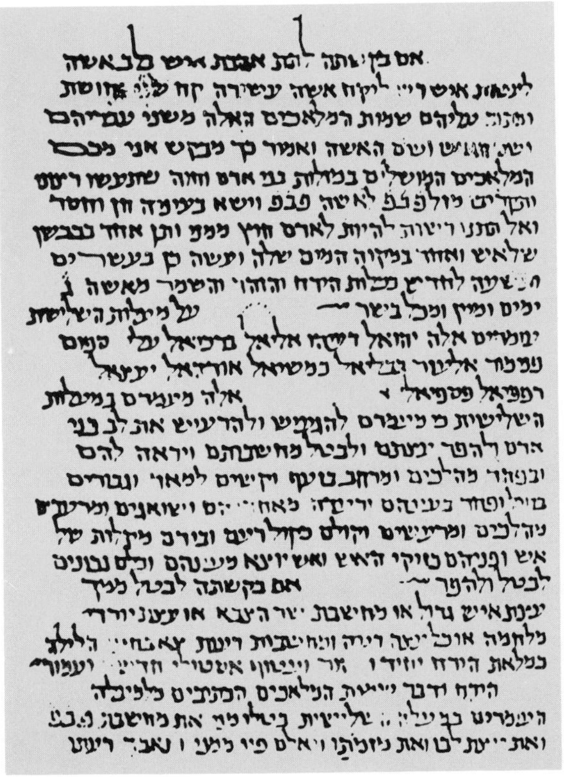

Part of the Genizah documents. At the end of the last century a large collection of documents from the synagogue in Cairo were investigated, and yielded much information about the history and religious practice of the Jews from the time of the Islamic conquests until the First Crusade.

In the 16th century exiles from Spain reached Cairo. Gradually the new and older communities merged. Arabic became the language of the Sephardim and Sephardi customs were taken over by the old community. It was a period of flourishing scholarship, which influenced the whole Diaspora.

In the early 19th century, Egypt became independent. The long suffering under Turkish governors ended and a new era began for the Jewish community. European schools were founded and new immigrants arrived from other Mediterranean countries. Banking and commerce prospered and Jews moved into new suburbs around the city. By 1917 there were 25,000 Jews in Cairo. They took their place in public life and in government. Joseph Cattavi, for example, who was minister of finance in 1923, was the son of Jacob Cattavi, who had been chief revenue officer of Egypt.

In 1947 Cairo had about 42,000 Jews, and the Zionist movement received much support over the years. The War of Independence which followed the establishment of the State of Israel in 1948 caused anti-Jewish riots in Egypt. Jewish property was seized then and again in 1956 after the *Sinai Campaign. Owing to the Arab-Israeli confrontations, Egyptian Jews were in a difficult position and most of them emigrated. In 1970 there were only a few hundred left in Cairo, some in the old quarter, others in mixed communities outside.

CALENDAR. In the Jewish calendar the months are reckoned according to the *moon, but the year is reckoned according to the sun. Unlike the Gregorian solar calendar used by the Western world, the Jewish month is initiated by the new moon. Unlike the lunar Muslim calendar, the months of the Jewish year always appear in the same season. This will be explained below.

The month of Nissan, which includes *Passover, is considered the first month since it celebrates the Exodus from Egypt, the event which marks the beginning of Jewish nationhood. "This month shall be unto you the beginning of months; it shall be the first month of the year to you." (Exodus 12:2).

The Jewish New Year, *Rosh Ha-Shanah, which is the anniversary of *Creation, is in Tishrei, the seventh month. The year is counted according to the number of years since Creation; for example, Rosh Ha-Shanah 1974 was the start of 5735, which is that number of years since the beginning of the world. (See also *Chronology). Months are often referred to by their number in the order. They are: Nissan, Iyyar, Sivan, Tammuz, Av, Elul, Tishrei, Ḥeshvan, Kislev, Tevet, Shevat, Adar, and in a leap year, Adar II.

The solar year is just over 365 days long and it

	Hebrew Month	Approx. English Month	Days
	Nissan	March-April	30
	Iyyar	April-May	29
	Sivan	May-June	30
	Tammuz	June-July	29
	Av	July-August	30
	Elul	August-Sept.	29
	Tishrei	Sept.-Oct.	30
	Heshvan	Oct.-Nov.	29-30
	Kislev	Nov.-Dec.	29-30
	Tevet	Dec.-Jan.	29
	Shevat	Jan.-Feb.	30
	Adar	Feb.-March	29
Leap Year	Adar Rishon	Feb.-March	30
	Adar Sheni	Feb.-March	29

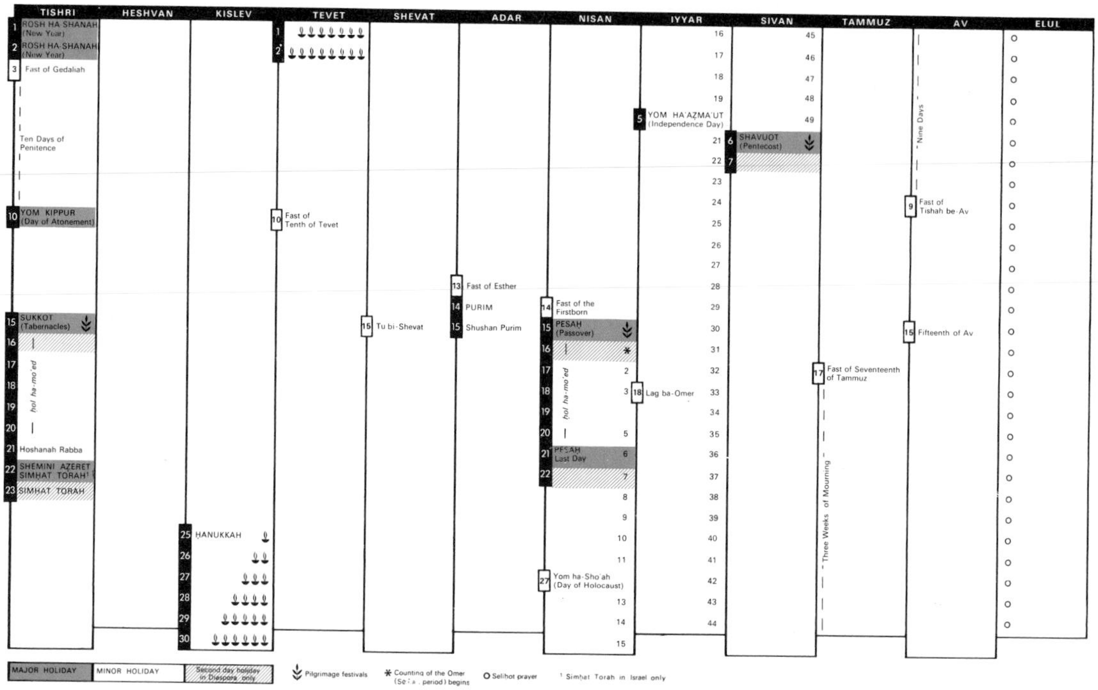

Calendar of festivals and fasts in the Jewish year. Note the different dating of festivals in Israel and in the Diaspora, and that the Sephardi and Ashkenazi dates of the *Seliḥot* prayer differ.

exceeds 12 lunar months by about 11 days. The cycle of the lunar year must, therefore, be adjusted to the solar year, because although the Jewish festivals are fixed according to dates in certain months, they must also be in specific seasons which depend on the solar year. If there were no adjustment, the months would wander through the seasons. Without any adaptation, Passover, the spring festival, would be celebrated eventually in winter, then in summer, and so on. The required adjustment is achieved by the addition of an extra month – Adar II – in seven years of each 19-year cycle. In the days of the Temple, the year to which a month was to be added was decided upon in that year according to climate or agricultural conditions. Later the leap years were fixed to be in the years 3, 6, 8, 11, 14, 17, and 19.

The monthly 'birth' of the moon, the *molad,* occurs when the moon is directly between the sun and the earth. Since the interval between each *molad* is approximately 29 and a half days, some months are 29 days, called *ḥaser,* or incomplete, while others are 30 days, called *shalem,* or complete. In the synagogue on the Sabbath before the *molad,* its exact time is announced, in units of days, hours, and *ḥalakim.* (One *ḥelek,* the smallest unit, is 1/1080 of an hour.) The day or days of Rosh Ḥodesh, the new month, are proclaimed at the same time.

It does not always follow that the day of the *molad* is the first day of the month, because adjustments need to be made to adhere to the true cycle of the calendar. In much the same way, the solar, or Gregorian, calendar adds February 29 every four years to adjust the solar cycle of a year which is actually 365 and one-quarter days.

The adjustments in the Jewish calendar, called *"deḥiyyot"* or postponements, are made usually in the "floating" months of Ḥeshvan and Kislev which may have either 29 or 30 days. The month of Adar II is another possible *deḥiyyah.* Two important reasons for using *deḥiyyot* are: 1) to delay Rosh Ha-Shanah which is the first day of Tishrei if the *molad* is at noon or later, and 2) to avoid the occurrence of Yom Kippur on Friday or Sunday and Hoshanah Rabba (See *Sukkot) on Shabbat, all for reasons of special religious observance.

The Jewish calendar in the form we have today was fixed by Hillel II over 1,600 years ago. Since then, the *molad* has been determined by mathematical-astronomical calculation, and the calendar can be fixed for an infinite number of years in advance. Prior to the fixed calendar, a month would consist of 29 days if witnesses appeared before the court on the 30th day stating that they saw the new moon. The court would then pronounce the new month on that

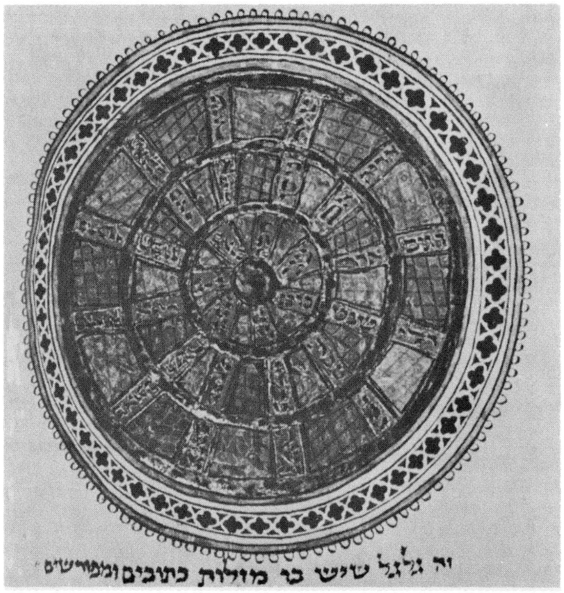

1

2

1. A Hebrew calendar from France, dated about 1280.
2. Omer-counting Table, Micrograph on parchment, 1823. The blessing is contained in the rectangle at the top; the 49 days of the *omer* are specified in a chain of squares and circles; and the scrolls in the center contain the prayers for *Kiddush* on Friday nights and the Grace after Meals.

day. If witnesses failed to appear, the month would automatically complete 30 days, and the new month would begin the following day. The fixing of the month is in itself a commandment in the Torah.

Seasons. The beginning of each of the four seasons is named a *tekufah*, literally, a circuit. The *tekufah* of Nissan denotes Spring, that of Tammuz Summer, that of Tishrei Fall, and that of Tevet Winter. The determination of the equinoxes and solstices is important only as it relates to the date of the first day in the Diaspora of the petition for *rain which is inserted in the *Amidah prayer from the 60th day after the autumnal equinox. For the 20th and 21st centuries this date falls on December 5 or 6. Every 28 years the *tekufah* of Nissan reverts to the same hour on the same day of the week as at the beginning. This 28 year cycle is name the *Maḥzor ha-Gadolah* or *Maḥzor Ḥammah* (respectively "Great Cycle" and "Cycle of the Sun").

The Day. Time is of major significance in Judaism. The day as defined in Jewish Law is a variable. Although all agree that night precedes the day in determining a full calendar day as it does in the account of the Creation of the world, the definition of the day is disputed among the rabbinic authorities. In general, it is accepted that "day" begins at dawn and ends at the appearance of the stars when "night" begins. An hour is equivalent to 1/12 of the day, whether the day consists of 14 hours or of 9 hours. All the commandments which have to be performed by a specific hour are dependent on this fact.

The Jew in observing his religious obligations must become very well aware of time – that irretrievable commodity.

CAMBRIDGE, English university city. Cambridge had a fairly important Jewish community in medieval times though the report that it dates from 1073 is unfounded. The original synagogue, already apparently disused, was assigned to the Franciscans in 1244. Nearly 50 householders figure in the Cambridge Jewry lists during the period from 1224 to 1240. In 1275 Edward I empowered his mother, Eleanor of Provence, to banish all Jews from her dower-towns, including Cambridge. In the 16th century, the university records list two converted Jewish teachers: John Immanuel Tremellius of Ferrara (1510-1580), "King's Reader of Hebrew" in 1549, and Philip Ferdinand, originally from Poland.

Until 1856 religious tests prevented Jews from obtaining degrees though not from studying at the university. There have since been many Jewish teachers and fellows and a high number of Jewish undergraduates. Toward the middle of the 18th century, a short-lived Jewish community existed. It was reestablished in 1847 and again in 1888. In 1968 the number of residents was small and the congregation was almost entirely comprised of students.

CANAAN, LAND OF, which God gave to the Children of Israel, was not a wilderness without people or history. When the Israelites arrived, Canaan was a populated, if not organized, area.

No single geographical definition for the land of Canaan exists in the Bible. The term occasionally indicates an extensive area that includes all of Palestine and Syria; at other times it is confined to a strip of land along the eastern shore of the Mediterranean. The most detailed description of the boundaries is to be found in Numbers 34:2-12.

The population of early Canaan was not of one people; the Canaanites are only one of several peoples who settled in the land that was given to the Israelites. At times, the term Amorite was used as a general name for the inhabitants. The Bible lists the following peoples as having lived in Canaan: Jebusites, Amorites, Girgashites, Hurites, Arkites, Sinites, Arvadites, Zemarites, and the Hamathites. Nevertheless, though the peoples varied, Canaan's population was basically of Semitic origin. This is indicated by place names such as Jericho, Megiddo, Gebal, and Sidon.

Canaan never existed as a unified political entity. Rather, it was split up into small units, each under the rule of a king. Because there were many kings, the battles for power between them were numerous. No less than 31 kings whom the Israelites fought during their conquest of Canaan are listed in Joshua 12.

The period of Israelite settlement, about 1200 b.c.e., marks the end of the Canaanite period in Palestine, although Canaanite culture endured in the large coastal towns of Phoenicia.

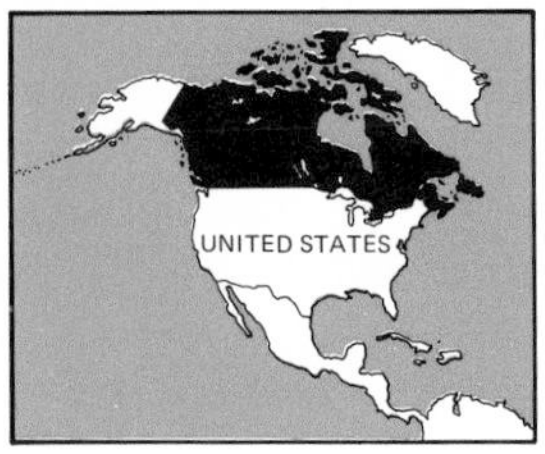

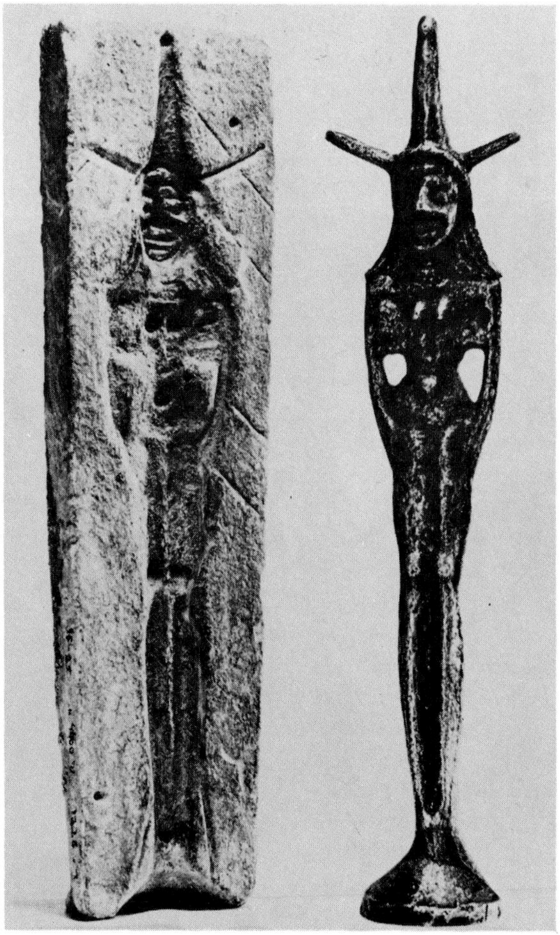
1

1. Canaanite statue of the goddess of fertility, Ashera. This bronze casting figure and cast were found in the temple at Nahariyyah, Israel, and date from 1750-1550 b.c.e.
2. In the foreground of the picture stand dignitaries invited to see off Jewish emigrants. The emigrants, standing in the background, are Displaced Persons bound for Canada, and they are standing while the Canadian National Anthem is played.

CANADA. Although relatively small – just over a quarter of a million Jews out of the population of 21 million Canadians – the Canadian Jewish community has shown numerous achievements in political, cultural and religious life.

The community dates from the year 1759, when the first settlers were merchants and fur traders associated with the Thirteen Colonies. At that time, Jewish families such as the *Hart, Joseph, and Judah families were active in leadership, local government, the military and the professions. Jewish life was concentrated mainly in the city of *Montreal, which until today is an important Jewish center. There the first congregation, She'arith Israel, was founded in 1768.

Throughout the 1800s, Jewish population growth was slow, and after 100 years of settlement, there were only 700 Jews in Canada. However, in 1881, with the assassination of Czar Alexander II and the

2

Russian pogroms, a large wave of immigration came to Canada. This marked the beginning of a new era of growth for the Canadian Jewish population. As a result, a string of Jewish communities and synagogues sprang up around the country, with a particularly large population concentration in *Toronto, where several congregations were founded in the 1880s.

After both World Wars there were again large influxes of Jews into Canada, resulting in the further growth of Jewish community life: more synagogues, improved Jewish education for both youth and adults, and organizations both religious and Zionist, as the Canadian community has always taken a positive attitude towards the State of Israel.

Jewish participation in Canadian life has been noteworthy and Jews have made great contributions especially in political life, government, the civil service and the arts. Jewish painters, sculptors, musicians, novelists, poets and composers are among the leading talents of the country. In politics, Canadian Jewry has long been concerned with the preservation of Jewish religious rights. As early as 1906, the Jewish community opposed the enactment of national Sunday observance laws. Jews played a crucial part in the enactment of Ontario's anti-discrimination laws in 1944 and 1951, and these laws set an example for the rest of the country. Canadian Jews established a committee on hate propaganda to recommend legislation against the spreading of racial and religious hatred. They also worked for Canadian action against anti-Semitism abroad, and in Germany in the 1930s, and in Russia and the Arab countries in the 1960s and 1970s.

Jews have been active members of parliament, and in fact, from 1917 until the present, the Montreal-Cartier district has always had a Jewish representative. Jews have served as mayors and cabinet members as well as judges, the most famous of whom is Bora Laskin, the first Jewish member of the Supreme Court of Canada.

Quebec, the capital city of the Canadian province of Quebec, did not allow Jews or Protestants to settle there until 1759, when the British captured Quebec from the French. The first Jew arrived in Quebec as early as 1767, yet its Jewish population has always remained small, ranging from 40 in 1851 to only 495 in 1961. Despite their small number, several Jews achieved social and professional prominence. Thus a Jew was the first chief of the Quebec Fire Brigade in 1790; a Jew was one of the founders of Canada's merchant marine and of the Banque Nationale, a

The Jewish Times

THE ONLY JEWISH PAPER PUBLISHED IN CANADA.

VOL. IV. MONTREAL, SHEBAT 11TH, 5661. FEBRUARY 1ST, 1901. No. 5

QUEEN VICTORIA.

The cover of the *Jewish Times,* Canada's first Jewish newspaper. This issue was published in Montreal in 1901, on the death of Queen Victoria.

member of the Quebec City Council, president of the Quebec Board of Trade, and president of the Stadacono Bank; and a Jew was the pioneer of hydro-electric development in Canada, using Montmorency Falls to light the city of Quebec.

In 1970 most of the Jewish population of Quebec City were the children and grandchildren of Jewish immigrants from Eastern Europe who had come to Quebec between 1890 and 1921. Approximately 80% of the Jews in the city in 1969 were merchants, and a few were clothing manufacturers, lawyers and doctors, and professors at Laval University, the French Catholic university in Quebec.

CANDLES. The warm, shimmering glow of candles has illuminated Jewish homes and synagogues for many centuries. Although horses have given way to automobiles and ancient handicrafts are being replaced by modern machines, the old-fashioned candle will continue to symbolize for Jews the spirit of God, the light of the Torah, the conclusion of the Sabbath and the memory of those who have passed away.

Before candles became commonplace, oil lamps were used for ritual purposes, including the *ner tamid* ("eternal light") suspended above the Ark in the synagogue, the *Ḥanukkah and Sabbath lights, and the

1

2

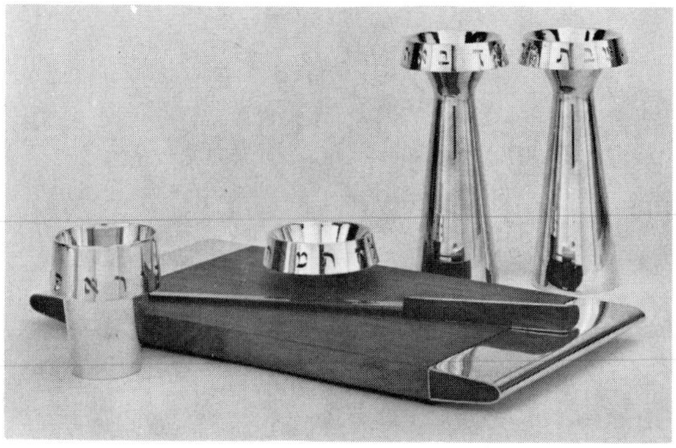
3

1. Pair of Sabbath candlesticks made in 1680, from Danzig.
2. "The Blessing over the Candles," by Isidor Kaufmann (1853-1921). The table is laid for the Sabbath meal, and the lady of the house, with a scarf over her hair raises her hands to cover her eyes while she recites the blessing over the candles.
3. Sabbath set by the Israel artist, Moshe Zabari, in silver and walnut. It consists of a wine cup and *ḥallah* tray and knife, a salt cellar and a pair of candlesticks.

flickering reminder of a loved one during the seven-day mourning period and on the anniversary of his death. In those days, the oil lamp was preferred to candles, which were often made from the fat of non-kosher animals. The invention of paraffin, a waxy substance extracted from petroleum, led to the widespread use of candles by the Jewish people, and it has continued up to our own times.

Women usher in the Sabbath each week by lighting candles and blessing God "who sanctified us by His commandments and commanded us to kindle the Sabbath light." On Saturday night, traditional Jewish families light a *havdalah* candle made of several wicks braided together, raise a cup of wine and sniff fragrant spices, thus bidding farewell to the Sabbath peace and beginning a new week. Sephardic Jews often use a single, unbraided candle for this ceremony. On the evening before Passover, the head of the household searches for the forbidden leaven *(bedikat ḥameẓ)* with the aid of a simple candle, and in various parts of the world, candles are carried on weekdays before the scroll of the Torah and held while it is being read in the synagogue. At weddings, too, the parents of the bride and groom sometimes hold candles when they escort the young couple to the *ḥuppah.*

Candle Tax. In Eastern Europe Jewish communities used to impose taxes on the candles used on the above occasions. In 1816, for example, communal representatives in Minsk levied a three-year candle tax on all Lithuanian Jews in order to support their poverty-stricken brethren in southern Russia. In other countries, the candle tax was imposed by governments, and Jewish tax farmers were often obliged to collect it.